Learning PostgreSQL

Create, develop, and manage relational databases
in real-world applications using PostgreSQL

Salahaldin Juba

Achim Vannahme

Andrey Volkov

BIRMINGHAM - MUMBAI

Learning PostgreSQL

First published: November 2015

Production reference: 1241115

Published by Packt Publishing Ltd.
Livery Place
35 Livery Street
Birmingham B3 2PB, UK.

ISBN 978-1-78398-918-8

www.packtpub.com

Credits

Authors

Salahaldin Juba

Achim Vannahme

Andrey Volkov

Reviewers

Ângelo Marcos Rigo

Dr. Isabel Rosa

Commissioning Editor

Julian Ursell

Acquisition Editors

Tushar Gupta

Greg Wild

Content Development Editor

Parita Khedekar

Technical Editor

Vijin Boricha

Copy Editors

Shruti Iyer

Sonia Mathur

Project Coordinator

Judie Jose

Proofreader

Safis Editing

Indexer

Monica Ajmera Mehta

Graphics

Disha Haria

Production Coordinator

Conidon Miranda

Cover Work

Conidon Miranda

About the Authors

Salahaldin Juba has over 10 years of experience in industry and academia, with a focus on database development for large-scale and enterprise applications. He holds a master's degree of science in environmental management and a bachelor's degree of engineering in computer systems.

I would like to express my deepest gratitude to my colleagues Achim Vannahme and Andrey Volkov for making this work possible. Also, I would like to thank all those who provided support, especially the Packt publishing team, especially the persons whom I interacted with—Vijin Boricha, Greg Wild, and Parita Khedekar—for their great help with proofreading, design, comments, and remarks.

I would also like to thank my mother, Wedad; my wife, Rana; and the rest of my family, who supported me despite all of the time that I had to devote to this book over them.

Achim Vannahme works as a senior software developer at a mobile messaging operator, where he focuses on software quality and test automation. He holds a degree in computer science and has over 10 years of experience in using Java and PostgreSQL in distributed and high-performance applications.

Andrey Volkov pursued his education in information systems in the banking sector. He started his career as a financial analyst in a commercial bank. Here, Andrey worked with a database as a data source for his analysis and soon realized that querying the database directly is much more efficient for ad hoc analyses than using any visual report-generating software. He joined the data warehouse team, and after a while, he led the team by taking up the position of a data warehouse architect. Andrey worked mainly with Oracle databases to develop logical and physical models of finance and accounting data, created them in a database, implemented procedures to load and process data, and performed analytical tasks. He was also responsible for teaching users how to use data warehouse and BI tools, and SQL training was a part of his job as well.

After many years of being greatly interested in the aspects of his job that were related to IT rather than accounting or banking, Andrey changed fields. Currently, he works as a database developer in a telecommunication company. Here, Andrey works mainly with PostgreSQL databases and is responsible for data modeling, implementing data structures in databases, developing stored procedures, integrating databases with other software components, and developing a data warehouse.

Having worked with both Oracle and PostgreSQL—the former is a leading commercial and the latter is one of the most advanced open source RDBMSes—he is able to compare them and recognize and evaluate the key advantages of both. Andrey's extensive experience, therefore, made him able and willing to work on this book.

About the Reviewers

Ângelo Marcos Rigo has a strong background in web development, which he has worked with since 1998, with a focus on content management systems, hibryd mobile apps and custom web based systems. He holds a degree in systems information and also has extensive experience in managing, customizing, and developing extensions for the moodle LMS. Ângelo can be reached on his website, http://www.u4w.com.br, for consultation. He has also reviewed, *Moodle Security*, *Packt Publishing*.

> I would like to thank my wife, Janaina de Souza, and my daughter, Lorena Rigo, for their support while I was away to review this book.

Dr. Isabel Rosa is a research associate at Imperial College London and one of the cofounders of Earthindicators. She has a PhD in computational ecology from Imperial College London and extensive experience in data mining and predictive modeling. For the last five years, Dr. Rosa worked as a researcher with Imperial College London. During her academic career, she acquired several skills such as statistical analysis, programming (R, C++, Python), working with geographic information systems (ArcGIS and QGIS), and creating databases (PostgreSQL/ PostGIS, SQLServer). Dr. Rosa is also the lead author and coauthor of several scientific papers published in top-quality scientific journals, such as Global Change Biology. She has presented her work at several national and international scientific conferences and is the lead coordinator of Land Use Forum (London).

www.PacktPub.com

Support files, eBooks, discount offers, and more

For support files and downloads related to your book, please visit www.PacktPub.com.

Did you know that Packt offers eBook versions of every book published, with PDF and ePub files available? You can upgrade to the eBook version at www.PacktPub.com and as a print book customer, you are entitled to a discount on the eBook copy. Get in touch with us at service@packtpub.com for more details.

At www.PacktPub.com, you can also read a collection of free technical articles, sign up for a range of free newsletters and receive exclusive discounts and offers on Packt books and eBooks.

https://www2.packtpub.com/books/subscription/packtlib

Do you need instant solutions to your IT questions? PacktLib is Packt's online digital book library. Here, you can search, access, and read Packt's entire library of books.

Why subscribe?

- Fully searchable across every book published by Packt
- Copy and paste, print, and bookmark content
- On demand and accessible via a web browser

Free access for Packt account holders

If you have an account with Packt at www.PacktPub.com, you can use this to access PacktLib today and view 9 entirely free books. Simply use your login credentials for immediate access.

Table of Contents

Preface

Picking the right database management system is a difficult task due to the vast number of options on the market. Depending on the business model, one can pick a commercial database or an open source database with commercial support. In addition to this, there are several technical and nontechnical factors to assess. When it comes to a relational database management system, PostgreSQL stands at the top for several reasons. The PostgreSQL slogan, "The world's most advanced open source database", shows the sophistication of PostgreSQL features and community confidence.

PostgreSQL is an open source object relational database management system. It emphasizes extensibility and competes with major relational database vendors such as Oracle, SQL server, and MySQL. Due to its rich extensions and open source license, it is often used for research purposes, but PostgreSQL code is also the base for many commercial database management systems such as Greenplum and Vertica. Furthermore, start-up companies often favor PostgreSQL due to its licensing costs and because there are a lot of companies that provide commercial support.

PostgreSQL runs on most modern operating systems, including Windows, Mac, and Linux flavors. Also, there are several extensions to access, manage, and monitor PostgreSQL clusters, such as pgAdmin III. PostgreSQL installation and configuration is moderately easy as it is supported by most packaging tools, such as yum and apt.

Database developers can easily learn and use PostgreSQL because it complies with ANSI SQL standards and comes with many client tools such as psql and pgAdmin III. Other than this, there are a lot of resources to help developers learn PostgreSQL; it has a very good documentation manual and a very active and organized community.

PostgreSQL can be used for both OLTP and OLAP applications. As it is ACID compliant, it can be used out of the box for OLTP applications. For OLAP applications, PostgreSQL supports Window functions, FDW, and table inheritance; there are many external extensions for this purpose as well.

Even though PostgreSQL is ACID compliant, it has very good performance as it utilizes state of the art algorithms and techniques. For example, PostgreSQL utilizes MVCC architecture to allow concurrent access to data. Also, PostgreSQL provides a very good analyzer and advanced features, such as data partitioning using table inheritance and constraint exclusion, to speed up the handling of very large data. PostgreSQL supports several types of indexes such as B-Tree, GiN, and GiST, and BRIN indexes are also supported by PostgreSQL 9.5 at the time of writing this book.

PostgreSQL is scalable thanks to the many replication solutions in the market, such as Slony and pgpool-II. Additionally, PostgreSQL supports out-of-the-box synchronous and asynchronous streaming replication. This makes PostgreSQL very attractive because it can be used to set up highly available and performant systems.

What this book covers

Chapter 1, *Relational Databases*, introduces relational database system concepts, including relational database properties, relational algebra, and database modeling. Also, it describes different database management systems such as graph, document, key value, and columnar databases.

Chapter 2, *PostgreSQL in Action*, provides first-hand experience in installing the PostgreSQL server and client tools on different platforms. This chapter also introduces PostgreSQL capabilities, such as out-of-the-box replication support and its very rich data types.

Chapter 3, *PostgreSQL Basic Building Blocks*, provides some coding best practices, such as coding conventions, identifier names, and so on. This chapter describes the PostgreSQL basic building blocks and the interaction between these blocks, mainly template databases, user databases, tablespaces, roles, and settings. Also, it describes basic data types and tables.

Chapter 4, *PostgreSQL Advanced Building Blocks*, introduces several building blocks, including views, indexes, functions, user-defined data types, triggers, and rules. This chapter provides use cases of these building blocks and compares building blocks that can be used for the same case, such as rules and triggers.

Chapter 5, *SQL Language*, introduces Structured Query Language (SQL) which is used to interact with a database, create and maintain data structures, and enter data into databases, change it, retrieve it, and delete it. SQL has commands related to Data Definition Language (DDL), Data Manipulation Language (DML), and Data Control Language (DCL). Four SQL statements form the basis of DML—SELECT, INSERT, UPDATE, and DELETE—which are described in this chapter.

The SELECT statement is examined in detail to explain SQL concepts such as grouping and filtering to show what SQL expressions and conditions are and how to use subqueries. Some relational algebra topics are also covered in application to joining tables.

Chapter 6, Advanced Query Writing, describes advanced SQL concepts and features, such as common table expressions and window functions. This helps you implement a logic that would not be possible without them, such as recursive queries. Other techniques explained here, such as the DISTINCT ON clause, the FILTER clause, or lateral subqueries, are not that irreplaceable. However, they can help make a query smaller, easier, and faster.

Chapter 7, Server-Side Programming with PL/pgSQL, describes PL/pgSQL. It introduces function parameters, such as the number of returned rows, and function cost, which is mainly used by the query planner. Also, it presents control statements such as conditional and iteration ones. Finally, it explains the concept of dynamic SQL and some recommended practices when using dynamic SQL.

Chapter 8, PostgreSQL Security, discusses the concepts of authentication and authorization. It describes PostgreSQL authentication methods and explains the structure of a PostgreSQL host-based authentication configuration file. It also discusses the permissions that can be granted to database building objects such as schemas, tables, views, indexes, and columns. Finally, it shows how sensitive data, such as passwords, can be protected using different techniques, including one-way and two-way encryption.

Chapter 9, The PostgreSQL System Catalog and System Administration Functions, provides several recipes to maintain a database cluster, including cleaning up data, maintaining user processes, cleaning up indexes and unused databases objects, discovering and adding indexes to foreign keys, and so on.

Chapter 10, Optimizing Database Performance, discusses several approaches to optimize performance. It presents PostgreSQL cluster configuration settings, which are used in tuning the whole cluster's performance. Also, it presents common mistakes in writing queries and discusses several approaches to increase performance, such as using indexes or table partitioning and constraint exclusion.

Chapter 11, Beyond Conventional Data types, discusses several rich data types, including arrays, hash stores, and documents. It presents use cases as well as operations and functions for each data type. Additionally, it presents full-text search.

Chapter 12, Testing, covers some aspects of the software testing process and how it can be applied to databases. Unit tests for databases can be written as SQL scripts or stored functions in a database. There are several frameworks that help us write unit tests and process the results of testing.

Chapter 13, PostgreSQL JDBC, introduces the JDBC API. It covers basic operations, including executing SQL statements and accessing their results as well as more advanced features such as executing stored procedures and accessing the metainformation of databases and tables.

Chapter 14, PostgreSQL and Hibernate, covers the concept of Object-Relational Mapping, which is introduced using the Hibernate framework. This chapter explains how to execute CRUD operations in Hibernate and fetch strategies and associative mappings and also covers techniques such as caching and pooling for performance optimization.

What you need for this book

In general, PostgreSQL server and client tools do not need an exceptional hardware. PostgreSQL can be installed on almost all modern platforms, including Linux, Windows, and Mac. Also, in the book, when a certain library is needed, the installation instructions are given.

The example provided in this book requires PostgreSQL version 9.4; however, most of the examples can be executed on earlier versions as well. In order to execute the sample code, scripts, and examples provided in the book, you need to have at least a PostgreSQL client tool installed on your machine—preferably psql—and access to a remote server running the PostgreSQL server. In a Windows environment, the cmd.exe command prompt is not very convenient; thus, the user might consider using Cygwin `http://www.cygwin.com/` or another alternative such as Powershell.

For some chapters, such as *Chapter 13, PostgreSQL JDBC* and *Chapter 14, PostgreSQL and Hibernate*, one needs to install a development kit (JDK). Also, it is convenient to use the NetBeans or Eclipse integrated development environment (IDE).

Who this book is for

If you are a student, database developer, or an administrator interested in developing and maintaining a PostgreSQL database, this book is for you. No knowledge of database programming or administration is necessary.

Conventions

In this book, you will find a number of text styles that distinguish between different kinds of information. Here are some examples of these styles and an explanation of their meaning.

Code words in text, database table names, folder names, filenames, file extensions, pathnames, dummy URLs, user input, and Twitter handles are shown as follows: "The `customer_service` associates the customer and the service relations."

A block of code is set as follows:

```
<hibernate-mapping package="carportal" schema="carportal_app">
  <class name="Account" table="account">
    <id name="accountID" column="account_id">
      <generator class="identity"/>
    </id>
```

Any command-line input or output is written as follows:

```
SELECT first_name, last_name, service_id
FROM customer AS c CROSS JOIN customer_service AS cs
WHERE c.customer_id=cs.customer_id AND c.customer_id = 3;
```

New terms and **important words** are shown in bold. Words that you see on the screen, for example, in menus or dialog boxes, appear in the text like this: "Another option is to use a Linux emulator such as **Cygwin** and **MobaXterm**."

 Warnings or important notes appear in a box like this.

 Tips and tricks appear like this.

Reader feedback

Feedback from our readers is always welcome. Let us know what you think about this book—what you liked or disliked. Reader feedback is important for us as it helps us develop titles that you will really get the most out of.

To send us general feedback, simply e-mail feedback@packtpub.com, and mention the book's title in the subject of your message.

If there is a topic that you have expertise in and you are interested in either writing or contributing to a book, see our author guide at www.packtpub.com/authors.

Customer support

Now that you are the proud owner of a Packt book, we have a number of things to help you to get the most from your purchase.

Downloading the example code

You can download the example code files from your account at http://www.packtpub.com for all the Packt Publishing books you have purchased. If you purchased this book elsewhere, you can visit http://www.packtpub.com/support and register to have the files e-mailed directly to you.

Errata

Although we have taken every care to ensure the accuracy of our content, mistakes do happen. If you find a mistake in one of our books—maybe a mistake in the text or the code—we would be grateful if you could report this to us. By doing so, you can save other readers from frustration and help us improve subsequent versions of this book. If you find any errata, please report them by visiting http://www.packtpub.com/submit-errata, selecting your book, clicking on the **Errata Submission Form** link, and entering the details of your errata. Once your errata are verified, your submission will be accepted and the errata will be uploaded to our website or added to any list of existing errata under the Errata section of that title.

To view the previously submitted errata, go to https://www.packtpub.com/books/content/support and enter the name of the book in the search field. The required information will appear under the **Errata** section.

Piracy

Piracy of copyrighted material on the Internet is an ongoing problem across all media. At Packt, we take the protection of our copyright and licenses very seriously. If you come across any illegal copies of our works in any form on the Internet, please provide us with the location address or website name immediately so that we can pursue a remedy.

Please contact us at copyright@packtpub.com with a link to the suspected pirated material.

We appreciate your help in protecting our authors and our ability to bring you valuable content.

Questions

If you have a problem with any aspect of this book, you can contact us at questions@packtpub.com, and we will do our best to address the problem.

1
Relational Databases

This chapter will provide a high-level overview of topics related to database development. Understanding the basic relational database concepts enables the developers to not only come up with clean designs, but also to master relational databases. This chapter is not restricted to learning PostgreSQL, but covers all relational databases.

The topics covered in this chapter include the following:

- **Database management systems**: Understanding the different database categories enables the developer to utilize the best in each world.
- **Relational algebra**: Understanding relational algebra enables the developers to master the SQL language, especially, SQL code rewriting.
- **Data modeling**: Using data modeling techniques leads to better communication.

Database management systems

Different database management systems support diverse application scenarios, use cases, and requirements. Database management systems have a long history. First we will quickly take a look at the recent history, and then explore the market-dominant database management system categories.

A brief history

Broadly, the term database can be used to present a collection of things. Moreover, this term brings to mind many other terms including data, information, data structure, and management. A database can be defined as a collection or a repository of data, which has a certain structure, managed by a **database management system (DBMS)**. Data can be structured as tabular data, semi-structured as XML documents, or unstructured data that does not fit a predefined data model.

In early days, databases were mainly aimed at supporting business applications; this led us to the well-defined relational algebra and relational database systems. With the introduction of object-oriented languages, new paradigms of database management systems appeared such as object-relational databases and object-oriented databases. Also, many businesses as well as scientific applications use arrays, images, and spatial data; thus, new models such as raster, map, and array algebra are supported. Graph databases are used to support graph queries such as the shortest path from one node to another along with supporting traversal queries easily.

With the advent of web applications such as social portals, it is now necessary to support a huge number of requests in a distributed manner. This has led to another new paradigm of databases called NoSQL (Not Only SQL) which has different requirements such as performance over fault tolerance and horizontal scaling capabilities.

In general, the timeline of database evolution was greatly affected by many factors such as:

- **Functional requirements**: The nature of the applications using a DBMS has led to the development of extensions on top of relational databases such as PostGIS (for spatial data) or even dedicated DBMS such as SCI-DB (for scientific data analytics).

- **Nonfunctional requirements**: The success of object-oriented programming languages has created new trends such as object-oriented databases. Object relational database management systems have appeared to bridge the gap between relational databases and the object-oriented programming languages. Data explosion and the necessity to handle terabytes of data on commodity hardware have led to columnar databases, which can easily scale up horizontally.

Database categories

Many database models have appeared and vanished such as the network model and hierarchal model. The predominant categories now in the market are relational, object-relational databases, and NoSQL databases. One should not think of NoSQL and SQL databases as rivals; they are complementary to each other. By utilizing different database systems, one can overcome many limitations, and get the best of different technologies.

The NoSQL databases

The NoSQL databases are affected by the CAP theorem, also known as Brewer's theorem. In 2002, S. Gilbert and N. Lynch published a formal proof of the CAP theorem in their article: "Brewer's conjecture and the feasibility of consistent, available, partition-tolerant web services". In 2009, the NoSQL movement began. Currently, there are over 150 NoSQL databases (`nosql-database.org`).

The CAP theorem

The CAP theorem states that it is impossible for a distributed computing system to simultaneously provide all three of the following guarantees:

- **Consistency**: All clients see (immediately) the latest data even in the case of updates.

- **Availability**: All clients can find a replica of some data even in the case of a node failure. That means even if some part of the system goes down, the clients can still access the data.

- **Partition tolerance**: The system continues to work regardless of arbitrary message loss or failure of part of the system.

The choice of which feature to discard determines the nature of the system. For example, one could sacrifice consistency to get a scalable, simple, and high-performance database management system.

Often, the main difference between a relational database and a NoSQL database is consistency. A relational database enforces ACID. ACID is the acronym for the following properties: Atomicity, Consistency, Isolation, and Durability. In contrast, many NoSQL databases adopt the **basically available soft-state, eventual-consistency (BASE)** model.

NoSQL motivation

A NoSQL database provides a means for data storage, manipulation, and retrieval for non-relational data. The NoSQL databases are distributed, open source and horizontally scalable. NoSQL often adopts the BASE model, which prizes availability over consistency, and informally guarantees that if no new updates are made on a data item, eventually all access to that data item will return the latest version of that data item. The advantages of this approach include the following:

- Simplicity of design
- Horizontal scaling and easy replication
- Schema free
- Huge amount of data support

We will now explore a few types of NoSQL databases.

Key value databases

The key value store is the simplest database store. In this database model, the storage, as its name suggests, is based on maps or hash tables. Some key-value databases allow complex values to be stored as lists and hash tables. Key-value pairs are extremely fast for certain scenarios, but lack the support for complex queries and aggregation. Some of the existing open source key-value databases are Riak, Redis, Memebase, and MemcacheDB.

Columnar databases

Columnar or column-oriented databases are based on columns. Data in a certain column in a two dimensional relation is stored together. Unlike relational databases, adding columns is inexpensive, and is done on a row-by-row basis. Rows can have a different set of columns. Tables can benefit from this structure by eliminating the storage cost of the null values. This model is best suited for distributed databases. HBase is one of the most famous columnar databases. It is based on the Google big table storage system. Column-oriented databases are designed for huge data scenarios, so they scale up easily. For small datasets, HBase is not a suitable architecture. First, the recommended hardware topology for HBase is a five-node or server deployment. Also, it needs a lot of administration, and is difficult to master and learn.

Document databases

A document-oriented database is suitable for documents and semi-structured data. The central concept of a document-oriented database is the notion of a document. Documents encapsulate and encode data (or information) in some standard formats or encodings such as XML, JSON, and BSON. Documents do not adhere to a standard schema or have the same structure; so, they provide a high degree of flexibility. Unlike relational databases, changing the structure of the document is simple, and does not lock the clients from accessing the data.

Document databases merge the power of relational databases and column-oriented databases. They provide support for ad-hoc queries, and can be scaled up easily. Depending on the design of the document database, MongoDB is designed to handle a huge amount of data efficiently. On the other hand, CouchDB provides high availability even in the case of hardware failure.

Graph databases

Graph databases are based on the graph theory, where a database consists of nodes and edges. The nodes as well as the edges can be assigned data. Graph databases allow traversing between the nodes using edges. Since a graph is a generic data structure, graph databases are capable of representing different data. A famous implementation of an open source commercially supported graph databases is Neo4j.

Relational and object relational databases

Relational database management systems are one of the most-used DBMSs in the world. It is highly unlikely that any organization, institution, or personal computer today does not have or use a piece of software that does not rely on RBDMS. Software applications can use relational databases via dedicated database servers or via lightweight RDBMS engines, embedded in the software applications as shared libraries.

The capabilities of a relational database management system vary from one vendor to another, but most of them adhere to the ANSI SQL standards. A relational database is formally described by relational algebra, and is modeled on the relational model. **Object-relational database (ORD)** are similar to relational databases. They support object-oriented model concepts such as:

- User defined and complex data types
- Inheritance

ACID properties

In a relational database, a single logical operation is called a transaction. The technical translation of a transaction is a set of database operations, which are create, read, update, and delete (CRUD). The simplest example for explaining a transaction is money transfer from one bank account to another, which normally involves debiting one account and crediting another. The ACID properties in this context could be described as follows:

- **Atomicity**: All or nothing, which means that if a part of a transaction fails, then the transaction fails as a whole.

- **Consistency**: Any transaction gets the database from one valid state to another valid state. Database consistency is governed normally by data constraints and the relation between data and any combination thereof. For example, imagine if one would like to completely purge his account on a shopping service. In order to purge his account, his account details, such as list of addresses, will also need to be purged. This is governed by foreign key constraints, which will be explained in detail in the next chapter.

- **Isolation**: Concurrent execution of transactions results in a system state that would be obtained if the transactions were executed serially.

- **Durability**: The transactions which are committed, that is executed successfully, are persistent even with power loss or some server crashes. This is done normally by a technique called **write-ahead log (WAL)**.

The SQL Language

Relational databases are often linked to the **Structured Query Language (SQL)**. SQL is a declarative programming language, and is the standard relational database language. **American National Standard Institute (ANSI)** and **International standard organization (ISO)** published the SQL standard for the first time in 1986, followed by many versions such as SQL:1999, SQL:2003, SQL:2006, SQL:2008, and so on.

The SQL language has several parts:

- **Data definition language (DDL)**: It defines and amends the relational structure.

- **Data manipulation language (DML)**: It retrieves and extracts information from the relations.

- **Data control language (DCL)**: It controls the access rights to relations.

Basic concepts

A relational model is a first-order predicate logic, which was first introduced by Edgar F. Codd. A database is represented as a collection of relations. The state of the whole database is defined by the state of all the relations in the database. Different information can be extracted from the relations by joining and aggregating data from different relations, and by applying filters on the data.

In this section, the basic concepts of the relational model are introduced using the top-down approach by first describing the relation, tuple, attribute, and domain.

 The terms relation, tuple, attribute, and unknown, which are used in the formal relational model, are equivalent to table, row, column, and null in the SQL language.

Relation

Think of a relation as a table with a header, columns, and rows. The table name and the header help in interpreting the data in the rows. Each row represents a group of related data, which points to a certain object.

A relation is represented by a set of tuples. Tuples should have the same set of ordered attributes. Attributes have a domain, that is, a type and a name.

Customer relation					
	customer_id	first_name	last_name	Email	Phone
Tuple →	1	Thomas	Baumann		6622347
Tuple →	2	Wang	Kim	kim@wang_kim.com	6622345
Tuple →	3	Christian	Bayer		6622919
Tuple →	4	Ali	Ahmad		3322123
	↑ Attribute	↑ Attribute	↑ Attribute	↑ Attribute	↑ Attribute

The relation schema is denoted by the relation name and the relation attributes. For example, customer (`customer_id`, `first_name`, `last_name`, and `Email`) is the relation schema for the customer relation. Relation state is defined by the set of relation tuples; thus, adding, deleting, and amending a tuple will change the relation to another state.

Tuple order or position in the relation is not important, and the relation is not sensitive to tuple order. The tuples in the relation could be ordered by a single attribute or a set of attributes. Also, a relation cannot have duplicate tuples.

A relation can represent entities in the real world, such as a customer, or can be used to represent an association between relations. For example, the customer could have several services, and a service can be offered to several customers. This could be modeled by three relations: `customer`, `service`, and `customer_service`. The `customer_service` relation associates the customer and the service relations. Separating the data in different relations is a key concept in relational database modeling. This concept called normalization is the process of organizing relation columns and relations to reduce data redundancy. For example, let us assume a collection of services is stored in the customer relation. If a service is assigned to multiple customers, that would result in data redundancy. Also, updating a certain service would require updating all its copies in the customer table.

Tuple

A tuple is a set of ordered attributes. They are written by listing the elements within parentheses () and separated by commas, such as (john, smith, 1971). Tuple elements are identified via the attribute name. Tuples have the following properties:

- `(a1,a2, a3, ...an) = (b1, b2,b3,...,bn )` if and only if `a1 = ba`, `a2=b2, ... an= bn`

- A tuple is not a set, the order of attributes matters.

    ○ `(a1, a2) ≠(a2, a1)`

    ○ `(a1, a1) ≠(a1)`

    ○ A tuple has a finite set of attributes

In the formal relational model, multi-valued attributes as well as composite attributes are not allowed. This is important to reduce data redundancy and increasing data consistency. This isn't strictly true in modern relational database systems because of the utilization of complex data types such as JSON and key-value stores. There is a lot of debate regarding the application of normalization; the rule of thumb is to apply normalization unless there is a good reason not to do so.

Another important concept is that of the unknown values, that is, `NULL` values. For example, in the customer relation, the phone number of a customer might be unknown. Predicates in relational databases uses three-valued logic (3VL), where there are three truth values: true, false, and unknown. In a relational database, the third value, unknown, can be interpreted in many ways, such as unknown data, missing data, or not applicable. The three-valued logic is used to remove ambiguity. Imagine two tuples in the customer relation with missing phone values; does that mean both have the same phone, that is, `NULL=NULL`? The evaluation of the expression `NULL=NULL` is also `NULL`.

		A		
		True	**False**	**Unknown**
B	**True**	True	True	True
	False	True	False	Unknown
	Unknown	True	Unknown	Unknown

Logical operator OR truth table

		A		
		True	**False**	**Unknown**
B	**True**	True	False	Unknown
	False	False	False	Unknown
	Unknown	True	False	Unknown

Logical AND truth table

A	**True**	**False**	**Unknown**
NOT A	False	True	Unknown

Logical NOT truth table

Attribute

Each attribute has a name and a domain, and the name should be distinct within the relation. The domain defines the possible set of values that the attribute can have. One way to define the domain is to define the data type and a constraint on this data type. For example, hourly wage should be a positive real number and bigger than five if we assume the minimum hourly wage is five dollars. The domain could be continuous, such as salary which is any positive real number, or discrete, such as gender.

The formal relational model puts a constraint on the domain: the value should be atomic. Atomic means that each value in the domain is indivisible. For instance, the `name` attribute domain is not atomic, because it can be divided into first name and last name. Some examples of domains are as follows:

- **Phone number**: Numeric text with a certain length.
- **Country code**: Defined by ISO 3166 as a list of two letter codes (ISO alpha-2) and three letter codes (ISO alpha-3). The country codes for Germany are DE and DEU for alpha-2 and alpha-3 respectively.

 It is good practice if you have lookup tables such as country code, currency code, and languages to use the already defined codes in ISO standards, instead of inventing your own codes.

Constraint

The relational model defines many constraints in order to control data integrity, redundancy, and validity.

- **Redundancy**: Duplicate tuples are not allowed in the relation.
- **Validity**: Domain constraints control data validity.
- **Integrity**: The relations within a single database are linked to each other. An action on a relation such as updating or deleting a tuple might leave the other relations in an invalid state.

We could classify the constraints in a relational database roughly into two categories:

- **Inherited constraints from the relational model**: Domain integrity, entity integrity, and referential integrity constraints.
- **Semantic constraint, business rules, and application specific constraints**: These constraints cannot be expressed explicitly by the relational model. However, with the introduction of procedural SQL languages such as PL/pgsql for PostgreSQL, relational databases can also be used to model these constraints.

Domain integrity constraint

The domain integrity constraint ensures data validity. The first step in defining the domain integrity constraint is to determine the appropriate data type. The domain data types could be `integer`, `real`, `boolean`, `character`, `text`, `inet`, and so on. For example, the data type of first name and e-mail address is text. After specifying the data type, check constraints, such as the mail address pattern, need to be defined.

- **Check constraint**: A check constraint can be applied to a single attribute or a combination of many attributes in a tuple. Let us assume that `customer_service` schema is defined as (`customr_id`, `service_id`, `start_date`, `end_date`, `order_date`). For this relation, we can have a check constraint to make sure that `start_date` and `end_date` are entered correctly by applying the following check (`start_date<end_date`).

- **Default constraint**: The attribute can have a default value. The default value could be a fixed value such as the default hourly wage of the employees , for example, $10. It may also have a dynamic value based on a function such as random, current time, and date. For example, in the `customer_service` relation, `order_date` can have a default value which is the current date.

- **Unique constraint**: A unique constraint guarantees that the attribute has a distinct value in each tuple. It allows null values. For example, let us assume we have a relation player defined as player (`player_id`, `player_nickname`). The player uses his ID to play with others; he can also pick up a nickname which is not used by someone else.

- **Not null constraint**: By default, the attribute value can be null. The not null constraint restricts an attribute from having a null value. For example, each person in the birth registry record should have a name.

Entity integrity constraint

In the relational model, a relation is defined as a set of tuples. By definition, the element of the set is distinct. This means that all the tuples in a relation must be distinct. The entity integrity constraint is enforced by having a primary key which is an attribute/set of attributes having the following characteristics:

- The attribute should be unique
- The attributes should be not null

Each relation must have only one primary key, but can have many unique keys. A candidate key is a minimal set of attributes which can identify a tuple. All unique, `not null` attributes can be candidate keys. The set of all attributes form a super key. In practice, we often pick up a single attribute to be a primary key instead of a compound key (key that consists of two or more attributes that uniquely identify a tuple) to reduce data redundancy, and to ease the joining of the relations with each other.

If the primary key is generated by the DBMS, then it is called a surrogate key. Otherwise, it is called a natural key. The surrogate key candidates can be sequences and **universal unique identifiers** (UUID). A surrogate key has many advantages such as performance, requirement change tolerance, agility, and compatibility with object relational mappers. More on surrogate keys will be covered in the following chapters.

Referential integrity constraints

Relations are associated with each other via common attributes. Referential integrity constraints govern the association between two relations, and ensure data consistency between tuples. If a tuple in one relation references a tuple in another relation, then the referenced tuple must exist. In the customer service example, if a service is assigned to a customer, then the service and the customer must exist as shown in the following example. For instance, in the `customer_service` relation, we cannot have a tuple with values (`5, 1,01-01-2014, NULL`), because we do not have a customer with `customer_id` equal to 5.

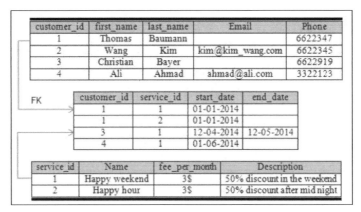

Association between customer and service

The lack of referential integrity constraints can lead to many problems such as:

- Invalid data in the common attributes
- Invalid information during joining of data from different relations.

Referential integrity constraints are achieved via foreign keys. A foreign key is an attribute or a set of attributes that can identify a tuple in the referenced relation. Since the purpose of a foreign key is to identify a tuple in the referenced relation, foreign keys are generally primary keys in the referenced relation. Unlike a primary key, a foreign key can have a null value. It can also reference a unique attribute in the referenced relation. Allowing a foreign key to have a null value enables us to model different cardinality constraints. Cardinality constraints define the participation between two different relations. For example, a parent can have more than one child; this relation is called one-to-many relationship, because one tuple in the referenced relation is associated with many tuples in the referencing relation. Also, a relation could reference itself. This foreign key is called a self-referencing or recursive foreign key. For example, a company acquired by another company:

company_id	Name	acquisitioned_by
1	Facebook	
2	WhatsApp	1
Primary key		**Foreign key**

Recursive foreign key

To ensure data integrity, foreign keys can be used to define several behaviors when a tuple in the referenced relation is updated or deleted. The following behaviors are called referential actions:

- **Cascade**: When a tuple is deleted or updated in the referenced relation, the tuples in the referencing relation are also updated or deleted.

- **Restrict**: The tuple cannot be deleted or the referenced attribute cannot be updated if it is referenced by another relation.

- **No action**: Similar to restrict, but it is deferred to the end of the transaction.

- **Set default**: When a tuple in the referenced relation is deleted or the referenced attribute is updated, then the foreign key value is assigned the default value.

- **Set null**: The foreign key attribute value is set to null when the referenced tuple is deleted.

Semantic constraints

Semantic integrity constraints or business logic constraints describe the database application constraints in general. Those constraints are either enforced by the business logic tier of the application program or by SQL procedural languages. Trigger and rule systems can also be used for this purpose. For example, the customer should have at most one active service at a time. Based on the nature of the application, one could favor using an SQL procedural language or a high-level programming language to meet the semantic constraints. The advantages of using the SQL programming language are:

- **Performance**: RDBMSs often have complex analyzers to generate efficient execution plans. Also, in some cases such as data mining, the amount of data that needs to be manipulated is very large. Manipulating the data using procedural SQL language eliminates the network data transfer. Finally, some procedural SQL languages utilize clever caching algorithms.

- **Last minute change**: For the SQL procedural languages, one could deploy bug fixes without service disruption.

Relational algebra

Relational algebra is the formal language of the relational model. It defines a set of closed operations over relations, that is, the result of each operation is a new relation. Relational algebra inherits many operators from set algebra. Relational algebra operations could be categorized into two groups:

- The first one is a group of operations which are inherited from set theory such as UNION, INTERSECTION, SET DIFFERENCE, and CARTESIAN PRODUCT, also known as CROSS PRODUCT.

- The second is a group of operations which are specific to the relational model such as SELECT and PROJECT.

Relational algebra operations could also be classified as binary and unary operations. Primitive relational algebra operators have ultimate power of reconstructing complex queries. The primitive operators are:

- SELECT (σ): A unary operation written as $\sigma_\varphi R$ where φ is a predicate. The selection retrieves the tuples in R, where φ holds.

- PROJECT (π): A unary operation used to slice the relation in a vertical dimension, that is, attributes. This operation is written as $\pi_{a1,a2...an} RO$, where $a1, a2, ..., an$ are a set of attribute names.

- CARTESIAN PRODUCT ($\times$): A binary operation used to generate a more complex relation by joining each tuple of its operands together. Let us assume that R and S are two relations, then $R \times S = \{r1, r2, ..., rn, s1, s2, ..., sn\}$, where $r1, r2, ..., rn \in R$ and $s1, s2, ..., sn \in S$.

- UNION ($\cup$): Appends two relations together; note that the relations should be union compatible, that is, they should have the same set of ordered attributes. Formally, $R \cup S = (r1, r2, ..., rn) \cup (s1, s2, ..., sn)$, where $(r1, r2, ..., rn) \in R$ and $(s1, s2, ..., sn) \in R$.

- DIFFERENCE ($/$ or -): A binary operation in which the operands should be union compatible. Difference creates a new relation from the tuples, which exist in one relation but not in the other. The set difference for the relation R and S can be given as $R / S = (r1, r2, ..., rn)$, where $(r1, r2, ..., rn) \in R$ and $(r1, r2, ..., rn) \notin S$.

- RENAME (ρ): A unary operation that works on attributes. It simply renames an attribute. This operator is mainly used in JOIN operations to distinguish the attributes with the same names but in different relation tuples. Rename is expressed as $\rho_{a/b} R$.

In addition to the primitive operators, there are aggregation functions such as sum, count, min, max, and average aggregates. Primitive operators can be used to define other relation operators such as left-join, right-join, equi-join, and intersection. Relational algebra is very important due to its expressive power in optimizing and rewriting queries. For example, the selection is commutative, so $\sigma_a \sigma_b R = \sigma_b \sigma_a R$. A cascaded selection may also be replaced by a single selection with a conjunction of all the predicates, that is, $\sigma_a \sigma_b R = \sigma_{a\,ANDb} R$.

The SELECT and PROJECT operations

SELECT is used to restrict tuples from the relation. If no predicate is given then the whole set of tuples is returned. For example, the query "give me the customer information where the customer_id equals to 2" is written as:

$$\sigma_{customer_{id}=2} \; customer$$

The selection is commutative; the query "give me all customers where the customer mail is known, and the customer first name is kim" is written in three different ways, as follows:

$$\sigma_{emails\ is\ not\ null} \left(\sigma_{first\_name=kim} customer \right)$$

$$\sigma_{first\_name=kim} \left(\sigma_{emails\ is\ not\ null} customer \right)$$

$$\sigma_{first\_name=kim\ AND\ emails\ is\ not\ null} \; customer$$

The selection predicates are certainly determined by the data types. For numeric data types, the comparison operator might be ($\neq, =, <, >, \geq, \leq$). The predicate expression can contain complex expressions and functions.

The equivalent SQL statement for the SELECT operator is the SELECT * statement, and the predicate is defined in the WHERE clause. Finally, the * means all the relation attributes; note that in the production environment, it is not recommended to use *. Instead, one should list all the relation attributes explicitly.

```
SELECT * FROM customer WHERE customer_id=2
```

The project operation could be visualized as vertical slicing of the table. The query: "give me the customer names" is written in relational algebra as follows:

$$\pi_{first\_name,last\_name} Customer$$

first_name	last_name
Thomas	Baumann
Wang	Kim
Christian	Bayer
Ali	Ahmad

The result of project operation

Duplicate tuples are not allowed in the formal relational model; the number of returned tuples from the project operator is always equal to or less than the number of total tuples in the relation. If a project operator's attribute list contains a primary key, then the resulting relation has the same number of tuples as the projected relation.

Cascading projections could be optimized as the following expression:

$$\pi_{att1}\left(\pi_{att1,}\pi_{att2}R\right)=\pi_{att1}R$$

The SQL equivalent for the PROJECT operator in SQL is SELECT DISTINCT. The DISTINCT keyword is used to eliminate duplicates. To get the result shown in the preceding expression, one could execute the following SQL statement:

```
SELECT DISTINCT first_name, last_name FROM customers;
```

The sequence of the execution of the PROJECT and SELECT operations can be interchangeable in some cases.

The query "give me the name of the customer with customer_id equal to 2" could be written as:

$$\sigma_{customer\_id=2}\left(\pi_{first\_name,last\_name}\ customer\right)$$

$$\pi_{first\_name,last\_name}\left(\sigma_{customer\_id=2}\ customer\right)$$

In other cases, the PROJECT and SELECT operators must have an explicit order as shown in the following example; otherwise, it will lead to an incorrect expression. The query "give me the last name of the customers where the first name is kim" could be written as the following expression:

$$\pi_{last\_name}\left(\sigma_{first\_name=kim}\ customer\right)$$

The RENAME operation

The Rename operation is used to alter the attribute name of the resultant relation, or to give a specific name to the resultant relation. The Rename operation is used to:

- Remove confusion if two or more relations have attributes with the same name
- Provide user-friendly names for attributes, especially when interfacing with reporting engines
- Provide a convenient way to change the relation definition, and still be backward compatible

The AS keyword in SQL is the equivalent of the RENAME operator in relational algebra. the following SQL example creates a relation with one tuple and one attribute, which is renamed PI.

```
SELECT 3.14::real AS PI;
```

The Set theory operations

The set theory operations are union, intersection, and minus (difference). Intersection is not a primitive relational algebra operator, because it is can be written using the union and difference operators:

$$A \cap B = \left(\left(A \cup B\right) - \left(A - B\right)\right) - \left(B - A\right)$$

The intersection and union are commutative:

$$A \cup B = \left(B \cup A\right)$$

$$A \cap B = \left(B \cap A\right)$$

For example, the query "give me all the customer IDs where the customer does not have a service assigned to him" could be written as:

$$\sigma_{customer\_id} customer - \sigma_{customer\_id} customer\_service$$

The CROSS JOIN (Cartesian product) operation

The CROSS JOIN operation is used to combine tuples from two relations into a single relation. The number of attributes in a single relation equals the sum of the number of attributes of the two relations. The number of tuples in the single relation equals the product of the number of tuples in the two relations. Let us assume A and B are two relations, and $C = A \times B$. Then:

$$number\ of\ attribute(C) = number\ of\ attributes(A) + number\ of\ attributes(B)$$

$$number\ of\ tuples(C) = number\ of\ tuples(A) * number\ of\ tuples(B)$$

The following image shows the cross join of customer and customer service, that is, $customer \times customer\_service$:

customer. customer_ id	first_name	last_ name	Email	phone	customer_ service. customer_ id	service_ id	start_ date	end_ date
1	Thomas	Baumann		6622347	1	1	01-01-2014	
2	Wang	Kim	kim@kim_wang.com	6622345	1	1	01-01-2014	
3	Christian	Bayer		6622919	1	1	01-01-2014	
4	Ali	Ahmad	ahmad@ali.com	3322123	1	1	01-01-2014	
1	Thomas	Baumann		6622347	1	2	01-01-2014	
2	Wang	Kim	kim@kim_wang.com	6622345	1	2	01-01-2014	
3	Christian	Bayer		6622919	1	2	01-01-2014	

customer. customer_ id	first_name	last_ name	Email	phone	customer_ service. customer_ id	service_ id	start_ date	end_ date
4	Ali	Ahmad	ahmad@ali.com	3322123	1	2	01-01-2014	
1	Thomas	Baumann		6622347	3	1	12-04-2014	12-05-2014
2	Wang	Kim	kim@kim_wang.com	6622345	3	1	12-04-2014	12-05-2014
3	Christian	Bayer		6622919	3	1	12-04-2014	12-05-2014
4	Ali	Ahmad	ahmad@ali.com	3322123	3	1	12-04-2014	12-05-2014
1	Thomas	Baumann		6622347	4	1	01-06-2014	
2	Wang	Kim	kim@kim_wang.com	6622345	4	1	01-06-2014	
3	Christian	Bayer		6622919	4	1	01-06-2014	
4	Ali	Ahmad	ahmad@ali.com	3322123	4	1	01-06-2014	

CROSS JOIN of customer and customer_service relations

For example, the query "for the customer with `customer_id` equal to 3, retrieve the customer name and the customer service IDs" could be written in SQL as follows:

```
SELECT first_name, last_name, service_id
FROM customer AS c CROSS JOIN customer_service AS cs
WHERE c.customer_id=cs.customer_id AND c.customer_id = 3;
```

In the preceding example, one can see the relationship between relational algebra and the SQL language. It shows how relational algebra could be used to optimize query execution. This example could be executed in several ways, such as:

Execution plan 1:

1. Select the customer where `customer_id = 3`.
2. Select the customer service where `customer_id = 3`.
3. Cross JOIN the relations resulting from steps 1 and 2.
4. Project `first_name`, `last_name`, and `service_id` from the relation resulting from step 3

Execution plan 2:

1. Cross JOIN `customer` and `customer_service`
2. Select all the tuples where

    `Customer_service.customer_id=customer.customer_id` and `customer.customer_id = 3`

3. Project `first_name`, `last_name`, and `service_id` from the relation resulting from step 2.

Each execution plan has a cost in terms of CPU and hard disk operations. The RDBMS picks the one with the lowest cost. In the preceding execution plans, the `RENAME` operator was ignored for simplicity.

Data modeling

Data models describe real-world entities such as customer, service, products, and the relation between these entities. Data models provide an abstraction for the relations in the database. Data models aid the developers in modeling business requirements, and translating business requirements to relations in the relational database. They are also used for the exchange of information between the developers and business owners.

In the enterprise, data models play a very important role in achieving data consistency across interacting systems. For example, if an entity is not defined, or is poorly defined, then this will lead to inconsistent and misinterpreted data across the enterprise. For instance, if the semantics of the customer entity is not defined clearly, and different business departments use different names for the same entity such as customer and client, this may lead to confusion in the operational departments.

Another common bad practice is to define business rules that describe how things should be done at the database level. This contradicts the "abstraction of concerns" and leads to fixed complex data structures. The business departments should define what needs to be done but not how.

Data model perspectives

Data model perspectives are defined by ANSI as follows:

- **Conceptual data model**: Describes the domain semantics, and is used to communicate the main business rules, actors, and concepts. It describes the business requirements at a high level and is often called a high-level data model. The conceptual model is the chain between developers and business departments in the application development life cycle.

- **Logical data model**: Describes the semantics for a certain technology, for example, the UML class diagram for object-oriented languages.

- **Physical data model**: Describes how data is actually stored and manipulated at the hardware level such as storage area network, table space, CPUs, and so on.

According to ANSI, this abstraction allows changing one part of the three perspectives without amending the other parts. One could change both the logical and the physical data models without changing the conceptual model. To explain, sorting data using bubble or quick sort is not of interest for the conceptual data model. Also, changing the structure of the relations could be transparent to the conceptual model. One could split one relation into many relations after applying normalization rules, or by using `enum` data types in order to model the lookup tables.

The entity-relation model

The entity-relation (ER) model falls in the conceptual data model category. It captures and represents the data model for both business users and developers. The ER model can be transformed into the relational model by following certain techniques.

Conceptual modeling is a part of the **Software development life cycle (SDLC)**. It is normally done after the functional and data requirements-gathering stage. At this point, the developer is able to make the first draft of the ER diagram as well as describe functional requirements using data flow diagrams, sequence diagrams, user case scenarios, user stories, and many other techniques.

During the design phase, the database developer should give great attention to the design, run a benchmark stack to ensure performance, and validate user requirements. Developers modeling simple systems could start coding directly. However, care should be taken when making the design, since data modeling involves not only algorithms in modeling the application but also data. The change in design might lead to a lot of complexities in the future such as data migration from one data structure to another.

While designing a database schema, avoiding design pitfalls is not enough. There are alternative designs, where one could be chosen. The following pitfalls should be avoided:

- **Data redundancy**: Bad database designs elicit redundant data. Redundant data can cause several other problems including data inconsistency and performance degradation. When updating a tuple which contains redundant data, the changes on the redundant data should be reflected in all the tuples that contain this data.

- **Null saturation**: By nature, some applications have sparse data, such as medical applications. Imagine a relation called diagnostics which has hundreds of attributes for symptoms like fever, headache, sneezing, and so on. Most of them are not valid for certain diagnostics, but they are valid in general. This could be modeled by utilizing complex data types like JSON, or by using vertical modeling like **entity-attribute-value** (**EAV**).

- **Tight coupling**: In some cases, tight coupling leads to complex and difficult-to-change data structures. Since business requirements change with time, some requirements might become obsolete. Modeling generalization and specialization (for example a part-time student is a student) in a tightly coupled way may cause problems.

Sample application

In order to explain the basics of the ER model, an online web portal to buy and sell cars will be modeled. The requirements of this sample application are listed as follows, and an ER model will be developed step-by-step:

- The portal provides the facility to register the users online, and provide different services for the users based on their categories.

- The users might be sellers or normal users. The sellers can create new car advertisements; other users can explore and search for cars.

- All users should provide there full name and a valid e-mail address during registration. The e-mail address will be used for logging in.

- The seller should also provide an address.

- The user can rate the advertisement and the seller's service quality.

- All users' search history should be maintained for later use.

- The sellers have ranks and this affects the advertisement search; the rank is determined by the number of posted advertisements and the user's rank.

- The car advertisement has a date and the car can have many attributes such as color, number of doors, number of previous owners, registration number, pictures and so on.

Entities, attributes, and keys

The ER diagram represents entities, attributes, and relationships. An entity is a representation of a real-world object such as car or a user. An attribute is a property of an object and describes it. A relationship represents an association between two or more entities.

The attributes might be composite or simple (atomic). Composite attributes can be divided into smaller subparts. A subpart of a composite attribute provides incomplete information that is semantically not useful by itself. For example, the address is composed of street name, building number, and postal code. Any one of them isn't useful alone without its counterparts.

Attributes could also be single-valued or multi-valued. The color of a bird is an example of a multi-valued attribute. It can be red and black, or a combination of any other colors. A multi-valued attribute can have a lower and upper bound to constrain the number of values allowed. In addition, some attributes can be derived from other attributes. Age can be derived from the birth date. In our example, the final rank of a seller is derived from the number of advertisements and the user ratings.

Finally, key attributes can identify an entity in the real world. A key attribute should be marked as a unique attribute, but not necessarily as a primary key, when physically modeling the relation. Finally, several attribute types could be grouped together to form a complex attribute.

Attribute symbol	Meaning
Attribute	Key attribute Example: E-mail address
Attribute	Attribute Example: Date of birth

Attribute symbol	Meaning
	Derived attribute Example: Age
	Multi-valued attribute Example: Car color
	Composite attribute Example: Address

Summary of the attribute notation for ER diagrams.

Entities should have a name and a set of attributes. They are classified into the following:

- Weak entity: Does not have key attributes of its own
- Strong entity or regular entity: Has a key attribute.

A weak entity is usually related to another strong entity. This strong entity is called the identifying entity. Weak entities have a partial key, aka "discriminator", which is an attribute that can uniquely identify the weak entity, and it is related to the identifying entity. In our example, if we assume that the search key is distinct each time the user searches for cars, then the search key is the partial key. The weak entity symbol is distinguished by surrounding the entity box with a double line.

Entity symbol	Meaning
Entity	Weak entity
Entity	Strong entity

ER entities symbols

The next image shows the preliminary design of the online. The user entity has several attributes. The name attribute is a composite attribute, and e-mail is a key attribute. The seller entity is a specialization of the user entity. The total rank is a derived attribute calculated by aggregating the user ratings and the number of advertisements. The color attribute of the car is multi-valued. The seller can be rated by the users for certain advertisements; this relation is a ternary relation, because the rating involves three entities which are car, seller, and user. The car picture is a subpart attribute of the advertisement. The following diagram shows that the car can be advertised more than once by different sellers. In the real world, this makes sense, because one could ask more than one seller to sell his car.

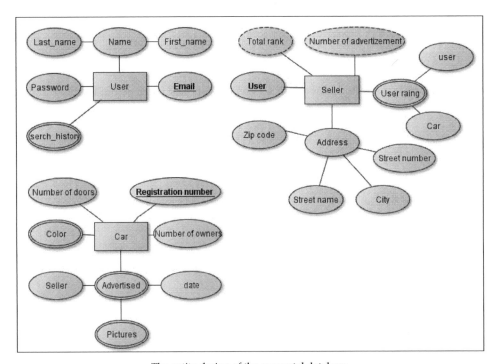

The entity design of the car portal database.

When an attribute of one entity refers to another entity, some relationships exist. In the ER model, these references should not be modeled as attributes but as relationships or weak entities. Similar to entities, there are two classes of relationships: weak and strong. Weak relationships associate the weak entities with other entities. Relationships can have attributes as entities. In our example, the car is advertised by the seller; the advertisement date is a property of the relationship.

Relationships have cardinality constraints to limit the possible combinations of entities that participate in a relationship. The cardinality constraint of car and seller is *1:N*; the car is advertised by one seller, and the seller can advertise many cars. The participation between seller and user is called total participation, and is denoted by a double line. This means that a seller cannot coexist alone, and he must be a user.

The many-to-many relationship cardinality constraint is denoted by *N:M* to emphasize different participation from the entities.

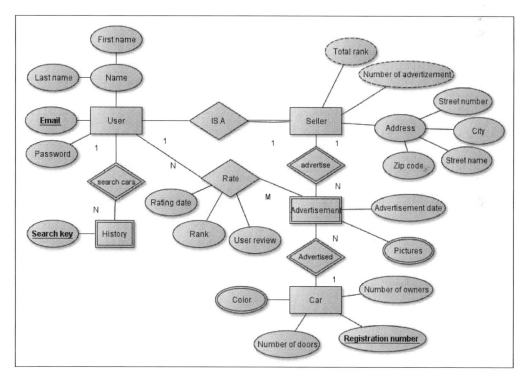

Car web portal ER diagram.

Up until now, only the basic concepts of ER diagrams have been covered. Some concepts such as (min, max) cardinality notation, ternary/n-ary relationships, generalization, specialization, and **Enhanced Entity relation diagrams (EER)** have not been discussed.

Mapping ER to Relations

The rules for mapping an ER diagram to a set of relations (that is, the database schema) are almost straightforward but not rigid. One could model an entity as an attribute, and then refine it to a relationship. An attribute which belongs to several entities can be promoted to be an independent entity. The most common rules are listed as follows (note that only basic rules have been covered, and the list is not exhaustive):

- Map regular entities to relations: If entities have composite attributes, then include all the subparts of the attributes. Pick one of the key attributes as a primary key.

- Map weak entities to relations, include simple attributes and the subparts of the composite attributes. Add a foreign key to reference the identifying entity. The primary key is normally the combination of the partial key and the foreign key.

- If a relationship has an attribute, and the relation cardinality is *1:1*, then the relation attribute can be assigned to one of the participating entities.

- If a relationship has an attribute, and the relation cardinality is *1:N*, then the relation attribute can be assigned to the participating entity on the N side. For example, the `advertisement_date` can be assigned to the car relation.

- Map many-to-many relationships, also known as *N:M*, to a new relation. Add foreign keys to reference the participating entities. The primary key is the composition of foreign keys. The `customer_service` relation is an example of many-to-many relationship.

- Map a multi-valued attribute to a relation. Add a foreign key to reference the entity that owns the multi-valued attribute. The primary key is the composition of the foreign key and the multi-valued attribute.

UML class diagrams

Unified modeling language (UML) is a standard developed by **Object Management Group (OMG)**. UML diagrams are widely used in modeling software solutions, and there are several types of UML diagrams for different modeling purposes including class, use case, activity, and implementation diagrams.

A class diagram can represent several types of associations, that is, the relationship between classes. They can depict attributes as well as methods. An ER diagram can be easily translated into a UML class diagram. UML class diagrams also have the following advantages:

- **Code reverse engineering**: The database schema can be easily reversed to generate a UML class diagram.

- **Modeling extended relational database objects**: Modern relational databases have several object types such as sequences, views, indexes, functions, and stored procedures. UML class diagrams have the capability to represent these objects types.

Summary

The design of a database management system is affected by the CAP theorem. Relational databases and NoSQL databases are not rivals but complementary. One can utilize different database categories in a single software application. In certain scenarios, one can use the key-value store as a cache engine on top of the relational database to gain performance.

Relational and object-relational databases are the market-dominant databases. Relational databases are based on the concept of relation, and have a very robust mathematical model. Object-relational databases such as PostgreSQL overcome the limitations of relational databases by introducing complex data types, inheritance, and rich extensions.

Relational databases are based on the relation, tuple, and the attribute concepts. They ensure data validity and consistency by employing several techniques such as entity integrity, constraints, referential integrity, and data normalization.

Modern RDBMS can capture semantic constraints by using SQL procedural languages, triggers, and rule systems. PostgreSQL can support several procedural languages including C, PL/pgSQL, PL/Python, and so on.

Relational algebra enables the developer to rewrite the SQL code in alternative ways. It also enables the RDBMS to generate, compare, and choose an execution plan from different execution plans. Relational algebra provides a closed set of operations which can be combined together to answer complex queries.

SQL is the standard relational database language. SQL standards are maintained by ISO, and SQL code is often compatible with different relational databases.

Data modeling is very important for communicating business requirements; it can help in achieving the concept of separation of concerns. There are several data modeling perspectives, namely, conceptual, logical, and physical perspectives.

In the next chapter, an overview of PostgreSQL will be introduced. The next chapter will discuss the advantages, history, capabilities, and forks of PostgreSQL. It also will show how one can install PostgreSQL on different platforms including Linux and Windows.

Downloading the example code

You can download the example code fies from your account at `http://www. packtpub.com` for all the Packt Publishing books you have purchased. If you purchased this book elsewhere, you can visit `http://www.packtpub.com/support` and register to have the files e-mailed directly to you.

2
PostgreSQL in Action

PostgreSQL (pronounced Post-Gres-Q-L) or postgres is an open source object relational database management system. It emphasizes extensibility, creativity, as well as compatibility. It competes with the major relational database vendors such as Oracle, MySQL, SQL servers, and others. It is used by different sectors including government agencies and the public and private sectors. It is a cross-platform DBMS, and runs on most modern operating systems including Windows, MAC, and Linux flavors. It conforms to SQL, and is ACID compliant.

An overview of PostgreSQL

PostgreSQL (http://www.postgresql.org/) has many rich features. It provides enterprise level services including performance, unique features, and scalability. It has a very supportive community and very good documentation.

PostgreSQL history

The name PostgreSQL is derived from post-ingres database. PostgreSQL history could be summarized as follows:

- **Academia**: University of California at Berkeley (UCB)
    - ○ **1977-1985, the Ingres project**: Michael Stonebraker created an RDBMS based on the formal relational model.
    - ○ **1986-1994, postgres**: Michael Stonebraker created postgres in order to support complex data types and the object relational model.
    - ○ **1995, Postgres95**: Andrew Yu and Jolly Chen changed the postgres POSTQUEL query language with an extended subset of SQL

- **Industry**

  ◦ **1996, PostgreSQL**: Several developers dedicated a lot of labor and time to stabilize postgres95. The first open source version was released on January 29, 1997. With the introduction of new features, enhancements, and due to it being an open source project, the postgres95 name was changed to PostgreSQL.

PostgreSQL begun at version 6, having a very strong starting point due to the advantage of several years of research and development. Being an open source project with a very good reputation, PostgreSQL attracted hundreds of developers. Currently, PostgreSQL has an uncountable number of extensions and a very active community.

The advantages of PostgreSQL

PostgreSQL provides many features that attract developers, administrators, architects, and companies.

Business advantages of PostgreSQL

PostgreSQL is a free **open source software** (**OSS**). It is released under the PostgreSQL license, which is similar to the BSD and MIT licenses. The PostgreSQL license is highly permissive, and PostgreSQL is not subject to monopoly and acquisition. This gives the company the following advantages:

- No associated licensing cost to PostgreSQL.

- Unlimited number of deployments of PostgreSQL.

- More profitable business model.

- PostgreSQL is SQL standards compliant; thus, finding professional developers is not very difficult. PostgreSQL is easy to learn, and porting code from one database vendor to PostgreSQL is cost efficient. Also, the PostgreSQL administrative tasks are easy to automate, thus reducing the staffing cost significantly.

- PostgreSQL is cross-platform, and it has drivers for all modern programming languages; so, there is no need to change the company policy regarding the software stack in order to use PostgreSQL.

- PostgreSQL is scalable, and it gives high performance.

- PostgreSQL is very reliable; it rarely crashes. Also, PostgreSQL is ACID compliant, which means that it can tolerate some hardware failure. In addition to that, it can be configured and installed as a cluster to ensure **high availability** (**HA**).

PostgreSQL user advantages

PostgreSQL is very attractive for developers, administrators, and architects. It has rich features that enable developers to perform tasks in an agile way. The following are some of the features that are attractive to developer:

- A new release almost every year; there have been 23 major releases until now, starting from Postgres95.

- Very good documentation and an active community enables developers to find and solve problems quickly. The PostgreSQL manual is over 2,500 pages.

- A rich extension repository enables developers to focus on business logic. Also, it enables developers to meet requirement changes easily.

- The source code is available free of charge. It can be customized and extended without huge effort.

- Rich clients and administrative tools enable developers to perform routine tasks such as describing database objects, exporting and importing data, and dumping and restoring databases very quickly.

- Database administration tasks do not require a lot of time, and can be automated.

- PostgreSQL can be integrated easily with other database management systems giving the software architecture a good flexibility for implementing software designs.

PostgreSQL applications

PostgreSQL can be used with a variety of applications. The main PostgreSQL application domains can be classified into two categories:

- **Online transactional processing (OLTP)**: OLTP is characterized by a large amount of CRUD operations, very fast processing of operations, and the maintaining of data integrity in a multi-access environment. Performance is measured in the number of transactions per second.

- **Online analytical processing (OLAP)**: OLAP is characterized by a small amount of requests, complex queries which involve data aggregation, huge amounts of data from different sources and with different formats, data mining, and historical data analysis.

OLTP is used to model business operations such as **customer relationship management (CRM)**. For example, the car web portal example in *Chapter 1, Relational Databases*, is an example of an OLTP application. OLAP applications are used for business intelligence, decision support, reporting, and planning. An OLTP database size is relatively small as compared to an OLAP database. OLTP normally follows relational model concepts, such as normalization ,when designing the database, while OLAP has less relation; the schema often has the shape of a star or a snowflake. Finally the data is deformalized.

In the car web portal example, we could have another database to store and maintain all the sellers' and users' historical data to analyze user preferences and seller activities. This database is an example of an OLAP application.

Unlike OLTP, OLAP's main operation is data retrieval. OLAP data is often generated by a process called ETL (extract, transform, and load). ETL is used to load data in to the OLAP database from different data sources and different formats.

PostgreSQL can be used out of the box for OLTP applications. For OLAP, there are many extensions and tools to support it, such as the PostgreSQL COPY command and **Foreign Data Wrappers (FDW)**.

Success stories

PostgreSQL is used in many application domains including communication, medical, geographical, and e-commerce applications. Many companies provide consultation as well as commercial services, such as migrating proprietary RDBMS to PostgreSQL in order to cut off the licensing costs. These companies often influence and enhance PostgreSQL by developing and submitting new features.

The following are a few companies that have used PostgreSQL:

- Skype uses PostgreSQL to store user chats and activities. Skype has also affected PostgreSQL by developing many tools called Skytools.

- Instagram is a social networking service that enables its user to share pictures and photos. Instagram has more than 100 million active users.

- The **American chemical society (ACS)** uses PostgreSQL to store more than one terabyte of data for the journal archive.

In addition to the companies mentioned in the preceding list, PostgreSQL is used by HP, WMware, and Heroku. PostgreSQL is used by many scientific communities and organizations, such as NASA, due to its extensibility and rich data types.

Forks

There are more than 20 PostgreSQL forks; PostgreSQL extensible APIs make postgres a great candidate for forking. Over the years, many groups forked PostgreSQL and contributed their findings to PostgreSQL. The following is a list of the popular PostgreSQL forks:

> A fork is an independent development of a software project based on another project.

- HadoopDB is a hybrid between the PostgreSQL RDBMS and MapReduce technologies to target analytical workload.

- Greenplum is a proprietary DBMS that was built on the foundation of PostgreSQL. It utilizes the shared-nothing and massively parallel processing (MPP) architectures. It is used as a data warehouse and for analytical workloads.

- The EnterpriseDB advanced server is a proprietary DBMS that provides Oracle with the capability to cap the oracle fees.

- **Postgres-XC (extensible cluster)** is a multi-master PostgreSQL cluster based on the shared-nothing architecture. It emphasis write-scalability, and provides the same APIs to applications as PostgreSQL.

- Vertica is a column-oriented database system that was started by Michael Stonebraker in 2005, and was acquisitioned by HP in 2011. Vertica reused the SQL parser, semantic analyzer, and standard SQL rewrites from the PostgreSQL implementation.

- Netzza, a popular data warehouse appliances solution, was started as a PostgreSQL fork.

- Amazon red shift is a popular data warehouse management system based on PostgreSQL 8.0.2. It is mainly designed for OLAP applications.

PostgreSQL architecture

PostgreSQL uses the client/server model, where the client and server programs can be on different hosts. The communication between the client and server is normally done via TCP/IP protocols or via Linux sockets. PostgreSQL can handle multiple connections from a client. A common PostgreSQL program consists of the following operating system processes:

- **Client process or program (frontend)**: The database frontend application performs a database action. The frontend can be a web server that wants to display a web page or a command-line tool to do maintenance tasks. PostgreSQL provides frontend tools such as **psql**, **createdb**, **dropdb**, and **createuser**.

- **Server process (backend)**: The server process manages database files, accepts connections from client applications, and performs actions on behalf of the client. The server process name is postgres.

PostgreSQL forks a new process for each new connection; thus, client and server processes communicate with each other without the intervention of the server main process (postgres), and they have a certain lifetime that is determined by accepting and terminating a client connection.

PostgreSQL abstract architecture

The aforementioned abstract conceptual PostgreSQL architecture gives an overview of the PostgreSQL capabilities and its interaction with the client, and the operating system. The PostgreSQL server could be divided roughly into four subsystems, as follows:

- **Process manager**: The process manager manages client connections such as forking and the terminating process.

- **Query processor**: When a client sends a query to PostgreSQL, the query is parsed by the parser, and then the *traffic cop* subsystem determines the query type. A utility query is passed to the utilities subsystem. Select, insert, update, and delete queries are rewritten by the rewriter following which an execution plan is generated by the planner. Finally, the query is executed and the result is returned to the client.

- **Utilities**: The utilities subsystem provides a means for maintaining the database such as claiming storage, updating statistics, and exporting and importing data with a certain format and logging.

- **Storage manager**: The storage manager handles the memory cache, disk buffers, and storage allocation.

Almost all PostgreSQL components can be configured, including a logger, planner, statistical analyzer, and storage manager. PostgreSQL configuration is governed by the nature of the application, such as OLAP and OLTP.

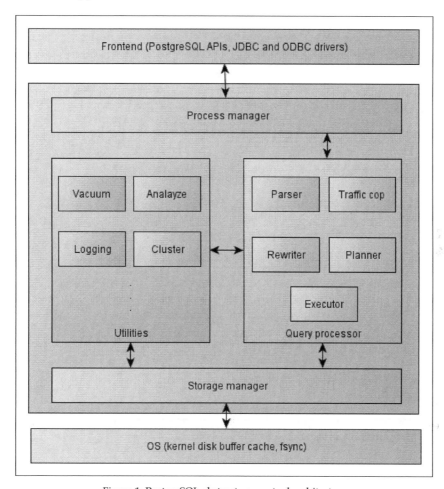

Figure 1: PostgreSQL abstract conceptual architecture

The PostgreSQL community

PostgreSQL has a very cooperative, active, and organized community. In the last 8 years, the PostgreSQL community has published eight major releases. Announcements are brought to the developers via the PostgreSQL weekly newsletter. There are dozens of mailing lists organized into categories such as user, developer, and associations. Examples of user mailing lists are pgsql-general, psql-doc, and psql-bugs. pgsql-general is a very important mailing list for beginners. All non-bugs-related questions regarding PostgreSQL installation, tuning, basic administration, PostgreSQL features, and general discussions are submitted to this list.

The PostgreSQL community runs a blog aggregation service called Planet PostgreSQL (`planet.postgrresql.org`). Several PostgreSQL developers and companies use this service to share their experience and knowledge.

PostgreSQL capabilities

PostgreSQL provides enterprise-level services which guarantee the continuation of the business.

Replication

Replication allows data from one database server to be replicated to another server. Replication is used mainly to achieve the following:

- **High availability**: A second server can take over if the primary server fails.
- **Load balancing**: Several servers can serve the same requests.
- **Faster execution**: A query is executed on several machines at once to gain performance.

PostgreSQL supports replication out of the box via streaming replication. Streaming replication is a master-slave replication that uses file-based log shipping. Streaming replication is a binary replication technique, because SQL statements are not analyzed. It is based on taking a snapshot of the master node, and then shipping the changes—the WAL files—from the master node to the slave node and replaying them on the slave. The master can be used for read/write operations, and the slave can be used to serve read requests. Streaming replication is relatively easy to set up and configure; it can support synchronous and asynchronous replications as well as cascading replication. In synchronous replication, a data modifying operation must be committed on all servers in order to be considered successful. In cascading replication, one could add a replica to a slave. This allows PostgreSQL to scale horizontally for read operations.

In addition to PostgreSQL streaming replication, there are several other open source solutions to target different workloads, such as:

- **Slony-1**: This is a master to multiple slave replication systems. Unlike PostgreSQL, it can be used with different server versions. So, one could replicate the 9.2 server data to the 9.4 server.

- **pgpool-II**: This is middleware between PostgreSQL and the client. In addition to replication, it can be used for connection pooling, load balancing, and parallel query execution.

- **Distributed Replicated Block Device (DRBD)**: A general solution for HA. It can be understood as a network RAID-1.

Security

PostgreSQL supports several authentication methods including trust, password, LDAB, GSSAPI, SSPI, Kerberos, ident-based, RADUIS, certificate, and PAM authentication. All database vulnerabilities are listed in the PostgreSQL security information web page—`http://www.postgresql.org/support/security/`—with information about the affected version, vulnerability class, and the affected component.

The PostgreSQL security updates are made available as minor updates. Also, known security issues are always fixed with the next major releases. Publishing security updates in minor updates makes it easy for a PostgreSQL administrator to keep PostgreSQL secure and up-to-date with minimal downtime.

PostgreSQL can control the database object access at several levels including database, table, view, function, sequence, and column. This enables PostgreSQL to have a great authorization control.

PostgreSQL can use encryption to protect data by hardware encryption. Also, one can encrypt certain information by utilizing the `pgcrypto` extension.

Extension

PostgreSQL can be extended to support new data types. PostgreSQL provides the `CREATE EXTENSION` command to load extensions to the current database. Also, PostgreSQL has a central distribution network (PGXN)—`www.pgxn.org`—which allows users to explore and download extensions. When installing the PostgreSQL binaries, the `postgresql-postgresql-contib` package contains many useful extensions such as `tablefunc`, which allows table pivoting and `pgcrypto` extension; the `README` file in the installation directory contains the summary information.

The ability of PostgreSQL to support extensions is a result of the following features:

- **PostgreSQL data types**: PostgreSQL has very rich data types. It supports primitive data types as well as some primitive data structures, such as arrays, out of the box. In addition to that, it supports complex data types, such as:

  - **Geometric data types**: Including point, line segment (`lseg`), path, polygon and box.

  - **Network address types**: Including `cidr`, `inet`, and `macaddr`.

  - **tsvector**: This is a sorted list of lexemes that enables postgres to perform full text search.

  - **Universal unique identifiers (UUID)**: UUID solves many problems related to databases, such as offline data generation.

  - **NoSQL**: It supports several NoSQL data types including XML, Hstore, and JSONB.

  - Enum, range and domain are user-defined data types with specific constraints, such as a set of allowed values, data range constraint, and check constraints.

  - Composite data type is a user-defined data type, where an attribute is composed of several attributes.

    The following example shows how to create a new composite type called `phone_number`. An equality operator is also created to check if two phone numbers are equal by comparing the area code and the line number.

    ```
    --This example shows how to create a composite data type.
    CREATE TYPE phone_number AS (
        area_code varchar(3),
        line_number varchar(7)
    );
    CREATE OR REPLACE FUNCTION phone_number_equal (phone_
    number,phone_number) RETURNS boolean AS
    $$
        BEGIN
            IF $1.area_code=$2.area_code AND
            $1.line_number=$2.line_number THEN
                RETURN TRUE ;
            ELSE
    ```

```
                        RETURN FALSE;
                END IF;
        END;
        $$
        LANGUAGE plpgsql;
        CREATE OPERATOR = (
            LEFTARG = phone_number,
            RIGHTARG = phone_number,
            PROCEDURE = phone_number_equal
        );
        --For test purpose
        SELECT row('123','222244')::phone_number =
        row('1','222244')::phone_number;
```

- **Supported languages**: PostgreSQL allows functions to be written in several languages. The PostgreSQL community supports the following languages: SQL, C, Python, PL/pgSQL, Perl, and Tcl. In addition to these, there are many externally maintained procedural languages, including Java, R, PHP, Ruby, and UNIX shell.

NoSQL capabilities

PostgreSQL is more than a relational database and an SQL language. PostgreSQL is now home to different NoSQL data types. The power of PostgreSQL and schema-less data stores enable the developers to build reliable and flexible applications in an agile way.

PostgreSQL supports the **JavaScript Simple Object Notation (JSON)** data type, which is often used for sharing data across different systems in modern RESTful web applications. In PostgreSQL release 9.4, PostgreSQL introduced another structured binary format for saving JSON documents instead of using the JSON format in the prior versions. The new data type is called JSONB. This data type eliminates the need for parsing a JSON document before it is committed to the database. In other words, PostgreSQL can ingest a JSON document at a speed comparable with document databases, while still maintaining compliance with ACID.

Key/value pairs are also supported by the PostgreSQL hstore extension. The Hstore is used to store semi-structured data, and it can be used in several scenarios to decrease the number of attributes that are rarely used and often contain null values.

Finally, PostgreSQL supports the **Extensible Markup Language (XML)** data type. XML is very flexible and it is often used to define document formats. XML is used in RSS, Atom, SOAP, and XHTML. PostgreSQL supports several XML functions to generate and create XML documents. Also, it supports xpath to find information in an XML document.

Foreign data wrapper

In 2011, PostgreSQL 9.1 was released with a read-only support for SQL / **Management of External Data (MED)** ISO/IEC 9075-9:2003 standard. SQL/MED defines **foreign data wrappers (FDW)** to allow the relational database to manage external data. Foreign data wrappers can be used to achieve data integration in a federated database system environment. PostgreSQL supports RDBMS, NoSQL, and file foreign data wrappers including Oracle, Redis, Mongodb, and delimited files.

A simple use case for FDW is to have one database server for analytical purposes, and then ship the result of this server to another server that works as a caching layer.

Also, FDW can be used for testing data changes. Imagine you have two databases, one with different data due to applying a certain development patch. One could use FDW to assess the effect of this patch by comparing the data from the two databases.

PostgreSQL supports postgres_fdw starting from release 9.3. postgres_fdw is used to enable data sharing and access between different PostgreSQL databases. It supports the SELECT, INSERT, UPDATE, and DELETE operations on foreign tables.

Performance

PostgreSQL has a proven performance. It employs several techniques to improve concurrency and scalability, including the following:

- **PostgreSQL locking system**: PostgreSQL provides several types of locks at the table and row levels. PostgreSQL is able to use more granular locks that prevent locking/blocking more than necessary; this increases concurrency and decreases the blocking time.

- **Indexes**: PostgreSQL provides four types of indexes: B-Tree, hash, **generalized inverted index (GIN)**, and the **Generalized Search Tree (GiST)** index. Each index type can be used for a certain scenario. For example, B-tree can be used for equality and range queries efficiently. GIST can be used for text search and for geospatial data. PostgreSQL supports partial, unique, and multicolumn indexes. It also supports indexes on expressions and operator classes.

- **Explain, analyze, vacuum, and cluster**: PostgreSQL provides several commands to boost performance and provide transparency. The EXPLAIN command shows the execution plan of an SQL statement. One can change some parameter settings such as memory settings, and then compare the execution plan before and after the change. The ANALYSE command is used to collect the statistics on tables and columns. The VACUUM command is used for garbage collection to reclaim unused hard disk space. The CLUSTER command is used for arranging data physically on the hard disk. All these commands can be configured based on the database workload.

- **Table inheritance and constraint exclusion**: Table inheritance allows the creation of tables with the same structure easily. Those tables are used to store subsets of data based on a certain criteria. This allows a very fast retrieval of information in certain scenarios, because only a subset of data is accessed when answering a query.

Very rich SQL constructs

PostgreSQL supports very rich SQL constructs. It supports correlated and non-correlated subqueries. It supports **common table expression (CTE)**, window functions, and recursive queries. Once developers have learned these SQL constructs, they will be able to write a crisp SQL code very quickly. Moreover, they will be able to write complex queries with minimal effort. The PostgreSQL community keeps adding new SQL features in each release; in release 9.4, three SQL clauses were added: FILTER, WITHIN GROUP, and the ALTER SYSTEM clause.

Installing PostgreSQL

PostgreSQL can be installed on almost all modern operating systems. It can be installed on all recent Linux distributions, Windows 2000 SP4 and later, FreeBSD, OpenBSD, Mac OS X, AIX, and Solaris. Also, PostgreSQL can work on various CPU architectures including x86, x86_64, IA64, and others. One can check if a platform (operating system and CPU architecture combination) is supported by exploring the PostgreSQL Build farm (http://buildfarm.postgresql.org/).

One can compile and install PostgreSQL from the source code or download its binary and install it.

 In order to automate PostgreSQL installation and to reduce server administrative tasks, it is recommended to use PostgreSQL binaries, which come with the operating system packaging system. This approach normally has one drawback: not up-to-date binaries.

Installing PostgreSQL on Ubuntu

Ubuntu is a Debian-based widely spread Linux operating system. Ubuntu uses the **Advanced Packaging Tool (APT)**, which handles software installation and removal on the Debian operating system and its variants.

Client installation

If you have a PostgreSQL server already installed and you need to interact with it, then you need to install the `postgresql-client` software package. In order to do so, open a terminal and execute the following command:

```
sudo apt-get install postgresql-client
```

With the installation of `postgrsql-client`, several tools are installed including the PostgreSQL interactive terminal (psql), which is a very powerful interactive frontend tool for PostgreSQL. To see the full list of installed programs, one can browse the installation directory. Note that the installation path might vary depending on the installed PostgreSQL version, and also depending on the operating system:

```
cd /usr/lib/postgresql/9.4/bin/

ls

clusterdb  createdb  createlang  createuser  dropdb  droplang  dropuser
pg_basebackup  pg_dump  pg_dumpall  pg_isready  pg_receivexlog  pg_
recvlogical  pg_restore  psql  reindexdb  vacuumdb
```

In order to connect to an existing PostgreSQL server using psql, one needs to specify the connection string, which might include the host, the database, the port, and the user name.

Another powerful frontend tool is `pgAdmin` which is used for PostgreSQL administration and development. Unlike psql: which is a terminal user interface, `pgAdmin` is a graphical user interface (GUI). `pgAdmin` is favored by beginners, while psql can be used for shell scripting.

In order to install pgAdmin, one should run the following command:

```
sudo apt-get install pgadmin3
```

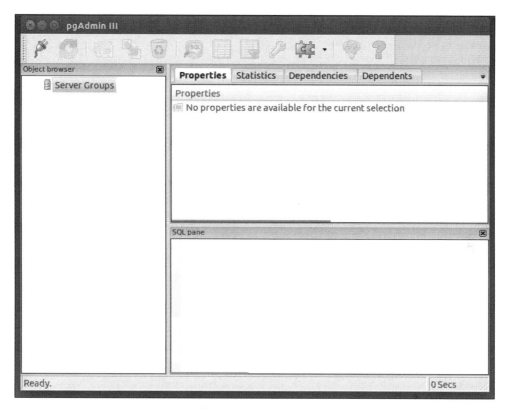

Figure 2: pgAdmin tool

Server installation

In order to install the server, one should run the following command:

```
sudo apt-get install postgresql
...
Creating config file /etc/postgresql-common/createcluster.conf with new
version

Creating config file /etc/logrotate.d/postgresql-common with new version
Building PostgreSQL dictionaries from installed myspell/hunspell
packages...
```

```
Removing obsolete dictionary files:
 * No PostgreSQL clusters exist; see "man pg_createcluster"
Processing triggers for ureadahead (0.100.0-16) ...
Setting up postgresql-9.4 (9.4.5-1.pgdg14.04+1) ...
Creating new cluster 9.4/main ...
  config /etc/postgresql/9.4/main
  data   /var/lib/postgresql/9.4/main
  locale en_US.UTF-8
Flags of /var/lib/postgresql/9.4/main set as ------------e-C
  port   5432
update-alternatives: using /usr/share/postgresql/9.4/man/man1/
postmaster.1.gz to provide /usr/share/man/man1/postmaster.1.gz
(postmaster.1.gz) in auto mode
 * Starting PostgreSQL 9.4 database server              [ OK ]
Setting up postgresql-contrib-9.4 (9.4.5-1.pgdg14.04+1) ...
Processing triggers for libc-bin (2.19-0ubuntu6.6) ...
```

The installation will give you information about the location of the PostgreSQL configuration files, data location, locale, port, and PostgreSQL status, as shown in the preceding code. PostgreSQL initializes a storage area on the hard disk called a database cluster. A database cluster is a collection of databases managed by a single instance of a running database server. That means, one can have more than one instance of PostgreSQL running on the same server by initializing several database clusters. These instances can be of different PostgreSQL server versions, or the same version.

The database cluster locale is en_US.UTF-8. By default, when a database cluster is created, the database cluster will be initialized with the locale setting of its execution environment. This can be controlled by specifying the locale when creating a database cluster. A configuration location enables a developer/administrator to control the behavior of the PostgreSQL database.

Another important package that should be installed is the postgresql-contrib, which contains community-approved extensions. To install postgresql-contib, use the command line and type the following:

```
sudo apt-get install postgresql-contrib
```

To check the installation, one can grep the postgres processes, as follows:

```
pgrep -a postgres
1091 /usr/lib/postgresql/9.4/bin/postgres -D /var/lib/postgresql/9.4/main
-c config_file=/etc/postgresql/9.4/main/postgresql.conf
```

```
1108 postgres: checkpointer process
1109 postgres: writer process
1110 postgres: wal writer process
1111 postgres: autovacuum launcher process
1112 postgres: stats collector process
```

The preceding query shows the server main process with two options: the `-D` option specifies the database cluster, and the `-c` option specifies the configuration file. Also, it shows many utility processes, such as `autovacuum`, and statistics collector processes.

One could also install the server and the client in one command, as follows:

```
sudo apt-get install postgresql postgresql-contrib  postgresql-client
pgadmin3
```

Basic server configuration

In order to access the server, we need to understand the PostgreSQL authentication mechanism. On Linux systems, one can connect to PostgreSQL by using a unix-socket or TCP/IP protocol. Also, PostgreSQL supports many types of authentication methods.

When a PostgreSQL server is installed, a new operating system user, as well as a database user, with the name `postgres` is created. This user can connect to the database server using peer authentication. The peer authentication gets the client's operating system user name, and uses it to access the databases that can be accessed. Peer authentication is supported only by local connections—connections that use unix-sockets. Peer authentication is supported by Linux distribution but not by Windows.

Client authentication is controlled by a configuration file named `pg_hba.conf`, where `pg` stands for postgres and `hba` stands for host-based authentication. To take a look at peer authentication, one should execute the following command:

```
$ grep -v '^#' /etc/postgresql/9.4/main/pg_hba.conf|grep 'peer'
local   all       postgres                        peer
local   all       all                             peer
```

The interpretation of the first line of the result is shown here: The `postgres` user can connect to all the databases by using unix-socket and the peer authentication method.

To connect to the database servers using the `postgres` user, first we need to switch the operating system's current user to `postgres`, and then invoke `psql`. This is done via the Linux command, `su`, as follows:

```
sudo su postgres
```

```
psql
# This also could be done as follows
# sudo -u postgres psql
```

The preceding query shows the psql interactive terminal. The select statement SELECT version (); was executed, and the PostgreSQL version information was displayed.

```
$ psql
psql (9.4.4)
Type "help" for help.


postgres=# SELECT version();
                                                    version

---------------------------------------------------------------------------
----------------------

 PostgreSQL 9.4.4 on i686-pc-linux-gnu, compiled by gcc (Ubuntu
4.8.2-19ubuntu1) 4.8.2, 32-bit
(1 row)
```

As shown in the preceding result, the installed version is PostgreSQL 9.4.4. The PostgreSQL version number has three digits. Major releases occur roughly on an annual basis, and usually change the internal format of the data. This means that the stored data's backward compatibility between major releases is not maintained. A major release is numbered by incrementing either the first or the second digit.

Minor releases are numbered by increasing the third digit of the release number, for example 9.3.3 to 9.3.4. Minor releases are only bug fixes.

Installing PostgreSQL on Windows

The installation of PostgreSQL on Windows is easier than Linux for beginners. One can download the PostgreSQL binaries from EnterpriseDB. The installer wizard will guide the user through the installation process. The installer will also launch the stack builder wizard, which is used to install the PostgreSQL drivers and many other utilities and extensions.

Unlike Ubuntu, the installation wizard gives the user the ability to specify the binaries location, the database cluster location, port, the postgres user password, and the locale:

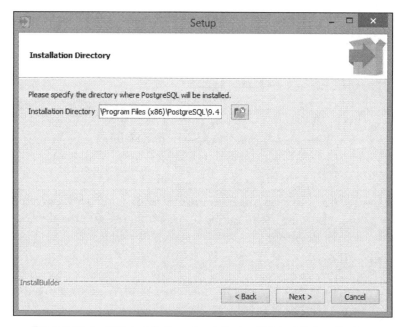

Figure 3: PostgreSQL installation wizard: PostgreSQL installation directory

Using the psql client is not very convenient in the latest version of Windows due to the lack of some capabilities such as copy, paste, and resizing in the Windows command prompt. pgAdmin is often used in the Windows operating system. Another option is to use a Linux emulator such as **Cygwin** and **MobaXterm**.

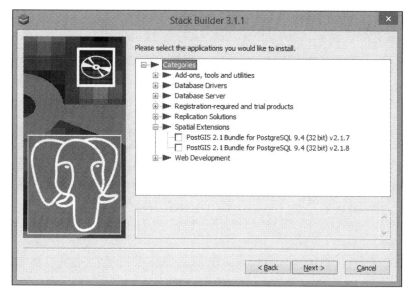

Figure 4: Stack builder

PostgreSQL in Windows is installed as a service; in order to validate the installation, one can view the service tab in the task manager utility.

The PostgreSQL clients

In addition to PgAdmin III and the psql client tools, there are a lot of vendors producing tools for PostgreSQL that cover different areas, such as database administration, modeling, development, reporting, ETL, and reverse engineering. In addition to the psql tool, PostgreSQL is shipped with several client tools, including the following:

- **Wrappers**: The wrappers are built around SQL commands such as CREATE USER. These wrappers facilitate the interaction between the database server and the developer, and automate the daily routine tasks.

- **Backup and replication**: PostgreSQL supports physical and logical backups. The physical backup is performed by taking a snapshot of the database files. The physical backup can be combined with WAL in order to achieve streaming replication or a hot standby solution. Logical backup is used to dump the database in the form of SQL statements. Unlike physical backup, one can dump and restore a single database.

- **Utilities**: PostgreSQL comes with several utilities to ease extraction of information and to help in diagnosing the problems.

The PostgreSQL community unifies the look and feel of the client tools as much as possible; this makes it easy to use and learn. For example, the connection options are unified across all client tools. The following screenshot shows the connection options for psql, which are common for other PostgreSQL clients as well.

Also, most PostgreSQL clients can use the environment variables supported by libpq such as PGHOST, PGDATABASE, and PGUSER. The libpq environment variables can be used to determine the default connection parameter values.

```
Connection options:
  -h, --host=HOSTNAME      database server host or socket directory (default: "/var/run/postgresql")
  -p, --port=PORT          database server port (default: "5432")
  -U, --username=USERNAME  database user name (default: "salahaldin")
  -w, --no-password        never prompt for password
  -W, --password           force password prompt (should happen automatically)
```

Figure 5: psql connection options

The psql client

The psql client is maintained by the PostgreSQL community, and it is a part of the PostgreSQL binary distribution. psql has many overwhelming features such as the following:

- **psql is configurable**: psql can be configured easily. The configuration might be applied to user session behavior such as commit and rollback, psql prompt, history files, and even shortcuts for predefined SQL statements.

- **Integration with editor and pager tools**: The psql query result can be directed to one's favorite pager such as less or more. Also, psql does not come with an editor, but it can utilize several editors. The following example shows the psql \ef meta tag—edit function—asking for editor selection on a Linux machine:

```
postgres=# \ef


Select an editor.  To change later, run 'select-editor'.
  1. /bin/ed
  2. /bin/nano        <---- easiest
  3. /usr/bin/vim.basic
  4. /usr/bin/vim.tiny


Choose 1-4 [2]:
```

- **Auto completion and SQL syntax help**: psql supports auto completion for database object names and SQL constructs.

```
postgres=# \h DEL
Command:     DELETE
Description: delete rows of a table
Syntax:
[ WITH [ RECURSIVE ] with_query [, ...] ]
DELETE FROM [ ONLY ] table_name [ * ] [ [ AS ] alias ]
    [ USING using_list ]
    [ WHERE condition | WHERE CURRENT OF cursor_name ]
    [ RETURNING * | output_expression [ [ AS ] output_name ] [, ...] ]
```

Figure 6: psql syntax help

- Query result format control: psql supports different formats such as html and latex.

The psql client tool is very handy in shell scripting, information retrieval, and learning the PostgreSQL internals. The following are some of the psql Meta commands that are often used daily:

- **\d+ [pattern]**: This describes all the relevant information for a relation. In PostgreSQL, the term relation is used for a table, view, sequence, or index. The following image shows the description of a pg_views view:

```
postgres=> \d+ pg_views
                View "pg_catalog.pg_views"
    Column    | Type | Modifiers | Storage  | Description
--------------+------+-----------+----------+-------------
 schemaname   | name |           | plain    |
 viewname     | name |           | plain    |
 viewowner    | name |           | plain    |
 definition   | text |           | extended |
View definition:
 SELECT n.nspname AS schemaname,
    c.relname AS viewname,
    pg_get_userbyid(c.relowner) AS viewowner,
    pg_get_viewdef(c.oid) AS definition
   FROM pg_class c
   LEFT JOIN pg_namespace n ON n.oid = c.relnamespace
  WHERE c.relkind = 'v'::"char";
```

Figure 7: \d meta command

- **\df+ [pattern]**: Describes a function
- **\z [pattern]**: Shows the relation access privileges

For shell scripting, there are several options that makes psql convenient, these options are:

- -A: The output is not aligned; by default, the output is aligned as shown in the following image:

- -q (quiet): This option forces psql not to write a welcome message or any other informational output.

- -t: This option tells psql to write the tuples only, without any header information.

- -X: This option informs psql to ignore the psql configuration that is stored in ~/.psqlrc file.

- -o: This option specifies psql to output the query result to a certain location.

- -F: This option determines the field separator between columns. This option can be used to generate **comma-separated values (CSV)**, which are useful for importing data to excel files.

- PGOPTIONS: psql can use PGOPTIONS to add command-line options to send to the server at run-time. This can be used to control statement behavior such as to allow indexing only, or to specify the statement timeout.

Let us assume that we would like to write a bash script to check the number of opened connections for determining if the database server is over-loaded for the Nagios monitoring system:

```bash
#!/bin/bash
connection_number=`PGOPTIONS='--statement_timeout=0' psql -AqXt -c
"SELECT count(*) FROM pg_stat_activity"`
case $connection_number in
[1-50]*)
echo "OK - $connection_number are used"
exit 0
;;
[50-100]*)
echo "WARNING - $connection_number are used"
exit 1
;;
# rest of case conditions ...
esac
```

The result of the command `psql -AqXt -d postgres -c "SELECT count(*) FROM pg_stat_activity"` is assigned to a bash variable, and then used in the bash script to determine the exit status. The options `-AqXt`, as discussed previously, cause psql to return only the result, without any decoration, as follows:

```
postgres@packet:/$ psql -AqXt -c "SELECT count(*) FROM pg_stat_activity"
1
```

Psql advanced settings

The psql client can be personalized. The psqlrc file is used to store the user preference for later use. There are several aspects of psql personalization, including:

- Look and feel
- Behavior
- Shortcuts

The following recipes show how one can personalize the psql client, add shortcuts, and control the statement transaction behavior:

- **Recipe 1**: Change the psql prompt to show the connection string information including the server name, database name, user name, and port. The psql variables PROMPT1, PROMPT2, and PROMPT3 can be used to customize the user preference. PROMPT1 and PROMPT2 are issued when creating a new command and a command expecting more input, respectively. The following example shows some of the prompt options; by default, when one connects to the database, only the name of the database is shown. The \set meta command is used to assign a psql variable to a value. In this case, it assigns PROMPT1 to (%n@%M:%>) [%/]%R%#%x >. The percent sign (%) is used as a placeholder for substitution. The substitutions in the example will be as follows:
  - %M: The full host name. In the example, [local] is displayed, because we use the Linux socket.
  - %>: The PostgreSQL port number.
  - %n: The database session user name.
  - %/: The current database name.
  - %R: Normally substituted by =; if the session is disconnected for a certain reason, then it is substituted with (!).
  - %#: Used to distinguish super users from normal users. The (#) hash sign indicates that the user is a super user. For a normal user, the sign is (>).
  - %x: The transaction status. The * sign is used to indicate the transaction block, and (!) sign to indicate a failed transaction block.

  Notice how PROMPT2 was issued when the SQL statement SELECT 1 was written over two lines. Finally, notice the * sign, which indicates a transaction block:

```
salahaldin@packet:~$ sudo -su postgres psql -d template1
[sudo] password for salahaldin:
psql (9.3.4)
Type "help" for help.

template1=# \set PROMPT1 '(%n@%M:%>) [%/]%R%#%x > '
(postgres@[local]:5432) [template1]=# > BEGIN;
BEGIN
(postgres@[local]:5432) [template1]=#* > \q
salahaldin@packet:~$ sudo -su postgres psql -d template1
psql (9.3.4)
Type "help" for help.

template1=# \set PROMPT1 '(%n@%M:%>) [%/]%R%#%x '
(postgres@[local]:5432) [template1]=# BEGIN;
BEGIN
(postgres@[local]:5432) [template1]=#* SELECT 1;
 ?column?
----------
        1
(1 row)

(postgres@[local]:5432) [template1]=#* SELECT
template1-# 1;
 ?column?
----------
        1
(1 row)

(postgres@[local]:5432) [template1]=#* SELECT ;
ERROR:  syntax error at or near ";"
LINE 1: SELECT ;
               ^
(postgres@[local]:5432) [template1]=#! █
```

Figure 8: psql PROMPT customization

- **Recipe 2**: Add a shortcut for a common query such as showing the current
  database activities. psql can be used to assign arbitrary variables using the
  \set" meta command. Again, the : symbol is used for substitution. The
  following example shows how one can add a shortcut for a query.
  The \x meta command changes the display setting to expanded display:

```
template1=# \set activity 'select datname, pid, usename, application_name,query, state from pg_stat_activity;'
template1=# \x
Expanded display is on.
template1=# :activity
-[ RECORD 1 ]----+----------------------------------------------------------------
datname          | template1
pid              | 4057
usename          | postgres
application_name | psql
query            | select datname, pid, usename, application_name,query, state from pg_stat_activity;
state            | active
```

Figure 9: Add shortcut to a query in psql

- **Recipe 3**: Control statement and transaction execution behavior. psql provides three variables, which are AUTOCOMMIT, ON_ERROR_STOP, and ON_ERROR_ROLLBACK.

  ○ ON_ERROR_STOP: By default, psql continues executing commands even after encountering an error. This is useful for some operations, including as dumping and restoring the whole database, where some errors can be ignored, such as missing extensions. However, in developing applications, such as deploying new application, errors cannot be ignored, and it is good to set this variable to ON. This variable is useful with the -f, \i, \ir options.

  ○ ON_ERROR_ROLLBACK: When an error occurs in a transaction block, one of three actions is performed depending on the value of this variable. When the variable value is off, then the whole transaction is rolled back—this is the default behavior. When the variable value is on, then the error is ignored, and the transaction is continued. The interactive mode ignores the errors in the interactive sessions, but not when reading files.

  ○ AUTOCOMMIT: An SQL statement outside a transaction, committed implicitly. To reduce human error, one can turn this option off:

```
postgres@packet:~$ echo -e 'SELECT 1/0;\nSELECT 1;\n'>/tmp/test_on_rollback_stop.sql
postgres@packet:~$ psql
psql (9.3.4)
Type "help" for help.

postgres=# \i /tmp/test_on_rollback_stop.sql
psql:/tmp/test_on_rollback_stop.sql:1: ERROR:  division by zero
 ?column?
----------
        1
(1 row)

postgres=# \set ON_ERROR_STOP ON
postgres=# \i /tmp/test_on_rollback_stop.sql
psql:/tmp/test_on_rollback_stop.sql:1: ERROR:  division by zero
postgres=#
```

Figure10: on_error_stop psql variable

The following figure shows the effect of the autocommit setting. This setting is quite useful because it allows the developer to rollback the unwanted changes. Note that when deploying or amending the database on life systems, it is recommended to make the changes within a transaction block, and also prepare a rollback script:

```
test=# CREATE TABLE test_autocommit AS SELECT 'testing autocommit default settings'::text;
SELECT 1
Time: 9,081 ms
test=# ROLLBACK;
NOTICE:  there is no transaction in progress
ROLLBACK
Time: 0,247 ms
test=# \set AUTOCOMMIT off
test=# CREATE TABLE test_autocommit_off AS SELECT 'testing autocommit when it is disabled'::text;
SELECT 1
Time: 8,916 ms
test=# ROLLBACK;
ROLLBACK
Time: 0,520 ms
test=# SELECT * /* only one table created*/ FROM pg_tables WHERE tablename IN ('test_autocommit', 'test_autocommit_off');
 schemaname |    tablename     | tableowner | tablespace | hasindexes | hasrules | hastriggers
------------+------------------+------------+------------+------------+----------+-------------
 public     | test_autocommit  | postgres   | NULL       | f          | f        | f
(1 row)

Time: 0,542 ms
test=#
```

Figure 11: Autocommit variable setting behavior

- **Other recipes**:

  - \timing: Shows the query execution time.

  - \pset null 'NULL': Displays null as NULL. This is important to distinguish an empty string from the NULL values. The \pset meta command is used to control the output formatting:

```
template1=# SELECT ''::text, NULL::text;
 text | text
------+------
      |
(1 row)

template1=# \timing
Timing is on.
template1=# SELECT ''::text, NULL::text;
 text | text
------+------
      |
(1 row)

Time: 0,153 ms
template1=# \pset null 'NULL'
Null display is "NULL".
template1=# SELECT ''::text, NULL::text;
 text | text
------+------
      | NULL
(1 row)

Time: 0,151 ms
```

Figure12: Enable timing and change null display settings in psql

For more information about psql, one should have a look at the psql manual pages or at the PostgreSQL documentation (`http://www.postgresql.org/docs/9.4/static/app-psql.html`).

PostgreSQL utility tools

Several PostgreSQL utility tools are wrappers around SQL constructs. The following table lists these wrappers and the equivalent SQL commands:

Tool name	SQL construct
dropdb	DROP DATABASE [IF EXISTS] name;
createdb	CREATE DATABASE name ...
dropuser	DROP ROLE [IF EXISTS] name [, ...]
createuser	CREATE ROLE name ...
droplang	DROP [PROCEDURAL] LANGUAGE [IF EXISTS] name [CASCADE | RESTRICT]
createlang	CREATE [OR REPLACE] [PROCEDURAL] LANGUAGE name
clusterdb	CLUSTER [VERBOSE] table_name [USING index_name] or CLUSTER [VERBOSE]
reindexdb	REINDEX { INDEX | TABLE | DATABASE | SYSTEM } name [FORCE]

Backup and replication

PostgreSQL supports physical and logical backup. The following tools are shipped with the postgresql-client package:

Tool name	Description
pg_dump	Creates a logical dump of a single PostgreSQL database into an SQL script file or archive file
pg_dumpall	Creates a logical dump for the whole PostgreSQL cluster
pg_restore	Restores a PostgreSQL database or PostgreSQL cluster from an archive file created by pg_dump or pg_dumpall
pg_basebackup	Dumps the whole database cluster by taking a snapshot of the hard disk
pg_receivexlog	Streams transaction logs from a PostgreSQL cluster

Utilities

PostgreSQL is shipped with two utilities: pg_config and pg_isready. pg_config. They come with the postgresql package, and are used to provide information about the installed version of PostgreSQL such as binaries and cluster folder location. pg_config provides valuable information since the PostgreSQL installation location and build information varies from one operating system to another. pg_isready checks the connection status of a PostgreSQL server and provides several exit codes to determine connection problems. Exit code zero means successfully connected. If the exit code is one, then the server is rejecting connections. If there is no response from the server, two will be returned as the exit code. Finally, exit code three indicates that no attempt is made to connect to the server.

In addition to the above, vacuumdb is used for garbage collection and for statistical data collection. vacuumdb is built around the PostgreSQL-specific statement, vacuum.

PgAdmin III

PgAdmin III is a very rich GUI tool for PostgreSQL administration and development. It is an open source and cross platform tool. It is available in several languages, and supports most of the PostgreSQL data encoding. It supports psql as a plugin, Slony-I replication, and the pgAgent job scheduling tool. It can be used for editing the PostgreSQL configuration files.

As shown earlier, PgAdmin III is installed by default on the Windows platform. The following are some of the PgAdmin III features for development:

* Basic editor but with syntax highlighting and auto completion.
* Database objects are rendered according to the PostgreSQL sever organization.
* Very convenient for extracting database object definitions.
* Comprehensive wizards to create database objects such as domain, functions, tables, and so on.
* Graphical representation of query execution plans.
* Graphical query builder.

psql will be used throughout this book, because it has many amazing features, such as shortcuts and customizations. Also, it can be used for scripting purposes.

Summary

PostgreSQL is an open source, object-oriented relational database system. It supports many advanced features and complies with the ANSI-SQL:2008 standard. It has won industry recognition and user appreciation. The PostgreSQL slogan "The world's most advanced open source database" reflects the sophistication of the PostgreSQL features. It is a result of many years of research and collaboration between academia and industry. Startup companies often favor PostgreSQL due to low licensing costs. PostgreSQL can aid profitable business models. PostgreSQL is also favored by many developers because of its capabilities and advantages.

PostgreSQL can be used for OLTP and OLAP applications. It is ACID compliant; thus, it can be used out of the box for OLTP applications. For OLAP applications, PostgreSQL supports the Windows functions, FDW, and table inheritance. Also, there are many external extensions for this purpose.

Several proprietary DBMSs are based on PostgreSQL. In addition to that, there are several open source forks which add new features and technologies to PostgreSQL such as MPP and MapReduce.

PostgreSQL has a very organized active community including users, developers, companies, and associations. The community contributes to PostgreSQL on a daily basis; many companies have contributed to PostgreSQL by publishing best practices or articles, submitting feature requests to the development group, submitting new features, and developing new tools and software.

In chapter three, the PostgreSQL building components will be introduced. Also, the user will be able to create their first database, and use some DDL statements such as CREATE TABLE and CREATE VIEWS.

3
PostgreSQL Basic Building Blocks

In this chapter, we will build a PostgreSQL database, and explore the basic building blocks of PostgreSQL. The conceptual model of a car web portal, which was presented in Chapter 1, *Relational Databases*, will be translated to a physical model. Also, some data modeling techniques, such as surrogate keys, will be discussed briefly and some coding best practices will be presented.

We will also take a look at the hierarchy of the database objects in PostgreSQL. This will help you to understand how to configure the database cluster and tune its settings. More detailed information will be presented to show the usage of template databases, user databases, roles, table spaces, schemas, configuration settings, and tables.

Database coding

The software engineering principles should be applied on database coding. Some of these principles are:

Database naming conventions

A naming convention describes how names are to be formulated. Naming conventions allow some information to be derived based on patterns, which helps the developer to easily search for and predict the database object names. Database naming conventions should be standardized across the organization. There is a lot of debate on how to name database objects. For example, some developers prefer to have prefixes or suffixes to distinguish the database object type from the names. For example, one could suffix a table or a view with tbl and vw respectively.

With regard to database object names, one should try to use descriptive names, and avoid acronyms and abbreviations if possible. Also, singular names are preferred, because a table is often mapped to an entity in a high programming language; thus, singular names lead to unified naming across the database tier and the business logic tier. Furthermore, specifying the cardinality and participation between tables is straightforward when the table names are singular.

In the database world, compound object names often use underscore but not camel case due to the ANSI SQL standard specifications regarding identifiers quotation and case sensitivity. In the ANSI SQL standard, non-quoted identifiers are case-insensitive.

In general, it is up to the developer to come up with a naming convention that suits his needs; in existing projects, do not invent any new naming conventions, unless the new naming conventions are communicated to the team members. In this book, we use the following conventions:

- The names of tables and views are not suffixed

- The database object names are unique across the database

- The identifiers are singulars including table, view, and column names

- Underscore is used for compound names

- The primary key is composed of the table name and the suffix "id"

- A foreign key has the same name of the referenced primary key in the linked table

- Use the internal naming conventions of PostgreSQL to rename the primary keys, foreign keys, and sequences

Do not use keywords to rename your database objects. The list of SQL keywords can be found at `http://www.postgresql.org/docs/current/static/sql-keywords-appendix.html`.

PostgreSQL identifiers

The length of PostgreSQL object names is 63 characters; PostgreSQL also follows ANSI SQL regarding case sensitivity. If you wanted to use the camel case for renaming database objects, you could achieve that by putting the identifier name in double quotes. PostgreSQL identifier names have the following constraints:

- The identifier name should start with an underscore or a letter. Letters can be Latin or non-Latin letters.

- The identifier name can be composed of letters, digits, underscore, and the dollar sign. For compatibility reasons, the use of the dollar sign is not recommended.

- The minimum length of the identifier is typically one, and the maximum length is 63.

In addition to the preceding points, it is not recommended to use keywords as table names.

Documentation

Documentation is essential for developers as well as business owners to understand the full picture. Documentation for database schema, objects, and code should be maintained. ER and class diagrams are very useful in understanding the full picture. There are tons of programs that support UML and ER diagrams. One can generate ER and UML diagrams by using graph editing tools such as yEd, which can be downloaded from http://www.yworks.com/en/products/yfiles/yed/. Another useful tool is SchemaSpy (http://schemaspy.sourceforge.net/), which generates a visual representation for table structures and the relation between tables. Also, there are many commercial UML modeling tools that support code reverse engineering.

Code documentation provide an insight into complex SQL statements. PostgreSQL uses -- and /**/ for single-line and multi-line comments respectively. The single line comment -- works on the rest of the line after the comment marker. Therefore, it can be used on the same line as the actual statement.

Finally, PostgreSQL allows the developer to store the database object description via the COMMENT ON command.

Version control system

It is a good idea to maintain your code using a revision control system such as GIT or SVN. When writing an SQL code, it is better to create an installation script and execute it in one transaction. This approach makes it easy to clean up if an error occurs.

Database objects have different properties: some are a part of the physical schema, and some control database access. The following is a proposal for organizing the database code in order to increase the **separation of concern (SoC)**:

- For each database in a PostgreSQL cluster, one should maintain the DDL script for objects that are part of the physical schema, and the DML script, which populates the tables with static data together. The state of an object in the physical schema is defined by the object structure and the data that is contained by this object; thus, the object cannot be recreated without being dropped first. Also, the structure of the physical schema object does not change often. In addition to that, the refactoring of some of the physical schema objects, such as tables, might require data migration. In other words, changing the definition of a physical schema object requires some planning.

- Store the DDL scripts for objects that are not part of the physical schema, such as views and functions, separately. Keeping the definitions of views and functions together allows the developer to refactor them easily. Also, the developer will be able to extract the dependency trees between these objects.

- Maintain the DCL script separately. This allows the developer to separate the security aspect from the functional requirements of the database. It allows the database developers and administrators to work closely without interfering with each other's work.

PostgreSQL objects hierarchy

Understanding the organization of PostgreSQL database logical objects helps in understanding object relations and interactions. PostgreSQL databases, roles, tablespaces, settings, and template languages have the same level of hierarchy, as shown in the following diagram:

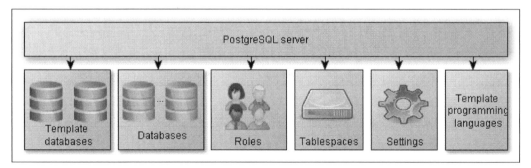

Top level component of the PostgreSQL server

Template databases

By default, when a database is created, it is cloned from a template database called `template1`. The template database contains a set of tables, views, and functions, which is used to model the relation between the user defined database objects. These tables, views, and functions are a part of the system catalog schema called `pg_catalog`.

 The schema is very close to the namespace concept in object-oriented languages. It is often used to organize the database objects, functionality, security access, or to eliminate name collision.

The PostgreSQL server has two template databases:

- `template1`: The default database to be cloned. It can be modified to allow global modification to all the newly created databases. For example, if someone intends to use a certain extension in all the databases, then they can install this extension in the `template1` database. Certainly, installing an extension in `template1` will not be cascaded to the already existing databases, but it will affect the databases that will be created after this installation.

- `template0`: A safeguard or version database, it has several purposes as follows:

    - If `template1` is corrupted by a user, then it can be used to fix `template1`.

    - It is handy, in restoring a database dump. When a developer dumps a database, all the extensions are also dumped. If the extension is already installed in `template1`, this will lead to a collision, because the newly created database already contains the extensions.

    - Unlike `template1`, `template0` does not contain encoding-specific or locale-specific data.

 One can create a database using a user database as a template. This is very handy for testing, database refactoring purposes, deployment plans, and so on.

User databases

One can have as many databases as one wants in a database cluster. A client connection to the PostgreSQL server can access only the data in a single database that is specified in the connection string. That means that data is not shared between the databases, unless the postgres foreign data wrapper or dblink extensions are used.

Every database in the database cluster has an owner and a set of associated permissions to control the actions allowed for a particular role. The privileges on PostgreSQL objects, which include databases, views, tables, and sequences, are represented in the psql client as follows:

```
<user>=<privileges>/granted by
```

If the user part of the privileges is not present, it means that the privileges are applied to the PostgreSQL special PUBLIC role.

The psql meta-command \l is used to list all the databases in the database cluster with the associated attributes:

```
postgres=# \x
Expanded display is on.
postgres=# \l
List of databases
-[ RECORD 1 ]-----+----------------------------
Name              | postgres
Owner             | postgres
Encoding          | UTF8
Collate           | English_United Kingdom.1252
Ctype             | English_United Kingdom.1252
Access privileges |
-[ RECORD 2 ]-----+----------------------------
Name              | template0
Owner             | postgres
Encoding          | UTF8
Collate           | English_United Kingdom.1252
Ctype             | English_United Kingdom.1252
Access privileges | =c/postgres
```

```
                      | postgres=CTc/postgres
-[ RECORD 3 ]-----+----------------------------
Name                  | template1
Owner                 | postgres
Encoding              | UTF8
Collate               | English_United Kingdom.1252
Ctype                 | English_United Kingdom.1252
Access privileges  | =c/postgres
                      | postgres=CTc/postgres
```

The database access privileges are the following:

- **Create (-C)**: The create access privilege allows the specified role to create new schemas in the database.

- **Connect (-c)**: When a role tries to connect to a database, the connect permissions is checked.

- **Temporary (-T)**: The temporary access privilege allows the specified role to create temporary tables. Temporary tables are very similar to tables, but they are not persistent, and they are destroyed after the user session is terminated.

In the preceding example, the postgres database has no explicit privileges assigned. Also notice that, the PUBLIC role is allowed to connect to the template1 database by default.

Encoding allows you to store text in a variety of character sets, including one byte character sets such as SQL_ASCII or multiple byte character sets such as UTF-8. PostgreSQL supports a rich set of character encodings. For the full list of character encodings, please visit http://www.postgresql.org/docs/current/static/multibyte.html.

In addition to these attributes, PostgreSQL has several other attributes for various purposes, including the following:

- **Maintenance**: The attribute datfrozenxid is used to determine if a database vacuum is required.

- **Storage management**: The dattablespace attribute is used to determine the database tablespace.

- **Concurrency**: The datconnlimit attribute is used to determine the number of allowed connections. -1 means no limits.

- **Protection**: The datallowconn attribute disables the connection to a database. This is used mainly to protect template0 from being altered.

The psql \c meta-command establishes a new connection to a database and closes the current one:

```
postgres=# \c template0
FATAL: database "template0" is not currently accepting connections
Previous connection kept
```

pg_catalog tables are regular tables, thus one can use the SELECT , UPDATE, and DELETE operations to manipulate them. Doing so is not recommended, and needs the utmost attention.

The catalog tables are very useful for automating some tasks, such as checking for tables with the same name, duplicate indexes, missing constraints, and so on. One should not change the catalog manually except in rare cases; there are SQL commands to perform the same task. The following example shows how one can alter the connection limit database property by using the ALTER database command, or by using the UPDATE statement, which is not recommended. The following example changes the datconnlimit value from -1 to 1, and then reset the value to -1 again:

```
postgres=# SELECT datconnlimit FROM pg_database WHERE datname=
'postgres';

 datconnlimit

--------------

            -1

(1 row)


postgres=# ALTER DATABASE postgres CONNECTION LIMIT 1;

ALTER DATABASE

postgres=# SELECT datconnlimit FROM pg_database WHERE datname=
'postgres';

 datconnlimit

--------------

            1

(1 row)


postgres=# UPDATE pg_database SET datconnlimit=-1 WHERE
datname='postgres';

UPDATE 1
```

```
postgres=# SELECT datconnlimit FROM pg_database WHERE datname=
'postgres';
 datconnlimit
--------------
           -1
(1 row)
```

Roles

Roles belong to the PostgreSQL server cluster and not to a certain database. A role can either be a database user or a database group. The role concept subsumes the concepts of users and groups in the old PostgreSQL versions. For compatibility reasons, with PostgreSQL version 8.1, the CREATE USER and CREATE GROUP SQL commands are still supported:

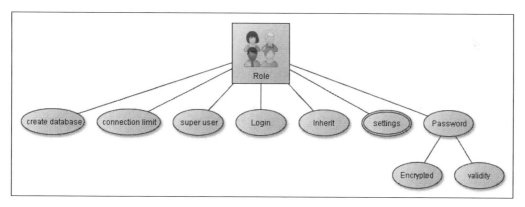

ER representation of role entity in PostgreSQL

The roles have several attributes, which are as follows:

- **Super user**: A super user role can bypass all permission checks except the login attribute.
- **Login**: A role with the login attribute can be used by a client to connect to a database.
- **Create database**: A role with the create database attribute can create databases.
- **Initiating replication**: A role with this attribute can be used for streaming replication.

- **Password**: The role password can be used with the md5 authentication method. Also, it can be encrypted. The password expiration can be controlled by specifying the validity period. Note that this password differs from the OS password.

- **Connection limit**: Connection limit specifies the number of concurrent connections that the user can initiate. Connection creation consumes hardware resources; thus, it is recommended to use connection pooling tools such as pgpool-II or pgbouncer, or some APIs such as apache DBCP or c3p0.

- **Inherit**: If specified, the role will inherit the privileges assigned to the roles that it is a member of. If not specified, Inherit is the default.

When a database cluster is created, the postgres super user role is created by default.

> CREATE USER is equivalent to CREATE ROLE with the LOGIN option, and CREATE GROUP is equivalent to CREATE ROLE with the NOLOGIN option.

A role can be a member of another role to simplify accessing and managing the database permissions; for example, one can create a role with no login, also known as group, and grant its permissions to access the database objects. If a new role needs to access the same database objects with the same permissions as the group, the new role could be assigned a membership to this group. This is achieved by the SQL commands GRANT and REVOKE, which are discussed in detail in *Chapter 8, PostgreSQL Security*.

> The roles of a cluster do not necessarily have the privilege to access every database in the cluster.

Tablespace

Tablespace is a defined storage location for a database or database objects. Tablespaces are used by administrators to achieve the following:

- **Maintenance**: If the hard disk partition runs out of space where the database cluster is created and cannot be extended, a tablespace on another partition can be created to solve this problem by moving the data to another location.

- **Optimization**: Heavily accessed data could be stored in fast media such as a **solid-state drive (SSD)**. At the same time, tables that are not performance critical could be stored on a slow disk.

The SQL statement to create tablespace is CREATE TABLESPACE.

Template procedural languages

Template procedural language is used to register a new language in a convenient way. There are two ways to create a programing language; the first way is by specifying only the name of the programing language. In this method, PostgreSQL consults the programing language template and determines the parameters. The second way is to specify the name as well as the parameters. The SQL command to create a language is CREATE LANGUAGE.

> In PostgreSQL versions older than 9.1, create extension can be used to install a programming language. The template procedural languages are maintained in the table pg_pltemplate. This table might be decommissioned in favor of keeping the procedural language information in their installation scripts.

Settings

The PostgreSQL settings control different aspects of the PostgreSQL server, including replication, write-ahead logs, resource consumption, query planning, logging, authentication, statistic collection, garbage collection, client connections, lock management, error handling, and debug options.

The following SQL command shows the number of PostgreSQL settings. Note that this number might differ slightly between different installations as well as customized settings:

```
postgres=# SELECT count(*) FROM pg_settings;
 count
-------
   239
(1 row)
```

Setting parameters

The setting names are case-insensitive. The setting value types can be the following:

- **Boolean**: 0, 1, true, false, on, off, or any case-insensitive form of the previous values. The ENABLE_SEQSCAN setting falls in this category.
- **Integer**: An integer might specify a memory or time value; there is an implicit unit for each setting such as second or minute. In order to avoid confusion, PostgreSQL allows units to be specified. For example, one could specify 128 MB as a shared_buffers setting value.

- **Enum**: These are predefined values such as ERROR and WARNING.
- **Floating point**: cpu_operator_cost has a floating point domain. cpu_operator_cost is used to optimize the PostgreSQL execution plans.
- **String**: A string might be used to specify the file location on a hard disk, such as the location of the authentication file.

Setting a context

The setting context determines how to change a setting value and when the change can take effect. The setting contexts are as follows:

- **Internal**: The setting cannot be changed directly. One might need to recompile the server source code or initialize the database cluster to change this. For example, the length of PostgreSQL identifiers is 63 characters.
- **Postmaster**: Changing a setting value requires restarting the server. Values for these settings are typically stored in the PostgreSQL postgresql.conf file.
- **Sighup**: No server restart is required. The setting change can be made by amending the postgresql.conf file, followed by sending a SIGHUP signal to the postgres server process.
- **Backend**: No server restart is required. They can also be set for a particular session.
- **Superuser**: Only a super user can change this setting. This setting can be set in postgresql.conf or via the SET command.
- **User**: This is similar to superuser, and is typically used to change the session-local values.

PostgreSQL provides the SET and SHOW commands to change and inspect the value of a setting parameter respectively. Those commands are used to change the setting parameters in the superuser and user context. Typically, changing the value of a setting parameter in the postgresql.conf file makes the effect global.

The settings can also have a local effect, and can be applied to different contexts such as session and table. For example, let us assume that you would like some clients to be able to perform the read-only operation; this is useful for configuring some tools such as Confluence (Atlassian). In this case, you can achieve that by setting the default_transaction_read_only parameter:

```
postgres=# SET default_transaction_read_only to on;
SET
```

```
postgres=# CREATE TABLE test_readonly AS SELECT 1;
ERROR:  cannot execute SELECT INTO in a read-only transaction
```

In the preceding example, the creation of a table has failed within the opened session; however, if one opens a new session and tries to execute the command CREATE TABLE, it will be executed successfully because the default value of the default_transaction_read_only setting is *off*. Setting the default_transaction_read_only parameter in the postgresql.conf file will have a global effect as mentioned earlier.

PostgreSQL also provides the pg_reload_conf() function, which is equivalent to sending the SIGHUP signal to the postgres process.

> In general, it is preferable to use pg_reload_conf(), because it is safer than the SIGHUP kill signal due to human error.

In order to set the database in the read-only mode in a Debian Linux distribution, one can do the following:

- Edit postgresql.conf and alter the value of default_transaction_read_only. This can be done in Ubuntu with the following commands:

  ```
  sudo su postgres
  CONF=/etc/postgresql/9.4/main/postgresql.conf
  sed -i "s/#default_transaction_read_only = off/default_transaction_read_only = on/" $CONF
  ```

- Reload the configuration by executing the pg_reload_conf() function:

  ```
  psql -U postgres -c "SELECT pg_reload_conf()"
   pg_reload_conf
  ----------------
   t
  (1 row)
  ```

One needs to plan carefully for changing the setting parameter values that require server down time. For noncritical changes, one can change the postgresql.conf file in order to make sure that the change will take effect when the server is restarted due to security updates. For urgent changes, one should follow certain processes, such as scheduling a down time and informing the user of this down time.

The developer, in general, is concerned with two settings categories, which are as follows:

- **Client connection defaults**: These settings control the statement behaviors, locale, and formatting.
- **Query planning**: These settings control the planner configuration, and give hints to the developer on how to rewrite SQL queries.

PostgreSQL high-level object interaction

To sum up, a PostgreSQL server can contain many databases, programming languages, roles, and tablespaces. Each database has an owner and a default tablespace; a role can be granted permission to access or can own several databases. The settings can be used to control the behavior of the PostgreSQL server on several levels, such as database and session. Finally, a database can use several programming languages:

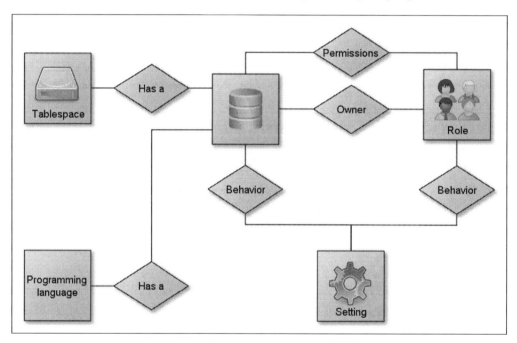

PostgreSQL main components conceptual relations

In order to create a database, one needs to specify the owner and the encoding of the database; if the encoding of template1 does not match the required encoding, template0 should be used explicitly.

For the car web high level objects interaction portal database, let us assume that the database owner is the `car_portal_role` role, and encoding is UTF8. In order to create this database, one can execute the following commands:

```
CREATE ROLE car_portal_role LOGIN;
CREATE DATABASE car_portal ENCODING 'UTF-8' LC_COLLATE 'en_US.UTF-8' LC_
CTYPE 'en_US.UTF-8' TEMPLATE template0 OWNER car_portal_app;;
```

PostgreSQL database components

A PostgreSQL database could be considered as a container for database schema; the database must contain at least one schema. A database schema is used to organize the database objects in a manner similar to namespaces in high programing languages.

Schema

Object names can be reused in different schema without conflict. The schema contains all the database named objects, including tables, views, functions, aggregates, indexes, sequences, triggers, data types, domains, and ranges.

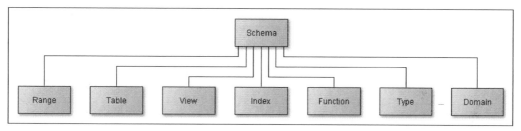

PostgreSQL schema as a database object container

By default, there is a schema called public in the template databases. That means, all the newly created databases also contain this schema. All users, by default, can access this schema implicitly. Again this is inherited from the template databases. Allowing this access pattern stimulates the situation where the server is not schema-aware. This is useful in small companies where there is no need to have complex security. Also, this enables smooth transition from the non-schema-aware databases.

Warning

In a multiuser and multidatabase environment set up, remember to revoke the ability for all users to create objects in the public schema. This is done by the following command in the newly created database, or in the `template1` database:

```
REVOKE CREATE ON SCHEMA public FROM PUBLIC;
```

When a user wants to access a certain object, he needs to specify the schema name and the object name separated by a period(`.`). If the database `search_path` setting does not contain this name, or if the developer likes to use full qualified names (for example, to select all the entries in `pg_database` in the `pg_catalog` schema), one needs to write the following command:

```
SELECT * FROM pg_catalog.pg_database;
```

Alternatively you can also use the following command:

```
TABLE pg_catalog.pg_database;
```

Qualified database object names are sometimes tedious to write, so many developers prefer to use the unqualified object name, which is composed of only the object name without the schema. PostgreSQL provides a `search_path` setting that is similar to the `using` directive in the C++ language. The search path is composed of schemas that are used by the server to search for the object. The default search path, as shown in the following code, is `$user, public`. If there is a schema with the same name as the user, then it will be used first to search for objects or creating new objects. If the object is not found in the schemas specified in the `search_path`, then an error will be thrown:

```
SHOW search_path;
--------------
 $user,public
```

Schema usages

Schemas are used for the following reasons:

- **Control authorization**: In a multi-user database environment, one can use schemas to group objects based on roles.

- **Organize database objects**: One can organize the database objects in groups based on the business logic. For example, historical and auditing data could be logically grouped and organized in a specific schema.

- **Maintain third-party SQL code**: The extensions available in the contribution package can be used with several applications. Maintaining these extensions in separate schemas enables the developer to reuse these extensions, and to update them easily.

In the car web portal, let us assume that we would like to create a schema named `car_portal_app`, owned by `car_portal_app` role. This can be done as follows:

```
CREATE SCHEMA car_portal_app AUTHORIZATION car_portal_app;
--The schema owner is the same as the schema name if not given
CREATE SCHEMA AUTHORIZATION car_portal_app;
```

For more information about the syntax of the `CREATE SCHEMA` command, one can use the psql \h meta-command, which displays the psql client tool inline help, or take a look at the PostgreSQL manual at `http://www.postgresql.org/docs/current/static/sql-createschema.html`.

Table

The `CREATE TABLE` SQL statement is very rich. It can be used for several purposes such as cloning a table, which is handy for database refactoring to create the uninstallation script to rollback changes. Also, it can be used to materialize the result of the `SELECT` SQL statement to boost performance, or for temporarily storing the data for later use.

 The PostgreSQL tables are used internally to model views and sequences.

In PostgreSQL, tables can be of different types:

- **Permanent table**: The table life cycle starts with table creation and ends with table dropping.

- **Temporary table**: The table life cycle is the user session. This is used often with procedural languages to model some business logic.

- **Unlogged table**: Operations on unlogged tables are much faster than on permanent tables, because data is not written into the WAL files. Unlogged tables are not crash-safe. Also, since streaming replication is based on shipping the log files, unlogged tables cannot be replicated to the slave node.

- **Child table**: A child table is a table that inherits one or more tables. The inheritance is often used with constraint exclusion to physically partition the data on the hard disk and to gain performance in retrieving a subset of data that has a certain value.

- The create table syntax is quite long; the full syntax of create table can be found at http://www.postgresql.org/docs/current/static/sql-createtable.html. The create table SQL command normally requires the following inputs:

  ○ Table name of the created table.

  ○ The table type.

  ○ The table storage parameters. These parameters are used to control the table storage allocation and several other administrative tasks.

  ○ The table columns, including the data type, default values, and constraint.

  ○ The cloned table name and the options to clone the table.

PostgreSQL native data types

When designing a database table, one should take care in picking the appropriate data type. When the database goes to production, changing the data type of a column might become a very costly operation, especially for heavily loaded tables. The cost often comes from locking the table, and in some cases, rewriting it. When picking a data type, consider a balance between the following factors:

- **Extensibility**: Can the maximum length of a type be increased or decreased without a full table rewrite and a full table scan?

- **Data type size**: Going for a safe option such as choosing big integers instead of integers, will cause more storage consumption.

PostgreSQL provides a very extensive set of data types. Some of the native data type categories are:

- Numeric type
- Character type
- Date and time types

These data types are almost common for all relational databases. Moreover, they are often sufficient for modeling traditional applications.

Numeric types

The following table shows various numeric types:

Name	Comments	Size	Range
smallint	SQL equivalent: `Int2`	2 bytes	-32768 to +32767
Int	SQL equivalent:`Int4` Integer is an alias for `int`	4 bytes	-2147483648 to +2147483647
Bigint	SQL equivalent: `Int8`	8 bytes	-9223372036854775808 to +9223372036854775807
Numeric or decimal	No difference in PostgreSQL	variable	up to 131072 digits before the decimal point; up to 16383 digits after the decimal point
real	Special values: Infinity	4 bytes	Platform dependent, at least 6 digit precision. Often the range is 1E-37 to 1E+37
Double precision	-Infinity NaN	8 bytes	Platform dependent, at least 15 digit precision, often the range is 1E-307 to 1E+308

Numeric data types

PostgreSQL supports various mathematical operators and functions, such as geometric functions and bitwise operations. The `smallint` data type can be used to save disk space, while `bigint` can be used if the integer range is not sufficient.

Serial types, namely smallserial, serial, and bigserial are wrappers on top of `smallint`, `int`, and `biginteger` respectively. Serial types are often used as surrogate keys, and by default, they are not allowed to have a `null` value. The serial type utilizes the sequences behind the scene. A sequence is a database object that is used to generate sequences by specifying the minimum, maximum, and increment values.

For example, the following code creates a table `customer` with a column `customer_id`:

```
CREATE TABLE customer (
    customer_id SERIAL
);
```

This will generate the following code behind the scene:

```
CREATE SEQUENCE custome_customer_id_seq;
CREATE TABLE customer (
customer_id integer NOT NULL DEFAULT nextval('customer_customer_id_seq')
);
ALTER SEQUENCE customer_customer_id_seq OWNED BY customer.Customer_id;
```

When creating a column with type serial, remember the following things:

- A sequence will be created with the name `tableName_columnName_seq`. In the preceding example, the sequence name is `customer_customer_id_seq`.
- The column will have a `Not Null` value constraint.
- The column will have a default value generated by the function `nextval()`.
- The sequence will be owned by the column, which means that the sequence will be dropped automatically if the column is dropped.

> The preceding example shows how PostgreSQL renames an object if the object name is not specified explicitly; PostgreSQL renames objects using the `{tablename}_{columnname(s)}_{suffix}` pattern, where the suffixes `pkey`, `key`, `excl`, `idx`, `fkey`, and `check` which stand for a primary key constraint, a unique constraint, an exclusion constraint, an index, a foreign key constraint, and a check constraint respectively.
>
> A common mistake when using the serial type is forgetting to grant proper permissions to the generated sequence.

Similar to the C language, the result of an integer expression is also an integer. So, the results of the mathematical operations 3/2 and 1/3 is 1 and 0 respectively. Thus, the fractional part is always truncated. Unlike C language, the postgres rounds off the numbers when casting a double value to int:

```
postgres=# SELECT CAST (5.9 AS INT) AS rounded_up, CAST(5.1 AS INTEGER)
AS rounded_down, 5.5::INT AS another_syntax;
 rounded_up | rounded_down | another_syntax
------------+--------------+----------------
          6 |            5 |              6
(1 row)
```

```
postgres=# SELECT 2/3 AS "2/3", 1/3 AS "1/3", 3/2 AS "3/2";
 2/3 | 1/3 | 3/2
-----+-----+-----
   0 |   0 |   1
(1 row)
```

The numeric and decimal types are recommended for storing monetary and other amounts where precision is required. There are three forms for defining a numeric or a decimal value:

- Numeric (precision, scale)
- Numeric (precision)
- Numeric

Precision is the total number of digits, while scale is the number of digits of the fraction part. For example, the number 12.344 has a precision of five and a scale of three. If a numeric type is used to define a column type without precision or scale, then the column can store any number with any precision and scale.

 If precision is not required, do not use the numeric and decimal types. Operations on numeric types are slower than floats and double precision.

Floating point and double precision are inexact; that means that the values in some cases cannot be represented in the internal binary format, and are stored as approximation.

Character types

The following table shows various character types:

Name	Comments	Trailing spaces	Maximum length
"char"	Equivalent to char(1) It must be quoted as shown in the name	Semantically insignificant	1
name	Equivalent to varchar(64) Used by postgres for object names	Semantically significant	64

Name	Comments	Trailing spaces	Maximum length
char(n)	Alias: character(n) Fixed length character where the length is n. Internally called bpchar (blank padded character)	Semantically insignificant	1 to 10485760(10*1024*1024)
Varchar(n)	Alias: character varying(n) Variable length character where the maximum length is n	Semantically significant	1 to 10485760
Text	Variable length character	Semantically significant	Unlimited

Character data types

PostgreSQL provides two general text types, which are char(n) and varchar(n) data types, where n is the number of characters allowed. In the char data type, if a value is less than the specified length, then trailing spaces are padded at the end of the value. Operations on the char data types ignore the trailing spaces. Take a look at the following example:

```
postgres=# SELECT 'a'::CHAR(2) = 'a '::CHAR(2);
 ?column?
----------
 t
(1 row)


postgres=# SELECT length('a          '::CHAR(10));
 length
--------
      1
(1 row)
```

It is not recommended to perform binary operations on varchar or text and char strings due to trailing spaces.

For both `char` and `varchar` data types, if the string is longer than the maximum allowed length, then:

- An error will be raised in the case of insert or update unless the extra characters are all spaces. In the latter case, the string will be truncated.

- In the case of casting, extra characters will be truncated automatically without raising an error.

The following example shows how mixing different data types might cause problems:

```
postgres=# SELECT 'a '::VARCHAR(2)='a '::text;
 ?column?
----------
 t
(1 row)
postgres=# SELECT 'a '::CHAR(2)='a '::text;
 ?column?
----------
 f
(1 row)
postgres=# SELECT 'a '::CHAR(2)='a '::VARCHAR(2);
 ?column?
----------
 t
(1 row)
postgres=# SELECT length ('a '::CHAR(2));
 length
--------
      1
(1 row)
postgres=# SELECT length ('a '::VARCHAR(2));
 length
--------
      2
(1 row)
```

The preceding example shows that `'a '::CHAR(2)` equals to `'a '::VARCHAR(2)`, but both have different lengths, which is not logical. Also, it shows that `'a '::CHAR(2)` is not equal to `'a '::text`. Finally, `'a '::VARCHAR(2)` equals `'a '::text`. The preceding example causes confusion because if a variable a is equal to b and b is equal to c, then a is equal to c according to mathematics.

The PostgreSQL text storage size depends on several factors, namely, the length of the text value, and the text decoding and compression. The text data type can be considered as an unlimited `varchar()` type. The maximum text size that can be stored is 1 GB, which is the maximum column size.

For fixed length strings, the character data type and the character varying data type consume the same amount of hard disk space. For variable length character, the character varying data type consumes less space, because character type appends the string with space. The following code shows the storage consumption for fixed and variable length texts for the character and character varying data types. It simply creates two tables, populates the tables with fictional data using fixed and variable length strings, and finally gets the table size in a human readable form:

```
CREATE TABLE char_size_test (
  size CHAR(10)
);
CREATE TABLE varchar_size_test(
  size varchar(10)
);
WITH test_data AS (
  SELECT substring(md5(random()::text), 1, 10) FROM
  generate_series (1, 1000000)
),
cahr _data_insert AS (
  INSERT INTO char_size_test SELECT * FROM test_data
)
INSERT INTO varchar_size_test SELECT * FROM test_date;
-- Get the table size in human readable form
SELECT pg_size_pretty(pg_relation_size ('char_size_test')) AS char_size_
test , pg_size_pretty(pg_relation_size ('varchar_size_test')) AS varchar_
size_test;
-- Delete the tables data
TRUNCATE char_size_test;
```

```
TRUNCATE varchar_size_test;
-- Insert data with fixed length
WITH test_date AS (
    SELECT substring(md5(random()::text), 1, (random()*
    10)::int) FROM generate_series (1, 1000000)
),
cahr _data_insert AS (
    INSERT INTO char_size_test SELECT * FROM test_date
)
INSERT INTO varchar_size_test SELECT * FROM test_date;


SELECT pg_size_pretty(pg_relation_size ('char_size_test')) AS char_size_
test , pg_size_pretty(pg_relation_size ('varchar_size_test')) AS varchar_
size_test;
-- Create tables
```

The varchar data type can be emulated by the text data type and a check constraint to check the text length. For example, the following code snippets are semantically equivalent:

```
CREATE TABLE emulate_varchar(
test VARCHAR(4)
);
--semantically equivalent to
CREATE TABLE emulate_varchar (
test TEXT,
CONSTRAINT test_length CHECK (length(test) <= 4)
);
```

In PostgreSQL, there is no difference in performance between the different character types, so it is recommended to use the text data type. It allows the developer to react quickly to the changes in business requirements. For example, one common business case is changing the text length, such as changing the length of a customer ticket number from six to eight characters due to length limitation, or changing how certain information are stored in the database. In such a scenario, if the data type is text, this could be done by amending the check constraint without altering the table structure.

Date and time types

The date and time data types are commonly used to describe the occurrence of events such as birth date. PostgreSQL supports the following date and time types:

Name	Storage size	Description	Low value	High value
Timestamp without time zone	8 bytes	Date and time without time zone equivalent to timestamp	4713 BC	294276 AD
Timestamp with time zone	8 bytes	Date and time with time zone equivalent to timestamptz	4713 BC	294276 AD
Date	4 bytes	Date only	4713 BC	5874897 AD
Time without time zone	8 bytes	Time of day	00:00:00	24:00:00
Time with time zone	12 bytes	Times of day only, with time zone	00:00:00+1459	24:00:00-1459
interval [fields]	16 bytes	Time interval	-178000000 years	178000000 years

Date/time data types

PostgreSQL stores timestamp with and without time zone in the **universal coordinated time (UTC)** format, and only time is stored without the time zone. This explains the identical storage size for both timestamp with time zone and time stamp without time zone.

There are two approaches for handling timestamp correctly. The first approach is to use timestamp without time zone, and let the client side handle the time zone differences. This is useful for in-house development, applications with only one time zone, and when the clients know the time zone differences.

The other approach is to use timestamp with time zone. The following are some of the best practices to avoid the common pitfalls when using `timestamptz`:

- Make sure to set the default time zone for all connections. This is done by setting the time zone configuration in the `postgresql.conf` file. Since PostgreSQL stores the timestamp with the time zone in UTC format internally, it is a good practice to set the default connection to UTC as well. Also, UTC helps in overcoming the potential problems due to **Daylight Saving Time** (DST).

- The time zone should be specified in each CRUD operation.

- Do not perform operations on timestamp without time zone and timestamp with time zone, this will normally lead to wrong results due to implicit conversion.

- Do not invent your own conversion; instead, use the database server to convert between the different time zones.

- Investigate the data types of high level languages to determine which type could be used with PostgreSQL without extra handling.

PostgreSQL has two important settings: `timezone` and `datestyle`. The `datestyle` has two purposes:

- **Setting the display format**: The `datestyle` specifies the `timestamp` and `timestamptz` rendering style.

- **Interpreting ambiguous data**: The `datestyle` specifies how to interpret `timestamp` and `timestamptz`.

The views `pg_timezone_names` and `pg_timezone_abbrevs` provide a list of the time zone names and abbreviations respectively. They also provide information regarding the time offset from UTC, and if the time zone is a DST. For example, the following code snippet sets the `timezone` setting to Jerusalem, and then retrieves the local date and time in Jerusalem:

```
postgres=> SET timezone TO 'Asia/jerusalem';
SET
postgres=> SELECT now();
             now
-------------------------------
 2014-08-27 23:49:49.611633+03
(1 row)
```

The PostgreSQL AT TIME ZONE statement converts the timestamp with or without the timezone to a specified time zone; its behavior depends on the converted type. The following example clarifies this construct:

```
postgres=> SHOW timezone;
 TimeZone
----------
 UTC
(1 row)


postgres=> \x
Expanded display is on.
postgres=> SELECT now(), now()::timestamp, now() AT TIME ZONE 'CST',
now()::timestamp AT TIME ZONE 'CST';
-[ RECORD 1 ]------------------------
now      | 2014-08-27 21:00:18.36009+00
now      | 2014-08-27 21:00:18.36009
timezone | 2014-08-27 15:00:18.36009
timezone | 2014-08-28 03:00:18.36009+00
```

The function now() returns the current timestamp with the time zone in the UTC format. Notice that the time zone offsite is +00. When casting the time stamp with the time zone to timestamp as in now()::timestamp, the time zone offsite is truncated. The now() AT TIME ZONE 'CST' expression converts the timestamp with the time zone UTC to timestamp in the specified time zone CST. Since the central standard time offset is -6, then six hours are deducted. The last expression now()::timestamp AT TIME ZONE 'CST' is reinterpreted as a timestamp as being in that time zone CST for the purpose of converting it to the connection default time zone UTC. So, the last expression is equivalent to the following:

```
postgres=> SELECT ('2014-08-27 21:00:18.36009'::timestamp AT time zone
'CST' AT TIME ZONE 'UTC')::timestamptz;
-[ RECORD 1 ]------------------------
timezone | 2014-08-28 03:00:18.36009+00
```

One can summarize the conversion between the timestamp with and without the time zone, as follows:

- The expression `timestamp without time zone AT TIME ZONE x` is interpreted as follows: the `timestamp` will be converted from the time zone x to the session time zone.

- The expression `timestamp with time zone AT TIME ZONE x` converts a `timestamptz` into a `timestamp` at the specified time zone x. The final result type is `timestamp`.

The date is recommended when there is no need to specify the time such as birth date, holidays, absence days, and so on.

Time with time zone storage is 12 bytes, 8 bytes are used to store the time, and 4 bytes are used to store the time zone. The time without time zone consumes only 8 bytes. Conversions between time zones can be made using the AT TIME ZONE construct.

Finally, the interval data type is very important in handling the timestamp operations as well as describing some business cases. From the point of view of functional requirements, the interval data type can represent a period of time such as estimation time for the completion of a certain task. The result type of the basic arithmetic operations such as + and - on timestamp, timestamptz, time, and time with time zone is of the type interval. The result of the same operations on date type is an integer. The following example shows `timestamptz` and date subtraction. Notice
the format of the specifying intervals:

```
SELECT '2014-09-01 23:30:00.000000+00'::timestamptz -'2014-09-01
22:00:00.000000+00'::timestamptz = Interval '1 hour, 30 minutes';
 ?column?
----------
 t
(1 row)
postgres=> SELECT '11-10-2014'::date -'10-10-2014'::date = 1;
 ?column?
----------
 t
(1 row)
```

The car web portal database

At this stage, one can convert the logical model of the car web portal presented in *Chapter 1, Relational Databases* to a physical model. To help the developer to create a table, one can follow this minimal check list:

- What is the primary key?
- What is the default value for each column?
- What is the type of each column?
- What are the constraints on each column or set of columns?
- Are permissions set correctly on tables, sequences, and schemas?
- Are foreign keys specified with the proper actions?
- What is the data life cycle?
- What are the operations allowed on the data?

For creating the car web portal schema, the formal relational model will not be applied strictly. Also, surrogate keys will be used instead of natural keys for the following reasons:

- Natural keys can change; one can change the current e-mail address to another one. Using a surrogate key guarantees that if a row is referenced by another row, then this reference is not lost, because the surrogate key has not changed.
- Incorrect assumptions about natural keys. Let us take e-mail address as an example. The general assumption about an e-mail address is that it identifies a person uniquely. This is not true; some e-mail service providers set policies such as e-mail expiration based on activity. Private companies might have general e-mail addresses such as contact@.., support@..., and so on. The same is applicable to phone and mobile numbers.
- Surrogate keys can be used to support a temporal database design within the relational database world. For example, some companies have a very strict security requirement, and data should be versioned for each operation.
- Surrogate keys often use compact data types such as integers. This allows for better performance than composite natural keys.

- Surrogate keys can be used in PostgreSQL to eliminate the effect of cross column statistic limitation. PostgreSQL collects statistics per single column. In some cases, this is not convenient because columns might be correlated. In this case, PostgreSQL gives a wrong estimation to the planner, and thus, imperfect execution plans are generated.

- Surrogate keys are better supported than the natural keys by object relational mappers such as hibernate.

Despite all these advantages of surrogate keys, it also has a few disadvantages:

- A surrogate key is auto generated, and the generation of the value might give different results. For example, one inserts a data in a test database and staging a database, and after the comparison of data, the data was not identical.

- A surrogate key is not descriptive. From the communication point of view, it is easier to refer to a person by a name instead of an auto generated number.

In the web car portal ER diagram, there is an entity with the name user. Since user is a reserved keyword, the name account will be used for creating the table. Note that to create a database object using a PostgreSQL keyword, the name should be quoted. The following example shows how to create a table user:

```
postgres=# \set VERBOSITY 'verbose'
postgres=# CREATE TABLE user AS SELECT 1;
ERROR:  42601: syntax error at or near "user"
LINE 1: CREATE TABLE user AS SELECT 1;
                     ^
LOCATION:   scanner_yyerror, src\backend\parser\scan.1:1053
postgres=# CREATE TABLE "user" AS SELECT 1;
SELECT 1
postgres=#
```

You can find the full list of reserved words at http://www.postgresql.org/docs/current/static/sql-keywords-appendix.html.

In the preceding example, the VERBOSITY setting for psql can be used to show error codes. Error codes are useful in detecting errors and trapping exceptions.

To create a table account, one can execute the following command:

```
CREATE TABLE account (
  account_id SERIAL PRIMARY KEY,
  first_name TEXT NOT NULL,
  last_name TEXT NOT NULL,
  email TEXT NOT NULL UNIQUE,
  password TEXT NOT NULL,
  CHECK(first_name !~ '\s' AND last_name !~ '\s'),
  CHECK (email ~* '^\w+@\w+[.]\w+$'),
  CHECK (char_length(password)>=8)
);
```

To summarize the user table:

- The account_id is defined as the primary key with type serial. The account_id is naturally unique and not null.

- The attributes first_name, last_name, email, and password are not allowed to have null values.

- The first_name and the last_name attributes are not allowed to have spaces.

- The password should be at least eight characters in length. In reality, the password length is handled in business logic, since passwords should not be stored in a plain text format in the database. For more information about securing the data, have a look at *Chapter 8, PostgreSQL Security*.

- The e-mail should match a certain regex expression. Note that the e-mail regular expression is really simplistic.

Behind the scene, the following objects are created:

- A sequence to emulate the serial type
- Two indices, both of them are unique. The first one is used for validation of the primary key—account_id. The second is used for the validation of the e-mail address.

To create the seller account, one can execute the following statement:

```
CREATE TABLE seller_account (
  seller_account_id SERIAL PRIMARY KEY,
  account_id INT UNIQUE NOT NULL REFERENCES
  account(account_id),
  number_of_advertizement advertisement INT DEFAULT 0,
  user_ranking float,
  total_rank float
);
```

As we can see, the seller account has a one-to-one relationship with the account. This is enforced by the `account_id` that consists of NOT NULL and UNIQUE constraints. Also, in this case, one can model the seller account as follows by marking the `account_id` as the primary key:

```
CREATE TABLE seller_account (
  account_id INT PRIMARY KEY REFERENCES
  account(account_id)
...
  );
```

The first design is more flexible and less ambiguous. First of all, the requirement might change, and the user account and the seller account relation might change from one-to-one to one-to-many. For example, the user concept might be generalized to handle companies where the company has several seller accounts.

Also, if a table references both the account and `seller_account` tables using a common column name such as `account_id`, then it will be difficult to distinguish which table is being referenced.

Summary

In this chapter, we explored the basic building blocks of PostgreSQL. There are several shared objects across the database cluster. These shared objects are roles, tablespaces, databases including template databases, template procedural languages, and some setting parameters. The tablespace is a defined storage used normally by the databases administrator for optimization or maintenance purposes.

The `template1` database is cloned each time a database is created. It can be loaded with extensions that should be available for all new databases. The `template0` database provides a fallback strategy in case the `template1` database is corrupted. Also, it can be used if the `template1` locale is not the required locale.

The role has several attributes such as login, superuser, createdb, and so on. The role is named a `user` in the old PostgreSQL version if it can log in to the database, and a group if it cannot. Roles can be granted to other roles; this allows the database administrators to manage permissions easily.

PostgreSQL has more than two hundred settings that control the database behavior. These settings can have different contexts, namely, internal, postmaster, backend, user, superuser, and sighup. To have a quick look at these settings, one can use the view `pg_settings`, which describes all the PostgreSQL settings.

The user database is the container for schemas, tables, views, functions, ranges, domain, sequences, and indexes. The database access permissions can be controlled via the `create`, `temporary`, and `connect` access privileges. Several aspects of the database behavior can be controlled by the `ALTER DATABASE` statement. The `pg_database` catalog table describes all the databases in the PostgreSQL cluster.

The schema is used to organize objects within the database. By default, each database has a public schema.

PostgreSQL provides a rich set of data types, including numeric, text, and date/time data types. Choosing a data type is an important task; thus, one should balance between extensibility and storage consumption when choosing a data type.

One should be careful when performing operations on a mixture of different data types due to implicit conversion. For example, one should know how the system behaves when comparing text data type with the varchar data type. This is applied to time and date data types.

Tables are the major building blocks in PostgreSQL; they are used internally to implement views as well as sequences. A table can be categorized as temporary or permanent. In streaming replication, unlogged tables are not replicated to the slave nodes.

4
PostgreSQL Advanced Building Blocks

In this chapter, the rest of the PostgreSQL building blocks, including views, indexes, functions, triggers, and rules, will be introduced. In addition to that, the web car portal schema will be revised. Several DDL commands, such as CREATE and ALTER, will also be introduced.

Since the lexical structure and several DML commands have not been introduced as yet, we will try to use very simple DML commands.

Views

A view can be seen as a named query, or as a wrapper around a SELECT statement. Views are essential building blocks of relational databases from the UML modeling perspective; a view can be thought of as a method for a UML class. Views share several advantages over procedures, so the following benefits are shared between views and stored procedures. Views can be used for the following purposes:

- Simplifying complex queries and increasing code modularity
- Tuning performance by caching the view results for later use
- Decreasing the amount of SQL code
- Bridging the gap between relational databases and OO languages—especially updatable views
- Implementing authorization at the row level by leaving out rows that do not meet a certain predicate

- Implementing interfaces and the abstraction layer between high level languages and relational databases
- Implementing last minute changes without redeploying the software

Unlike stored procedures, the views dependency tree is maintained in the database; thus, altering a view might be forbidden due to a cascading effect.

It is essential to know the way in which views are designed. The following is some general advice to keep in mind for handling views properly:

 In PostgreSQL, one cannot find a dangling view due to the maintenance of the view's dependency tree. However, this might happen in the case of a stored procedure.

- The view definition should be crisp: the view should meet the current business need instead of potential future business needs. It should be designed to provide a certain functionality or service. Note that, the more attributes in the view, the more effort required to re-factor this view. In addition to that, when the view aggregates data from many tables and is used as an interface, there might be a degradation in performance due to many factors (for example bad execution plans due to outdated statistics for some tables, execution plan time generation, and so on).
- Views dependency—when implementing complex business logic in the database using views and stored procedures, the database refactoring, especially for base tables, might turn out to be very expensive. To solve this issue, consider migrating the business logic to the application business tier.
- Take care of business tier needs—some frameworks, such as the object relational mappers, might require specific needs such as a unique key. This can be achieved via the windows `row_number` function.

In PostgreSQL, the view is internally modeled as a table with a _RETURN rule. So, the following two pieces of code are equivalent:

```
CREATE VIEW test AS SELECT 1 AS one;

CREATE TABLE test (one INTEGER);

CREATE RULE "_RETURN" AS ON SELECT TO test DO INSTEAD
    SELECT 1;
```

The preceding example is for the purpose of explanation only, it is not recommended to play with the PostgreSQL catalogue, including the reserved rules, manually. Moreover, note that a table can be converted to a view but not vice versa.

When one creates views, the created tables are used to maintain the dependency between the created views. So when executing the following query:

```
SELECT * FROM test;
```

We actually execute the following:

```
SELECT * FROM(SELECT 1) AS test;
```

To understand views dependency, let us build a view using another view, as follows:

```
--date_trunc function is similar to trunc function for numbers,
CREATE VIEW day_only AS
SELECT date_trunc('day', now()) AS day;
CREATE VIEW month_only AS
SELECT date_trunc('month', day_only.day)AS month FROM day_only;
```

The preceding views, month_only and day_only, are truncating the time to day and month respectively. The month_only view depends on the day_only view. In order to drop the day_only view, one can use one of the following options:

1. First drop the month_only view followed by the day_only view:

   ```
   car_portal=# DROP VIEW day_only;
   ERROR:  cannot drop view day_only because other objects depend on it
   DETAIL:  view month_only depends on view day_only
   HINT:  Use DROP ... CASCADE to drop the dependent objects too.
   car_portal=# DROP VIEW month_only;
   DROP VIEW
   car_portal=# DROP VIEW day_only;
   DROP VIEW
   ```

2. Use the CASCADE option when dropping the view:

   ```
   car_portal=# DROP VIEW day_only CASCADE;
   NOTICE:  drop cascades to view month_only
   DROP VIEW
   ```

View synopsis

In the view synopsis shown next, the CREATE keyword is used to create a view, while the REPLACE keyword is used to redefine the view if it already exists. The view attribute names can be given explicitly, or they can be inherited from the SELECT statement:

```
CREATE [ OR REPLACE ] [ TEMP | TEMPORARY ] [ RECURSIVE ] VIEW name [ (
column_name [, ...] ) ]
    [ WITH ( view_option_name [= view_option_value] [, ... ] ) ]
    AS query
    [ WITH [ CASCADED | LOCAL ] CHECK OPTION ]
```

The following example shows how to create a view that lists only the user information without the password. This might be useful for implementing data authorization to restrict the applications for accessing the password. Note that the view column names are inherited from the SELECT list, as shown by the \d in the account_information meta command:

```
CREATE VIEW account_information AS
SELECT
  account_id,
  first_name,
  last_name,
  email
FROM
  account;


car_portal=# \d account_information
View "public.account_information"
   Column    |  Type   |  Modifiers
------------+---------+-----------
 account_id | integer |
 first_name | text    |
 last_name  | text    |
 email      | text    |
```

The view account information column names can be assigned explicitly as shown in the following example. This might be useful when one needs to change the view column names:

```
CREATE VIEW account_information (account_id,first_name,last_name,email)
AS

SELECT

  account_id,

  first_name,

  last_name,

 email

FROM

  account;
```

When replacing the view definition using the REPLACE keyword, the column list should be identical before and after the replacement, including the column type, name, and order. The following example shows what happens when trying to change the view column order:

```
car_portal=# CREATE OR REPLACE VIEW account_information AS

SELECT

account_id,

last_name,

first_name,

email

FROM

account;

ERROR:  cannot change name of view column "first_name" to "last_name"
```

Views categories

Views in PostgreSQL can be categorized in one of the following categories on the basis of their usage:

- **Temporary views**: A temporary view is dropped automatically at the end of a user session. If the TEMPORARY or TEMP keywords are not used, then the life cycle of the view starts with view creation and ends with the action of dropping it.

- **Recursive views**: A recursive view is similar to the recursive functions in high level languages. The view column list should be specified in recursive views. Recursion in relational databases, such as in recursive views or recursive **common table expressions** (CTEs), can be used to write very complex queries specifically for hieratical data.

- **Updatable views**: Updatable views allow the user to see the view as a table. This means that the developer can perform INSERT, UPDATE and DELETE on views similar to tables. Updatable views can help in bridging the gap between an object model and a relational model to some extent, and they can help in overcoming problems like polymorphism.

- **Materialized views**: A materialized view is a table whose contents are periodically refreshed based on a certain query. Materialized views are useful for boosting the performance of some queries, which require a longer execution time and are executed frequently on static data. One could perceive materialized views as a caching technique.

Since recursion will be covered in the following chapters, we will focus here on the updatable and materialized views.

Materialized views

The materialized view synopsis differs a little bit from the normal view synopsis. Materialized views are a PostgreSQL extension, but several databases, such as Oracle, support it. As shown in the following synopsis below, a materialized view can be created in a certain TABLESPACE, which is logical since materialized views are physical objects:

```
CREATE MATERIALIZED VIEW table_name
    [ (column_name [, ...] ) ]
    [ WITH ( storage_parameter [= value] [, ... ] ) ]
    [ TABLESPACE tablespace_name ]
    AS query
    [ WITH [ NO ] DATA ]
```

At the time of creation of a materialized view, it can be populated with data or left empty. If it is not populated, retrieving data from the unpopulated materialized view will raise an ERROR. The REFRESH MATERIALIZED VIEW statement can be used to populate a materialized view. The following example shows an attempt to retrieve data from an unpopulated materialized view:

```
car_portal=# CREATE MATERIALIZED VIEW test_mat_view AS SELECT 1 WITH NO
DATA;
car_portal=# SELECT * FROM test_mat_view;
ERROR:  materialized view "test_mat_view" has not been populated
HINT:  Use the REFRESH MATERIALIZED VIEW command.
car_portal=# REFRESH MATERIALIZED VIEW test_mat_view;
```

```
REFRESH MATERIALIZED VIEW
car_portal=# SELECT * FROM test_mat_view;
 ?column?
----------
        1
(1 row)
```

Materialized views are often used with data warehousing. In data warehousing, several queries are required for business analyses and for decision support. The data in this kind of applications does not usually change, but the calculation and aggregation of this data is often a costly operation. In general, a materialized view can be used for the following:

- Generating summary tables and keeping summary tables up-to-date
- Caching the results of recurring queries

Since materialized views are tables, they also can be indexed, leading to a great performance boost.

In our web car portal application, let us assume that we need to create a monthly summary report for the previous month to see which car was searched for the most . Let us also assume that the user search key has the following pattern:

Keyword1=value1&keyword2&value2& … & keywordn=valuen

For example, a search key could be :brand=opel&manufacturing_date=2013. The summary report can be created using the following query:

```
CREATE MATERIALIZED VIEW account_search_history AS
SELECT
  Key,
  count(*)
FROM
 (SELECT
    regexp_split_to_table(search_key, '&') AS key
 FROM
    account_history
 WHERE
    search_date >= date_trunc('month', now()-INTERVAL '1
    month') AND
    search_date < date_trunc('month', now())) AS FOO
```

```
GROUP BY key;


car_portal=# SELECT * FROM account_search_history;
    key       |  count
------------+-------
 brand=opel |    2
 model=2013 |    1
(2 rows)
```

The preceding query requires a lot of calculation because of the aggregation function, and also due to the big amount of data in the table. In our car web portal, if we have a million searches per month, that would mean a million records in the database. The query uses the following functions and predicates:

- The predicate `regexp_split_to_table(search_key, '&')` is used to split each search key and return the result as a table or set
- The count (`*`) is used to count the number of times the key is used in a search
- The predicate `search_date >= ...` is used to get the search keys for the previous month

For completion purposes in our example, the generation of the materialized views should be automated using cron job in Linux or the job scheduler software. Additionally, the names of the generated materialized views should be suffixed with the month, since we need to generate a summary table for the search keys each month.

Updatable views

By default, simple PostgreSQL views are auto-updatable. Auto-updatable means that one could use the view with the **DELETE**, **INSERT** and **UPDATE** statements to manipulate the data of the underlying table. If the view is not updatable (which is not simple) due to the violation of one of the following constraints, the trigger and rule systems can be used to make it updatable. The view is automatically updatable if the following conditions are met:

1. The view must be built on top of a table or an updatable view.

2. The view definition must not contain the following clauses and set operators at the top level: DISTINCT, WITH, GROUP BY, OFFSET, HAVING, LIMIT, UNION, EXCEPT, and INTERSECT.

3. The view's select list must be mapped to the underlying table directly without using functions and expressions. Moreover, the columns in the select list should not be repeated.

4. The security_barrier property must not be set.

The preceding conditions promise that the view attributes can be mapped directly to the underlying table attributes.

In the web car portal, let us assume that we have a view that shows only the accounts that are not seller accounts. This can be done as follows:

```
CREATE VIEW user_account AS
SELECT
account_id,
..first_name,
..last_name,
..email,
..password
FROM
..account
WHERE
..account_id NOT IN (
....SELECT account_id FROM seller_account);
```

The preceding view is updatable by default; thus, one can insert and update the view content as follows:

```
car_portal=# INSERT INTO user_account VALUES (default, 'test_first_name',
'test_last_name','test@email.com', 'password');
INSERT 0 1
car_portal=# DELETE FROM user_account WHERE first_name = 'test_first_
name';
DELETE 1
```

In the case of an auto-updatable view, one cannot modify the base table if it does not contain data. For example, let us insert an account with a seller account, and then try to delete it:

```
car_portal=# WITH account_info AS (
INSERT INTO user_account
VALUES (default,'test_first_name','test_last_name','test@email.
com','password')
RETURNING account_id)
INSERT INTO seller_account (account_id, street_name, street_number, zip_
code, city) SELECT account_id, 'test_street', '555', '555', 'test_city'
FROM account_info;
INSERT 0 1

car_portal=# DELETE FROM user_account WHERE first_name = 'test_first_
name';
DELETE 0
```

In the preceding example, notice that the insert to the user account was successful, while the DELETE command did not delete any row.

If one is uncertain whether a view is auto updatable or not, he/she can verify this information using the information schema by checking the value of the is_insertable_into flag, as follows:

```
car_portal-# SELECT table_name, is_insertable_into FROM information_
schema.tables WHERE table_name = 'user_account';
  table_name   | is_insertable_into
---------------+--------------------
 user_account  | YES
(1 row)
```

Indexes

An index is a physical database object that is defined on a table column or a list of columns. In PostgreSQL, there are many types of indexes and several ways to use them. Indexes can be used, in general, to do the following:

- Optimize performance: an index allows an efficient retrieval of a small number of rows from the table. The small number is often determined by the total number of rows in the table and execution planner settings.

- Validate constraints, instead of checking constraints. An index can be used to validate the constraints on several rows. For example, the UNIQUE check constraint creates a unique index on the column behind the scenes.

Let us take a look at the `account_history` table in the car web portal example. The unique constraint, `UNIQUE (account_id, search_key, search_date)`, has two purposes: the first purpose is to define the validity constraint for inserting the search key into the table only once each day, even if the user searches for the key several times. The second purpose is to retrieve the data quickly. Let us assume that we would like to show the last 10 searches for the user. The query for performing this will be as follows:

```
SELECT search_key FROM account_history WHERE account_id = <account> GROUP
BY search_key ORDER BY max(search_date) limit 10;
```

The preceding query returns only 10 records containing the different `search_key` ordered by `search_date`. If we assume that the search `account_history` contains millions of rows, then reading all the data will take a lot of time. In this case, this is not true, because the unique index will help us in reading the columns only for this particular customer. To understand how PostgreSQL uses indexes, let us populate the table with fictional data.

- **Fictional data 1**: Two users and four search keys for each—in total, eight records will be inserted into the table:

```
WITH test_account AS( INSERT INTO account VALUES (1000, 'test_
first_name', 'test_last_name','test@email.com', 'password'),

(2000, 'test_first_name2', 'test_last_name2','test2@email.com',
'password2') RETURNING account_id

),car AS ( SELECT i as car_model FROM (VALUES('brand=BMW'),
('brand=WV')) AS foo(i)

),manufacturing_date AS ( SELECT  'year='|| i as date FROM
generate_series (2015, 2014, -1) as foo(i))

INSERT INTO account_history (account_id, search_key,

search_date) SELECT account_id, car.car_model||'&'||manufacturing_
date.date, current_date

FROM test_account, car, manufacturing_date;
```

To understand how the data is generated, we simply created a cross join, as discussed in *Chapter 1*, *Relational Databases*. Since we have two brands and two manufacturing dates, we generated four combinations. To see the generated date, let us execute the preceding query for the test account with `account_id`, which has the value `1000`:

```
car_portal=# SELECT search_key FROM account_history WHERE account_
id = 1000 GROUP BY (search_key) ORDER BY max(search_date) limit
10;

    search_key

--------------------

 brand=BMW&year=2014

 brand=WV&year=2014

 brand=BMW&year=2015

 brand=WV&year=2015

(4 rows)
```

For small data, PostgreSQL prefers to perform a sequential scan simply due
to the execution cost. On a small data set, a sequential scan is faster than
an index scan. To get the execution plan, one can execute the following
command:

```
car_portal=# EXPLAIN SELECT search_key FROM account_history WHERE
account_id = 1000 GROUP BY search_key ORDER BY max(search_date)
limit 10;
                                    QUERY PLAN

-----------------------------------------------------------------
--------------------

 Limit  (cost=38.64..38.67 rows=10 width=23)

   -> Sort  (cost=38.64..39.43 rows=313 width=23)

        Sort Key: (max(search_date))

        -> HashAggregate  (cost=28.75..31.88 rows=313 width=23)

             -> Seq Scan on account_history  (cost=0.00..25.63
rows=625 width=23)

                  Filter: (account_id = 1000)

(6 rows)
```

- **Fictional data 2**: Use the same preceding code, and keep increasing the
  number of test accounts, manufacturing dates, and the car models to generate
  a big data set, as follows. Keep generating the execution plan until you get an
  index scan:

```
...
(5000, 'test_first_name5', 'test_last_name5','test5@email.com',
'password5')

...

SELECT i as car_model FROM (VALUES('brand=BMW'), ('brand=WV'),
('brand=Opel'), ('brand=Fiat'), ('brand=Siat')) AS foo(i)

...

SELECT  'year='|| i as date FROM generate_series (2015, 1980, -1)
as foo(i)
```

With a big data set, PostgreSQL performs an index scan instead of a
sequential scan to retrieve the data. The following shows the execution plan
with an index scan for the preceding query:

```
car_portal=# EXPLAIN SELECT search_key FROM account_history WHERE
account_id = 1000 GROUP BY search_key ORDER BY max(search_date)
limit 10;

QUERY PLAN
------------------------------------------------------------------
------------------------------------------------------------------
-----
 Limit  (cost=26.07..26.09 rows=10 width=24)
   -> Sort  (cost=26.07..26.19 rows=50 width=24)
        Sort Key: (max(search_date))
        -> HashAggregate  (cost=24.49..24.99 rows=50 width=24)
              -> Bitmap Heap Scan on account_history
(cost=10.18..23.26 rows=246 width=24)
                    Recheck Cond: (account_id = 1000)
                    -> Bitmap Index Scan on account_history_
account_id_search_key_search_date_key  (cost=0.00..10.12 rows=246
width=0)
                          Index Cond: (account_id = 1000)
(8 rows)
```

The PostgreSQL planner decides whether to use an index based on the
execution plan cost. For the same query with different parameters, the
planner might pick a different plan based on the data histogram.

Index types

PostgreSQL supports different indexes; each index can be used for a certain scenario or a data type.

- **B-tree index**: This is the default index in PostgreSQL when the index type is not specified with the CREATE INDEX command. The "B" stands for balanced, which means that the data on both sides of the tree is roughly equal. B-tree can be used for equality, ranges, and null predicates. The B-tree index supports all PostgreSQL data types.

- **Hash indexes**: Hash indexes are not well supported in PostgreSQL. They are not transaction-safe, and are not replicated to the slave nodes in streaming replication. They are useful for equality predicates, but since a B-tree index can support this use case, it is not recommended to use the Hash indexes.

- **Generalized inverted index (GIN)**: The GIN index is useful when several values need to map to one row. It can be used with complex data structures such as arrays and full-text searches.

- **Generalized Search Tree (GiST)**: The GiST indexes allow building of general balanced tree structures. They are useful in indexing geometric data types, as well as full-text search.

- **Block range index (BRIN)**: This will be introduced in PostgreSQL 9.5. The BRIN index is useful for very large tables where the size is limited. A BRIN index is slower than a B-tree index, but requires less space than the B-tree.

Partial indexes

A partial index indexes only a subset of the table data that meets a certain predicate; the WHERE clause is used with the index. The idea behind a partial index is to decrease the index size, thus making it more maintainable and faster to access. Let us assume that we would like to introduce a data life cycle for some tables. For the advertisement table in the car web portal, suppose that we would like to keep the advertisement for a certain period of time after deletion to enable the seller to revive their advertisement easily. The deletion operation will be emulated by adding a column called advertisement_deletion_date and a job scheduler task to clean up the advertisements that have been deleted. For the SQL part, this could be done as follows:

```
car_portal=# ALTER TABLE advertisement ADD column advertisement_deletion_
date TIMESTAMP WITH TIME ZONE;

ALTER TABLE
```

In order to retrieve the dead advertisement quickly, one could use the partial index on the `advertisement_deletion_date`, as follows:

```
CREATE INDEX ON advertisement(advertisement_id) WHERE advertisement_
deletion_date IS NOT NULL;
CREATE INDEX
```

The preceding index will help in retrieving the dead advertisement quickly without creating an index on the whole advertisement table.

Indexes on expressions

As stated earlier, an index could be created on a table column or multiple columns. It can also be created on expressions and function results. In the account table, let us assume that we would like to search for an account with the first name `foo`. Also, let us assume that the names are stored in the database in different cases such as `Foo`, `foo`, and `fOo`, and that there is an index on the `first_name`. To get the accounts, one can use the `lower()` and `upper()` functions or the case insensitive regular expressions operator `~*`. The queries can be written as follows:

```
 car_portal=# INSERT INTO account values (DEFAULT, 'fOo', 'bar', 'foo@
bar.com', md5('foo'));
INSERT 0 1
car_portal=# SELECT * FROM account WHERE first_name ~* '^foo$';
 account_id | first_name | last_name |     email     |        password
------------+------------+-----------+---------------+---------------------
-------------
          1 | fOo        | bar       | foo@bar.com   |
acbd18db4cc2f85cedef654fccc4a4d8
(1 row)
car_portal=# SELECT * FROM account WHERE lower(first_name) = 'foo';
 account_id | first_name | last_name |     email     |        password
------------+------------+-----------+---------------+---------------------
-------------
          1 | fOo        | bar       | foo@bar.com   |
acbd18db4cc2f85cedef654fccc4a4d8
(1 row)
```

The two preceding approaches will not use an index scan, which is the preferable method, because only one row is retrieved. When using the lower (first_name) function, the value of the function is not determined unless the function is executed. Thus, the index cannot be used. For the regular expressions, the expression might match one or more values. To solve this, an index on the lower () function can be used as follows, and the lower () function should then be used instead of regex:

```
CREATE index ON account(lower(first_name));
SELECT * FROM account WHERE lower(first_name) = 'foo';
```

Another usage of the expression indexes is to find rows by casting a data type to another data type. For example, the birth of a child can be stored as a timestamp; however, we often search for a birth date and not the birth time.

Unique indexes

The unique index guarantees the uniqueness of a certain value in a row across the whole table. In the account table, the email column has a unique check constraint. This is implemented by the unique index, as shown by the \d meta command:

```
car_portal=# \d account
                        Table "car_portal_app.account"
   Column   |  Type   |                       Modifiers
------------+---------+-------------------------------------------------------
------------
 account_id | integer | not null default nextval('account_account_id_
seq'::regclass)
 first_name | text    | not null
 last_name  | text    | not null
 email      | text    | not null
 password   | text    | not null
Indexes:
    "account_pkey" PRIMARY KEY, btree (account_id)
    "account_email_key" UNIQUE CONSTRAINT, btree (email)
    "account_lower_idx" btree (lower(first_name))
Check constraints:
...
Referenced by:
...
```

Note that in the index section of the \d command there are three indexes; the `account_email_key` is a B-tree index for the email column.

 In the PostgreSQL renaming conventions, the suffixes for unique and normal indexes are `key` and `idx` respectively.

One can also use the unique and partial indexes together. For example, let us assume that we have a table called employee, where each employee must have a supervisor except for the company head. We can model this as a self-referencing table, as follows:

```
CREATE TABLE employee (employee_id INT PRIMARY KEY, supervisor_id INT);

ALTER TABLE employee ADD CONSTRAINT supervisor_id_fkey FOREIGN KEY
(supervisor_id) REFERENCES employee(employee_id);
```

To guarantee that only one row is assigned to a supervisor, we can add the following unique index:

```
CREATE UNIQUE INDEX ON employee ((1)) WHERE supervisor_id IS NULL;
```

The unique index on the constant expression (1) will allow only one row with a null value. With the first insert of a null value, a unique index will be built using the value 1. A second attempt to add a row with a null value will cause an error, because the value 1 is already indexed:

```
car_portal=# INSERT INTO employee VALUES (1, NULL);

INSERT 0 1

car_portal=# INSERT INTO employee VALUES (2, 1);

INSERT 0 1

car_portal=# INSERT INTO employee VALUES (3, NULL);

ERROR:  duplicate key value violates unique constraint "employee_expr_
idx"

DETAIL:  Key ((1))=(1) already exists.
```

Multicolumn indexes

A multicolumn index can be used for a certain pattern of query conditions. Suppose a query has a pattern similar to the following:

```
SELECT * FROM table WHERE column1 = constant1 and column2= constant2 AND
... columnn = constantn;
```

In this case, an index can be created on `column1`, `column2`,..., and `columnn`, where n is less than or equal to `32`. Currently, only B-tree, GIN, and GiST support multicolumn indexes. When creating a multicolumn index, the column order is important. A multicolumn index can be used to retrieve data if the leftmost columns are used with equality and inequality expressions on the first column that does not have any equality expressions.

Since the multicolumn index size is often big, the planner might prefer to perform a sequential scan rather than reading the index.

Best practices on indexes

It is often useful to index columns that are used with predicates and foreign keys. This enables PostgreSQL to use an index scan instead of a sequential scan. The benefits of indexes are not limited to the SELECT statements, but the DELETE and UPDATE statements can also benefit from it. There are some cases where an index is not used, and this is often due to the small table size. In big tables, one should plan the space capacity carefully, since the index size might be very big. Also note that indexes have a negative impact on the INSERT statements, since amending the index comes with a cost.

There are several catalogue tables and functions that help in maintaining the indexes. The first view is `pg_stat_all_indexes`, which gives the statistics about the index usage. In the following example, we can see that the index `account_history_account_id_search_key_search_date_key` is never used, which is fine in this case, since the database has just been created:

```
car_portal=# SELECT * FROM pg_stat_all_indexes WHERE schemaname = 'car_
portal_app' limit 1;
  relid  | indexrelid |   schemaname    |    relname    |
indexrelname                         | idx_scan | idx_tup_read | idx_tup_
fetch

---------+------------+-----------------+-----------------+----------------+----------------
-----------------------------------+----------+--------------+------
---------
 8053962 |    8053971 | car_portal_app  | account_history | account_
history_account_id_search_key_search_date_key |        0 |              0
|          0
(1 row)
```

The function pg_index_size can be used with the pg_size_pretty function to get the index size in a human-readable form, as follows:

```
car_portal=# SELECT pg_size_pretty(pg_indexes_size ('car_portal_app.
account_pkey'));
 pg_size_pretty
----------------
 0 bytes
(1 row)
```

When creating an index, make sure that the index does not exist, otherwise one could end up with duplicate indexes. PostgreSQL does not raise a warning when creating duplicate indexes, as shown in the following example:

```
car_portal=# CREATE index on car_portal_app.account(first_name);
CREATE INDEX
car_portal=# CREATE index on car_portal_app.account(first_name);
CREATE INDEX
```

In some cases, an index might be bloated; PostgreSQL provides the REINDEX command, which is used to rebuild the index. Note that the REINDEX command is a blocking command. To solve this, one can create another index identical to the original index concurrently to avoid locks. Creating an index concurrently is often preferred with a live system, but it requires more work than creating a normal index. Moreover, creating an index concurrently has some caveats; in some cases index creation might fail, leading to an invalid index. An invalid index can be dropped or rebuilt using the DROP and REINDEX statements respectively.

Let us assume that we have a table called a, and an index on this table called a_index. Let us also assume that the index is bloated, and we need to build it. The following two pieces of code could be considered equivalent with one difference, that is, the locking behavior:

```
--- create a test table
car_portal=# CREATE TABLE a (id int);
CREATE TABLE
car_portal=# CREATE INDEX a_index ON a(id);
CREATE INDEX
```

```
--- Piece of code1: cause locks
car_portal=# REINDEX INDEX a_index;
REINDEX
--- Piece of code 2: No locks
car_portal=# CREATE INDEX concurrently a_index_1 ON a(id);
CREATE INDEX
car_portal=# DROP index a_index;
DROP INDEX
car_portal=# ALTER INDEX a_index_1 RENAME TO a_index;
ALTER INDEX
```

PostgreSQL indexes is a huge topic. Indexes can also be used to answer certain queries without doing a table scan at all. They can, additionally, be used to speed up sorting operations. Also, they can be used for anchored and non-anchored text searches using operator classes and operator families. Finally, PostgreSQL supports full-text searches using the GIN and GiST indexes and the text search types: tsvector and tsquery.

Functions

A PostgreSQL function is used to provide a distinct service, and is often composed of a set of declarations, expressions, and statements. PostgreSQL has very rich built-in functions for almost all the existing data types. In this chapter, we will focus on user-defined functions. However, details about the syntax and function parameters will be covered in the following chapters.

PostgreSQL native programming languages

PostgreSQL supports out-of-the-box user-defined functions to be written in C, SQL and PL/pgSQL. There are also three other procedural languages that come with the standard PostgreSQL distribution: PL/Tcl, PL/Python, and PL/Perl. However, one needs to create the language in order to use them via the CREATE EXTENSION PostgreSQL command or via the createlang utility tool.

The simplest way to create a language and make it accessible to all the databases is to create it in template1, directly after the PostgreSQL cluster installation. Note that one does not need to perform this step for C, SQL, and PL/pgSQL.

For beginners, the most convenient languages to use are SQL and PL/pgSQL since they are supported directly. Moreover, they are highly portable, and do not need special care during the upgrading of the PostgreSQL cluster. Creating functions in the C language is not as easy as creating it in SQL or PL/pgSQL, but since C language is a general programing language, one could use it to create very complex functions to handle complex data types such as images.

Creating a function in the C language

In the following example, we will create a factorial function in the C language; this can be used as a template for creating more complex functions. One can create a PostgreSQL C function in four steps, as follows:

1. Install the PostgreSQL server development library.

2. Define your function in C, create a make file, and compile it as a shared library (.so). In order to do that, one needs to read the PostgreSQL documentation provided at http://www.postgresql.org/docs/9.4/ static/xfunc-c.html.

3. Specify the location of the shared library that contains your function. The easiest way to do this is to provide the library's absolute path when creating the function, or by copying the created function-shared library to the PostgreSQL library directory.

4. Create the function in your database using the CREATE FUNCTION command.

To install the PostgreSQL development library, one can use the apt tool, as follows:

```
sudo apt-get install postgresql-server-dev-9.4
```

In C language development, the make tools are often used to compile the C code. The following is a simple make file to compile the factorial function:

```
MODULES = fact

PG_CONFIG = pg_config
PGXS = $(shell $(PG_CONFIG) --pgxs)
INCLUDEDIR = $(shell $(PG_CONFIG) --includedir-server)
include $(PGXS)

fact.so: fact.o
  cc -shared -o fact.so fact.o

fact.o: fact.c
  cc -o fact.o -c fact.c $(CFLAGS) -I$(INCLUDEDIR)
```

The source code of the factorial `fact` for the abbreviation C function is given as follows:

```c
#include "postgres.h"
#include "fmgr.h"

#ifdef PG_MODULE_MAGIC
  PG_MODULE_MAGIC;
#endif

Datum fact(PG_FUNCTION_ARGS);

PG_FUNCTION_INFO_V1(fact);

Datum
fact(PG_FUNCTION_ARGS) {
  int32   fact = PG_GETARG_INT32(0);
  int32 count = 1, result = 1;

  for (count = 1; count <= fact; count++)
    result = result * count;


  PG_RETURN_INT32(result);
 }
```

The last step is to compile the code, copy the library to the PostgreSQL libraries location, and create the function:

```
make -f makefile
cp fact.so $(pg_config --pkglibdir)/
psql -d template1 -c "CREATE FUNCTION fact(INTEGER) RETURNS INTEGER AS
'fact', 'fact' LANGUAGE C STRICT;"
psql -d template1 -c "SELECT fact(5);"
 fact
------
  120
(1 row)
```

Writing C functions is quite complicated as compared to the SQL and PL/pgSQL functions. They might even cause some complications in upgrading the database if they are not well maintained.

Creating functions in the SQL language

Creating SQL functions is quite easy. The following is a function that determines if a view is updatable or not:

```
CREATE OR REPLACE FUNCTION is_updatable_view (text) RETURNS BOOLEAN AS
$$
  SELECT is_insertable_into='YES' FROM information_schema.tables WHERE
table_type = 'VIEW' AND table_name = $1
$$
LANGUAGE SQL;
```

The body of the SQL function can be composed of several SQL statements; the result of the last SQL statement determines the function return type. An SQL PostgreSQL function cannot be used for constructing dynamic SQL statements, since the function argument can only be used to substitute data values but not identifiers. The following snippet is not valid in an SQL function:

```
CREATE FUNCTION ...
--$1 is used to substitute table name
SELECT * FROM $1;
```

Creating a function in the PL/pgSQL language

The PL/pgSQL language is a full-fledged and preferable choice for usage on a daily basis. It can contain a variable declaration, conditional and looping construct, exception trapping, and so on.

The following function returns the factorial of an integer:

```
CREATE OR REPLACE FUNCTION fact(fact INT) RETURNS INT AS
$$
DECLARE
count INT = 1;
result INT = 1;
BEGIN
  FOR count IN 1..fact LOOP
```

```
    result = result* count;
  END LOOP;
  RETURN result;
END;
$$
LANGUAGE plpgsql;
```

PostgreSQL function usages

PostgreSQL can be used in several scenarios. For example, some developers use functions as an abstract interface with higher programming languages to hide the data model. Additionally, functions can have several other usages such as:

- Performing complex logic that is difficult to perform with SQL
- In Dynamic SQL, a function argument can be used to pass table and views' names via the EXECUTE statement
- Performing actions before or after the execution of an SQL statement via the trigger system
- Performing exception handling and additional logging via the EXCEPTION blocks and RAISE statement respectively
- Cleaning the SQL code by reusing the common code, and bundling the SQL codes in modules

PostgreSQL function dependency

When using PostgreSQL functions, one needs to be careful not to end with dangling functions, since the dependency between functions in not well maintained in the PostgreSQL system catalogue. The following example shows how one can end up with a dangling function:

```
CREATE OR REPLACE FUNCTION test_dep (INT) RETURNS INT AS $$
BEGIN
RETURN $1;
END;
$$
LANGUAGE plpgsql;
```

```
CREATE OR REPLACE FUNCTION test_dep_2(INT) RETURNS INT AS
$$
BEGIN
RETURN test_dep($1);
END;
$$
LANGUAGE plpgsql;
DROP FUNCTION test_dep(int);
SELECT test_dep_2 (5);


ERROR:  function test_dep(integer) does not exist
LINE 1: SELECT test_dep($1)
                    ^
HINT:  No function matches the given name and argument types. You might
need to add explicit type casts.
QUERY:  SELECT test_dep($1)
CONTEXT:  PL/pgSQL function test_dep_2(integer) line 3 at RETURN
```

In the preceding example, two functions were created with one dependent on the other. The test_dep() function was dropped leaving the test_depend_2() as a dangling function.

PostgreSQL function categories

When creating a function, it is marked as *volatile* by default if the volatility classification is not specified. If the created function is not volatile, it is important to mark it as *stable* or *immutable*, because this will help the optimizer to generate the optimal exaction plans. PostgreSQL functions can have one of the following three volatility classifications:

- **Volatile**: The volatile function can return a different result on successive calls even if the function argument did not change, or it can change the data in the database. The random() function is a volatile function.

- **Stable and immutable**: These functions cannot modify the database, and are guaranteed to return the same result for the same argument. The stable function provides this guarantee within statement scope, while the immutable function provides this guarantee globally, without any scope.

For example, the `random()` function is volatile, since it will give a different result for each call. The function `round()` is immutable because it will always give the same result for the same argument. The function current time is stable, since it will always give the same result within the statement or transaction, as shown next:

```
car_portal=# SELECT current_time;
     timetz
----------------
 15:54:50.32-08
(1 row)


car_portal=# BEGIN;
BEGIN
car_portal=# SELECT current_time;
     timetz
----------------
 15:54:55.464-08
(1 row)


car_portal=# SELECT 'some time has passed';
       ?column?
----------------------
 some time has passed
(1 row)


car_portal=# SELECT current_time;
     timetz
----------------
 15:54:55.464-08
(1 row)
```

PostgreSQL anonymous functions

PostgreSQL provides the DO statement, which can be used to execute anonymous code blocks. The DO statement reduces the need for creating shell scripts for administration purposes. However, one should note that all PostgreSQL functions are transactional, so if one would like to create indexes on partitioned tables, for example, shell scripting is a better alternative.

In the web_car portal schema, let us assume that we would like to have another user who can perform only select statements. This can be done by executing the following code block:

```
car_portal=# CREATE user select_only;
CREATE ROLE
car_portal=# DO $$DECLARE r record;
BEGIN
    FOR r IN SELECT table_schema, table_name FROM
    information_schema.tables
            WHERE   table_schema = 'car_portal_app'
    LOOP
        EXECUTE 'GRANT SELECT ON ' || quote_ident(r.table_schema) || '.'
|| quote_ident(r.table_name) || ' TO select_only';
    END LOOP;
END$$;
DO
car_portal=# \z account
```

```
                                    Access privileges
    Schema     |   Name   | Type  |            Access privileges
| Column access privileges
----------------+----------+-------+----------------------------------------
-+------------------------
 car_portal_app | account  | table | car_portal_app=arwdDxt/car_portal_
app+|
               |          |       | select_only=r/car_portal_app
|
(1 row)
```

PostgreSQL user-defined data types

PostgreSQL provides two methods for implementing user-defined data types through the following commands:

- **CREATE DOMAIN**: The CREATE DOMAIN command allows developers to create a user-defined data type with constraints. This helps in making the source code more modular.

- **CREATE TYPE**: The CREATE TYPE command is often used to create a composite type, which is useful in procedural languages, and is used as the return data type. Also, one can use the create type to create the ENUM type, which is useful in decreasing the number of joins, specifically for lookup tables.

Often, developers tend not to use the user-defined data types, and use flat tables instead due to a lack of support on the driver side, such as JDBC and ODBC. Nonetheless, in JDBC, the composite data types can be retried as Java objects and parsed manually.

The PostgreSQL CREATE DOMAIN command

Domain is a data type with optional constraints, and as with other database objects it should have a unique name within the schema scope.

The first use case of domains is to use it for common patterns. For example, a text type that does not allow null values and does not contain spaces is a common pattern. In the web car portal, the first_name and the last_name columns in the account table are not null. They should also not contain spaces, and are defined as follows:

```
CREATE TABLE account (
...
..first_name TEXT NOT NULL,
  last_name TEXT NOT NULL,
..CHECK(first_name !~ '\s' AND last_name !~ '\s'),
...
);
```

One can replace the text data type and the constraints by creating a domain and using it for defining the `first_name` and the `last_name` data type, as follows:

```
CREATE DOMAIN text_without_space_and_null AS TEXT NOT NULL CHECK (value
!~ '\s');
```

In order to test the `text_without_space_and_null` domain, let us use it in a table definition, and execute several INSERT statements, as follows:

```
CREATE TABLE test_domain (
  test_att text_without_space_and_null
);
INSERT INTO test_domain values ('hello');
INSERT INTO test_domain values ('hello  with space');
-- This error is raised: ERROR: value for domain text_without_space_and_
null violates check constraint "text_without_space_and_null_check"

INSERT INTO test_domain values (NULL);
-- This error is raised: ERROR:  domain text_without_space_and_null does
not allow null values
```

Another good use case for creating domains is to create distinct identifiers across several tables, since some people tend to use numbers instead of names to retrieve information.

One can do that by creating a sequence and wrapping it with a domain:

```
CREATE SEQUENCE global_id_seq;
CREATE DOMAIN global_id INT DEFAULT NEXTVAL('global_id_seq') NOT NULL;
```

Finally, one can alter the domain using the ALTER DOMAIN command. If a new constraint is added to the domain, it will cause all the attributes using this domain to be validated against the new constraint. One can control this by suppressing the constraint validation on old values and then cleaning up the tables individually. For example, let us assume we would like to have a constraint on the text length of the `text_without_space_and_null` domain; this can be done as follows:

```
ALTER DOMAIN text_without_space_and_null ADD CONSTRAINT text_without_
space_and_null_length_chk check (length(value)<=15);
```

The preceding SQL statement will fail due to data violation if an attribute is using this domain, and the attribute value length is more than 15 characters. So, to force the newly created data to adhere to the domain constraints and to leave the old data without validation, one can still create it as follows:

```
ALTER DOMAIN text_without_space_and_null ADD CONSTRAINT text_without_
space_and_null_length_chk check (length(value)<=15) NOT VALID;
```

After data clean up, one can also validate the constraint for old data by the ALTER DOMAIN ... VALIDATE CONSTRAINT option.

Finally, the \dD+ Psql meta command can be used for describing the domain, as follows:

```
\dD+ text_without_space_and_null
```

The PostgreSQL CREATE TYPE command

Composite data types are very useful in creating functions, especially when the return type is a row of several values. For example, let us assume that we would like to have a function that returns the seller_id, seller_name, number of advertisements, and the total rank for a certain customer account. The first step is to create a type, as follows:

```
CREATE TYPE seller_information AS (seller_id INT, seller_name TEXT,
number_of_advertisements BIGINT, total_rank float);
```

Then we can use the newly created data type as the return type of the function, as follows:

```
CREATE OR REPLACE FUNCTION seller_information (account_id INT ) RETURNS
seller_information AS
$$
  SELECT
    seller_id,
    first_name || last_name as seller_name,
    count(*),
    sum(rank)::float/count(*)
  FROM
    account INNER JOIN
    seller_account ON (account.account_id =
    seller_account.account_id) LEFT JOIN
    advertisement ON (advertisement.seller_account_id =
    seller_account.seller_account_id)LEFT JOIN
```

```
  advertisement_rating ON
    (advertisement.advertisement_id =
  advertisement_rating.advertisement_id)
WHERE
  account.account_id = $1
GROUP BY
  seller_id,
  first_name,
  last_name
$$
LANGUAGE SQL;
```

CREATE TYPE could be also used to define enums; an enum type is a special data type that enables an attribute to be assigned one of the predefined constants. The usage of the enum data types reduces the number of joins needed to create some queries; thus, it makes the SQL code more compact and easier to understand. In the advertisement_rating table, we have a column with the rank name, which is defined as follows:

```
CREATE TABLE advertisement_rating (
  ...
rank INT NOT NULL,
CHECK (rank IN (1,2,3,4,5))
  ...
);
```

In the preceding example, the given code is not semantically clear. For example, some people might consider 1 as the highest rank, while others might consider 5 as the highest rank. To solve this, one could use the lookup table, as follows:

```
CREATE TABLE rank (
  rank_id SERIAL PRIMARY KEY,
  rank_name TEXT NOT NULL
);
INSERT INTO rank VALUES (1, 'poor') , (2, 'fair'), (3, 'good') , (4,
'very good') ,( 5, 'excellent');


CREATE TABLE advertisement_rating (
  ...
rank INT NOT NULL REFERENCES rank(rank_id),
);
```

In this preceding approach, the user can explicitly see the rank table entries. Moreover, the rank table entries can be changed to reflect new business needs, such as to make ranking from 1 to 10. Additionally, in this approach, changing the rank table entries will not lock the "advertisement rating" table, since the ALTER TABLE command will not be needed to change the check constraint CHECK (rank IN (1, 2, 3, 4, 5)). The disadvantage of this approach lies in retrieving the information of a certain table that is linked to several lookup tables, since the tables need to be joined together. In our example, we need to join advertisement_rating and the rank table to get the semantic of rank_id in the advertisement_rating table, as follows:

```
SELECT
  advertisement_rating_id,
  ...,
  rank_id,
  rank_name
FROM
  advertisement_rating INNER JOIN
  rank ON (advertisement_rating.rank_id = rnk.rank_id);
```

Another approach to model the rank is to use the enum data types, as follows:

```
CREATE TYPE rank AS ENUM ('poor', 'fair', 'good', 'very good',
'excellent');
```

The psql \dT meta command is used to describe the enum data type. One could also use the function enum_range, as follows:

```
car_portal=# SELECT enum_range(null::rank);
                enum_range
----------------------------------------
 {poor,fair,good,"very good",excellent}
(1 row)
```

The enum data type order is determined by the order of the values in the enum at the time of its creation. So in our example, poor always comes first, as shown in the following example:

```
CREATE TABLE rank_type_test (
  id SERIAL PRIMARY KEY,
  rank rank
);
```

```
INSERT into rank_type_test(rank) VALUES ('poor') , ('fair'), ('very
good') ,( 'excellent'), ('good'), ('poor') ;


SELECT * FROM rank_type_test ORDER BY rank ASC;
 id |    rank
----+-----------
 17 | poor
 22 | poor
 18 | fair
 21 | good
 19 | very good
 20 | excellent
(6 rows)
```

The enum PostgreSQL data types are type safe, and the different enum data types cannot be compared with each other. Moreover, the enum data types can be altered, and new values can be added. Unfortunately, it is not possible to take out the old values.

Triggers and rule systems

PostgreSQL provides triggers and rules systems to automatically perform a certain function when an event like INSERT, UPDATE, or DELETE is performed.

> Triggers and rules cannot be defined on the SELECT statements except for the _RETURN, which is used in the internal implementation of PostgreSQL views.

From the functionality point of view, the trigger system is more generic; it can be used to implement complex actions more easily than rules. However, both trigger and rule systems can be used to implement the same functionality in several cases.

From the performance point of view, rules tend to be faster than triggers; but triggers tend to be simpler and more compatible with other RDBMs, since the rule system is a PostgreSQL extension.

The PostgreSQL rule system

Creating a rule will either rewire the default rule, or create a new rule for a specific action on a specific table or view. In other words, a rule on an insert action can change the insert action behavior, or can create a new action for the insert. When using the rule system, one needs to note that it is based on the C macro system. This means one can get strange results when it is used with volatile functions such as random(), and sequence functions such as nextval(). The following example shows how tricky the rule system can be. Let us assume that we would like to audit the table for car. For this reason, a new table called car_log will be created to keep a track of all the actions on the car table, such as UPDATE, DELETE, and INSERT. One can achieve this by using the trigger system, as follows:

```
CREATE TABLE car_log (LIKE car);


ALTER TABLE car_log
ADD COLUMN car_log_action varchar (1) NOT NULL,
ADD COLUMN car_log_time TIMESTAMP WITH TIME ZONE NOT NULL;
CREATE RULE car_log AS
    ON INSERT TO car
    DO ALSO
        INSERT INTO car_log (car_id, number_of_owners,
        regestration_number, number_of_doors, car_log_action,
        car_log_time)
        VALUES (new.car_id, new.number_of_owners,
        new.regestration_number, new.number_of_doors, 'I', now());
```

The preceding code creates the car_log table, which has a structure similar to the car table. The car_log table also has two additional attributes to log the actions: such as insert (indicated in the example as I), and the action time. The preceding code also creates a rule on the car table to cascade the insert on the car table to the car_log table. To test the code, let us insert a record, and examine the contents of the car_log table, as follows:

```
car_portal=# INSERT INTO car (car_id, number_of_owners, regestration_
number, number_of_doors) VALUES (1, 2, '2015xyz', 3);
INSERT 0 1
car_portal=# SELECT * FROM car;
-[ RECORD 1 ]-------+--------
car_id              | 1
number_of_owners    | 2
```

```
regestration_number | 2015xyz

number_of_doors     | 3


car_portal=# SELECT * FROM car_log;
-[ RECORD 1 ]-------+---------------------------
car_id              | 1
number_of_owners    | 2
regestration_number | 2015xyz
number_of_doors     | 3
car_log_action      | I
car_log_time        | 2015-02-04 10:48:56.779-08
```

As the preceding example shows, everything goes as expected. One record is inserted in the `car_log` table, and that record is identical to the one inserted in the `car` table. However, as said earlier, the rules system is built on macros, which cause some issues, as shown in the following example:

```
car_portal=# TRUNCATE car cascade;

NOTICE:  truncate cascades to table "advertisement"

...

TRUNCATE TABLE

car_portal=# ALTER sequence car_car_id_seq RESTART;

ALTER SEQUENCE

car_portal=# INSERT INTO car (car_id, number_of_owners, regestration_
number, number_of_doors) VALUES (DEFAULT, 2, '2015xyz', 3);

INSERT 0 1

car_portal=# SELECT * FROM ONLY car;
-[ RECORD 1 ]-------+--------
car_id              | 1
number_of_owners    | 2
regestration_number | 2015xyz
number_of_doors     | 3


car_portal=# SELECT * FROM car_log;
-[ RECORD 1 ]-------+---------------------------
car_id              | 2
number_of_owners    | 2
```

```
regestration_number | 2015xyz

number_of_doors     | 3

car_log_action      | I

car_log_time        | 2015-02-04 10:56:48.553-08
```

In the preceding example, the car table is truncated, and car_car_id_seq is restarted to compare the results easily. Note that the records in the car table and the car_log tables are not identical. The car_id in the car table is 1 while in the car_log table it is 2. One can notice that the DEFAULT keyword is used to indicate the car_id which is nextval('car_car_id_seq'::regclass), shown as follows:

```
car_portal=# \d car
                        Table "car_portal_app.car"
       Column          |  Type   |                  Modifiers
-----------------------+---------+----------------------------------------
-------------
 car_id                | integer | not null default nextval('car_car_id_
seq'::regclass)
...
```

The car_log rule caused the sequence to be executed another time, because it did not substitute NEW.car_id with 1, but substituted it with nextval('car_car_id_seq'::regclass) instead.

Writing rules is often quicker than writing triggers, and the code is crisper and shorter. A common case of using rules is to ignore the CRUD operation on the table in order to protect the table against data changes. This scenario can be used to protect lookup tables or to ignore the CRUD operations, for example. In the car web portal database, let us assume that we would like to disable the logging of the user's search. A very simple technique to do so without changing the client codes is as follows:

```
CREATE RULE account_search_log_insert AS
    ON INSERT TO account_search_history
    DO INSTEAD NOTHING;
```

When creating a rule, one can have a conditional rule, that is, one can rewrite the action if a certain condition is met, as shown in the following rule synopsis. However, one cannot have conditional rules for INSERT, UPDATE, and DELETE on views without having unconditional rules. To solve this problem, one can create an unconditional dummy rule. Rules on views are one way of implementing updatable views.

```
CREATE [ OR REPLACE ] RULE name AS ON event
    TO table_name [ WHERE condition ]
    DO [ ALSO | INSTEAD ] { NOTHING | command | ( command ; command ... )
}
```

where event can be one of:

```
SELECT | INSERT | UPDATE | DELETE
```

Finally, when defining rules, one should take care of infinite recursion, similar to triggers. Wrong rule definitions can cause the error: ERROR: infinite recursion detected in rules for relation ....

The PostgreSQL trigger system

PostgreSQL triggers a function when a certain event occurs on a table, view, or foreign table. Triggers are executed when a user tries to modify the data through any of the **data manipulation language (DML)** events, including INSERT, UPDATE, DELETE, or TRUNCATE. The trigger synopsis is as follows:

```
CREATE [ CONSTRAINT ] TRIGGER name { BEFORE | AFTER | INSTEAD OF } {
event [ OR ... ] }
    ON table_name
    [ FROM referenced_table_name ]
    [ NOT DEFERRABLE | [ DEFERRABLE ] { INITIALLY IMMEDIATE |
    INITIALLY DEFERRED } ]
    [ FOR [ EACH ] { ROW | STATEMENT } ]
    [ WHEN ( condition ) ]
    EXECUTE PROCEDURE function_name ( arguments )
```

where event can be one of:

```
INSERT
UPDATE [ OF column_name [, ... ] ]
DELETE
TRUNCATE
```

The trigger time context is one of the following:

- BEFORE: This is applied on tables only, and is fired before the constraints are checked and the operation is performed. It is useful for checking data constraints on several tables. It is not possible to model using the referential integrity constraints.

- AFTER: This too is applied on tables only, and is fired after the operation is performed. It is useful for cascading the changes to other tables. An example use case is data auditing.

- INSTEAD OF: This is applied on views, and is used to make views updatable.

When the trigger is marked for each row, then the trigger function will be executed for each row that has been affected by the CRUD operation. A statement trigger is only executed once per operation. When the WHEN condition is supplied, then only the rows that fulfill the condition will be handled by the trigger. Finally, triggers can be marked as CONSTRAINT to control when they can be executed; the trigger can be executed after the end of the statement or at the end of the transaction. The constraint trigger must be AFTER and FOR EACH ROW, and the firing time constraint triggers controlled by the following options:

- DEFERRABLE: This marks the trigger as deferrable, which will cause the trigger firing to be postponed till the end of the transaction.

- INITIALLY DEFERRED: This specifies the time when the trigger is to be executed. This means that the trigger will be executed at the end of the transaction.

- NOT DEFERRABLE: This is the default behavior of the trigger, which will cause the trigger to be fired after each statement in the transaction.

- INITIALLY IMMEDIATE: This specifies the time when the trigger is to be executed. This means that the trigger will be executed after each statement.

Trigger names define the execution order of the triggers, which have the same firing time context alphabetically.

The firing time options: DEFERRABLE, INITIALLY DEFERRED, NOT DEFERRABLE, and INITIALLY IMMEDIATE, can also be applied to constraint. These options are useful when PostgreSQL interacts with external systems such as memcached. For example, let us assume that we have a trigger on a table that is cached; whenever the table is updated, the cache is also updated. Since the caching system is not transactional, we can postpone the update until the end of the transaction to guarantee data consistency.

To explain the trigger system, let us redo the `car_log` table example using triggers. First of all, notice that the trigger type is AFTER trigger, since `data` should first be checked against the `car` table constraint before inserting it in the new table. To create a trigger, one needs to create a function, as follows:

```
CREATE OR REPLACE FUNCTION car_log_trg () RETURNS TRIGGER AS
$$
BEGIN
  IF TG_OP = 'INSERT' THEN
    INSERT INTO car_log SELECT NEW.*, 'I', NOW();
  ELSIF TG_OP = 'UPDATE' THEN
    INSERT INTO car_log SELECT NEW.*, 'U', NOW();
  ELSIF TG_OP = 'DELETE' THEN
    INSERT INTO car_log SELECT OLD.*, 'D', NOW();
  END IF;
  RETURN NULL; --ignored since this is after trigger
END;
$$
LANGUAGE plpgsql;
```

To create the trigger, one needs to execute the following statement:

```
CREATE TRIGGER car_log AFTER INSERT OR UPDATE OR DELETE ON car FOR EACH
ROW EXECUTE PROCEDURE car_log_trg ();
```

The TRIGGER function should fulfill the following requirements:

- **Return type**: The TRIGGER function should return the trigger pseudo type.
- **Return value**: The TRIGGER function must return a value. The value is often NULL for AFTER ... EACH ROW and for statement-level triggers or record/row with the exact structure of the table that fired the trigger.
- **No arguments**: The trigger function must be declared without an argument, even if one needs to pass an argument to it. The passing of an argument is achieved via the TG_ARG variable.

When the trigger function is created, several variables, such as TG_ARG and NEW, are created automatically. Other variables that are created are listed in the following table:

Trigger variable	Data type	Description
NEW	RECORD	It holds the row that is inserted or updated. In the case of statement level trigger, it is NULL.
OLD	RECORD	It holds the old row that is updated or deleted. In the case of statement level trigger, it is NULL.
TG_NAME	NAME	The trigger name.
TG_OP	NAME	The trigger operation, which can have one of the following values: INSERT UPDATE DELETE TRUNCATE
TG_WHEN	NAME	The time when the trigger is fired. It can have one of the following values: AFTER BEFORE
TG_RELID	OID	The relation OID. One can get the relation name by casting it to text using regclass::text.
TG_TABLE_NAME	NAME	The trigger table name.
TG_TABLE_SCHEMA	NAME	The trigger table schema name.
TG_NARG	INTEGER	Number of arguments passed to the trigger.
TG_ARG[]	TEXT array	The trigger argument. The indexing starts from zero and a wrong index returns NULL.

For a row-level trigger, which is fired BEFORE the actual operation, returning null values will cancel the operation. This means that the next trigger will not be fired, and the affected row will not be deleted, updated, or inserted. For the trigger that is fired AFTER the operation or a statement-level trigger, the return value will be ignored; however, the operation will be aborted if the trigger function raises an exception or an error due to the relational database's transactional behavior.

In the preceding auditing example, if one changes the car table definition such as adding or dropping a column, the trigger function on the car table will fail, leading to the ignoring of the newly inserted or updated row. One could solve this by using exception trapping in the trigger definition.

Triggers with arguments

In the following example, another general auditing technique will be presented which can be applied to several tables, while some table columns can be excluded from auditing.

The new editing techniques use the hstore extension. hstore defines a hash map data type, and provides a set of functions and operators to handle this data type. In the new auditing technique, the table rows will be stored as a hash map. The first step is to create the hstore extension and a table where the audited data will be stored, as follows:

```
SET search_path to car_portal_app;
CREATE extension hstore;
CREATE TABLE car_portal_app.log
(
  schema_name text NOT NULL,
  table_name text NOT NULL,
  old_row hstore,
  new_row hstore,
  action TEXT check (action IN ('I','U','D')) NOT NULL,
  created_by text NOT NULL,
  created_on timestamp without time zone NOT NULL
);
```

The second step is to define the trigger function, as follows:

```
CREATE OR REPLACE FUNCTION car_portal_app.log_audit() RETURNS trigger  AS
$$
DECLARE
  log_row log;
  excluded_columns text[] = NULL;
```

```
BEGIN
  log_row = ROW (
    TG_TABLE_SCHEMA::text,
    TG_TABLE_NAME::text,
    NULL,
    NULL,
    NULL,
    current_user::TEXT,
    current_timestamp
    );


  IF TG_ARGV[0] IS NOT NULL THEN
    excluded_columns = TG_ARGV[0]::text[];
  END IF;


  IF (TG_OP = 'INSERT') THEN
    log_row.new_row = hstore(NEW.*) - excluded_columns;
    log_row.action ='I';
  ELSIF (TG_OP = 'UPDATE' AND (hstore(OLD.*) -
  excluded_columns!= hstore(NEW.*)-excluded_columns))
  THEN
      log_row.old_row = hstor(OLD.*) - excluded_columns;
    log_row.new_row = hstore(NEW.* )- excluded_columns;
    log_row.action ='U';
  ELSIF (TG_OP = 'DELETE') THEN
    log_row.old_row = hstore (OLD.*) - excluded_columns;
    log_row.action ='D';
  ELSE
    RETURN NULL; -- update on excluded columns
  END IF;


  INSERT INTO log SELECT log_row.*;


  RETURN NULL;
END;
$$ LANGUAGE plpgsql;
```

The preceding function defines a variable `log_row` of type `log`, and populates this variable with the trigger table name, trigger table schema, current user, and the current timestamp using the row construct. Moreover, the preceding trigger function parses `TG_ARGV` to determine if some columns need to be excluded from auditing. Note that the excluded columns are passed as a text array. Finally, the trigger function populates `log.action`, `log.old_row`, and `log.new_row` based on the `TG_OP` variable.

To apply the preceding trigger on the car table, assuming that the `number_of_doors` attribute should be excluded from tracking, one can create the trigger as follows:

```
CREATE TRIGGER car_log_trg  AFTER INSERT OR UPDATE OR DELETE ON car_
portal_app.car FOR EACH ROW EXECUTE PROCEDURE log_audit('{number_of_
doors}');
```

The array lateral `{number_of_doors}` is passed to the function `log_audit` and accessed via the `TG_ARG` variable. Finally, the expression `hstore(NEW.*) - excluded_columns` is used to convert the `NEW` variable to the `hstore` type, and then delete the keys specified in the `excluded_columns` array from the converted `hstore`. The following example shows the trigger behavior for the insert statement:

```
car_portal=# INSERT INTO car_portal_app.car (car_id, number_of_owners,
registration_number, number_of_doors) VALUES (DEFAULT, 1, '2015abcde',
5);
INSERT 0 1


car_portal=# TABLE car_portal_app.log;
-[ RECORD 1 ]-------------------------------------------------------
----------------
schema_name | car_portal_app
table_name  | car
old_row     |
new_row     | "car_id"=>"10", "number_of_owners"=>"1", "registration_
number"=>"2015abcde"
action      | I
created_by  | postgres
created_on  | 2015-02-14 11:56:47.483
```

Using triggers to make views updatable

For views that are not automatically updatable, the trigger system can be used to make them updatable. The view `seller_account_information`, which shows the information about the seller account, is not automatically updatable, as shown next:

```
CREATE OR REPLACE VIEW seller_account_info AS
SELECT
    account.account_id,
    first_name,
    last_name,
    email,
    password,
    seller_account_id,
    total_rank,
    number_of_advertisement,
    street_name,
    street_number,
    zip_code ,
    city
FROM
    account INNER JOIN
    seller_account ON (account.account_id =
    seller_account.account_id);


car_portal=# SELECT is_insertable_into FROM information_schema.tables
WHERE table_name = 'seller_account_info';
-[ RECORD 1 ]------+---
is_insertable_into | NO
```

The following trigger function assumes that `account_id` and `seller_account_id` are always generated using the default values, which are the sequences generated automatically when creating a serial data type. This is often a good approach and relieves the developer from checking the table for a unique constraint before inserting new rows, and in keeps the primary key values without big gaps. Furthermore, the trigger function assumes that the primary keys cannot be changed for the same reason. Changing the primary keys might also cause problems when the default foreign keys options, cascade delete and cascade update, are not used. Finally, note that the trigger functions return NEW for the INSERT and UPDATE operations, OLD for the DELETE operation, and NULL in the case of an exception.

Returning the proper value is important to detect the number of rows that are affected by the operation. It is also very important to return the proper value when using the RETURNING keyword, as shown in the following TRIGGER function code:

```
CREATE OR REPLACE FUNCTION seller_account_info_update () RETURNS TRIGGER
AS
$$
DECLARE
  acc_id INT;
  seller_acc_id INT;
BEGIN
  IF (TG_OP = 'INSERT') THEN
    WITH inserted_account AS (
      INSERT INTO car_portal_app.account (account_id,
      first_name, last_name, password, email)
      VALUES (DEFAULT, NEW.first_name, NEW.last_name,
      NEW.password, NEW.email) RETURNING account_id
      ), inserted_seller_account AS (INSERT INTO
      car_portal_app.seller_account(seller_account_id,
      account_id, total_rank, number_of_advertisement,
      street_name, street_number, zip_code, city)
      SELECT
      nextval('car_portal_app.
      seller_account_seller_account_id_seq'::regclass),
      account_id, NEW.total_rank,
      NEW.number_of_advertisement, NEW.street_name,
      NEW.street_number, NEW.zip_code, NEW.city FROM
      inserted_account RETURNING account_id,
      seller_account_id
      ) SELECT account_id, seller_account_id INTO
      acc_id, seller_acc_id FROM
      inserted_seller_account;
      NEW.account_id = acc_id;
      NEW.seller_account_id = seller_acc_id;
      RETURN NEW;
    ELSIF (TG_OP = 'UPDATE' AND OLD.account_id =
    NEW.account_id AND OLD.seller_account_id =
    NEW.seller_account_id) THEN
      UPDATE car_portal_app.account
      SET first_name = new.first_name, last_name =
      new.last_name, password= new.password, email =
      new.email
```

```
    WHERE account_id = new.account_id;

    UPDATE car_portal_app.seller_account

    SET total_rank = NEW.total_rank,
    number_of_advertisement=
    NEW.number_of_advertisement, street_name=
    NEW.street_name, street_number =
    NEW.street_number, zip_code = NEW.zip_code, city =
    NEW.city

    WHERE seller_account_id = NEW.seller_account_id;

    RETURN NEW;


  ELSIF (TG_OP = 'DELETE') THEN

    DELETE FROM car_portal_app.seller_account WHERE
    seller_account_id = OLD.seller_account_id;

    DELETE FROM car_portal_app.account WHERE
    account_id = OLD.account_id;

    RETURN OLD;

  ELSE

    RAISE EXCEPTION 'An error occurred for %
    operation', TG_OP;

    RETURN NULL;

  END IF;

END;

$$

LANGUAGE plpgsql;
```

To run and test the trigger function, let us execute the following SQL statements:

```
CREATE  TRIGGER seller_account_info_trg INSTEAD OF INSERT OR UPDATE
OR DELETE ON car_portal_app.seller_account_info FOR EACH ROW  EXECUTE
PROCEDURE seller_account_info_update ();


car_portal=# INSERT INTO car_portal_app.seller_account_info (first_name,
last_name, password, email, total_rank, number_of_advertisement, street_
name, street_number, zip_code, city) VALUES

('test_first_name', 'test_last_name', 'test_password', 'test_email@test.
com', NULL, 0, 'test_street_name', 'test_street_number', 'test_zip_code',
'test_city') RETURNING account_id, seller_account_id;

 account_id | seller_account_id

------------+-------------------
         14 |                 8
```

```
(1 row)


INSERT 0 1

car_portal=# UPDATE car_portal_app.seller_account_info set email = 'teat@
test.com' RETURNING seller_account_id;
 seller_account_id
-------------------
                 8
(1 row)


UPDATE 1

car_portal=# DELETE FROM car_portal_app.seller_account_info;
DELETE 1
```

Summary

In this chapter, indexes, views, functions, user-defined data types, and the rule and trigger systems have been discussed.

The view is a named query or a wrapper around a SELECT statement. It can be used as a data access layer, provides an abstraction level, and controls data privileges and permissions.

A view in PostgreSQL can be categorized as temporary, materialized, updatable, and recursive. Simple views in PostgreSQL are automatically updatable. To make the complex views updatable, one can use the rule and trigger systems.

Indexes are physical database objects defined on a table column, a set of columns, and expressions. Indexes are often used to optimize performance or to validate data.

There are several techniques for building indexes, including B-tree, hash, GIN, GiST, and BRIN. B-tree is the default indexing method. Hash indexes are not recommended, especially in the case of streaming replication. GIN and GiST are useful for indexing complex data types and for full-text searches.

There are several types of indexes; each type can be used for a different use case. For example, partial index indexes only a subset of the data that meets a certain predicate. The unique index is often used to validate data such as the uniqueness of the primary keys. Finally, a multicolumn index can be used for specific data retrieval scenarios.

The information about indexes can be retrieved from the pg_catalog statistics, and can be used for maintenance purposes. When an index is bloated, one can create a concurrent index instead of reindexing it. Note that the creation of concurrent indexes will not lock the database table.

PostgreSQL functions provide distinct services, and have usages similar to views. Functions can be written in C, SQL, and PL/pgsql without extra extensions. One important usage of the functions is to assist in maintaining the database. This can be done easily without using external scripting, such as Bash, by utilizing anonymous functions.

Specifying the function category as stable, volatile, or immutable is very important because it helps the optimizer to generate the optimal execution plan. Unfortunately, the interdependency between functions is not recorded in the database catalogue. This means one should take great care when writing complex logic using functions.

User-defined data type can be created using the CREATE DOMAIN, and CREATE TYPE commands. Some user-defined data types such as ENUM can greatly reduce the number of joins, thus leading to more understandable and efficient SQL code.

PostgreSQL triggers and rules are used to execute an action when a certain event occurs. They can be used alternately in several scenarios. One needs to be careful when using rules with volatile functions, because they have some side effects.

5
SQL Language

Structured Query Language (**SQL**) is used to set up the structure of the database, to manipulate the data in the database and to query the database. This chapter will be dedicated to the **Data Manipulation Language** (**DML**).

After reading this chapter, you will understand the concept of SQL and the logic of SQL statements. You will be able to write your own SQL queries and manipulate the data using this language.

The complete reference of SQL can be found in the official PostgreSQL documentation at `http://www.postgresql.org/docs/current/static/sql.html`.

So, the topics we are going to cover in this chapter are as follows:

- SQL fundamentals
- Lexical structure
- Select
- Update
- Delete

Code examples in this chapter are based on the car portal database described in the previous chapters. The scripts to create the database and fill it with data can be found in the attached media in the `Chapter 6` folder. They are called `schema.sql` and `data.sql`.

All the code examples of this chapter can be found in the file `examples.sql`.

Refer to *Chapter 2*, *PostgreSQL in Action* for details on how to use the PSQL console.

SQL fundamentals

SQL is used to manipulate the data in the database and to query the database. Also, SQL is used to define the structure of the data. You already know that from the previous chapters. In general, SQL consists of three parts:

- **Data Definition Language (DDL)**
- **Data Manipulation Language (DML)**
- **Data Control Language (DCL)**

The first part is used to create and manage the structure of the data, the second part is used to manage the data itself, and the third part—to control access to the data. Usually, the data structure is defined only once and then it is rarely changed. But the data is constantly inserted into the database, changed or retrieved. For that reason, DML is used much more often than DDL.

SQL is not an imperative programming language, which makes it different from many other languages. To be more specific, one cannot define a detailed algorithm of how the data should be processed, and this might make an impression of lack of control of the data. In imperative languages, the developer usually specifies it in very detailed level: where to take the data from and how to do it, how to iterate through the array of records, and when and how to process them. If it is necessary to process the data from multiple sources, the developer should implement the relationship between them in the application layer rather than in the database.

SQL, in contrast, is a declarative language. In other words: to get the same result in other languages, the developer writes a whole story. In SQL, the developer writes only one major sentence and leaves details for the database. In SQL, one just defines the format in which it is needed to get the data from the database, specifies the tables where the data is stored and states the rules for processing the data. The exact order of these operations and the actual algorithm for processing them are chosen by the database, and the developer should not care about it.

But this black-box behavior should not be treated as something bad. First, the box is not completely black: there are ways to know how the data is processed by the database engine, and there are ways to control it. And second, the logic in the SQL statement is very deterministic. Even if it is not clear how the database is processing the query on a low level, the logic of the process and the result of the query is entirely determined by the SQL statement.

This determines the size of a statement (smallest standalone element of execution). In Java, for example, every operation such as assignment a value to a variable is logically processed as a separate item of an algorithm. In contrast, the logic of SQL implies that the whole algorithm is executed all at once, as one statement. There is no way to get the state of the data at any intermediate step of the execution of the query. But this does not limit the complexity of the logic of the query. It is possible to implement any sophisticated algorithm in a single SQL statement. And usually it takes less time to implement complex logic in SQL than in any lower-level language. Developers operate with logical relational data structures and do not need to implement their own algorithms of data processing on a physical level. This is what makes SQL so powerful.

Another good thing about SQL is that there is a standard for the language, and every modern relation database supports SQL. Although different databases could support different features and implement their own dialect of SQL, the basics of the language are the same. PostgreSQL also has its own SQL dialect, and we will point out some differences to the other RDBMS. By the way, at the beginning of its history, postgres did not support SQL. It was added in 1994 and after a while the database was renamed PostgreSQL to indicate that fact.

SQL lexical structure

The minimal SQL instruction that can be executed by the database engine is called a statement. Also it can be called a command or query. For example, each of the following is a statement:

```
SELECT car_id, number_of_doors FROM car_portal_app.car;
DELETE FROM car_portal_app.a;
SELECT now();
```

SQL commands are terminated by a semicolon (;). End of input also terminates the command, but that depends on the tools used.

SQL statements can contain:

- Keywords determine what exactly it is required from the database to be done
- Identifiers refer to the objects in the database—tables, their fields, functions, and so on
- Constants are parts of expressions whose values are specified directly in the code

- Operators determine how the data is processed in the expressions
- Special characters, such as parenthesis, brackets, commas, and so on, which have other meanings than simply being an operator
- Whitespaces separate words from each other
- Comments are used to describe a particular line of code

Keywords are words such as SELECT or UPDATE. They have special meaning in SQL. They are names of statements or parts of statements. The full list of keywords can be found in the documentation at http://www.postgresql.org/docs/current/static/sql-keywords-appendix.html.

Identifiers are the names of the database objects. Objects such as tables or views can be referred by the name of the schema where it belongs to (see *Chapter 3, PostgreSQL Basic Building Blocks*) followed by the dot symbol (.) and the name of the object. That is called a qualified object name. If the name of the schema is included in the search_path setting or if the object belongs to the current user's schema, then it is not required to use the schema name when referring to the object. In that case, it is called an unqualified object name. Names of the fields of tables are used in the same way: table name, then dot (.) and field name. In some cases, it is not necessary to specify table the name, for example, when only one table is queried, and in other cases, it is possible to use a table alias.

SQL is not case sensitive. Both keywords and identifiers can contain any letters (a-z), digits (0-9), underscores (_) or dollar signs ($). But they cannot start with a digit or dollar sign. That makes them similar to each other and without knowing the language, sometimes it is difficult to say if some word is a keyword or an identifier. Usually, keywords are typed in upper case.

In identifiers, it is still possible to use symbols other than those mentioned earlier, by double-quoting them. Also it is possible to create objects with the same names as keywords but is not recommended.

Constants in SQL are also called literals. PostgreSQL supports three types of implicitly typed constants: numbers, strings and bit strings. To use constant values of any other data type, implicit or explicit conversion should be performed.

Numeric constants contain digits and optionally decimal point, and exponent sign. These are examples of selecting valid numeric constants:

```
SELECT 1, 1.2, 0.3, .5, 1e15, 12.65e-6;
```

String constants should be quoted. There are two kinds of syntax of string constants in PostgreSQL: single quoted constants like in SQL standard, and PostgreSQL-specific dollar-quoted constants. Putting a letter E before the string constant makes it possible to use C-style backslash escaped characters such as \n for a new line, or \t for tabulation. A single quote character (') inside a literal should be doubled (") or used as an escape string (\). Putting a letter U with an ampersand before the string without any spaces in between allows you tu specify unicode characters by their code after a backslash.

The examples would be:

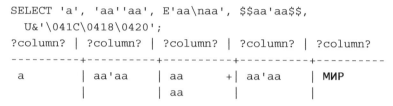

The first is simple — a letter a. The second will have a single quote in the middle. The third has C-style new line sequence: \n. The next string is dollar-quoted. And the last has unicode characters (the word means "peace" in Russian).

Dollar-quoted string constants always have the same value as it was written. No escape sequences are recognized and any kind of quotes are part of the string except for dollar-quote when it is written in the same way as in the beginning. Dollar-quoted strings can have their names set between the dollar signs, which makes it possible to use one dollar-quoted string inside another, like this:

```
SELECT $str1$SELECT $$dollar-quoted string$$;$str1$;
  ?column?
  ---------------------------------
  SELECT $$dollar-quoted string$$;
```

Here the sequences $str1$ are the quotes, and another double dollar inside the literal does not terminate the string. That's why it is very common to use dollar-quoted string to define a function body that is usually given to the PostgreSQL server as a string literal.

Bit strings are preceded by a letter B and can contain only digits 0 or 1. Alternatively, they can be preceded by a letter X and contain any digits, along with letters A-F. In that case, they are hexadecimal strings. Most of the time bit strings are converted to a numeric data type:

```
SELECT B'01010101'::int, X'AB21'::int;
 int4 | int4
------+-------
   85 | 43809
```

Operators are basic elements of data processing. They are used in SQL expressions. They take one or two arguments and return a value. The examples of operators can be addition (+), subtraction (-), and so on. PostgreSQL supports a wide range of operators for all data types. In the statements, operators look like sequences of characters from the list: + - * / < > = ~ ! @ # % ^ & | ` ?.

When several operators are used in the same expression, they are executed in a specific order. Some operators, such as multiplication (*) or division (/), have higher precedence among others, and some other operators such as logical or comparison operators have lower precedence. The operators with the same precedence are executed from left to right. The full list of operators and their precedence can be found in the documentation at http://www.postgresql.org/docs/current/static/sql-syntax-lexical.html#SQL-SYNTAX-OPERATORS.

Special characters include:

- Parenthesis (()): These are used to control the precedence of operations or to group expressions. Also they can have special meaning in the syntax of particular SQL command. And they are used as a part of a function name.

- Brackets ([]): These are used to select elements from an array.

- Colons (:): These are used to access parts of arrays.

- Double colons (::): These are used for type casing.

- Commas (,): These are used to separate elements of a list.

- Periods (.): These are used to separate schema, table and column names from each other.

- Semicolon (;): This is used to terminate a statement.

- Asterisk (*): This is used to refer to all the fields of a table or all the elements of composite value.

Whitespaces separate words from each other. In SQL, any number of spaces, new lines, or tabulations are considered as a single whitespace.

Comments can be used in any part of SQL code. The server ignores comments treating them as whitespace. Comments are quoted in pairs of /* and */. Also, the whole line of code can be commented by using double dash (--). In this case, comment starts from double dash and ends at the end of the line.

Simply speaking, DML has only four types of statements:

- INSERT is used to put new data into the database
- UPDATE is used to change the data
- DELETE is used to delete the data
- SELECT is used to retrieve the data

The structure of every statement is strict and human readable, though the syntax of each statement is different. A complete list of detailed syntax diagrams can be found in the PostgreSQL documentation at http://www.postgresql.org/docs/current/static/sql-commands.html. In this chapter, the main elements of each statement will be described.

SELECT will be the first because it is the most used command and because very often it is used as an element of other commands. SQL allows that: it is possible to nest commands, using a result of one command as an input for another command. That nested queries are called subqueries.

Querying the data with the SELECT statement

SELECT statements or SELECT queries or just queries are used to retrieve data from the database. SELECT queries can have different sources: tables, views, functions or the VALUES command. All of them are relations or can be treated as relations or return relations, which functions can do. The output of SELECT is also a relation which in general can have multiple columns and contain many rows. Since the result and the source of the query have the same nature in SQL, it is possible to use one SELECT query as a source for another statement. But in this case, both queries are considered as parts of one bigger query. The source of the data, output format, filters, grouping, ordering and required transformations of the data are specified in the code of the query.

In general, SELECT queries do not change the data in the database and could be considered as read-only, but there is an exception. If a volatile function is used in the query, then the data can be changed by the function.

The structure of the SELECT query

Let's start with a simple example. We will use the sample database of the car web portal, which was described in previous chapters. The sample database is used by the web portal application.

To connect to the database, the following command is used:

```
> psql -h localhost car_portal
```

There is a table called `car` that contains information about the cars registered in the system. Suppose it is necessary to query the database to get the information about cars that have 3 doors. They should be sorted by their ID. The output should be limited to 5 records due to pagination in the user interface. The query will look like this:

```
SELECT car_id, registration_number, manufacture_year
  FROM car_portal_app.car
  WHERE number_of_doors=3
  ORDER BY car_id
  LIMIT 5;
```

And the result:

```
car_id | registration_number | manufacture_year
-------+---------------------+------------------
     2 | VSVW4565            |             2014
     5 | BXGK6290            |             2009
     6 | ORIU9886            |             2007
     7 | TGVF4726            |             2009
     8 | JISW6779            |             2013
(5 rows)
```

The syntax and the logic of the query are the following. The query starts from the keyword SELECT which determines the type of statement. Therefore, this keyword is always required. The keyword is followed by the comma-separated list of the fields to be retrieved from the database. Instead of the list, it is possible to use an asterisk (*) which would mean that all the fields from the table are selected.

The name of the table is specified after the FROM keyword. It is possible to get the data from several tables at the same time. The filter criteria - predicate - is after the WHERE keyword. The sorting rule is at the end after ORDER BY. And the keyword LIMIT makes the database return not more than 5 rows even if the number of records in the table is larger.

These parts of the query — the keywords and the following expressions are called clauses, such as the FROM clause, the WHERE clause, and so on.

All of these clauses have their own purpose and logic. They must follow each other in the specific order. And none of them is mandatory. The simplified syntax diagram for the SELECT statement is as follows:

```
SELECT [DISTINCT | ALL]
  <expression>[[AS] <output_name>][, …]
[FROM <table>[, <table>… | <JOIN clause>…]
[WHERE <condition>]
[GROUP BY <expression>|<output_name>|<output_number>
  [,…]]
[HAVING <condition>]
[ORDER BY  <expression>|<output_name>|<output_number>
  [ASC | DESC] [NULLS FIRST | LAST] [,…]]
[OFFSET <expression>]
[LIMIT <expression>];
```

Some elements were not included here such as the WINDOW clause, the WITH clause or FOR UPDATE. A complete syntax diagram can be found in the documentation at http://www.postgresql.org/docs/current/static/sql-select.html.

Some of the omitted elements will be described in the next chapters.

There is no part of the SELECT statement that is always mandatory. For example, the query might be simpler if no ordering or filtering is needed:

```
SELECT * FROM car_portal_app.car;
```

Even the FROM clause is not mandatory. When one needs to evaluate an expression that does not take any data from the database, the query takes this form:

```
SELECT 1;
 ?column?
----------
        1
```

That can be considered as Hello world in SQL. Note that the FROM clause is optional in PostgreSQL but in other RDBMS such as Oracle the FROM keyword may be required.

Logically, the sequence of the operations performed by the SELECT query is as follows:

- Take all the records from all the source tables. If there are subqueries in the FROM clause, they are evaluated first.

- Build all possible combinations of those records and discard the combinations that do not follow the JOIN conditions or set some fields to NULL in case of outer joins.

- Filter out the combinations that do not match the condition of the WHERE clause.

- Build groups based on the values of the expressions of the GROUP BY list.

- Filter the groups that match the HAVING conditions.

- Evaluate expressions of the Select-list.

- Eliminate duplicated rows if DISTINCT is specified.

- Apply the set operations UNION, EXCEPT, or INTERSECT.

- Sort rows according to the ORDER BY clause.

- Discard records according to OFFSET and LIMIT.

In fact PostgreSQL optimizes that algorithm by performing the steps in a different order or even simultaneously. For example, if LIMIT 1 is specified, then it does not make sense to retrieve all the rows from the source tables, but only one that matches the WHERE condition.

Select-list

After the SELECT keyword, one should specify the list of fields or expressions to get from the database. This list is called Select-list. It defines the structure of the query result: the number, names, and type of the selected values.

Every expression in Select-list has a name in the output of the query. The names, when not provided by the user, are assigned automatically by the database and in most cases the name reflects the source of the data: a name of a column when a field from a table is selected, or a name of a function when one is used. In other cases, the name will look like ?column?. It is possible and in many cases, it totally makes sense to provide a different name to a selected expression. This is done using the AS keyword, like this:

```
SELECT car_id AS identifier_of_the_car ...
```

In the result, the column `car_id` from the table `car` will be named `identifier_of_the_car`. The keyword `AS` is optional. The output column name follows the rules for any SQL identifier. It is possible to use the same name for several columns in a single `SELECT` query. Double quoted names could be used, for example, when some report is generated by the `SELECT` query without any subsequent processing. In that case, it may make sense to use more human readable column names:

```
SELECT car_id "Identifier of the car" ...
```

In many cases, it is convenient to use an asterisk (*) instead of Select-list. Asterisk represents all the fields from all the tables specified in the `FROM` clause. And it is possible to use an asterisk for each table separately, like this:

```
SELECT car.*, car_model.marke ...
```

In this example, all fields are selected from table `car` and only one field — `marke` — from `car_model`.

It is considered a bad practice to use * in situations where the query is used in other code: in applications, stored procedures, view definitions, and so on. It is not recommended because in case of using *, the output format depends not on the code of the query but on the structure of the data. And if the data structure changes, the output format also changes which will break the application using it. But if you explicitly specify all the output fields in the query and afterwards add another column in the input table, this will not change the output of the query and will not break the application.

So, in our example instead of `SELECT * ...`, it is safer to use:

```
SELECT car_id, number_of_owners, regestration_number,
number_of_doors, car_model_id, mileage ...
```

SQL expressions

Expressions in the Select-list are called value expressions or scalar expressions. That is because each expression in the Select-list always returns only one value (but the value can be an array).

Scalar expressions can also be called SQL expressions or simply expressions.

Each expression in SQL has its data type. It is determined by the data type(s) of the input. In many cases, it is possible to explicitly change the type of the data. Each item of the Select-list becomes a column in the output dataset of a type that the corresponding expression has.

SQL expressions can contain:

- Column names (most of the cases)
- Constants
- Operator invocations
- Parenthesis to control operations precedence
- Function calls
- Aggregate expressions (we will discuss them later)
- Scalar subqueries
- Type casts
- Conditional expressions

This list is not complete. There are several other cases of using SQL expressions that are not covered by this chapter.

Column names can be qualified and unqualified. Qualified means that the name of the column is preceded by the table name and optionally the schema name, all separated by the period (.) symbol. Unqualified are just names of the fields without table references. Qualified column names must be used when several tables in the FROM clause have columns with the same name. Unqualified naming in this case will cause an error "column reference is ambiguous". That means the database cannot understand which column is meant there. It is possible to use table alias instead of table name, and in case of using subqueries or functions, the alias must be used.

An example of using qualified names in Select-list is as follows:

```
SELECT car.car_id, car.number_of_owners
  FROM car_portal_app.car;
```

SQL supports all common operators as most of the other languages: logical, arithmetic, string, binary, date/time, and so on. We will discuss logical operators later in reference to SQL conditions. An examples of using arithmetic operators in expressions would be:

```
SELECT 1+1 AS two, 13%4 AS one, -5 AS minus_five,
  5! AS factorial, |/25 AS square_root;
 two | one | minus_five | factorial | square_root
-----+-----+------------+-----------+-------------
   2 |   1 |         -5 |       120 |           5
```

Also, in PostgreSQL, it is possible to create user-defined operators.

Function calls can also be a part of an SQL expression. To call an SQL function one should use its name and the arguments in parenthesis. Like this:

```
SELECT substring('this is a string constant',11,6);
  substring
  ----------
  string
```

A function named `substring` was executed here. Three arguments were passed to the function: a string and two integers. This function extracts a part from, given string starting from the character specified by the second argument and having specified length.

By default, PostgreSQL assigns to the output column the same name as the function.

If a function has no arguments it is still necessary to use parenthesis to indicate that it is a function name and not a field name or another identifier or a keyword.

Another thing that makes SQL very flexible and powerful is scalar subqueries, which can be used as a part of the value expression. It allows the developer to combine the results of different queries together. Scalar subqueries or scalar queries are queries that return exactly one column and one or zero records. They have no special syntax and their difference from non-scalar queries is nominal.

Consider the example:

```
SELECT (SELECT 1) + (SELECT 2) AS three;
  three
  ----------
       3
```

Here, the result of one scalar query which returns the value of 1 is added to the result of another scalar query returning 2. The result of the whole expression is 3.

Type casting means changing the data type of a value.

Type casts have several syntax patterns with the same meaning:

- `CAST ( <value> AS <type>)`
- `<value>::<type>`
- `<type> '<value>'`
- `<type> (<value>)`

The first is a common SQL syntax that is supported in most databases. The second is PostgreSQL specific. The third is only applicable for string constants is and usually used to define constants of other types but string or numeric. The last is function-like and can be applied only for types whose names are also existing function names, which is not very convenient. That's why this syntax is not widely used.

In many cases, PostgreSQL can do implicit type conversion. For example, the concatenation operator || takes two operands of type string. But if one tries to concatenate a string with a number, PostgreSQL will convert the number to a string automatically:

```
SELECT 'One plus one equals ' || (1+1) AS str;
        str
----------------------
One plus one equals 2
```

A conditional expression is an expression returning different results depending on some condition. It is similar to an IF — THEN — ELSE statement in other programming languages. The syntax is as follows:

```
CASE WHEN <condition1> THEN <expression1> [WHEN <condition2> THEN
<expression2> ...] [ELSE <expression n>] END
```

The behavior is understandable from the syntax: if the first condition is met, then the result of the first expression is returned, if the second condition is met, then the second expression is used, and so on. If no condition is met, then the expression specified in the ELSE part is evaluated. Each <condition> is an expression returning Boolean (true or false) result. All expressions used after the keyword THEN should return result of the same type or at least of compatible types.

The number of condition-expression pairs should be one or more. ELSE is optional and when ELSE is not specified and the no condition's result is true, then the CASE expression returns NULL.

CASE can be used in any place where the SQL expression is used. CASE expressions can be nested, that is they can be put one inside another. The order of evaluating conditions is the same as specified in the expression. That means for any condition, it is known that all preceding conditions have returned false. And if any condition returns true, subsequent conditions are not evaluated at all.

There is a simplified syntax for the CASE expression. When all the conditions implement checking of equality of the same expression to several values, it is possible to use it like this:

```
CASE <checked_expression> WHEN <value1> THEN <result1> [WHEN <value2>
THEN <result2> ...] [ELSE <result_n>] END
```

This means when the value of checked_expression is equal to value1, the result1 is returned, and so on.

This is an example of using CASE:

```
SELECT
  CASE
    WHEN now() > date_trunc('day', now()) +
      interval '12 hours'
    THEN 'PM'
    ELSE 'AM' END;
 case
 ------
 PM
```

Here, the current time is compared to midday (the current time is truncated to day, which gives midnight and then time interval of 12 hours is added). When the current time is more than midday, the expression returns the sting PM, otherwise it returns AM.

A single SQL expression can have many operators, functions, type casts, and so on. The length of an SQL expression has no limits in language specification. The Select-list is not the only place where SQL expressions can be used. In fact, they are used almost everywhere in SQL statements. For example, one can order the results of the query based on some SQL expression, as a sorting key. In an INSERT statement they are used to calculate values of the fields for newly inserted records. SQL expressions that return Boolean values are used as conditions.

PostgreSQL supports the short-circuit evaluation of the expressions and it sometimes it skips the evaluation of the part of the expression when it does not affect the result. For example, when evaluating the expression false AND z(), PostgreSQL will not call the function because the result of the AND operator is false, regardless of the result of the z() function call.

DISTINCT

Another thing related to the Select-list is pair of keywords DISTINCT and ALL, which can be used right after the SELECT keyword. When DISTINCT is specified, only unique rows from the input dataset will be returned. ALL returns all the rows, this is the default.

Consider the examples:

```
SELECT ALL marke FROM car_portal_app.car_model;
     marke
--------------
 Audi
 Audi
 Audi
 Audi
 BMW
 BMW
...
(99 rows)
and
SELECT DISTINCT marke FROM car_portal_app.car_model;
     marke
--------------
 Ferrari
 GMC
 Citroen
 UAZ
 Audi
 Volvo
...
(25 rows)
```

The input in both cases is the same: the table with the car models. But the first query returned 99 records while the second only returned 25. This is because the first returned all the rows that were in the input table. The second query selected only the unique rows. DISTINCT removes duplicate records based on the Select-list, not on the data in the input table. For example, if only the first letter of the name of the manufacturer is selected the result will be even shorter because some names start from the same letter:

```
SELECT DISTINCT substring(marke, 1, 1) FROM car_portal_app.car_model;
 substring
```

```
----------
 H
 S
 C
 J
 L
 I
 ...
(21 rows)
```

DISTINCT also works when several columns are selected. In that case, DISTINCT will remove duplicated combinations of all the column values.

FROM clause

The source of the rows for the query is specified after the FROM keyword. It is called the FROM clause. The query can select rows from zero, one, or more sources. When no source is specified, the FROM keyword should be omitted. The source of the rows for the query can be any of:

- Table
- View
- Function
- Subquery
- Values

When multiple sources are specified, they should be separated by a comma, or the JOIN clause should be used.

It is possible to set aliases for tables in the FROM clause. The optional keyword AS is used for that:

```
SELECT a.car_id, a.number_of_doors
  FROM car_portal_app.car AS a;
car_id | number_of_doors
--------+-----------------
      1 |               5
      2 |               3
      3 |               5
 ...
```

In the preceding example, the table name `car_portal_app.car` was substituted by its alias `a` in the Select-list. If an alias is used for a table or view in the FROM clause, in the Select-list (or anywhere else) it is no longer possible to refer to the table by its name. Subqueries when used in the FROM clause must have an alias. Also aliases are often used when self-join is performed, which means using the same table several times in the FROM clause.

Selecting from multiple tables

It is possible to select records from several sources at a time. Consider the following examples. There are two tables each having three rows:

```
SELECT * FROM car_portal_app.a;
 a_int | a_text
-------+--------
     1 | one
     2 | two
     3 | three
(3 rows)


SELECT * FROM car_portal_app.b;
 b_int | b_text
-------+--------
     2 | two
     3 | three
     4 | four
(3 rows)
```

When records are selected from both of them, we get the combinations of all their rows :

```
SELECT * FROM car_portal_app.a, car_portal_app.b;
 a_int | a_text | b_int | b_text
-------+--------+-------+--------
     1 | one    |     2 | two
     1 | one    |     3 | three
     1 | one    |     4 | four
     2 | two    |     2 | two
     2 | two    |     3 | three
     2 | two    |     4 | four
     3 | three  |     2 | two
     3 | three  |     3 | three
     3 | three  |     4 | four
(9 rows)
```

All possible combinations of records are called Cartesian product and usually it does not make much sense. In most cases, the user is interested in certain combinations of rows, when rows from one table match rows from another table based on some criteria. For example, it may be necessary to select only the combinations when the integer fields of both the tables have equal values. To get it the query should be changed:

```
SELECT *
  FROM car_portal_app.a, car_portal_app.b
  WHERE a_int=b_int;
 a_int | a_text | b_int | b_text
-------+--------+-------+--------
     2 | two    |     2 | two
     3 | three  |     3 | three
(2 rows)
```

This condition (a_int=b_int) join the tables. The joining conditions could be specified in the WHERE clause but in most cases it is better to put them into a FROM clause to make it more visible that they are here for joining and not for filtering the result of the join, though there is no formal difference.

The JOIN keyword is used to add join conditions to the FROM clause. The following query has the same logic and the same results as the previous one:

```
SELECT *
FROM car_portal_app.a JOIN car_portal_app.b ON a_int=b_int;
```

The JOIN condition may be specified using any of these three ways:

```
<first table> JOIN <second table> ON <condition>
```

The condition can be any. It's even not necessary to include fields from the joined tables.

```
<first table> JOIN <second table> USING (<field list>)
```

The join is based on the equality of all the fields specified in the comma separated <field list>. The fields should exist in both tables with the same name. So this syntax is not flexible enough.

```
<first table> NATURAL JOIN <second table>
```

Here, the join is based on the equality of all the fields that have the same name in both tables.

Usage of USING or NATURAL JOIN syntax has a drawback which is similar to the usage of * in the Select-list. It is possible to change the structure of the tables, for example, by adding another column or renaming them, in a way which does not make the query invalid but changes the logic of the query. This will cause errors that are very difficult to find.

What if not all rows from the first table can be matched to a row in the second table? In our example, only rows with integer values 2 and 3 exist in both tables. And when we join on the condition a_int=b_int, only those two rows are selected from the tables. The rest of the rows are not selected. This kind of the join is called inner join. It can be shown as a filled area on the diagram, like this:

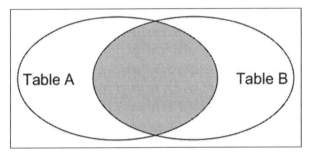

Inner join

When all the records from one table are selected, regardless of the existence of matching records in the other table, it is called an outer join. There are three types of outer joins. Look at the following diagrams:

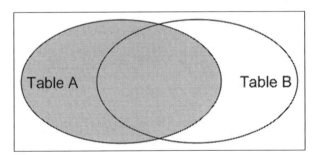

Left outer join

If all records are selected from the first table, along with only those records that match the joining condition from the second – it is a left outer join.

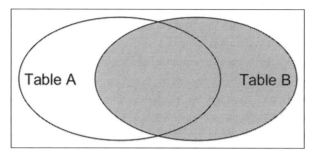

Right outer join

When all records from the second table are selected , along with only the matching records from the first table – it is a right outer join.

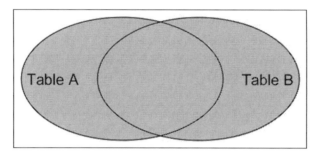

Full outer join

And when all the records from both tables are selected – it is a full outer join.

In SQL syntax, the words `inner` and `outer` are optional. Consider the following code example:

```
SELECT *
FROM car_portal_app.a JOIN car_portal_app.b ON a_int=b_int;
 a_int | a_text | b_int | b_text
-------+--------+-------+--------
     2 | two    |     2 | two
     3 | three  |     3 | three
(2 rows)
```

```
SELECT *
FROM car_portal_app.a LEFT JOIN car_portal_app.b ON a_int=b_int;
 a_int | a_text | b_int | b_text
-------+--------+-------+--------
     1 | one    |       |
     2 | two    |     2 | two
     3 | three  |     3 | three
(3 rows)


SELECT *
FROM car_portal_app.a RIGHT JOIN car_portal_app.b ON a_int=b_int;
 a_int | a_text | b_int | b_text
-------+--------+-------+--------
     2 | two    |     2 | two
     3 | three  |     3 | three
       |        |     4 | four
(3 rows)


SELECT *
FROM car_portal_app.a FULL JOIN car_portal_app.b ON a_int=b_int;
 a_int | a_text | b_int | b_text
-------+--------+-------+--------
     1 | one    |       |
     2 | two    |     2 | two
     3 | three  |     3 | three
       |        |     4 | four
(4 rows)
```

Note that the Cartesian product is not the same as the result of the full outer join. Cartesian product means all possible combinations of all records from the tables without any specific matching rules. Full outer join returns pairs of records when they that match the join conditions. And the records that do not have a pair in other table are returned separately. Outer joins return empty values (NULLs) in columns that correspond to the table where no matching record is found.

Since it is possible to query not only tables but also views, functions and subqueries, it is also possible to join them using the same syntax as for joining tables:

```
SELECT *
  FROM car_portal_app.a
  INNER JOIN
    (SELECT * FROM car_portal_app.b WHERE b_text = 'two') subq
    ON a.a_int=subq.b_int;
 a_int | a_text | b_int | b_text
```

```
-------+--------+-------+--------
   2 | two    |     2 | two
```

In the example, the subquery got the alias `sq` and it was used in the join condition.

Also, it is possible to join more than two tables. In fact, every join clause joins all the tables before the `JOIN` keyword with one table right after the keyword.

For example, this is correct:

```
SELECT *
  FROM table_a
    JOIN table_b ON table_a.field1=table_b.field1
    JOIN table_c ON table_a.field2=table_c.field2
      AND table_b.field3=table_c.field3;
```

At the moment of `JOIN table_c`, the table `table_a` has been mentioned already in the `FROM` clause, therefore it is possible to refer to that table.

However, this is not correct:

```
SELECT *
  FROM table_a
    JOIN table_b ON table_b.field3=table_c.field3
    JOIN table_c ON table_a.field2=table_c.field2
```

The code will cause an error because at `JOIN table_b`, the table `table_c` has not been there yet.

The Cartesian product can also be implemented using the `JOIN` syntax. The keywords `CROSS JOIN` are used for that. The following code:

```
SELECT * FROM car_portal_app.a CROSS JOIN car_portal_app.b;
```

Is equivalent to:

```
SELECT * FROM car_portal_app.a, car_portal_app.b;
```

The join condition in `INNER JOIN` in the logic of the query has the same meaning as a condition for filtering the rows in the `WHERE` clause. So the two following queries are the same:

```
SELECT * FROM car_portal_app.a INNER JOIN car_portal_app.b ON a.a_
int=b.b_int;
SELECT * FROM car_portal_app.a, car_portal_app.b WHERE a.a_int=b.b_
int;
```

But this is not the case for outer joins. There is no way to implement an outer join with the `WHERE` clause in PostgreSQL, though it may be possible in other databases.

Self-joins

It is possible to join a table with itself. It is called self-join. Self-join has no special syntax. In fact, all the data sources in the query are considered as independent even though they could be the same. Suppose one wants to know about each record of a table and how many records exist with a bigger value than the field a_int. The following query can be used for that:

```
SELECT t1.a_int AS current, t2.a_int AS bigger
  FROM car_portal_app.a t1
    INNER JOIN car_portal_app.a t2
      ON t2.a_int > t1.a_int;
 current | bigger
---------+--------
       1 |      2
       1 |      3
       2 |      3
(3 rows)
```

The table a is joined to itself. From the logic of the query, it does not matter if two different tables are joined or if the same table is used twice. To be able to reference the fields of the table and distinguish the instances of the table, the table aliases are used. The first instance is called t1 and the second t2. From the results, it is visible that for the value 1 there are two bigger values: 2 and 3; and for the value 2 only one bigger value of 3 exists. The examined value is in the column named current and the bigger values are in the column of the same name.

The value 3 is not selected because there are no values bigger than 3. But if one wants to explicitly show that, LEFT JOIN is used:

```
SELECT t1.a_int AS current, t2.a_int AS bigger
  FROM car_portal_app.a t1
    LEFT JOIN car_portal_app.a t2
      ON t2.a_int > t1.a_int;
 current | bigger
---------+--------
       1 |      2
       1 |      3
       2 |      3
       3 |
(4 rows)
```

WHERE clause

In many cases, after the rows are taken from the input tables, they should be filtered. It is done via the WHERE clause. The filtering condition is specified after the WHERE keyword. The condition is an SQL expression returning a Boolean value. That's why the syntax of the WHERE condition is the same as in the expressions in the Select-list. This is specific for PostgreSQL. In other databases, it may not be possible to use Boolean values in the Select-list, which makes SQL conditions different from SQL expressions. But in PostgreSQL, the difference is only in the data type of a returned value.

Simple examples of the WHERE conditions can be:

```
SELECT * FROM car_portal_app.car_model
  WHERE marke='Peugeot';
SELECT * FROM car_portal_app.car WHERE mileage < 25000;
SELECT * FROM car_portal_app.car
  WHERE number_of_doors > 3
    AND number_of_owners <= 2;
```

Although there is no formal difference between SQL expressions and SQL conditions in PostgreSQL, usually all expressions returning a Boolean type are called conditional expressions or just conditions. And they are mostly used in the WHERE clause, in conditional expressions like CASE or in the JOIN clause.

Logical operators are usually used in conditional expressions. They are AND, OR and NOT. They take Boolean arguments and return Boolean values. Logical operators are evaluated in the following order: NOT, AND, OR. But they have lower priority than any other operators. PostgreSQL tries to the optimize evaluation of logical expressions. For example, when the OR operator is evaluated, and it is known that the first operand has the true value, PostgreSQL may not evaluate the second operand at all, because the result of OR is already known. For that reason, PostgreSQL may change the actual order of evaluating expressions on purpose to get the results faster.

Sometimes that might cause problems. For example, it is not possible to divide by zero, and in case one wanted to filter rows based on the result of division, this would not be correct:

```
SELECT * FROM t WHERE a<>0 AND b/a>0.5
```

Because it is not guaranteed that PostgreSQL will evaluate the first condition (a<>0) before the second, and in case a = 0, this could cause an error. To be secure one should use a CASE statement because the order of evaluation of CASE conditions is determined by the statement:

```
SELECT * FROM t
    WHERE CASE WHEN a=0 THEN false ELSE b/a>0.5 END
```

There are some other operators or expressions returning Boolean values that are used in conditional expressions:

- Comparison operators
- Pattern matching operators
- The OVERLAPS operator
- Row and array comparison constructs
- Subquery expressions
- Any function returning Boolean or convertible to Boolean values

As if in the Select-list, functions can be used in the WHERE clause as well as anywhere in the expression. Suppose one wants to search for car models whose name is four letters long. This can be done by using a length function:

```
SELECT * FROM car_portal_app.car_model
    WHERE length(model)=4;
 car_model_id |   marke    | model
--------------+------------+-------
           47 | KIA        | Seed
           57 | Nissan     | GT-R
           70 | Renault    | Clio
 ...
```

Comparison operators

Comparison operators are < (less), > (more), <= (equal or less), >= (equal or more), = (equal) and <> or != (not equal—those two are synonyms). These operators can compare not only numbers but any values that can be compared, for example dates, or strings.

There is a BETWEEN construct that also relates to comparing:

```
x BETWEEN a AND b
```

The preceding code is equivalent to:

```
x>=a AND a<=b
```

The OVERLAPS operator checks to see if two ranges of dates overlap or not. An example would be:

```
SELECT 1 WHERE (date '2014-10-15', date '2014-10-31')
  OVERLAPS (date '2014-10-25', date '2014-11-15');
 ?column?
----------
        1
```

Comparison operators have different precedence: >= and <= have the highest priority. Then comes BETWEEN, then OVERLAPS, then < and >. And = has the lowest priority.

Pattern matching

Pattern matching is always about strings. There are two similar operators: LIKE and ILIKE. They check if a string matches a given pattern. Only two wildcards can be used in the pattern: underscore (_) for exactly one character (or number) and percent sign (%) for any number of any characters, including an empty string.

LIKE and ILIKE are the same except that the first is case-sensitive and second is not.

For example, to get car models whose names start with s and have exactly four characters, one can use the following query:

```
SELECT * FROM car_portal_app.car_model
  WHERE model ILIKE 's_ _ _';
 car_model_id |   marke    | model
--------------+------------+-------
           47 | KIA        | Seed
```

There are another two pattern matching operators: SIMILAR and ~. They check for pattern matching using regular expressions. The difference between them is that SIMILAR uses regular expression syntax defined in SQL standard, while ~ uses **Portable Operating System Interface (POSIX)** regular expressions.

In this example, one selects all car models whose names consist of exactly two words:

```
SELECT * FROM car_portal_app.car_model
 WHERE model ~ '^\w+\W+\w+$';
car_model_id |     marke     |    model
-------------+---------------+-------------
          21 | Citroen       | C4 Picasso
          33 | Ford          | C-Max
          34 | Ford          | S-Max
...
```

Row and array comparison constructs

Row and array comparison constructs are used to make multiple comparisons between values, groups of values and arrays.

The expression IN is used for checking if a value equals to any of the values from a list. The expression is as follows:

```
a IN (1, 2, 3)
```

The preceding code will return true if a equals to 1, 2 or 3. It is a shorter way of implementing the following:

```
(a = 1 OR a = 2 OR a = 3)
```

SQL allows the use of array types that mean several elements as a whole in one single value. This can be used for enriching comparison conditions. For example, this checks if a is bigger than any of x, y or z:

```
a > ANY (ARRAY[x, y, z])
```

The preceding code is equivalent to:

```
(a >  x OR a > y OR a > z)
```

This checks if a is bigger than either x, y, or z:

```
a >  ALL (ARRAY[x, y, z])
```

The preceding code is equivalent to:

```
(a > x AND a > y AND a > z )
```

The keywords IN, ALL, and ANY (which has a synonym SOME) can also be used in subquery expressions with the same logic. A result of subquery can be used in any place where it is possible to use a set of values or an array. This makes it possible, for instance, to select records from one table, when some values exist in an other table. For example, here car models are selected when there is a car of that model:

```
SELECT * FROM car_portal_app.car_model
  WHERE car_model_id IN
    (SELECT car_model_id FROM car_portal_app.car);
 car_model_id |      marke      |     model
--------------+-----------------+--------------
            2 | Audi            | A2
            3 | Audi            | A3
            4 | Audi            | A4
...
(86 rows)
```

Sometimes an IN expression can be replaced by inner join, but not always. Consider the example:

```
SELECT car_model.*
  FROM car_portal_app.car_model
    INNER JOIN car_portal_app.car USING (car_model_id);

 car_model_id |      marke      |     model
--------------+-----------------+--------------
            2 | Audi            | A2
            2 | Audi            | A2
            2 | Audi            | A2
            3 | Audi            | A3
            3 | Audi            | A3
            4 | Audi            | A4
            4 | Audi            | A4
...
(229 rows)
```

Although the same table is queried and the same columns are returned, the number of records is bigger. That is because there are many cars of the same model, and for them, the model is selected several times.

The NOT IN construct with a subquery is sometimes very slow because the check for the nonexistence of a value is more expensive than the opposite.

Grouping and aggregation

In all previous examples, the number of records returned by the SELECT query is the same as the number of rows from the input table (or tables) after filtering. In other words, every row from any of the source table (or joined tables) becomes exactly one row in the query result. Rows are processed one by one.

But SQL provides a way to get some aggregated result of processing several records at a time and get the result in one single row. The easiest example would be counting the total number of records in the table. The input is all the records of a table. The output is one single record. Grouping and aggregation is used for this.

GROUP BY clause

The GROUP BY clause is used for grouping. Grouping means splitting the whole input set of records into several groups with a view to have only one result row for each group. Grouping is performed on the basis of a list of expressions. All records that have the same combination of values of grouping expressions are grouped together. That means the groups are identified by the values of expressions defined in the GROUP BY clause. Usually, it makes sense to include those expressions in the Select-list, in order to make it visible which group is referred to by the result row.

For example:

```
SELECT a.marke, a.model
  FROM car_portal_app.car_model a
    INNER JOIN car_portal_app.car b
     ON a.car_model_id=b.car_model_id
  GROUP BY a.marke, a.model;
    marke      |     model
---------------+--------------
 Opel          | Corsa
 Ferrari       | 458 Italia
 Peugeot       | 308
 Opel          | Insignia
 ...
(86 rows)
```

Here, the list of all the car models that are used in the table car is selected. Each record in the result set represents a group of records from the source tables relating to the same car model. In fact, this query gives the same result as SELECT DISTINCT marke, model... without GROUP BY but the logic is different. DISTINCT removes duplicated values, but GROUP BY groups duplicated values together.

It is almost useless just to group rows. Usually, it is necessary to do some computing on the groups. In the last case, it would be interesting to know how many cars of which model are in the system. This is done by aggregation. Aggregation means performing calculation, on a group of records returning a single value for the whole group. This is done by the special aggregating functions that are used in the Select-list. To get the number of cars, one needs to use the `count` function:

```
SELECT a.marke, a.model, count(*)
  FROM car_portal_app.car_model a
    INNER JOIN car_portal_app.car b
      ON a.car_model_id=b.car_model_id
  GROUP BY a.marke, a.model;
    marke      |     model      | count
---------------+----------------+-------
 Opel          | Corsa          |   6
 Ferrari       | 458 Italia     |   4
 Peugeot       | 308            |   3
 Opel          | Insignia       |   4
 ...
(86 rows)
```

There are several aggregating functions available in PostgreSQL. The most frequently used are `count`, `sum`, `max`, `min`, and `avg` for computing, respectively the number of records in the group, the sum of any numeric expression for all the records in the group, the biggest, the lowest and average value of any expression. There are some other aggregating functions such as `corr`, which computes the correlation coefficient of the two given arguments, `stddev` — for standard deviation, `string_agg`, which concatenates the string values of an expression, and others.

When grouping and aggregation is used, the records are grouped. This means several records become one. Therefore, no other expressions except the aggregation functions and expressions from the GROUP BY list can be included in the Select-list. If it is done, the database will raise an error:

```
SELECT a_int, a_text
  FROM car_portal_app.a
  GROUP BY a_int;
ERROR:  column "a.a_text" must appear in the GROUP BY clause or be
used in an aggregate function
```

But it is possible to create new expressions based on the expressions from the GROUP BY list. For example, if we have GROUP BY a, b, it is possible to SELECT a+b.

What if it is needed to group all of the records of the table together, not on the basis of the values of some field, but the whole table? To do that one should include aggregating functions in the Select-list (and only them!) and not use the GROUP BY clause:

```
SELECT count(*) FROM car_portal_app.car;
 count
-------
   229
(1 row)
```

If all the records of a table are grouped without any GROUP BY expressions, then exactly one group exists. Note that the SQL queries that have aggregating functions in the Select-list and do not have the GROUP BY clause always return exactly one row, even if there are no rows in the input tables, or if all of them are filtered out. For example:

```
SELECT count(*)
FROM car_portal_app.car WHERE number_of_doors = 15;
 count
-------
     0
(1 row)
```

There are no cars with 15 doors. If the table is selected with this WHERE condition, no rows will be returned. But if one uses count(*), the aggregating function will return a row with a value of zero.

It is possible to count the number of unique values of the expression with count(DISTINCT <expression>). For example:

```
SELECT count(*), count(DISTINCT car_model_id)
  FROM car_portal_app.car;
 count | count
-------+-------
   229 |    86
```

Here, the first column has the total number of cars. The second column is the number of the car models to which the cars belong. Since some cars are of the same model, the number of models is lower than the total number of the cars.

HAVING clause

Aggregating functions are not allowed in the WHERE clause but it is possible to filter groups that follow a certain condition. This is different from filtering in the WHERE clause because WHERE filters input rows, and groups are calculated afterwards. The filtering of the groups is done by the HAVING clause. That is very similar to the WHERE clause but only aggregating functions are allowed there. The HAVING clause is specified after the GROUP BY clause. Suppose one needs to know which car models have a number of cars greater than 5. This can be done by using a subquery:

```
SELECT marke, model FROM
(
  SELECT a.marke, a.model, count(*) c
    FROM car_portal_app.car_model a
      INNER JOIN car_portal_app.car b
        ON a.car_model_id=b.car_model_id
    GROUP BY a.marke, a.model
) subq
WHERE c >5;
  marke   | model
----------+-------
 Opel     | Corsa
 Peugeot  | 208
(2 rows)
```

But the simpler and clearer way is to do it via a HAVING clause:

```
SELECT a.marke, a.model
  FROM car_portal_app.car_model a
    INNER JOIN car_portal_app.car b
      ON a.car_model_id=b.car_model_id
  GROUP BY a.marke, a.model
  HAVING count(*)>5;
  marke   | model
----------+-------
 Opel     | Corsa
 Peugeot  | 208
```

Ordering and limiting the results

The results of the query are not ordered by default. The order of the rows is not defined and may depend on their physical place on the disc, the joining algorithm, or on other factors. But in many cases it is required to have the result set sorted. This is done with the ORDER BY clause. The list of expressions whose values should be sorted is specified after the ORDER BY keywords. At the beginning, the records are sorted on the basis of the first expression of the ORDER BY list. If some rows have the same value for the first expression, they are sorted by the values of the second expression, and so on.

After each item of the ORDER BY list it is possible to specify if the order should be ascending or descending. That is done by specifying the keywords ASC or DESC after the expression. Ascending is the default. NULL values are considered larger than any other values by default but it is possible to explicitly define that NULLs should precede other rows by specifying NULLS FIRST or NULLS LAST if NULLs should be at the end.

It is not required for the ORDER BY clause to contain the same expressions as the Select-list but it usually does. So, to make it more convenient, it is allowed to use in the ORDER BY list the output column names that are assigned to the expression in the Select-list instead of fully qualified expressions. Also, it is possible to use the numbers of the columns.

So, these examples are equivalent:

```
SELECT number_of_owners, manufacture_year,
    trunc(mileage/1000) as kmiles
  FROM car_portal_app.car
  ORDER BY number_of_owners, manufacture_year,
    trunc(mileage/1000) DESC;

SELECT number_of_owners, manufacture_year,
    trunc(mileage/1000) as kmiles
  FROM car_portal_app.car
  ORDER BY number_of_owners, manufacture_year,
    kmiles DESC;

SELECT number_of_owners, manufacture_year,
    trunc(mileage/1000) as kmiles
  FROM car_portal_app.car
  ORDER BY 1, 2, 3 DESC;
```

Sometimes it is necessary to limit the output of the query to a certain number of rows and discard the rest. That is done by specifying that number after the `LIMIT` keyword. For example:

```
SELECT * FROM car_portal_app.car_model LIMIT 5;
 car_model_id | marke | model
--------------+-------+-------
            1 | Audi  | A1
            2 | Audi  | A2
            3 | Audi  | A3
            4 | Audi  | A4
            5 | Audi  | A5
(5 rows)
```

The preceding code returns only 5 rows regardless of the fact that the actual number of records in the table is bigger. This is sometimes used in scalar subqueries that should not return more than 1 record.

Another similar task is to skip several rows at the beginning of the output. This is done by the using keyword `OFFSET`. `OFFSET` and `LIMIT` can be used together:

```
SELECT * FROM car_portal_app.car_model OFFSET 5 LIMIT 5;
 car_model_id | marke | model
--------------+-------+-------
            6 | Audi  | A6
            7 | Audi  | A8
            8 | BMW   | 1er
            9 | BMW   | 3er
           10 | BMW   | 5er
(5 rows)
```

The typical use case for `OFFSET` and `LIMIT` is the implementation of paginated output in web applications. For example, if ten rows are displayed on a page, then on third page the rows 21-30 should be shown. Then `OFFSET 20 LIMIT 10` is used. In most cases of using `OFFSET` and `LIMIT`, the rows should be ordered, otherwise it is not determined which records are not shown. The keywords are then specified after the `ORDER BY` clause.

Subqueries

Subqueries are a very powerful feature of SQL. They can be used almost everywhere in the query. The most obvious way to use subqueries is in the FROM clause as a source for the main query:

```
SELECT * FROM
(
  SELECT car_model_id, count(*) c
    FROM car_portal_app.car
    GROUP BY car_model_id
) subq
WHERE c = 1;
 car_model_id | c
--------------+---
            8 | 1
           80 | 1
...
(14 rows)
```

When subqueries are used in the FROM clause they must have an alias. In the preceding example, the subquery is given the name subq.

Also, subqueries can be used in SQL conditions in the IN expressions:

```
SELECT car_id, registration_number
FROM car_portal_app.car
WHERE car_model_id IN
(
  SELECT car_model_id
    FROM car_portal_app.car_model
    WHERE marke='Peugeot'
);
 car_id | registration_number
--------+---------------------
      1 | MUWH4675
     14 | MTZC8798
     18 | VFZF9207
...
(18 rows)
```

Scalar subqueries can be used everywhere in expressions: in the Select-list, WHERE clause, GROUP BY clause, and so on. Even in LIMIT:

```
SELECT (SELECT count(*) FROM car_portal_app.car_model)
FROM car_portal_app.car
LIMIT (SELECT MIN(car_id)+2 FROM car_portal_app.car);
 count
-------
    99
    99
    99
(3 rows)
```

This is a PostgreSQL specific feature. Not every RDBMS supports subqueries in every place where expression is allowed.

It is not possible to refer to the internal elements of one subquery from inside of another. But subqueries can refer to the elements of main query. For example, if it is necessary to count cars for each car model, and select the top five most popular models, it can be done by using subquery in this way:

```
SELECT marke, model,
  (
    SELECT count(*)
      FROM car_portal_app.car
      WHERE car_model_id = main.car_model_id
  )
  FROM car_portal_app.car_model main
  ORDER BY 3 DESC
  LIMIT 5;
  marke   |  model    | count
----------+-----------+-------
 Peugeot  | 208       |     7
 Opel     | Corsa     |     6
 Jeep     | Wrangler  |     5
 Renault  | Laguna    |     5
 Peugeot  | 407       |     5
(5 rows)
```

In the example the subquery in the Select-list refers to the table of the main query by its alias main. The subquery is executed for each record received from the main table, using the value of car_model_id in the WHERE condition.

Subqueries can be nested. It means it is possible to use subqueries inside another subqueries.

Set operations – UNION, EXCEPT, and INTERSECT

Set operations are used to combine the results of several queries. It is different from joining, although the same results often can be achieved by joining.

Joining means placing the records of two tables, one table with another table *horizontally*. The result of joining is that the number of columns equal to the sum of the numbers of columns of the source tables, and the number of records will depend on the join conditions.

Combining means putting the result of one query *on top* of the result of another query. The number of columns stays the same, but the number of rows is the sum of the rows from the sources.

There are three set operations:

- UNION: This appends the result of one query to the result of another query
- INTERSECT: This returns the records that exist in the results of both queries
- EXCEPT: This returns the records from the first query that do not exist in the result of the second query — the difference

The syntax of set operations is as follows:

```
<query1> UNION <query2>;
<query1> INTERSECT <query2>;
<query1> EXCEPT <query2>;
```

It is possible to use several set operations in one statement:

```
SELECT a, b FROM t1
UNION
SELECT c, d FROM t2
INTERSECT
SELECT e, f FROM t3;
```

The priority of all set operations is the same. That means logically they are executed in the same order as used in the code. But the records can be returned in a different order that is not predicted, unless the ORDER BY clause is used. In this case, the ORDER BY clause is applied after all of the set operations. And for that reason, it does not make sense to put ORDER BY into the subqueries.

All set operations by default remove duplicated records as if SELECT DISTINCT is used. To avoid this and return all the records, the ALL keyword should be used, which is specified after the name of the set operation:

```
<query1> UNION ALL <query2>.
```

The set operations can be used to find the difference between the two tables. For example:

```
SELECT 'a', * FROM
(
  SELECT * FROM car_portal_app.a
  EXCEPT ALL
  SELECT * FROM car_portal_app.b
) v1
UNION ALL
SELECT 'b', * FROM
(
  SELECT * FROM car_portal_app.b
  EXCEPT ALL
  SELECT * FROM car_portal_app.a
) v2;
 ?column? | a_int | a_text
----------+-------+--------
 a        |     1 | one
 b        |     4 | four
(2 rows)
```

From the results of that query, you can find out that the row one exists in the table a but does not exist in the table b. And the row four exists in the table b, but not in a.

It is possible to append one set of records to another only when they have the same number of columns and they have respectively the same data types, or compatible data types. The output names for the columns are always taken from the first subquery, even if they are different in subsequent queries.

In other RDBMS, set operations can have different names, for example, in Oracle EXCEPT is called MINUS.

Dealing with NULLs

NULL is a special value that any field or expression can have, except for when it is explicitly forbidden. NULL means the absence of any value. It can also be treated as an unknown value in some cases. In relation to logical values, NULL is neither true nor false. Working with NULLs can be confusing because almost all operators when take NULL as an argument, return NULL. And if one tries to compare some values and one of them is NULL the result will also be NULL, which is not true. For example, the query

```
SELECT * FROM t WHERE a > b
```

This will return no records if a or b have NULL value. That can be expected, but for the following condition this is not so clear:

```
SELECT * FROM t WHERE a = b
```

Here, if both a and b have a value of NULL, the record still will not be selected. The equal operator (=) returns NULL if any of the arguments is NULL, and since WHERE filters rows only when the condition is true, the record is not selected. Similarly, the following will never return any record, even if a has a NULL value:

```
SELECT * FROM t WHERE a = NULL
```

To check the expression for having NULL value, a special operator is used: IS NULL. The previous query, if it is necessary to also select records when both a and b are NULL, should be changed this way:

```
SELECT * FROM t WHERE a = b OR (a IS NULL AND b IS NULL)
```

There is a special construct, that can be used to check the equivalence of expressions taking NULL into account: IS NOT DISTINCT FROM. The preceding example can be implemented in the following way, which has the same logic:

```
SELECT * FROM t WHERE a IS NOT DISTINCT FROM b
```

Logical operators are different. They can sometimes return not null value even if they take NULL as an argument. For logical operators NULL means an unknown value. Operator AND always returns false when one of the operands is false, even if the second is NULL. Or always returns true if one of the arguments if true. In all other cases, the result is unknown, therefore NULL:

```
SELECT true AND NULL, false AND NULL, true OR NULL,
  false OR NULL, NOT NULL;
 ?column? | ?column? | ?column? | ?column? | ?column?
----------+----------+----------+----------+----------
          | f        | t        |          |
```

Functions can treat NULL values differently. Their behavior is determined by their code. Most built-in functions return NULL if any of the arguments are NULL.

Aggregating functions work with NULL values in a different way. They work with many rows and therefore many values. In general, they ignore NULL. Sum calculates the total of all not-null values and ignores NULL. Sum returns NULL only when all the received values are NULL. For avg, max and min it is the same. But for count it is different. count returns the number of not-null values. So if all the values are NULL, count returns zero.

In contrast to some other databases in PostgreSQL, empty string is not NULL. Consider the example:

```
SELECT a IS NULL, b IS NULL, a = b
  FROM (SELECT ''::text a, NULL::text b) v;
?column? | ?column? | ?column?
----------+----------+----------
    f     | t        |
```

There are a couple of functions designed to deal with NULL values: COALESCE and NULLIF.

The COALESCE function takes any number of arguments of the same data type or compatible types. It returns the value of the first of its arguments that is not null:

```
COALESCE(a, b, c)
```

The preceding code is equivalent to:

```
CASE
    WHEN a IS NOT NULL THEN a
    WHEN b IS NOT NULL THEN b
    ELSE c END
```

NULLIF takes two arguments and returns NULL if they are equal. Otherwise it returns the value of the first argument. This is somehow the opposite of COALESCE:

```
NULLIF (a, b)
```

The preceding code is equivalent to:

```
CASE WHEN a = b THEN NULL ELSE a END
```

Another aspect of NULL values is that they are ignored by unique constraints. This means if a field of a table is defined as unique, it is still possible to create several records having a NULL value of that field. Also b-tree indexes which are most commonly used, do not index NULL values. Consider the query as follows:

```
SELECT * FROM t WHERE a IS NULL
```

The preceding code will not use an index if it is created on the column a.

Changing the data in the database

Data can be inserted into database tables, updated or deleted from the database. Respectively, statements are used for this: INSERT, UPDATE and DELETE.

INSERT statement

The INSERT statement is used to insert new data into tables in the database. The records are always inserted into only one table.

The INSERT statement has the following syntax:

```
INSERT INTO <table_name> [(<field_list>)]
{VALUES (<expression_list>)[,...]}|{DEFAULT VALUES}|<SELECT query>;
```

The name of the table into which the records are inserted is specified after the INSERT INTO keywords. There are two options for using the INSERT statement, which have different syntax: to insert one or several individual records, or to insert the whole dataset of many records.

To insert several records one should use VALUES clause. The list of the values to insert is specified after the VALUES keyword. Items of the list correspond to the fields of the table according to their order. If it is not necessary to set the values for all the fields, the names of the fields whose values should be set are specified in parenthesis after the table name. The skipped fields will then get their default values, if defined, or they will be set to NULL. The number of items in the VALUES list must be the same as the number of fields after the table name:

```
INSERT INTO car_portal_app.a (a_int) VALUES (6);
```

Another way to set default values to the field is to use the DEFAULT keyword in the VALUES list. If default is not defined for the field, a NULL-value will be set:

```
INSERT INTO car_portal_app.a (a_text) VALUES (default);
```

It is also possible to set all fields to their default values using the keywords DEFAULT VALUES:

```
INSERT INTO car_portal_app.a DEFAULT VALUES;
```

And it is possible to insert multiple records using VALUES syntax:

```
INSERT INTO car_portal_app.a (a_int, a_text) VALUES (7, 'seven'), (8,
'eight');
```

This option is PostgreSQL-specific. Some other databases allow inserting only one row at a time.

In fact, in PostgreSQL the VALUES clause is a standalone SQL command. Therefore, it can be used as a subquery in any SELECT query:

```
SELECT * FROM (VALUES (7, 'seven'), (8, 'eight')) v;
column1 | column2
---------+---------
      7 | seven
      8 | eight
(2 rows)
```

When the records to insert are taken from another table or view, a SELECT query is used instead of the VALUES clause:

```
INSERT INTO car_portal_app.a
SELECT * FROM car_portal_app.b;
```

The result of the query should match the structure of the table: have the same number of columns of compatible types.

It is possible to use the table in which the records are inserted, in the SELECT query. For example, to duplicate the records in the table, the following statement can be used:

```
INSERT INTO car_portal_app.a
SELECT * FROM car_portal_app.a;
```

By default, the INSERT statement returns the number of inserted records. But it is also possible to return the inserted records themselves, or some of their fields. The output of the statement is then similar to the output of the SELECT query. The RETURNING keyword, with the list of fields to return, is used for this:

```
INSERT INTO car_portal_app.a
SELECT * FROM car_portal_app.b
RETURNING a_int;
 a_int
-------
     2
     3
     4
(3 rows)
```

UPDATE statement

The UPDATE statement is used to change the data in the records of a table without changing their number. It has the following syntax:

```
UPDATE <table_name>
SET <field_name> = <expression>[, ...]
[FROM <table_name> [JOIN clause]]
[WHERE <condition>];
```

There are two ways of using the UPDATE statement. The first is similar to the simple SELECT statement, and is called sub-select. The second is based on other tables, and is similar to the SELECT statement from multiple tables. In most cases, the same result can be achieved by using any of those methods.

In PostgreSQL, only one table can be updated at a time. Other databases may allow the updating of multiple tables at the same time under certain conditions.

UPDATE using sub-select

The expression for a new value is the usual SQL expression. It is possible to refer to the same field in the expression. In that case the old value is used:

```
UPDATE t SET f = f+1 WHERE a = 5;
```

It is common to use a subquery in the UPDATE statements. To refer to the updated table from a subquery the table should have an alias:

```
UPDATE car_portal_app.a u SET a_text =
  (SELECT b_text FROM car_portal_app.b
    WHERE b_int = u.a_int);
```

If the subquery returns no result, the field value is set to NULL.

The WHERE clause is similar to the one used in the SELECT statement. If the WHERE statement is not specified, all the records are updated.

UPDATE using additional tables

The second way of updating rows in the table is to use the FROM clause in a similar manner as it is done in the SELECT statement:

```
UPDATE car_portal_app.a SET a_int = b_int FROM car_portal_app.b WHERE
a.a_text=b.b_text;
```

All rows from a, for which there are rows in b with the same value of the text field, were updated. The new value for the numeric field was taken from the table b. Technically, it is nothing but an inner join of the two tables. But the syntax here is different. Since table a is not part of the FROM clause, using the usual `join` syntax is not possible and the tables are joined on the condition of the WHERE clause. But if another table was used it would have been possible to join it to the table b using the join syntax, inner or outer.

The FROM syntax of the UPDATE statement can seem more obvious in many cases. For example, the following statement performs the same changes to the table as the previous, but it is less clear:

```
UPDATE car_portal_app.a SET a_int =
  (SELECT b_int FROM car_portal_app.b
    WHERE a.a_text=b.b_text)
WHERE a_text IN (SELECT b_text FROM car_portal_app.b);
```

Another advantage of the FROM-syntax is that in many cases it is much faster.

On the other hand, this syntax can have unpredictable results in cases where for a single record of the updated table there are several matching records from the tables of the FROM clause.

For example:

```
UPDATE car_portal_app.a SET a_int = b_int FROM car_portal_app.b;
```

This query is syntactically correct. However, it is known that in the table b there is more than one record. And which of them will be selected for every updated row is not determined, since no WHERE condition is specified. The same happens when the WHERE clause does not define the one-to-one matching rule:

```
UPDATE car_portal_app.a SET a_int = b_int
   FROM car_portal_app.b
   WHERE b_int>=a_int;
```

For each record of table a there is more than one record from table b where, b_int is more or equal to a_int. That's why the result of this update is undefined. However, PostgreSQL will allow this to be executed.

For this reason, one should be careful when uses this way of doing updates.

The update query can return updated records if the RETURNING clause is used as it is in the INSERT statement:

```
UPDATE car_portal_app.a SET a_int = 0 RETURNING *;
 a_int | a_text
-------+--------
     0 | one
     0 | two
...
```

DELETE statement

The DELETE statement is used to remove records from the database. As with UPDATE, there are two ways of deleting: using sub-select or using another table or tables. The sub-select syntax is as follows:

```
DELETE FROM <table_name> [WHERE <condition>];
```

Records that follow the condition will be removed from the table. If the WHERE clause is omitted, then all the records will be deleted.

Delete based on another tables is similar to using the FROM clause of the UPDATE statement. But instead of FROM, the USING keyword should be used because FROM is already used in the syntax of the DELETE statement:

```
DELETE FROM car_portal_app.a
USING car_portal_app.b WHERE a.a_int=b.b_int;
```

The preceding statement will delete all the records from a when there is a record in b with the same value of the numeric field. This is equivalent to:

```
DELETE FROM car_portal_app.a
WHERE a_int IN (SELECT b_int FROM car_portal_app.b);
```

As well as UPDATE and INSERT, the DELETE statement can return deleted rows when the RETURNING keyword is used:

```
DELETE FROM car_portal_app.a RETURNING *;
 a_int | a_text
-------+--------
     0 | one
     0 | two
...
```

TRUNCATE statement

Another statement that can also change the data but not the data structure is TRUNCATE. It clears the table completely and almost instantly. It has the same effect as the DELETE statement without the WHERE clause. So, it is useful on large tables:

```
TRUNCATE TABLE car_portal_app.a;
```

Summary

SQL is used to interact with the database: create and maintain the data structures, put data into the database, change it, retrieve it and delete it. SQL has commands related to DDL , DML and DCL. The four SQL statements form the basis of DML: SELECT, INSERT, UPDATE and DELETE. They were described in this chapter.

The SELECT statement was examined in detail to explain SQL concepts such as grouping and filtering, to show what are SQL expressions and conditions, and to explain how to use subqueries. Also, some relational algebra topics were covered in section to join tables.

In the next chapters, the more complicated topics are covered: some advanced SQL features and techniques, and the programming language PL/pgSQL, which can be used to implement functions in PostgreSQL.

6
Advanced Query Writing

In this chapter, we will discuss some SQL features supported by PostgreSQL, that were not covered in the previous chapters. Some advanced techniques will also be described.

The same sample database as was used in the previous chapters is used in the code examples. It is recommended to recreate the sample database in order to get the same results as shown in the examples.

In this chapter, we are going to cover the following topics:

- Common table expression
- Window functions
- Advanced SQL
- Transaction isolation and Multiversion Concurrency Control

The code examples in this chapter are based on the car portal database described in the previous chapters. The scripts for creating the database and filling it with data (`schema.sql` and `data.sql`) can be found in the code bundle in the `Chapter 6` folder.

All the code examples of this chapter can be found in the file `examples.sql`.

Common table expressions

Although SQL is a declarative language, it provides a way of implementing the logic of sequential execution of code or of reusing code. **Common table expressions** (CTE) is a feature that makes it possible to define a subquery, give it a name, and then use it at several places in the main query.

The simplified syntax diagram for CTE is as follows:

```
WITH <subquery name> AS (
<subquery code>)
[, ...]
SELECT <Select list> FROM <subquery name>;
```

In the preceding syntax diagram, subquery code is a query that returns results of which will be used in the primary query as if it was a real table. The subquery in parenthesis, after the keyword AS, is a common table expression. It can also be called a substatement or an auxiliary statement. The query after the WITH block is the primary or main query. The whole statement itself is called the WITH query. It is possible to use not only the SELECT statements in CTE but also the INSERT, UPDATE, or DELETE statements.

It is possible to use several CTEs in one WITH query. Every CTE has its name defined before the keyword AS. The main query can reference a CTE by its name. A CTE can also refer to another CTE by name. A CTE can refer only to the CTEs that were written before the referencing one.

The references to CTEs in the primary query can be treated as table names. In fact, PostgreSQL executes the CTEs only once, stores the results, and reuses them instead of executing subqueries each time they occur in the main query. This makes them similar to tables.

CTEs may help developers in organizing SQL code, as follows:

```
WITH pre_select AS
(
  SELECT car_id, number_of_owners, car_model_id
    FROM car_portal_app.car
    WHERE manufacture_year >= 2010
),
joined_data AS
(
  SELECT car_id, marke, model, number_of_owners
    FROM pre_select
      INNER JOIN car_portal_app.car_model
        ON  pre_select.car_model_id= car_model.car_model_id
),
minimal_owners AS
(
  SELECT min(number_of_owners) AS min_number_of_owners
    FROM pre_select
)
```

```
SELECT car_id, marke, model, number_of_owners
  FROM joined_data
    INNER JOIN minimal_owners
      ON joined_data.number_of_owners =
        minimal_owners.min_number_of_owners;
```

car_id	marke	model	number_of_owners
2	Opel	Corsa	1
3	Citroen	C3	1
11	Nissan	GT-R	1
36	KIA	Magentis	1

...

(25 rows)

In the preceding example, the logic part of the query is presented as a sequence of actions—filtering in pre_select and then joining in joined_data. The other part, that is, calculating the minimal number of owners, is executed in a dedicated subquery, minimal_owners. This makes the implementation of the query logic similar to that of an imperative programming language.

The use of CTEs in the preceding example does not make the whole query faster; however, there are situations where the use of CTEs can increase performance. Moreover, sometimes it is not possible to implement the logic in any other way but by using CTEs. In the following sections, some of those situations are discussed in detail.

The order of execution of the CTEs is not defined. PostgreSQL aims to execute only the main query. If the main query contains references to the CTEs, then PostgreSQL will execute them first. If the SELECT CTE is not referenced by the main query, directly or indirectly, then it is not executed at all. Data-changing sub statements are always executed.

Reusing SQL code with CTE

When the execution of a subquery takes too much time, and the subquery is used in the statement more than once, it makes sense to put it in the WITH clause to reuse its results. This makes the query faster, because PostgreSQL executes the subqueries from the WITH clause only once, saves the results in the memory or on disk, depending on their size, and then reuses them.

For example, let's take the car portal database. Suppose it is required to find newer car models. That would require the calculation of the average age of each model of the cars, and then selecting the models with an age lower than the average age among all the models.

This can be done in the following way:

```
SELECT marke, model, avg_age
  FROM (
    SELECT car_model_id,
        avg(EXTRACT(YEAR FROM now())-manufacture_year)
          AS avg_age
      FROM car_portal_app.car
      GROUP BY car_model_id
    ) age_subq1
    INNER JOIN car_portal_app.car_model
      ON car_model.car_model_id = age_subq1.car_model_id
  WHERE avg_age < (SELECT avg(avg_age) FROM
        (
          SELECT avg(EXTRACT(YEAR FROM now())
              -manufacture_year) avg_age
            FROM car_portal_app.car
            GROUP BY car_model_id
        ) age_subq2
      );
    marke       |     model     |     avg_age
---------------+---------------+-------------------
 BMW           | 1er           |         1
 BMW           | X6            |         2.5
 Mercedes Benz | A klasse      |         1.5
...
(41 rows)
```

The function EXTRACT used in the query returns the integer value of the given part of the date expression. In the preceding example, the function is used to retrieve the year from the current date. The difference between the current year and manufacture_year is the age of a car.

There are two subqueries that are similar: the same table is queried and the same grouping and aggregation are performed. That makes it possible to use the same subquery twice when it is used as a CTE:

```
WITH age_subq AS
(
  SELECT car_model_id,
      avg(EXTRACT(YEAR FROM now())-manufacture_year)
        AS avg_age
    FROM car_portal_app.car
    GROUP BY car_model_id
)
```

```
SELECT marke, model, avg_age
  FROM age_subq
    INNER JOIN car_portal_app.car_model
      ON car_model.car_model_id = age_subq.car_model_id
  WHERE avg_age < (SELECT avg(avg_age) FROM age_subq);
    marke       |     model     |      avg_age
--------------+---------------+-------------------
  BMW           | 1er           |                 1
  BMW           | X6            |               2.5
  Mercedes Benz | A klasse      |               1.5
  ...
(41 rows)
```

The result of both the queries is the same. But the first query took 1.9 milliseconds to execute and the second one took 1.0 milliseconds. Of course, in absolute values the difference is nothing. But relatively, the WITH query is almost twice as fast. And if the number of records in the tables was in millions, then the absolute difference would be substantial.

Another advantage of using a CTE in this case is that the code became smaller and easier. That is another use case for the WITH clause. Long and complicated subqueries can be formatted as CTEs in order to make the whole query smaller and more understandable, even if it does not affect the performance.

Sometimes, it is better not to use CTE. For example, one could decide to preselect some columns from the table thinking it would help the database to perform the query because of the reduced amount of information to process. In that case, the query would be the following:

```
WITH car_subquery AS
(
  SELECT number_of_owners, manufacture_year,
      number_of_doors
    FROM car_portal_app.car
)
SELECT number_of_owners, number_of_doors
  FROM car_subquery
  WHERE manufacture_year = 2008;
```

But that has the opposite effect. PostgreSQL does not push the WHERE clause from the primary query to the substatement. The database will retrieve all the records from the table, take three columns from them, and store this temporary dataset in the memory. Then, the temporary data will be queried using the predicate, manufacture_year = 2008. If there was an index on manufacture_year, it would not be used because it is the temporary data being queried and not the real table.

For that reason, the following query is executed five times faster than the preceding one even though it seems almost the same:

```
SELECT number_of_owners, number_of_doors
  FROM car_portal_app.car
  WHERE manufacture_year = 2008;
```

Recursive and hierarchical queries

It is possible to refer a substatement from itself. Statements like that are called recursive queries. Recursive queries must have a special structure that indicates to the database that the subquery is recursive. The structure of a recursive query is as follows:

```
WITH RECURSIVE <subquery_name> (<field list>) AS
(
<non-recursive term>
UNION [ALL|DISTINCT]
<recursive term>
)
[,...]
<main query>
```

Both, non-recursive and recursive terms, are subqueries that must return the same number of fields of the same types. The names for the fields are specified in the declaration of the whole recursive query; therefore, it does not matter which names are assigned to the fields in the subqueries.

The non-recursive term is also called an anchor subquery while the recursive term is also known as an iterating subquery.

A non-recursive or anchor subquery is a starting point of the execution of a recursive query. It cannot refer to the name of the recursive query. It is executed only once. The results of the non-recursive term are passed to the recursive term, which can reference the whole recursive query by its name. If the recursive term returns rows, they are passed to the recursive term again. This is called iteration. Iteration is repeated as long as the result of the recursive term is not empty. The result of the whole query is all the rows returned by the non-recursive term and all the iterations of the recursive term. If the keywords UNION ALL are used, then all the rows are returned. If UNION DISTINCT or just UNION is used, then the duplicated rows are removed from the result set.

Note that the algorithm of a recursive subquery implies iterations but not recursion. However, in SQL standard, these kind of queries are called recursive. In other databases, the same logic can be implemented in a similar manner, but the syntax can be slightly different.

For example, the following recursive query can be used to calculate factorial values:

```
WITH RECURSIVE subq (n, factorial) AS
(
  SELECT 1, 1
  UNION ALL
  SELECT n+1, factorial*(n+1) from subq WHERE n <5
)
SELECT * FROM subq;
 n | factorial
---+-----------
 1 |         1
 2 |         2
 3 |         6
 4 |        24
 5 |       120
(5 rows)
```

Here, SELECT 1, 1 is the anchor subquery. It returns one row (the fields n and factorial have values of 1 and 1), which is passed to the subsequent iterating subquery. The first iteration adds one to the value of the field n and multiplies the value of the factorial by (n+1), which gives the values 2 and 2; it then passes the result row to the next iteration. The second iteration returns the values 3 and 6, and so on. The last iteration returns a row where the value of the field n equals 5. That row is filtered out in the WHERE clause of the iterating subquery; that's why the following iteration returns nothing and the execution stops at that point. So, the whole recursive subquery returns a list of five numbers, from 1 to 5, and their factorial values.

Note that if no WHERE clause was specified, the execution would never stop, which would cause an error at the end.

The preceding example is quite easy to implement without recursive queries. PostgreSQL provides a way to generate a series of numeric values and use them in subqueries. But there is a task that cannot be solved without recursive queries, and that is: querying a hierarchy of objects.

There is no hierarchical data in the car portal database, so in order to illustrate the technique, we need to create some sample data. A typical hierarchy implies the existence of a parent-child relationship between objects, where an object can be a parent and a child at the same time. Suppose there is a family: **Alan** has two children, **Bert** and **Bob**. **Bert** also has two children: **Carl** and **Carmen**. **Bob** has one child: **Cecil**, who has two children, **Dave** and **Den**. The relationships are shown in the next image:

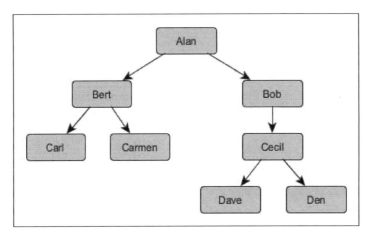

An hierarchical relationship

In the database, the hierarchy can be stored in a simple table of two columns: parent and child.

```
CREATE TABLE family (parent text, child text);
INSERT INTO family VALUES (NULL, 'Alan'),
('Alan', 'Bert'), ('Alan', 'Bob'), ('Bert', 'Carl'), ('Bert',
'Carmen'), ('Bob', 'Cecil'), ('Cecil', 'Dave'), ('Cecil', 'Den');
```

The first inserted record with a NULL value for parent indicates that there is no information about Alan's parent. The table is not normalized, but it does not matter for the example.

Suppose it is required to build a full bloodline for all the children in the family. It is not possible to do so by just joining tables, because each join will process only one level of hierarchy, but in general, the number or levels is not given.

The following recursive query will solve the problem:

```
WITH RECURSIVE genealogy (bloodline, parent, level) AS
(
  SELECT child, child, 0
    FROM family WHERE parent IS NULL
  UNION ALL
  SELECT g.bloodline || ' -> ' || f.child, f.child,
      g.level + 1
    FROM family f, genealogy g
    WHERE f.parent = g.parent
)
SELECT bloodline, level FROM genealogy;
          bloodline             | level
--------------------------------+-------
 Alan                           |    0
 Alan -> Bert                   |    1
 Alan -> Bob                    |    1
 Alan -> Bert -> Carl           |    2
 Alan -> Bert -> Carmen         |    2
 Alan -> Bob -> Cecil           |    2
 Alan -> Bob -> Cecil -> Dave   |    3
 Alan -> Bob -> Cecil -> Den    |    3
(8 rows)
```

In the non-recursive term, the start of the hierarchy is selected. Here it is a child who has no parent. His name is an initial value for the bloodline. On the first iteration in the recursive term, his children are selected. Their names are added to the bloodline field with a separator - >. On the second iteration, the children of the children are selected, and so on. When no more children are found, the execution stops. The value in the field level is incremented on each iteration so that the number of iterations is visible in the results.

There is a potential problem with those hierarchical queries. If the data contained cycles, the recursive query would never stop if written in the same way as the preceding code. For example, let's add another record into the table family:

```
INSERT INTO family VALUES ('Bert', 'Alan');
```

Now there is a cycle in the data: Alan is a child of his own child. To run the query, it is necessary to somehow make the query stop. That can be done by checking if the child being processed is already included in the bloodline, as follows:

```
WITH RECURSIVE genealogy
    (bloodline, parent, level, processed) AS
(
    SELECT child, child, 0, ARRAY[child]
      FROM family WHERE parent IS NULL
    UNION ALL
    SELECT g.bloodline || ' -> ' || f.child,
          f.child, g.level + 1, processed || f.child
      FROM family f, genealogy g
      WHERE f.parent = g.parent
        AND NOT f.child = ANY(processed)
)
SELECT bloodline, level FROM genealogy;
            bloodline            | level
---------------------------------+-------
 Alan                            |    0
 Alan -> Bert                    |    1
 Alan -> Bob                     |    1
 Alan -> Bert -> Carl            |    2
 Alan -> Bert -> Carmen          |    2
 Alan -> Bob -> Cecil            |    2
 Alan -> Bob -> Cecil -> Dave    |    3
 Alan -> Bob -> Cecil -> Den     |    3
(8 rows)
```

The result is the same as in the previous example. The field processed is an array which contains the names of all the processed children. In fact, it has the same data as the field bloodline, but in a way that is more efficient to analyze. In each iteration, the name of the processed child is added to the array. Additionally, in the WHERE clause of the recursive term, the name of the child is checked so that it is not equal to any element of the array.

There are some limitations to the implementation of recursive queries. The use of aggregation is not allowed in the recursive term. Moreover, the name of the recursive subquery can be referenced only once in the recursive term.

Changing data in multiple tables at a time

Another very useful application of CTEs is performing several data-changing statements at once. This is done by including the INSERT, UPDATE, and DELETE statements in the CTEs. The results of any of those statements can be passed to the following CTEs or to the primary query by specifying the RETURNING clause. As well as for SELECT statements, the maximal number of changing data common table expressions is not defined.

For example, suppose one wants to add a new car to the car portal database and there is no corresponding car model in the car_model table. To do this, one needs to enter a new record in the car_model, take the ID of the new record, and use that ID to insert the data into the car table:

```
car_portal=# INSERT INTO car_portal_app.car_model (marke, model)
VALUES ('Ford','Mustang') RETURNING car_model_id;
car_model_id
--------------
          100
(1 row)
INSERT 0 1
car_portal=# INSERT INTO car_portal_app.car (number_of_owners,
registration_number, manufacture_year, number_of_doors, car_model_id,
mileage)
   VALUES (1, 'GTR1231', 2014, 4, 100, 10423);
INSERT 0 1
```

Sometimes, it is not convenient to perform two statements while storing the intermediate ID number somewhere. The WITH queries provide a way to make the changes in both the tables at the same time:

```
car_portal=# WITH car_model_insert AS
(
  INSERT INTO car_portal_app.car_model (marke, model)
    VALUES ('Ford','Mustang') RETURNING car_model_id
)
INSERT INTO car_portal_app.car
  (number_of_owners, registration_number,
    manufacture_year, number_of_doors, car_model_id,
    mileage)
  SELECT 1, 'GTR1231', 2014, 4, car_model_id, 10423
    FROM car_model_insert;
INSERT 0 1
```

As mentioned earlier, the CTEs that change the data are always executed. It does not matter if they are referenced in the primary query directly or indirectly. However, the order of their execution is not determined. One can influence that order by making them dependent on each other.

What if several CTEs change the same table or use the results produced by each other? There are some principles for their isolation and interaction:

- For sub-statements:
    - All the sub-statements work with the data as it was at the moment of the start of the whole WITH query.
    - They don't see the results of each other's work. For example, it is not possible for the DELETE sub-statement to remove a row that was inserted by another INSERT sub-statement.
    - The only way for passing information of the processed records from a data changing CTE to another CTE is by using the RETURNING clause.

- For triggers defined on the tables being changed:
    - **For the BEFORE triggers**: Statement-level triggers are executed just before the execution of each sub-statements. Row-level triggers are executed just before the changing of every record. This means that a row-level trigger for one sub-statements can be executed before a statement-level trigger for another sub-statement even if the same table is changed.
    - **For the AFTER triggers**: Both, statement-level and row-level triggers are executed after the whole WITH query. They are executed in groups per every sub-statement: first row-level then statement-level. That means that a statement-level trigger for one sub-statements can be executed before a row-level trigger for another sub-statement, even if the same table is changed.
    - The statements inside the code of the triggers do see the changes in data that were made by other sub-statements.

- For the constraints defined on the tables being changed, assuming they are not set to DEFERRED:

  - ° PRIMARY KEY and UNIQUE constraints are validated for every record at the moment of insert or update of the record. They take into account the changes made by other sub-statements.

  - ° CHECK constraints are validated for every record at the moment of insert or update of the record. They do not take into account the changes made by other sub-statements.

  - ° FOREIGN KEY constraints are validated at the end of the execution of the whole WITH query.

A simple example of dependency and interaction between CTEs would be as follows:

```
car_portal=# CREATE TABLE t (f int UNIQUE);
CREATE TABLE
car_portal=# INSERT INTO t VALUES (1);
INSERT 0 1
car_portal=# WITH del_query AS (DELETE FROM t)
INSERT INTO t VALUES (1);
ERROR:  duplicate key value violates unique constraint "t_f_key"
```

The last query failed because PostgreSQL tried to execute the main query before the CTE. But if one creates a dependency that will make the CTE execute first, then the record will be deleted and the new record will be inserted. In that case, the constraint will not be violated:

```
car_portal=#  WITH del_query AS
(DELETE FROM t RETURNING f)
INSERT INTO t SELECT 1
WHERE (SELECT count(*) FROM del_query) IS NOT NULL;
INSERT 0 1
```

In the preceding code snippet, the WHERE condition in the main query does not have any practical meaning because the result of COUNT is never NULL. However, since the CTE is referenced in the query, it is executed before the execution of the main query.

Window functions

Apart from grouping and aggregation, PostgreSQL provides another way to perform computations based on the values of several records. It can be done by using the window functions. Grouping and aggregation implies the output of a single record for every group of input records. Window functions can do similar things, but they are executed for every record, and the number of records in the output and the input is the same:

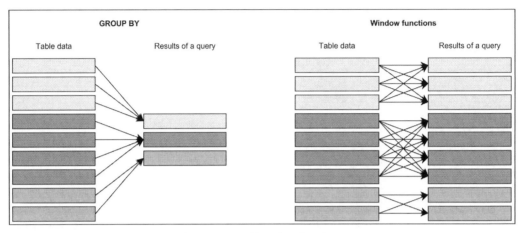

GROUP BY and Window functions

In the preceding diagram, the rectangles represent the records of a table. Let's assume that the color of the rectangles indicates the value of a field, used to group the records. When GROUP BY is used in a query, each distinct value of that field will create a group, and each group will become a single record in the results of the query. That was explained in *Chapter 5*, *SQL Language*. Window functions can access the values of other records of the same group (which is called a partition in this case), although the number of records stays the same. When window functions are used, no grouping is necessary, although possible.

Window functions are evaluated after grouping and aggregation. For that reason, the only places in the SELECT query where the window functions are allowed are Select-List and the ORDER BY clause.

Window definition

The syntax of the window functions is as follows:

```
<function_name>(<function_arguments>)
OVER(
[PARTITION BY <expression_list>]
[ORDER BY <order_by_list>]
[{ROWS | RANGE} <frame_start> |
 {ROWS | RANGE} BETWEEN <frame_start> AND <frame_end>])
```

The construct in the parenthesis, after the OVER keyword, is called the window definition. The last part of the window definition, which starts with ROWS, is called a frame clause. The syntax of frame_start and frame_end is described later.

Window functions, in general, work like aggregating functions. They process sets of records. These sets are built separately for each processed record. That's why, unlike the normal aggregating functions, window functions are evaluated for each row.

For each record, a set of rows to be processed by a window function is built in the following way:

At the beginning, the PARTITION BY clause is processed. All the records that have the same values as all the expressions in the expression_list on the current row, are taken. The set of those rows is called a partition. The current row is also included in the partition. In fact, the PARTITION BY clause has the same logic and syntax as the GROUP BY clause of the SELECT statement, except that it is not possible to refer to the output column names or numbers in PARTITION BY. In other words, while processing each record, a window function will take a look into all the other records to check if any of them falls into the same partition as the current one. If no PARTITION BY is specified, it means that all the rows will be included in a single partition at this step.

Next, the partition is sorted according to the ORDER BY clause which has the same syntax and logic as the ORDER BY clause in the SELECT statement. Again, no references to the output column names or numbers are allowed here. If the ORDER BY clause is omitted, then all the records of the set are considered to have the same precedence.

In the end, the frame clause is processed. It means taking a subset from the whole partition to pass it to the window function. The subset is called a window frame. The frame has its starting and ending points. The start of the frame, which is referenced by `frame_start` in the preceding syntax diagram, can be any of the following:

- UNBOUNDED PRECEDING: The very first record of the partition.
- <value> PRECEDING: A record, that is <value> number of records before the current one. <value> is an integer expression which cannot return a negative value and which cannot use aggregating functions or other window functions. "0 PRECEDING" points to the current row.
- CURRENT ROW: The current row itself.
- <value> FOLLOWING: A record, that is <value> number of records after the current record.

The ending point—`frame_end`—can be any one of the following:

- <value> PRECEDING
- CURRENT ROW
- <value> FOLLOWING
- UNBOUNDED PRECEDING—the very last record of the partition.

The starting point should precede the ending point. That's why, for example, ROWS BETWEEN CURRENT ROW AND 1 PRECEDING is not correct.

A window frame can be defined using the ROWS mode or the RANGE mode. It affects the meaning of the CURRENT ROW. In the ROWS mode, the CURRENT ROW points to the current record itself. In the RANGE mode, the CURRENT ROW points to the first or to the last record that has the same position when sorted according to the ORDER BY clause. First or last will be chosen with a view to make the frame wider.

If `frame_end` is omitted, then CURRENT ROW is used instead.

If the whole frame clause is omitted, then the frame will be built using the RANGE UNBOUNDED PRECEDING definition.

Look at the following example of a window definition:

```
OVER (PARTITION BY a ORDER BY b ROWS BETWEEN UNBOUNDED PRECEDING AND 5
FOLLOWING)
```

The preceding definition means that for every row, all the records with the same value of the field a will form the partition. Then, the partition will be ordered in an ascending manner by the values of the field b, and the frame will contain all the records from the first to the fifth one following the current row.

The WINDOW clause

The window definitions can be quite long, and in many cases, it is not convenient to use them in the Select-list. PostgreSQL provides a way to define windows and give them names that can be used in the OVER clause in window functions. This is done by using the WINDOW clause of the SELECT statement, which is specified after the HAVING clause, as follows:

```
SELECT
    count() OVER w,
    sum(b) OVER w,
    avg(b) OVER (w ORDER BY c ROWS BETWEEN 1 PRECEDING
        AND 1 FOLLOWING)
FROM table1
WINDOW w AS (PARTITION BY a)
```

The predefined window can be used as is. In the preceding example, the window functions count and sum do that. The window definition can also be further detailed like it is for the function avg in the example. The syntactical difference is the following: to reuse the same window definition, the window name should be specified after the OVER keyword, without parenthesis. To extend the window definition with the ORDER BY or frame clause, one should use the name of the window inside the parenthesis.

When the same window definition is used several times, PostgreSQL will optimize the execution of the query by building partitions only once and then reusing the results.

Using window functions

All aggregating functions can be used as window functions, with the exception of ordered-set and hypothetical-set aggregates. User defined aggregating functions can also be used as window functions. The presence of an OVER clause indicates that the function is a window function.

When the aggregating function is used as a window function, it will aggregate the rows that belong to the window frame of a current row.

The typical use cases for the window functions are computing statistical values of different kinds. Take the car portal database for example. There is a table called advertisement that contains information about the advertisements that users create. Suppose it is required to analyze the quantity of advertisements that the users create over a period of time. The query which generates the report would be as follows:

```
WITH monthly_data AS (
    SELECT date_trunc('month', advertisement_date) AS
        month, count(*) as cnt
    FROM car_portal_app.advertisement
    GROUP BY date_trunc('month', advertisement_date)
)
SELECT to_char(month, 'YYYY-MM') as month, cnt,
    sum(cnt) OVER (w ORDER BY month) AS cnt_year,
    round(avg(cnt) OVER (ORDER BY month
        ROWS BETWEEN 2 PRECEDING AND 2 FOLLOWING),1)
        AS mov_avg,
    round(cnt/sum(cnt) OVER w *100,1) AS ratio_year
FROM monthly_data
WINDOW w AS (PARTITION BY date_trunc('year',month));
```

month	cnt	cnt_year	mov_avg	ratio_year
2014-01	42	42	41.3	5.7
2014-02	51	93	45.3	7.0
2014-03	31	124	57.4	4.2
2014-04	57	181	69.6	7.8
2014-05	106	287	73.2	14.5
2014-06	103	390	81.2	14.1
2014-07	69	459	86.2	9.4
2014-08	71	530	74.2	9.7
2014-09	82	612	60.8	11.2
2014-10	46	658	54.4	6.3
2014-11	36	694	49.8	4.9
2014-12	37	731	35.2	5.1
2015-01	48	48	32.5	84.2
2015-02	9	57	31.3	15.8
(14 rows)

In the WITH clause, the data is aggregated on a monthly basis. In the main query, the window w is defined as implying partitioning by year. This means that every window function that uses the window w will work with the records of the same year as the current record.

The first window function, sum, uses the window w. Since ORDER BY is specified, each record has its place in the partition. The Frame clause is omitted, which means that the frame, RANGE BETWEEN UNBOUNDED PRECEDING AND CURRENT ROW is applied. That means, the function calculates the sum of the values for the records from the beginning of each year till the current month. It is the cumulative total on an yearly basis.

The second function, avg, calculates the moving average. For each record, it calculates the average value of five records—ranging from two preceding the current record to the second one following the current one. It does not use a predefined window, because the moving average does not take the year into account. Only the order of the values matters.

The third window function, sum, uses the same window definition again. It calculates the sum of the values for the whole year.

There are several window functions that are different from aggregating functions. They are used to get the values of other records within the partition, calculate the rank of the current row among all rows, and generate row numbers.

For example, let's extend the report of the previous example. Suppose, it is necessary to calculate the difference in the quantity of advertisements for each month against the previous months and against the same month of the previous year. Suppose it is also required to get the rank of the current month. The query would be as follows:

```
WITH monthly_data AS (
    SELECT date_trunc('month', advertisement_date) AS
        month, count(*) as cnt
    FROM car_portal_app.advertisement
    GROUP BY date_trunc('month', advertisement_date)
)
SELECT to_char(month,'YYYY-MM') as month,
    cnt,
    cnt - lag(cnt) OVER (ORDER BY month) as prev_m,
    cnt - lag(cnt, 12) OVER (ORDER BY month) as prev_y,
    rank() OVER (w ORDER BY cnt DESC) as rank
  FROM monthly_data
```

```
WINDOW w AS (PARTITION BY date_trunc('year',month))
ORDER BY month DESC;
```

```
 month   | cnt | prev_m | prev_y | rank
---------+-----+--------+--------+------
 2015-02 |   9 |    -39 |    -42 |    2
 2015-01 |  48 |     11 |      6 |    1
 2014-12 |  37 |      1 |        |   10
 2014-11 |  36 |    -10 |        |   11
 2014-10 |  46 |    -36 |        |    8
 2014-09 |  82 |     11 |        |    3
 2014-08 |  71 |      2 |        |    4
 2014-07 |  69 |    -34 |        |    5
 2014-06 | 103 |     -3 |        |    2
 2014-05 | 106 |     49 |        |    1
 2014-04 |  57 |     26 |        |    6
 2014-03 |  31 |    -20 |        |   12
 2014-02 |  51 |      9 |        |    7
 2014-01 |  42 |        |        |    9
(14 rows)
```

The `lag` function returns the value of a given expression for the record, which is the given number of records before the current one (default is 1). In the first occurrence of the function in the example, it returns the value of the field `cnt` in the previous record, which corresponds to the previous month.

The second `lag` returns the value of `cnt` for twelve previous records.

The `rank` function returns the rank of the current row within the partition. It returns the rank with gaps. That means that if two records have the same position according to the `ORDER BY` clause, both of them will get the same rank. The next record will get the rank after the next rank.

Other window functions are as follows:

- `lead`: This returns the value of a given expression evaluated for the record that is the given number of records after the current row.

- `first_value`, `last_value`, `nth_value`: This returns the value of a given expression evaluated for the first record, last record, or nth record of the frame respectively.

- row_number: This returns the number of the current row within the partition.
- dense_rank: This returns the rank of the current row without gaps.
- percent_rank and cume_dist: These return the relative rank of the current row. The difference is that the first function uses rank and the second uses row_number as a numerator for the calculations.
- ntile: This divides the partition into the given number of equal parts and returns the integer number of the part where the current record belongs.

A more detailed description of these functions is available in the documentation at http://www.postgresql.org/docs/current/static/functions-window.html.

Window functions with grouping and aggregation

Since window functions are evaluated after grouping, it is possible to use aggregating functions within the window functions, but not the other way around.

A code like the following is right:

```
sum( count(*) ) OVER()
```

This will also work: sum(a) OVER(ORDER BY count(*))

However, the code, sum(count(*) OVER()),is wrong.

For example, to calculate the rank of the seller accounts by the number of advertisements they give, the following query can be used:

```
SELECT seller_account_id,
    dense_rank() OVER(ORDER BY count(*) DESC)
  FROM car_portal_app.advertisement
  GROUP BY seller_account_id;


seller_account_id | dense_rank
------------------+-----------
               26 |          1
              128 |          2
               28 |          2
              126 |          2

...
```

Advanced SQL

In the following sections, some other advanced SQL techniques will be introduced:

- The DISTINCT ON clause, which helps finding the first records in groups
- The set returning functions, which are functions that return relations
- LATERAL joins, which allow subqueries to reference each other
- Some special aggregating functions

Selecting the first records

Quite often it is necessary to find the first records based on some criteria. For example, let's take the car_portal database; suppose it is required to find the first advertisement for each car_id in the advertisement table.

Grouping can help in this case. It will require a subquery to implement the logic:

```
SELECT advertisement_id, advertisement_date, adv.car_id,
    seller_account_id
  FROM car_portal_app.advertisement adv
  INNER JOIN
  (
    SELECT car_id, min(advertisement_date) min_date
      FROM car_portal_app.advertisement
      GROUP BY car_id
  ) first ON adv.car_id=first.car_id AND
    adv.advertisement_date = first.min_date;
```

However, if the ordering logic is complex and cannot be implemented by using the function min, that approach will not work.

Although window functions can solve the problem, they are not always convenient to use:

```
SELECT DISTINCT first_value(advertisement_id) OVER w
    AS advertisement_id,
  min(advertisement_date) OVER w
    AS advertisement_date,
  car_id, first_value(seller_account_id) OVER w
```

```
    AS seller_account_id
FROM car_portal_app.advertisement
WINDOW w AS (PARTITION BY car_id ORDER BY
    advertisement_date);
```

In the preceding code, `DISTINCT` is used to remove the duplicates which where grouped together in the previous example.

PostgreSQL provides an explicit way of selecting the first record within each group. The `DISTINCT ON` keywords are used for that. The syntax is as follows:

```
SELECT DISTINCT ON (<expression_list>) <Select-List>

...

ORDER BY <order_by_list>
```

In the preceding code snippet, for each distinct combination of values of `expression_list`, only the first record will be returned by the `SELECT` statement. The `ORDER BY` clause is used to define a rule to determine which record is the first. `Expression_list` from `DISTINCT ON` must be included in the `ORDER BY` list.

For the task being discussed, it can be applied in the following way:

```
SELECT DISTINCT ON (car_id) advertisement_id,
    advertisement_date, car_id, seller_account_id
  FROM car_portal_app.advertisement
  ORDER BY car_id, advertisement_date;
```

Set returning functions

Functions in PostgreSQL can return not only single values but also relations. They are called set returning functions.

There is a quite typical task for every SQL developer: to generate a sequence of integers, each in a separate record. This sequence or relation can have many use cases. For example, suppose it is necessary to select data from the `car_portal` database to count the number of cars for each year of manufacture, from 2010 till 2015; and it is required to show zero for the years where no cars exist at all. The simple `SELECT` statement from the only table, `car`, cannot be used to implement that logic. It is not possible to see the records that are absent from the table data itself. That's why it would be useful if a table with the numbers from 2010 to 2015 existed. Then it could be outer-joined to the results of the query.

One could create that table in advance, but it is not a very good idea, because the number of records necessary in that table is not known in advance; and if one created a very big table, it would be just a waste of disk space in most cases.

There is a `generate_series` function called which serves exactly that purpose. It returns a set of integers with the given start and stop values. The query for the example would be as follows:

```
SELECT years.manufacture_year, count(car_id)
  FROM generate_series(2010, 2015) as
      years (manufacture_year)
    LEFT JOIN car_portal_app.car
      ON car.manufacture_year = years.manufacture_year
  GROUP BY years.manufacture_year
  ORDER BY 1;
manufacture_year | count
------------------+-------
            2010 |    11
            2011 |    12
            2012 |    12
            2013 |    21
            2014 |    16
            2015 |     0
(6 rows)
```

In the preceding query, the `generate_series` function returns six integers from 2010 to 2015. That set has an alias `t`. The table `car` is left-joined to the set of integers and then, all the years can be seen in the output result set.

It is possible to specify a step when calling `generate_series`:

```
SELECT * FROM generate_series(5, 11, 3);
generate_series
-----------------
               5
               8
              11
(3 rows)
```

The `generate_series` function can also return a set of timestamp values:

```
SELECT * FROM generate_series('2015-01-01'::date,
  '2015-01-31'::date, interval '7 days');
   generate_series
-----------------------
 2015-01-01 00:00:00-05
 2015-01-08 00:00:00-05
 2015-01-15 00:00:00-05
 2015-01-22 00:00:00-05
 2015-01-29 00:00:00-05
(5 rows)
```

There are a couple of other set-returning functions designed to work with arrays:

- `generate_subscripts`: This generates numbers that can be used to reference the elements in a given array for the given dimension(s). This function is useful for enumerating the elements of an array in an SQL statement.
- `unnest`: This transforms a given array into a set or rows where each record corresponds to an element of the array.

Set-returning functions are also called table functions.

Table functions can return sets of rows of a predefined type, like `generate_series` returns a set of `int` or `bigint` (depending on the type of input argument). Moreover, they can return a set of abstract type records. That allows a function to return different numbers of columns depending on their implementation. But SQL requires that the row structure of all input relations is defined so that the optimizer can parse the query and build the execution plan. That's why all table functions that return sets of records, when used in a query, must be followed by a definition of their row structure:

```
function_name [AS] alias (column_name column_type [, ...])
```

The output of several set-returning functions can be combined together as if they were joined on the position of each row. The ROWS FROM syntax is used for this, as follows:

```
ROWS FROM (function_call [,…]) [[AS] alias (column_name [,...])]
```

The preceding construct will return a relation. The number of rows is equal to the largest output of the functions. Each column corresponds to the respective function in the ROWS FROM clause. If a function returns fewer rows than other functions, the missing values will be set to NULL. For example:

```
SELECT foo.a, foo.b FROM
  ROWS FROM (
    generate_series(1,3), generate_series(1,7,2)
  ) AS foo(a, b);
a | b
---+---
 1 | 1
 2 | 3
 3 | 5
   | 7
(4 rows)
```

Lateral subqueries

Subqueries were discussed in the previous chapter. However, it is worth mentioning one specific pattern of using them in more detail.

It is very convenient to use subqueries in the Select-list. They are used in the SELECT statements, for example, to create calculated attributes when querying a table. Let's take the car portal database again. Suppose it is necessary to query the table car to retrieve information about the cars. For each car, it is required to assess its age by comparing it with the age of the other cars of the same model. Furthermore, it is required to query the number of cars of the same model.

These two additional fields can be generated by scalar subqueries, as follows:

```
SELECT car_id, manufacture_year,
    CASE WHEN manufacture_year <=
      (SELECT avg(manufacture_year)
        FROM car_portal_app.car
        WHERE car_model_id = c.car_model_id
      ) THEN 'old' ELSE 'new' END as age,
    (SELECT count(*) FROM car_portal_app.car
      WHERE car_model_id = c.car_model_id
    ) AS same_model_count
```

```
FROM car_portal_app.car c;
```

```
car_id | manufacture_year | age | same_model_count
--------+------------------+-----+------------------
     1 |             2008 | old |                3
     2 |             2014 | new |                6
     3 |             2014 | new |                2
  ...
(229 rows)
```

The power of those subqueries is that they can refer to the main table in their WHERE clause. That makes them easy. It is also very simple to add more columns in the query by adding other subqueries. On the other hand, there is a problem here: performance. The car table is scanned by the database server once for the main query, and then it is scanned two times again for each retrieved row, that is, for the age column and for the same_model_count column.

It is possible, of course, to calculate those aggregates once for each car model independently and then join the results with the car table:

```
SELECT car_id, manufacture_year,
    CASE WHEN manufacture_year <= avg_year
      THEN 'old' ELSE 'new' END as age,
    same_model_count
  FROM car_portal_app.car
    INNER JOIN (
      SELECT car_model_id,
          avg(manufacture_year) avg_year,
          count(*) same_model_count
        FROM car_portal_app.car
        GROUP BY car_model_id
    ) subq USING (car_model_id);
```

```
car_id | manufacture_year | age | same_model_count
--------+------------------+-----+------------------
     1 |             2008 | old |                3
     2 |             2014 | new |                6
     3 |             2014 | new |                2
  ...
(229 rows)
```

The result is the same and the query is 20 times faster. However, this query is only good for retrieving many rows from the database. If it is required to get the information about only one car, the first query will be faster.

One can see that the first query could perform better if it was possible to select two columns in the subquery in the Select-list. But that is not possible. Scalar queries can return only one column.

There is yet another way of using subqueries. It combines the advantages of the subqueries in the Select-list, which can refer to the main table, with the subqueries in the FROM clause, which can return multiple columns. This can be done via lateral subqueries that were added in PostgreSQL version 9.3. Putting the LATERAL keyword before the subquery code in the FROM clause makes it possible to reference any preceding items of the FROM clause from the subquery.

The query would be as follows:

```
SELECT car_id, manufacture_year,
       CASE WHEN manufacture_year <= avg_year
         THEN 'old' ELSE 'new' END as age,
       same_model_count
    FROM car_portal_app.car c,
      LATERAL (SELECT avg(manufacture_year) avg_year,
          count(*) same_model_count
        FROM car_portal_app.car
        WHERE car_model_id = c.car_model_id) subq;
car_id | manufacture_year | age | same_model_count
--------+------------------+-----+------------------
     1 |             2008 | old |                3
     2 |             2014 | new |                6
     3 |             2014 | new |                2
...

(229 rows)
```

This query is approximately two times faster than the first one, and is the best one for retrieving only one row from the car table.

When it comes to set-returning functions, it is not necessary to use the LATERAL keyword. All functions that are mentioned in the FROM clause can use the output of any preceding functions or subqueries:

```
SELECT a, b FROM
  generate_series(1,3) AS a,
  generate_series(a, a+2) AS b;
a | b
---+---
 1 | 1
 1 | 2
 1 | 3
 2 | 2
 2 | 3
 2 | 4
 3 | 3
 3 | 4
 3 | 5
(9 rows)
```

In the preceding query, the first function that has the alias a returns three rows. For each of those three rows, the second function is called, returning three more rows.

Advanced usage of aggregating functions

There are several aggregating functions that are executed in a special way.

The first group of such aggregating functions are called ordered-set aggregates. They take into account not just the values of the argument expressions but also their order. They are related to statistics and calculate percentile values.

Percentile is the value of a group in which the given percentage of other values is less than that of the group. For example, if a value is at the 95th percentile, it means it is higher than 95 percent of the other values. In PostgreSQL, one can calculate a continuous or discrete percentile. A discrete percentile is one of the actual values of a group, while a continuous percentile is an interpolated value between two actual values. It is possible to calculate the percentile for a given fraction, or several percentile values for a given array of fractions.

For example, the query regarding the distribution of the number of advertisements per car:

```
SELECT percentile_disc(ARRAY[0.25, 0.5, 0.75])
    WITHIN GROUP (ORDER BY cnt)
  FROM (
    SELECT count(*) cnt
      FROM car_portal_app.advertisement
      GROUP BY car_id) subq;
```

```
percentile_disc
-----------------
 {2,3,5}
(1 row)
```

The result means that there are, at the most, two advertisements for 25 percent of the cars, three advertisements for 50 percent of the cars, and five advertisements for 75 percent of the cars in the database.

The syntax of the ordered-set aggregating functions differs from the normal aggregates and uses a special construct, WITHIN GROUP (ORDER BY expression). The expression here is actually an argument of a function. Here, not just the order of the rows but the values of the expressions as well affect the result of the function. In contrast to the ORDER BY clause of the SELECT query, only one expression is possible here, and no references to the output column numbers are allowed.

Another ordered-set aggregating function is mode. It returns the most frequently appearing value of the group. If two values appear the same number of times, then the first of them will be returned.

For example, the following query gets the ID of the most frequent car model in the database:

```
SELECT mode() WITHIN GROUP (ORDER BY car_model_id)
FROM car_portal_app.car;
```

```
mode
------
    64
(1 row)
```

To get the same result without this function will require self-join or ordering and limiting the result. Both are more expensive operations.

Another group of aggregates that use the same syntax are the hypothetical-set aggregating functions. They are `rank`, `dense_rank`, `percent_rank`, and `cume_dist`. There are window functions with the same names. Window functions take no argument and they return the result for the current row. Aggregate functions have no current row because they are evaluated for a group of rows. But they take an argument: the value for the hypothetical current row.

For example, the aggregate function `rank` returns the rank of a given value in the ordered set as if that value existed in the set:

```
SELECT rank(2) WITHIN GROUP (ORDER BY a)
  FROM generate_series(1,10,3) a;
rank

------

    2

(1 row)
```

In the preceding query, the value 2 does not exist in the output of `generate_series` (it returns `1..4..7..10`). But if it existed, it would take the second position in the output.

Another topic worth mentioning about aggregating functions is the `FILTER` clause.

The `FILTER` clause filters the rows that are passed to the particular aggregating function based on a given condition. For example, suppose it is required to count the number of cars in the database for each car model separately, for each number of doors. If one groups the records by these two fields, the result will be correct but not very convenient to use in reporting:

```
SELECT car_model_id, number_of_doors, count(*)
  FROM car_portal_app.car
  GROUP BY car_model_id, number_of_doors;
car_model_id | number_of_doors | count
--------------+-----------------+-------
          47 |               4 |     1
          42 |               3 |     2
          76 |               5 |     1
          52 |               5 |     2

...
```

The FILTER clause makes the output much clearer:

```
SELECT car_model_id,
    count(*) FILTER (WHERE number_of_doors = 2) doors2,
    count(*) FILTER (WHERE number_of_doors = 3) doors3,
    count(*) FILTER (WHERE number_of_doors = 4) doors4,
    count(*) FILTER (WHERE number_of_doors = 5) doors5
  FROM car_portal_app.car
  GROUP BY car_model_id;
car_model_id | doors2 | doors3 | doors4 | doors5
-------------+--------+--------+--------+--------
          43 |      0 |      0 |      0 |      2
           8 |      0 |      0 |      1 |      0
          11 |      0 |      2 |      1 |      0
          80 |      0 |      1 |      0 |      0
...
```

Note that the cars with a number of doors other that is than from 2 to 5 will not be counted by the query.

The same result can be achieved by calling functions, as follows:

```
count(CASE WHEN number_of_doors = 2 THEN 1 END) doors2
```

However, the FILTER clause method is easier and shorter.

Transaction isolation and multiversion concurrency control

There is a fundamental concept is called transaction in relational databases. Transaction is a unit of data change. PostgreSQL implements a set of principles related to transaction processing, which is called ACID:

- **Atomicity**: Every transaction can be fixed (saved or committed) only as a whole. If one part of a transaction fails, the whole transaction is aborted and no changes are saved at all.

- **Consistency**: All data integrity constraints are checked and all triggers are processed before a transaction is fixed. If any constraint is violated, then the transaction cannot be fixed.

- **Isolation**: A database system manages concurrent access to the data objects by parallel transactions in a way that guarantees that the results of their execution is the same as if they were executed serially, one after the other.

- **Durability**: If a transaction is fixed, the changes it has made to the data are written to the non-volatile memory (disk). So, even if the system crashes or is powered-off immediately after that, the result of the transaction will persist in the database.

Simply speaking, transactions are a mechanism that allows the database user to save or discard any changes he has made in the data. To start a transaction, one should use the SQL command BEGIN and COMMIT to save the result of one's work. To abort a transaction without saving, the user can use ROLLBACK. A transaction can include only one statement or it can include many of them. The size of the transaction has no defined limit, they can be very big. If no transaction is started explicitly, PostgreSQL will automatically run each single SQL statement within its own transaction. For example, if an UPDATE statement has updated several rows and then fails to update another one, then all the rows that have been updated already will be returned back to their original versions as if the UPDATE was never executed.

PostgreSQL implements a special mechanism that maintains data consistency and transaction isolation. It is called **multiversion concurrency control** (**MVCC**). In short, it means that each transaction works with a consistent snapshot of data as it was some time ago, without taking into account the changes made by other transactions that are not finished yet.

When it comes to accessing the same data object by several concurrent transactions, the way they interact with each other is determined by the level of transaction isolation. There are four levels of transaction isolation defined in SQL standard: Read uncommitted, Read committed, Repeatable read, and Serializable. The difference between them is the phenomena that they prevent from appearing.
Those phenomena are:

- **Dirty read**: A transaction can read data that was written by another transaction, which is not committed yet.

- **Nonrepeatable read**: When rereading data, a transaction can find that the data has been modified by another transaction that has just committed. The same query executed twice can return different values for the same rows.

- **Phantom read**: This is similar to nonrepeatable read, but it is related to new data, created by another transaction. The same query executed twice can return different numbers of records.

The following table shows which phenomena are not allowed by the SQL standard at different isolation levels:

Isolation level	Dirty read	Nonrepeatable read	Phantom read
Read uncommitted			
Read committed	Not allowed		
Repeatable read	Not allowed	Not allowed	
Serializable	Not allowed	Not allowed	Not allowed

PostgreSQL does not explicitly support the Read uncommitted isolation level. Furthermore, Phantom reads do not actually appear at the Repeatable read isolation level, which makes it quite similar to Serializable. The actual difference between Repeatable read and Serializable is that Serializable guarantees that the result of the concurrent transactions will be exactly the same as if they were executed serially one after another, which is not always true for Repeatable read.

The isolation level for the transaction can be set when the transaction is started. This command: BEGIN ISOLATION LEVEL REPEATABLE READ; will start a transaction with a Repeatable read isolation level. The default isolation level in PostgreSQL is Read committed.

Transactions will block each other when they try to access the same data, and the result of the statement will depend on whether the concurrent transaction commits or aborts. For example, suppose there are two transactions, A and B. Transaction A has updated a record, increasing the value of a field by one. Transaction B tries to do the same with the same record. But the result of the update of transaction B will depend on what transaction A will do further. If transaction A commits, then B should increment a new value. If transaction A aborts, then B should use the old value. So transaction B will wait until transaction A is finished.

It is possible that this blocking will lead to a situation of deadlock. It can happen if the transaction A, in turn, tries to update another record which has been previously updated by transaction B. In that case, A will wait for B while it is waiting for A. PostgreSQL detects deadlocks and automatically terminates the transactions causing those situations.

Another more complicated issue related to the concurrent access is serialization errors. Again, suppose there are two transactions that run at the Serializable isolation level. Transaction A updates a record, increasing the value of a field by 1. Transaction B tries to do the same with the same record. Again, it will be blocked until transaction A is finished. If A is aborted, then B will continue. But if A is committed, it will not allow B to continue. That is because both A and B work with the snapshots of data at the moment of the start of the transactions. Both of them will update a field from its original state and set it to the same new value. But the result of these operations will be different from what could have been if the transactions were executed one after another. In this situation, transaction B will fail with an error "could not serialize access".

To block transactions and monitor serialization anomalies, PostgreSQL uses the mechanism of locks. Locks are special objects in the database that are obtained by transactions and associated with data objects: rows or tables. A data object cannot be locked by more than one transaction. So, when a transaction wants to update a record, it will first lock it. If another transaction tries to update the same record, it will also try to lock it but since it is already locked, the transaction will wait. Locks are created automatically by the database when it processes SQL statements and released when the transaction is finished.

Database applications can manage concurrent access to shared resources by obtaining locks explicitly. To lock a record or several records, an application should use the SELECT statement with the locking clause. The locking clause, that is, FOR UPDATE is added to the very end of the statement. This will not only return the records as any other SELECT statement, but also make PostgreSQL lock those records against concurrent updates or deletions until the current transaction is finished:

```
SELECT * FROM car_portal_app.car WHERE car_model_id = 5 FOR UPDATE;
```

This will lock all the records in the table car that satisfy the condition. If another instance of the application tries to execute the same query, it will be blocked until the transaction is committed or aborted. If an application does not want to wait, the locking clause can be supplemented by the NOWAIT keyword. In that case, if a lock cannot be acquired, then the statement will immediately report an error.

It is also possible to explicitly create table-level locks by using the SQL LOCK command.

The third option is using the so-called advisory locks. They are not related to a data object, but are associated with a certain key value specified by the application. They are created and released by the application, and can be used when, for some reason, the default MVCC model is not suitable to manage concurrent access.

Detailed information about concurrency control is available in the documentation at `http://www.postgresql.org/docs/current/static/mvcc.html`.

Summary

This chapter described the advanced SQL concepts and features like common table expressions and window functions. These features allow implementing a logic that would not be possible without them, that is, recursive queries.

The other techniques explained here, like the DISTINCT ON clause, the FILTER clause or lateral subqueries, are not that irreplaceable. But they can help in making a query smaller, easier, and faster.

SQL can be used to implement a very complicated logic. However, in difficult cases, the queries can become overcomplicated and very hard to maintain. Moreover, sometimes it is not possible to do some things in pure SQL. In those cases, one needs a procedural language to implement an algorithm. The next chapter will introduce one of them: PL/pgSQL.

7

Server-Side Programming with PL/pgSQL

The ability to write functions in PostgreSQL is an amazing feature. One can perform any task within the scope of the database server. These tasks might be related directly to data manipulation such as data aggregation and auditing, or can be used to perform miscellaneous services such as statistics collection, monitoring, system information acquisition, and job scheduling.

In this chapter, our focus is the PL/pgSQL language. PL/pgSQL can be considered as the default PostgreSQL, which is a full-fledged procedural language. As mentioned earlier in *Chapter 4*, *PostgreSQL Advanced Building Blocks*, PL/pgSQL is installed by default in PostgreSQL.

Introduction

PL/pgSQL has been influenced by the PL/SQL language, which is the Oracle stored procedural language. PL/pgSQL is a complete procedural language with rich control structures and full integration with the PostgreSQL trigger, index, rule, user defined data type, and operator objects.

There are several advantages of using PL/pgSQL; they are as follows:

- It is easy to use and learn
- It has very good support and documentation
- It has very flexible result data types, and it supports polymorphism
- It can return scalar values and sets using different return methods

SQL language and PL/pgSQL – a comparison

As shown in *Chapter 4, PostgreSQL Advanced Building Blocks*, one can write functions in C, SQL, and PL/pgSQL. There are some pros and cons of each approach. One can think of an SQL function as a wrapper around a parameterized SELECT statement. SQL functions can be in-lined into the calling subquery leading to a better performance. Also, since the SQL function execution plan is not cashed as in PL/pgSQL, it often behaves better than PL/pgSQL. Moreover, caching in PL/pgSQL can have some surprisingly bad side effects such as caching of sensitive time stamp values, as shown in the documentation that can be found at http://www.postgresql.org/docs/current/interactive/plpgsql-implementation.html.

Finally, with the introduction of CTE, recursive CTE, window functions, and LATERAL JOINS, one can perform complex logic using only SQL.

> If the function logic can be implemented in SQL, use an SQL function instead of PL/PGSQL.

The PL/pgSQL function execution plan is cached; caching the plan can help in reducing the execution time, but it can also hurt it in case the plan is not optimal for the provided function parameters.

From a functionality point of view, PL/pgSQL is much more powerful than SQL for writing functions. PL/pgSQL supports several features that the SQL functions cannot support, including the following:

- It provides the ability to raise exceptions as well as to raise messages at different levels such as notice and debug.
- It supports constructing of dynamic SQL using the EXECUTE command.
- It provides EXCEPTION handling.
- It has a complete set of assignment, control, and loop statements.
- It supports cursors.
- It is fully integrated with the PostgreSQL trigger system. SQL functions cannot be used with triggers.

PostgreSQL function parameters

In Chapter 4, *PostgreSQL Advanced Building Blocks*, we discussed the function categories *immutable*, *stable*, and *volatile*. In this section, we will continue with other function options. These options are not PL/pgSQL language-specific.

Function authorization-related parameters

The first parameters are related to security, and can have one of the following values:

* SECURITY DEFINER
* SECURITY INVOKER

The default value for this option is SECURITY INVOKER, which indicates that the function will be executed with the privileges of the user who calls it. The SECURITY DEFINER functions will be executed using the privileges of the user who created it. For the SECURITY INVOKER functions, the user must have the permissions to execute the CRUD operations in the function; otherwise, the function will raise an error. The SECURITY INVOKER functions are very useful in defining triggers, or for promoting the user to perform tasks only supported by the function.

To test these security parameters, let us create two dummy functions, and execute them in different sessions, as follows:

```
psql -U postgres -h localhost -d car_portal

car_portal=# CREATE FUNCTION test_security_definer () RETURNS  TEXT AS $$
SELECT 'current_user :'||current_user || ' session_user: ' || session_
user; $$ LANGUAGE SQL SECURITY DEFINER;

CREATE FUNCTION

car_portal=# CREATE FUNCTION test_security_invoker () RETURNS  TEXT AS $$
SELECT 'current_user :'||current_user || ' session_user: ' || session_
user; $$ LANGUAGE SQL SECURITY INVOKER;

CREATE FUNCTION

car_portal=# SELECT test_security_definer();

test_security_definer

-------------------------------------------------

current_user :postgres session_user: postgres

(1 row)
```

```
car_portal=# SELECT test_security_invoker();
test_security_invoker
-----------------------------------------------
current_user :postgres session_user: postgres
(1 row)
car_portal=# \q
$ psql -U car_portal_app -h localhost -d car_portal
car_portal=> SELECT test_security_invoker();
test_security_invoker
-------------------------------------------------------------
current_user :car_portal_app session_user: car_portal_app
(1 row)

car_portal=> SELECT test_security_definer();
test_security_definer
-----------------------------------------------------
current_user :postgres session_user: car_portal_app
(1 row)
```

The two functions `test_security_definer` and `test_security_invoker` are identical except for the security parameter. When the two functions are executed by a postgres user, the result of the two functions is identical to `current_user` `:postgres session_user: postgres`. This is simply because the one who created the function and the one who called it is the same user.

When the user `car_portal_app` executes the two preceding functions, the result of the `test_security_definer` function is `current_user :postgres session_user: car_portal_app`. In this case, the `session_user` is `car_portal_app`, since it has started the session using a psql client. However, the `current_user` who executes the SELECT statement SELECT `'current_user :'||current_user || ' session_user: ' || session_user;` is postgres.

Function planner-related parameters

The following three parameters are used by the planner to determine the cost of executing the function, the number of rows that are expected to be returned, and whether the function pushes down when evaluating predicates. These parameters are:

- **Leakproof**: Leakproof means that the function has no side effects. It does not reveal any information about its argument. For example, it does not throw error messages about its argument. This parameter affects the views with the `security_barrier` parameter.

- **Cost**: It declares the execution cost per row; the default value for the C language function is `1`, and for PL/pgSQL it is `100`. The cost is used by the planner to determine the best execution plan.

- **Rows**: The estimated number of returned rows by the function if the function is a returning set. The default value is `1000`.

To understand the effect of the rows, let us consider the following example:

```
CREATE OR REPLACE FUNCTION a() RETURNS SET OF INTEGER AS $$
   SELECT 1;
$$
LANGUAGE SQL;

EXPLAIN SELECT * FROM a() CROSS JOIN (Values(1),(2),(3)) as foo;
                            QUERY PLAN
---------------------------------------------------------------------
 Nested Loop   (cost=0.25..47.80 rows=3000 width=8)
    -> Function Scan on a   (cost=0.25..10.25 rows=1000 width=4)
    -> Materialize   (cost=0.00..0.05 rows=3 width=4)
          -> Values Scan on "*VALUES*"   (cost=0.00..0.04 rows=3 width=4)
(4 rows)
```

The `SQL` function return type is `SET OF INTEGER`, which means that the planner expected more than one row to be returned from the function. Since the `ROWS` parameter is not specified, the planner uses the default value which is `1000`. Finally, due to `CROSS JOIN`, the total estimated number of rows is `3000`, which is calculated as *3 * 1000*.

In the preceding example, a wrong estimation is not critical. However, in a real life example, where one might have several joins, the error of rows estimation will be propagated and amplified leading to bad execution plans.

The COST function parameter determines when the function will be executed such as:

- It determines the function execution order
- It determines if the function call can be pushed down

The following example shows how the execution order for functions is affected by the function cost. Let us assume we have two functions, as follows:

```
CREATE OR REPLACE FUNCTION slow_function (anyelement) RETURNS BOOLEAN AS
$$
BEGIN
  RAISE NOTICE 'Slow function %', $1;
  RETURN TRUE;
END;
$$
LANGUAGE PLPGSQL COST 10000;
```

```
CREATE OR REPLACE FUNCTION fast_function (anyelement) RETURNS BOOLEAN AS
$$
BEGIN
  RAISE NOTICE 'Fast function %', $1;
  RETURN TRUE;
END;
$$
LANGUAGE PLPGSQL COST 0.0001;
```

The fast_function and the slow_function are identical except for the cost parameter:

```
EXPLAIN SELECT * FROM pg_language WHERE lanname ILIKE '%sql%' AND slow_
function(lanname) AND fast_function(lanname);
                                QUERY PLAN
-------------------------------------------------------------------------
----------------------
```

```
Seq Scan on pg_language   (cost=0.00..101.05 rows=1 width=114)

    Filter: (fast_function(lanname) AND (lanname ~~* '%sql%'::text) AND
slow_function(lanname))

(2 rows)
```

```
EXPLAIN SELECT * FROM pg_language WHERE fast_function(lanname) AND slow_
function(lanname) AND lanname ILIKE '%sql%';
                                        QUERY PLAN
----------------------------------------------------------------------
----------------------
Seq Scan on pg_language   (cost=0.00..101.05 rows=1 width=114)

    Filter: (fast_function(lanname) AND (lanname ~~* '%sql%'::text) AND
slow_function(lanname))

(2 rows)
```

The preceding two SQL statements are identical, but the predicates are shuffled. Both statements give the same execution plan. Notice how the predicates are arranged in the filter execution plane node. The `fast_function` is evaluated first followed by the `ILIKE` operator, and finally, the `slow_function` is pushed.

When executing one of the preceding statements, one will get the following result:

```
SELECT * FROM pg_language WHERE lanname ILIKE '%sql%' AND slow_
function(lanname)AND fast_function(lanname);
NOTICE:  Fast function internal
NOTICE:  Fast function c
NOTICE:  Fast function sql
NOTICE:  Slow function sql
NOTICE:  Fast function plpgsql
NOTICE:  Slow function plpgsql
lanname | lanowner | lanispl | lanpltrusted | lanplcallfoid | laninline |
lanvalidator | lanacl

---------+----------+---------+--------------+---------------+-----------
+--------------+--------
sql     |       10 | f       | t            |               |         0 |
         0
|       2248 |
plpgsql |       10 | t       | t            |               |     11751 |
     11752
|      11753 |
(2 rows)
```

Notice that `fast_function` was executed four times, and `slow_function` was executed only twice. This behavior is known as short-circuit evaluation. `slow_function` is executed only when `fast_function` and the `ILIKE` operator have returned `true`.

In PostgreSQL, the `ILIKE operator` is equivalent to the `~~*` operator, and `LIKE` is equivalent to the `~~` operator.

As discussed in *Chapter 4*, *PostgreSQL Advanced Building Blocks*, views can be used to implement authorization, and they can be used to hide data from some users. The function cost parameter can be exploited in the earlier versions of postgres to crack views; however, this has been improved by the introduction of the `LEAKPROOF` and `SECURITY_BARRIER` flags.

To be able to exploit the function cost parameter to get data from a view, several conditions should be met, some of which are as follows:

- The function cost should be very low
- The function should be marked as `LEAKPROOF`. Note that only super users are allowed to mark functions as `LEAKPROOF`.
- The view security barrier flag should not be set.
- The function should be executed and not ignored due to short-circuit evaluation.

Meeting all these conditions is very difficult; the following code shows a hypothetical example of exploiting views:

```
CREATE OR REPLACE VIEW pg_sql_pl AS
SELECT lanname FROM pg_language WHERE lanname ILIKE '%sql%';
-- Only super user can do that
ALTER FUNCTION fast_function(anyelement)  LEAKPROOF;
SELECT * FROM pg_sql_pl WHERE fast_function(lanname);
NOTICE:  Fast function internal
NOTICE:  Fast function c
NOTICE:  Fast function sql
NOTICE:  Fast function plpgsql
lanname
--------
```

```
sql

plpgsql

(2 rows)
```

In the preceding example, the view itself should not show c and `internal`. By exploiting the function cost, the function was executed before executing the filter `lanname ILIKE '%sql%';` exposing information that will never be shown by the view.

 Since only superusers are allowed to mark a function as leak proof, exploiting the function cost in the newer versions of postgres is not possible.

Function configuration-related parameters

Function configuration-related parameters are the setting parameters. These parameters can be used to determine the resources such as the amount of memory required to perform an operation—work_mem—, or they can be used to determine the execution behavior, such as disabling a sequential scan or nested loop joins. Certainly, only parameters which have the context of the user can be used.

The SET clause causes the specified setting parameter to be set with a specified value when the function is entered; the same setting parameter value is reset back to its default value when the function exits. The parameter configuration setting can be set explicitly for the whole function, can be overwritten locally inside the function, and can inherit the value from the session setting using the FROM CURRENT clause.

These configuration parameters are often used to tweak the function performance in the case of limited resources, legacy code, bad design, wrong statistics estimation, and so on. For example, let us assume that a function behaves badly due to database normalization. In this case, refactoring the database might be expensive to perform. To solve this problem, one could alter the execution plan by enabling or disabling some settings, as show in the following example:

```
car_portal=# SET enable_seqscan TO OFF;

SET

car_portal=# CREATE OR REPLACE FUNCTION configuration_test () RETURNS
VOID AS

$$

BEGIN
```

```
RAISE NOTICE 'Current session enable_seqscan value: %', (SELECT setting
FROM pg_settings WHERE name ='enable_seqscan')::text;
RAISE NOTICE 'Function work_mem: %', (SELECT setting FROM pg_settings
WHERE name ='work_mem')::text;


---
---SQL statement here will use index scan when possible
---
SET LOCAL enable_seqscan TO TRUE;
RAISE NOTICE 'Override session enable_seqscan value: %', (SELECT setting
FROM pg_settings WHERE name ='enable_seqscan')::text;
---
---SQL statement here will use index scan when possible
---
END;
$$
LANGUAGE PLPGSQL
SET enable_seqscan FROM current
SET work_mem = '10MB';
CREATE FUNCTION
car_portal=# SELECT configuration_test () ;
NOTICE:  Current session enable_seqscan value: off
NOTICE:  Function work_mem: 10240
NOTICE:  Override session enable_seqscan value: on
-[ RECORD 1 ]------+-
configuration_test |
```

The PostgreSQL PL/pgSQL control statements

The PostgreSQL control structure is an essential part of the PL/pgSQL language; it enables developers to code very complex business logic inside PostgreSQL.

Declaration statements

The general syntax of a variable declaration is as follows:

```
name [ CONSTANT ] type [ COLLATE collation_name ] [ NOT NULL ] [ {
DEFAULT | := | = } expression ];
```

Let's see what the keywords mean:

- `name`: The name should follow the naming rules discussed in *Chapter 3, PostgreSQL Basic Building Blocks*. For example, the name should not start with an integer.

- `CONSTANT`: The variable cannot be assigned another value after the initialization. This is useful in defining constant variables such as Pi.

- `type`: The type of variable can be simple such as integer, user defined data type, pseudo type, record, and so on. Since a type is created implicitly on creating a table, one can use this type to declare a variable.

> In PostgreSQL, the following two declarations are equivalent; however, the second declaration is more portable with Oracle.
> ```
> Myrow tablename ;
> Myrow tablename%ROWTYPE;
> ```

- `NOT NULL`: Not null causes a runtime error to be raised if the variable is assigned to null. Not null variables must be initialized.

- `DEFAULT`: Causes the initialization of the variable to be delayed until the block is entered. This is useful in defining a timestamp variable to indicate when the function is called but not the function pre-compilation time.

- Expression is a combination of one or more explicit values, operators, and functions that can be evaluated to another value.

The PostgreSQL PL/pgSQL function body is composed of nested blocks with an optional declaration section and a label. Variables are declared in the declare section of the block, shown as follows:

```
[<<label>>]
[ DECLARE
declarations]
BEGIN
statements
END [label];
```

The BEGIN and END keywords are not used in this context to control transactional behavior, but only for grouping. The declaration section is used for declaring variables, and the label is used to give a name for the block as well as to give fully qualified names to the variables. Finally, in each PL/pgSQL function, there is a hidden block labeled with the function name that contains predefined variables such as FOUND. To understand the function block, let us take a look at the following code, which defines the factorial function in a recursive manner:

```
CREATE OR REPLACE FUNCTION factorial(INTEGER ) RETURNS INTEGER AS $$
BEGIN
  IF $1 IS NULL OR $1 < 0 THEN
    RAISE NOTICE 'Invalid Number';
    RETURN NULL;
  ELSIF $1 = 1 THEN
    RETURN 1;
  ELSE
    RETURN factorial($1 - 1) * $1;
  END IF;
END;
$$ LANGUAGE 'plpgsql'
```

The block defines the variable scope; in our example, the scope of the argument variable $1 is the whole function. Also, as shown in the example, there is no declaration section.

To understand the scope between different code blocks, let us write the factorial function in a slightly different manner, which is as follows:

```
CREATE OR REPLACE FUNCTION factorial(INTEGER ) RETURNS INTEGER AS $$
DECLARE
  fact ALIAS FOR $1;
BEGIN
  IF fact IS NULL OR fact < 0 THEN
    RAISE NOTICE 'Invalid Number';
    RETURN NULL;
  ELSIF fact = 1 THEN
    RETURN 1;
  END IF;
```

```
DECLARE

   result INT;

BEGIN

   result = factorial(fact - 1) * fact;

   RETURN result;

END;

END;

$$ LANGUAGE 'plpgsql'
```

The preceding function is composed of two blocks: the variable `fact` is an alias for the first argument. In the sub-block, the `result` variable is declared with a type integer. Since the `fact` variable is defined in the upper block, it can also be used in the sub-block. The `result` variable can be used only in the sub-block.

Assignment statements

The assignment operators `:=` and `=` are used to assign an expression to a variable, as follows:

```
variable { := | = } expression;
```

For the variable names, one should choose names that do not conflict with the column names. This is important when writing parameterized SQL statements.

The `=` operator is supported not only for PostgreSQL version 9.4 but also for the previous versions. Unfortunately, the documentations for the previous versions does not mention it. Moreover, since the `=` operator is used in SQL for equality comparison, it is preferable to use the `:=` operator to reduce confusion.

In certain contexts, it is important to pick up the right assignment operator:

- When assigning a default value, one should use the `=` operator, as indicated in the documentation at `http://www.postgresql.org/docs/current/interactive/sql-createfunction.html`.

- For named notations in a function call, one should use the `:=` operator, as shown in the documentation at `http://www.postgresql.org/docs/current/interactive/sql-syntax-calling-funcs.html#SQL-SYNTAX-CALLING-FUNCS-NAMED`.

The following example shows a case when one cannot use = and =: interchangeably:

```
CREATE OR REPLACE FUNCTION cast_numeric_to_int (numeric_value
numeric, round boolean = TRUE /*correct use of "=". Using ":="
will raise a syntax error */)
RETURNS INT AS
$$
BEGIN
RETURN (CASE
          WHEN round = TRUE  THEN  CAST (numeric_value AS INTEGER)
          WHEN numeric_value>= 0 THEN CAST (numeric_value -.5 AS INTEGER)
          WHEN numeric_value< 0 THEN CAST (numeric_value +.5 AS INTEGER)
          ELSE NULL
       END);
END;
$$ LANGUAGE plpgsql;
car_portal=# SELECT cast_numeric_to_int(2.3, round:= true /*correct use
of :=*/);
cast_numeric_to_int
--------------------
                  2
(1 row)


car_portal=# SELECT cast_numeric_to_int(2.3, round= true );
ERROR:  column "round" does not exist
LINE 1: SELECT cast_numeric_to_int(2.3, round= true );
```

The assignment expression can be a single atomic value such as pi = 3.14, or it can be a row:

```
DO $$
DECLARE
  test record;
BEGIN
  test =: ROW (1,'hello', 3.14);
  RAISE notice '%', test;
END;
$$
```

Finally, it can be a result of the evaluation of the SELECT statement, as shown in the following example. Note that the SELECT statement should not return a set:

```
car_portal=# DO $$
DECLARE
number_of_accounts INT:=0;
BEGIN
number_of_accounts:= (SELECT COUNT(*) FROM car_portal_app.account)::INT;
RAISE NOTICE 'number_of accounts: %', number_of_accounts;
END;$$
LANGUAGE plpgSQL;
NOTICE:   number_of accounts: 1
DO
```

There are other techniques for assigning values to the variables from a query that returns a single row:

```
SELECT select_expressions INTO [STRICT] targets FROM ...;
INSERT ... RETURNING expressions INTO [STRICT] targets;
UPDATE ... RETURNING expressions INTO [STRICT] targets;
DELETE ... RETURNING expressions INTO [STRICT] targets;
```

Often, the expressions are column names, while the targets are variable names. In the case of select into, the target can be of the type record.

The query INSERT ... RETURNING is often used to return the default value of a certain column; this can be used to define the ID of a primary key using the SERIAL and BIGSERIAL data types, which is shown as follows:

```
CREATE TABLE test (
  id SERIAL PRIMARY KEY,
  name TEXT NOT NULL
);


DO $$
DECLARE
  auto_generated_id INT;
BEGIN
  INSERT INTO test(name) VALUES ('Hello World') RETURNING id INTO
  auto_generated_id;
```

```
      RAISE NOTICE 'The primary key is: %', auto_generated_id;
END
$$;
--- the result of executing the above
--NOTICE:  The primary key is: 1
--DO
```

 One could get the default value when inserting a row in plain SQL using CTE, as follows:
```
WITH get_id AS (
    INSERT INTO test(name) VALUES ('Hello World')
    RETURNING id
) SELECT * FROM get_id;
```

Finally, one could use qualified names to perform assignment; in trigger functions, one could use NEW and OLD to manipulate the values of these records.

Conditional statements

PostgreSQL supports the IF and CASE statements, which allow a conditional execution based on a certain condition. PostgreSQL supports the IF statement construct, as follows:

```
IF boolean_expression THEN statement [statement]...
  [ELSIF boolean_expression THEN statement [statement]...]
    [ELSIF boolean_expression THEN statement [statement]...]...
  [ELSE statement [statement]...] END IF;
```

The case statement comes in two forms, as follows:

```
CASE search-expression
    WHEN expression [, expression [ ... ]] THEN
statements
[ WHEN expression [, expression [ ... ]] THEN
statements
    ... ]
[ ELSE
statements ]
END CASE;
```

```
CASE

    WHEN boolean-expression THEN

statements

[ WHENboolean-expression THEN

statements

    ... ]

[ ELSE

statements ]

END CASE;
```

To understand the IF statement, let us assume that we would like to convert the advertisement rank to text, as follows:

```
CREATE OR REPLACE FUNCTION cast_rank_to_text (rank int) RETURNS TEXT AS
$$
DECLARE
  rank ALIAS FOR $1;
  rank_result TEXT;
BEGIN
  IF rank = 5 THEN
    rank_result = 'Excellent';
  ELSIF rank = 4 THEN
    rank_result = 'Very Good';
  ELSIF rank = 3 THEN
    rank_result = 'Good';
  ELSIF rank = 2 THEN
    rank_result ='Fair';
  ELSIF rank = 1 THEN
    rank_result ='Poor';
  ELSE
    rank_result ='No such rank';
  END IF;
  RETURN rank_result;
END;
$$
Language plpgsql;
```

```
--- to test the function
SELECT n,cast_rank_to_text(n) FROM generate_series(1,5) as foo(n);
```

When any branch of the IF statement is executed due to the IF condition being met, then the execution control returns to the first statement after END IF, assuming the RETURN statement is not executed inside this branch. If none of the conditions are met for IF or ELSIF, then the ELSE branch will be executed. Also note that one could nest all the control structures; so, one can have an IF statement inside another one.

The following code snippet implements the preceding function using the CASE statement:

```
CREATE OR REPLACE FUNCTION cast_rank_to_text (rank int) RETURNS TEXT AS
$$
DECLARE
   rank ALIAS FOR $1;
   rank_result TEXT;
BEGIN
   CASE rank
   WHEN 5 THEN rank_result = 'Excellent';
   WHEN 4 THEN rank_result = 'Very Good';
   WHEN 3 THEN rank_result = 'Good';
   WHEN 2 THEN rank_result ='Fair';
   WHEN 1 THEN rank_result ='Poor';
   ELSE rank_result ='No such rank';
   END CASE;
   RETURN rank_result;
END;
$$
Language plpgsql;
```

In the CASE statement, if any branch of the case matches the selector, the execution of the case is terminated and the execution control goes to the first statement after CASE. Moreover, in the previous form of CASE, one cannot use it to match NULL values, since NULL equality is NULL. To overcome this limitation, one should specify the matching condition explicitly using the second form of CASE statement, as follows:

```
CREATE OR REPLACE FUNCTION cast_rank_to_text (rank int) RETURNS TEXT AS
$$
DECLARE
```

```
    rank ALIAS FOR $1;
    rank_result TEXT;
BEGIN
  CASE
  WHEN rank=5 THEN rank_result = 'Excellent';
  WHEN rank=4 THEN rank_result = 'Very Good';
  WHEN rank=3 THEN rank_result = 'Good';
  WHEN rank=2 THEN rank_result ='Fair';
  WHEN rank=1 THEN rank_result ='Poor';
  WHEN rank IS NULL THEN RAISE EXCEPTION 'Rank should be not NULL';
  ELSE rank_result ='No such rank';
  END CASE;
  RETURN rank_result;
END;
$$
Language plpgsql;
--- to test
SELECT cast_rank_to_text(null);
```

Finally, the CASE statement raises an exception if no branch is matched and the ELSE branch is not specified, as follows:

```
DO
$$
DECLARE
i int := 0;
BEGIN
case WHEN i=1 then
        RAISE NOTICE 'i is one';
END CASE;
END;
$$
LANGUAGE plpgsql;
ERROR:  case not found
HINT:   CASE statement is missing ELSE part.
CONTEXT:  PL/pgSQL function inline_code_block line 5 at CASE
```

Iteration

Iteration is used to repeat a block of statements to achieve a certain goal. With iteration, one often needs to specify the starting point and the ending condition. In PostgreSQL, there are several statements for iterating through the results and for performing looping, including LOOP, CONTINUE, EXIT, FOR, WHILE, and FOR EACH.

The loop statement

The basic LOOP statement has the following structure:

```
LOOP
  Statements
END LOOP;
```

To understand the LOOP statement, let us rewrite the factorial function, as follows:

```
CREATE OR REPLACE FUNCTION factorial (fact int) RETURNS BIGINT AS
$$
DECLARE
  result bigint = 1;
BEGIN
  IF fact = 1 THEN
    RETURN 1;
  ELSIF fact IS NULL or fact < 1 THEN
    RAISE EXCEPTION 'Provide a positive integer';
  ELSE
    LOOP
      result = result*fact;
      fact = fact-1;
      EXIT WHEN fact = 1;
    END Loop;
  END IF;
  RETURN result;
END;
$$
LANGUAGE plpgsql;
```

In the preceding code, the conditional EXIT statement is used to prevent infinite looping by exiting the LOOP statement. When an EXIT statement is encountered, the execution control goes to the first statement after the LOOP. To control the execution of the statements inside the LOOP statement, PL/pgSQL also provides the CONTINUE statement, which works somewhat like the EXIT statement. Thus, instead of forcing termination, the CONTINUE statement forces the next iteration of the loop to take place, skipping any code in between.

> The usage of the CONTINUE and EXIT statements, especially in the middle of a code block, is not encouraged because it breaks the execution order, which makes the code harder to read and understand.

The while loop statement

The WHILE statement keeps executing a block of statements while a particular condition is met. Its syntax is as follows:

```
WHILE boolean-expression LOOP
    statements
END LOOP ;
```

The following example uses the while loop to print the days of the current month:

```
DO
$$
DECLARE
  first_day_in_month date := date_trunc('month',
  current_date)::date;
  last_day_in_month date := (date_trunc('month', current_date)+
  INTERVAL '1 MONTH - 1 day')::date;
  counter date = first_day_in_month;
BEGIN
  WHILE (counter <= last_day_in_month) LOOP
    RAISE notice '%', counter;
    counter := counter + interval '1 day';
  END LOOP;

END;
$$
LANGUAGE plpgsql;
```

The for loop statement

PL/pgSQL provides two forms of the FOR statement, and they are used to:

- Iterate through the rows returned by an SQL query
- Iterate through a range of integer values

The syntax of the `for` loop statement is:

```
FOR index_name IN [ REVERSE ] expression1 .. expression2 [ BY expression
] LOOP
    statements
END LOOP;
```

`index_name` is the name of a local variable of the type integer. This local variable scope is the FOR loop. Statements inside the loop can read this variable, but cannot change its value. Finally, one can change this behavior by defining the variable in the declaration section of the outer block. `expression1` and `expression2` must be evaluated to integer values; if `expression1` equals `expression2` then the FOR loop is run only once.

The REVERSE key word is optional, and it is used to define the order in which the range will be generated (ascending or descending). If REVERSE is omitted, then `expression1` should be smaller than `expression2`, otherwise the loop will not be executed. Finally, BY defines the steps between two successive numbers in the range. Note that the BY value should always be a positive integer. The following example shows a FOR loop iterating over a negative range of numbers in the reverse order:

```
DO
$$
BEGIN
FOR j IN REVERSE -1 .. -10 BY 2 LOOP
    Raise notice '%', j;
END LOOP;
END;
$$
LANGUAGE plpgsql;
--- output should be
NOTICE:   -1
NOTICE:   -3
```

```
NOTICE:   -5
NOTICE:   -7
NOTICE:   -9
```

To iterate through the result of a set query, the syntax is different, as follows:

```
[ FOR index_name IN { cursor  | ( select_statement )} LOOP
       statement...
END LOOP ;
```

index_name is a local variable in the outer block. Its type is not restricted to simple types such as integer and text. However, its type might be a composite or a RECORD data type. In PL/pgSQL, one could iterate over a cursor result or over a SELECT statement result.

Cursor is a special data object that can be used to encapsulate a SELECT query, and then to read the query result a few rows at a time.

The following example shows all the database names:

```
DO $$
DECLARE
  database RECORD;
BEGIN
  FOR database IN SELECT * FROM pg_database LOOP
    RAISE notice '%', database.datname;
  END LOOP;
END;
$$;
--- output should be like
NOTICE:   template1
NOTICE:   template0
NOTICE:   postgres
...
```

Returning from the function

The PostgreSQL return statement is used for terminating the function, and for returning the control to the caller. The return statement has different forms such as RETURN, RETURN NEXT, RETURN QUERY, RETURN expression, RETURN QUERY EXECUTE, and so on. The return statement can return a single value or a set to the caller, as will be shown in this chapter. In this context, let us consider the following anonymous function:

```
postgres=# DO $$

BEGIN

RETURN;

RAISE NOTICE 'This statement will not be executed';

END

$$

LANGUAGE plpgsql;

DO

postgres=#
```

As shown in the preceding example, the function is terminated before the execution of the RAISE statement due to the RETURN statement.

Returning void

A void type is used in a function for performing some side effects such as logging; the built-in function pg_sleep is used to delay the execution of a server process in seconds:

```
\df pg_sleep
```

```
                       List of functions
   Schema    |   Name    | Result data type | Argument data types |  Type
-------------+-----------+------------------+---------------------+--------
 pg_catalog  | pg_sleep  | void             | double precision    | normal
```

Returning a single row

PL/pgSQL can be used to return a single row from a function; an example of this type is the factorial function.

Some developers refer to PL/pgSQL and SQL functions returning a single-row, single-column scalar variable as scalar functions.

The return type can be base, composite, domain, pseudo type, or domain data type. The following function returns a JSON representation of a certain account:

```
CREATE OR REPLACE FUNCTION car_portal_app.get_account_in_json (account_id
INT) RETURNs JSON AS

$$

  SELECT row_to_json(account) FROM car_portal_app.account WHERE
  account_id = $1;

$$

LANGUAGE SQL;

-- For test

WITH inserted_account AS (

  INSERT into car_portal_app.account VALUES (DEFAULT,
  'first_name', 'last_name', 'account@example.com','some_pass')
  RETURNING account_id

) SELECT  car_portal_app.get_account_in_json (account_id) FROM inserted_
account;

--Result

"{"account_id":15,"first_name":"first_name","last_name":"last_
name","email":"account@example.com","password":"some_pass"}"
```

Returning multiple rows

Set Returning Functions (SRFs) can be used to return a set of rows. The row type can either be base type such as integer, composite, table type, pseudo type, or domain type.

To return a set from a function, the keyword SETOF is used to mark the function as an SRF, as follows:

```
CREATE OR REPLACE FUNCTION advertisement_in_last_7_days() RETURNS SETOF
car_portal_app.advertisement AS $$

  SELECT * FROM car_portal_app.advertisement WHERE
  advertisement_date >= now() -INTERVAL '7 days';

$$ LANGUAGE SQL;


--To test

SELECT * FROM advertisement_in_last_7_days()
```

If the return type is not defined, one could:

- Define a new data type and use it
- Use return table
- Use output parameters and record data type

Let us assume that we would like to return only the `car_id` and the `account_seller_id`, as in this case, we do not have a data type. Thus, the preceding function can be written as:

```
CREATE OR REPLACE FUNCTION advertisement_in_last_7_days() RETURNS TABLE
(car_id INT, seller_account_id INT) AS $$

BEGIN

  RETURN QUERY SELECT a.car_id, a.seller_account_id FROM car_portal_app.
advertisement a WHERE advertisement_date >= now() -INTERVAL '7 days';

END;

$$ LANGUAGE plpgSQL;


--To TEST
SELECT * FROM advertisement_in_last_7_days()
```

Note that in the preceding function, we use an alias; else, PL/pgSQL will raise an error, as follows:

```
ERROR:  column reference "car_id" is ambiguous

...

DETAIL:  It could refer to either a PL/pgSQL variable or a table column.

QUERY:  SELECT car_id, seller_account_id FROM
```

Moreover, in this function, RETURN QUERY is used only to show a different option in returning a query result.

The preceding function can also be written using the OUT variables; actually, the return table is implemented internally as indicated by the error using the OUT variables, as follows:

```
CREATE OR REPLACE FUNCTION advertisement_in_last_7_days(OUT car_id INT,
OUT seller_account_id INT) RETURNS SETOF RECORD AS $$

BEGIN

  RETURN QUERY SELECT a.car_id, a.seller_account_id FROM car_portal_app.
advertisement a WHERE advertisement_date >= now() -INTERVAL '7 days';

END;

$$ LANGUAGE plpgsql;
```

Function predefined variables

The PL/pgSQL functions have several special variables that are created automatically in the top-level block. For example, if the function returns a trigger, then several variables such as NEW, OLD, and TG_OP are created.

In addition to the trigger special values, there is a Boolean variable called FOUND. This is often used in combination with DML and PERFORM statements to conduct sanity checks. The value of the FOUND variable is affected by the SELECT, INSERT, UPDATE, DELETE, and PERFORM statements. These statements set FOUND to true if at least one row is selected, inserted, updated, or deleted.

The PERFORM statement is similar to the SELECT statement, but it discards the result of the query. Finally, the EXECUTE statement does not change the value of the FOUND variable. The following examples show how the FOUND variable is affected by the INSERT and PERFORM statements:

```
DO $$
BEGIN
  CREATE TABLE t1(f1 int);
  --- Set FOUND to true
  INSERT INTO t1 VALUES (1);
  RAISE NOTICE '%', FOUND;
  --- Set FOUND to false
  PERFORM* FROM t1 WHERE f1 = 0;
  RAISE NOTICE '%', FOUND;
  DROP TABLE t1;
END;
$$LANGUAGE plpgsql;
--- output
NOTICE:  t
NOTICE:  f
```

In addition to the preceding query, one could get the last OID — object identifier — for an inserted row as well as the affected number of rows by using the INSERT, UPDATE, and DELETE statements via the following commands:

```
GET DIAGNOSTICS variable = item;
```

Assuming that there is variable called i of type integer, one can get the affected number of rows, as follows:

```
GET DIAGNOSTICS i = ROW_COUNT;
```

Exception handling

One could trap and raise errors in PostgreSQL using the exception and raise statements. Errors can be raised by violating data integrity constraints, or by performing illegal operations such as assigning text to integers, dividing an integer or float by zero, out-of-range assignments, and so on. By default, any error occurrence inside a PL/pgSQL function causes the function to abort the execution and roll back the changes. To be able to recover from errors, PL/pgSQL can trap the errors using the EXCEPTION clause. The syntax of the exception clause is very similar to the PL/pgSQL blocks. Moreover, PostgreSQL can raise errors using the RAISE statement. To understand exception handling, let us consider the following helping function:

```
CREATE OR REPLACE FUNCTION check_not_null (value anyelement ) RETURNS
VOID AS
$$
BEGIN
  IF (value IS NULL) THEN
    RAISE EXCEPTION USING ERRCODE = 'check_violation';
  END IF;
END;

$$ LANGUAGE plpgsql;
```

The check_not_null statement is a polymorphic function, which simply raises an error with a check_violation SQLSTATE. Calling this function and passing the NULL value as an argument will cause an error, as follows:

```
SELECT check_not_null(null::text);
ERROR:  check_violation
```

In order to properly determine when the exception is raised and why, PostgreSQL defines several categories of error codes. *PostgreSQL Error Codes* can be found at `http://www.postgresql.org/docs/current/interactive/errcodes-appendix.html`. For example, raising an exception by the user without specifying the ERRCODE will set the SQLSTATE to P001, while a unique violation exception will set the SQLSTATE to 23505. Errors can be matched in the EXCEPTION clause either by the SQLSTATE or by the condition name, as follows:

```
WHEN unique_violation THEN ...
WHEN SQLSTATE '23505' THEN ...
```

Finally, one could provide a customized error message and SQLSTATE when raising an exception such that the ERRCODE should be five digits and/or uppercase ASCII letters other than 00000, as follows:

```
DO
$$
BEGIN
RAISE EXCEPTION USING ERRCODE = '1234X', MESSAGE = 'test customized
SQLSTATE:';
EXCEPTION WHEN SQLSTATE  '1234X' THEN
  RAISE NOTICE '% %', SQLERRM, SQLSTATE;
END;

$$ LANGUAGE plpgsql;
--output
--NOTICE:  test customized SQLSTATE: 1234X
```

To trap an exception, let us rewrite the factorial function, and let us assume that the factorial function should return null if the provided argument is null:

```
CREATE OR REPLACE FUNCTION factorial(INTEGER ) RETURNS BIGINT AS $$
DECLARE
  fact ALIAS FOR $1;

BEGIN
  PERFORM check_not_null(fact);
  IF fact > 1 THEN
    RETURN factorial(fact - 1) * fact;
  ELSIF fact IN (0,1) THEN
    RETURN 1;
```

```
   ELSE
     -- Negative values
     RETURN NULL;
   END IF;

EXCEPTION
   WHEN check_violation THEN
     RETURN NULL;
   WHEN OTHERS THEN
     RAISE NOTICE '% %', SQLERRM, SQLSTATE
END;
$$ LANGUAGE 'plpgsql'

-- in psql client
\pset null 'NULL'
--Null display is "NULL".
SELECT * FROM factorial(null::int);
 factorial
-----------
      NULL
(1 row)
```

The `factorial` function did not raise an error, because the error is trapped in the EXCEPTION clause and a NULL value is returned instead. Notice that the matching is performed using the condition name instead of SQLSTATE. The special condition name OTHERS matches any error; this is often used as a safe fallback when unexpected errors occur.

In handling exceptions, if SQLERRM and SQLSTATE are not deterministic enough to know the exception cause, one could get more information about the exception using GET STACKED DIAGNOSTICS:

```
GET STACKED DIAGNOSTICS variable { = | := } item [ , ... ];
```

The item is a keyword identifying a status value related to the exception. For example, the item keywords COLUMN_NAME, TABLE_NAME, and SCHEMA_NAME indicate the names of the column, table, and schema involved in the exception.

Dynamic SQL

Dynamic SQL is used for building and executing queries on the fly. Unlike the static SQL statement, a dynamic SQL statement full text is unknown, and can change between successive executions. These queries can be DDL, DCL, and DML statements. Dynamic SQL is used for reducing repetitive tasks. For example, one could use dynamic SQL to create table partitioning for a certain table on a daily basis, add missing indexes on all foreign keys, or add data auditing capabilities to a certain table without major coding effects. Another important use of dynamic SQL is to overcome the side effects of PL/pgSQL caching, as queries executed using the EXECUTE statement are not cached.

Dynamic SQL is achieved via the EXECUTE statement. The EXECUTE statement accepts a string and simply evaluates it. The synopsis to execute a statement is given as follows:

```
EXECUTE command-string [ INTO [STRICT] target ] [ USING expression [, ...
] ];
```

Executing DDL statements in dynamic SQL

In some cases, one needs to perform operations at the database object level such as tables, indexes, columns, roles, and so on. For example, a database developer would like to vacuum and analyze a specific schema object, which is a common task after deployment of updating the statistics. For example, to vacuum the car_portal_app schema, one could write the following script:

```
SET search_path TO car_portal_app;

DO $$

DECLARE

table_name text;

BEGIN

  FOR table_name IN SELECT tablename FROM pg_tables WHERE schemaname =
'car_portal_app' LOOP

    EXECUTE 'ANALYZE ' || table_name;

  END LOOP;

END;

$$;
```

Executing DML statements in dynamic SQL

Some applications might interact with data in an interactive manner. For example, one might have a billing data generated on a monthly basis. Also, some applications filter data on different criteria defined by the user. In such cases, dynamic SQL is very convenient.

For example, in the car portal application, search functionality is needed for getting accounts using the dynamic predicate, as follows:

```
CREATE OR REPLACE FUNCTION get_account (predicate TEXT) RETURNS SETOF
account AS
$$
BEGIN
  RETURN QUERY EXECUTE 'SELECT * FROM account WHERE ' || predicate;
END;
$$
LANGUAGE plpgsql;
-- For test
--SELECT * FROM get_account ('true');
--SELECT * FROM get_account (E'first_name=\'test\'');
```

Dynamic SQL and the caching effect

As mentioned earlier, PL/pgSQL caches execution plans. This is quite good if the generated plan is expected to be static. For example, the following statement is expected to use an index scan because of selectivity. In this case, caching the plan saves some time, and thus, increases performance:

```
SELECT * FROM account WHERE account_id =<INT>
```

In other scenarios however, this is not true. For example, let us assume we have an index on the `advertisement_date` column, and we would like to get the number of advertisements since a certain date, as follows:

```
SELECT count (*) FROM car_portal_app.advertisement WHERE advertisement_
date >= <certain_date>;
```

In the preceding query, the entries from the advertisement table can be fetched from the hard disk either by using the index scan or using the sequential scan based on selectivity, which depends on the provided `certain_date` value. Caching the execution plan of such a query will cause serious problems; thus, writing the function as follows is not a good idea:

```
CREATE OR REPLACE FUNCTION get_advertisement_count (some_date timestamptz
) RETURNS BIGINT AS $$

BEGIN

  RETURN  (SELECT count (*) FROM car_portal_app.advertisement WHERE
advertisement_date >=some_date)::bigint;

END;

$$

LANGUAGE plpgsql;
```

To solve the caching issue, one could rewrite the above function either using the SQL language function or by using the PL/pgSQL execute command, as follows:

```
  CREATE OR REPLACE FUNCTION get_advertisement_count (some_date
timestamptz ) RETURNS BIGINT AS $$

DECLARE

  count BIGINT;

BEGIN

EXECUTE 'SELECT count (*) FROM car_portal_app.advertisement WHERE
advertisement_date >= $1' USING some_date INTO count;

  RETURN count;

END;

$$

LANGUAGE plpgsql;

-- To test

SELECT get_advertisement_count(now() -INTERVAL '1 year');
```

Recommended practices when using dynamic SQL

Dynamic SQL can cause security issues if not handled carefully; dynamic SQL is vulnerable to the SQL injection technique. SQL injection is used for executing SQL statements that reveal secure information, or even for destroying the data in the database.

A very simple example of a PL/pgSQL function vulnerable to SQL injection is as follows:

```
CREATE OR REPLACE FUNCTION can_login (user text, pass text) RETURNS
BOOLEAN AS $$
DECLARE
stmt TEXT;
result bool;
BEGIN
    stmt = E'SELECT COALESCE (count(*)=1, false) FROM account
    WHERE email = \''|| $1 || E'\'  and password = \''||$2||E'\'';
    RAISE NOTICE '%' , stmt;
    EXECUTE stmt INTO result;
    RETURN result;
END;
$$
LANGUAGE plpgsql
```

The preceding function returns `true` if the e-mail and the password match. To test this function, let us insert a row and try to inject some code, as follows:

```
car_portal=# INSERT INTO account VALUES (DEFAULT, 'test', 'injection',
'test@injet_db.com', 'test_pass' );
INSERT 0 1
car_portal=# SELECT can_login('test@injet_db.com', 'test_pass');
NOTICE:  SELECT COALESCE (count(*)=1, false) FROM account WHERE email =
'test@injet_db.com'  and password = 'test_pass'
 can_login
-----------
 t
(1 row)


car_portal=# SELECT can_login('test@injet_db.com', 'wrong_pass');
NOTICE:  SELECT COALESCE (count(*)=1, false) FROM account WHERE email =
'test@injet_db.com'  and password = 'wrong_pass'
 can_login
-----------
```

```
 f
(1 row)
```

```
car_portal=# SELECT can_login(E'test@injet_db.com\'--', 'wrong_pass');
NOTICE:  SELECT COALESCE (count(*)=1, false) FROM account WHERE email =
'test@injet_db.com'--'  and password = 'wrong_pass'
 can_login
-----------
 t
(1 row)
```

Notice that the function returns true even when the password does not match the password stored in the table. This is simply because the predicate was commented, as shown by the raise notice:

```
 SELECT COALESCE (count(*)=1, false) FROM account WHERE email = 'test@
injet_db.com'--'  and password = 'wrong_pass'
```

To protect the code against this technique, one could follow these practices:

- For parameterized dynamic SQL statements, use the `USING` clause.
- Use the `format` function with appropriate interpolation to construct your queries. Note that `%I` escapes the argument as an identifier and `%L` as a literal.
- Use `quote_ident()`, `quote_literal()`, and `quote_nullable()` to properly format your identifiers and literal.

One way to write the preceding function is as follows:

```
CREATE OR REPLACE FUNCTION can_login (text, pass text) RETURNS BOOLEAN AS
$$
DECLARE
stmt TEXT;
result bool;
BEGIN
    stmt = format('SELECT COALESCE (count(*)=1, false) FROM
    account WHERE email =  %Land password = %L', $1,$2);
    RAISE NOTICE '%' , stmt;
    EXECUTE stmt INTO result;
    RETURN result;
END;
$$
LANGUAGE plpgsql;
```

Summary

PostgreSQL provides a complete programming language called PL/pgSQL, which is integrated with the PostgreSQL trigger system. The PL/pgSQL and SQL languages can be used to code very complex logic. One should use the SQL functions when possible. With the introduction of advanced query writing techniques such as window function and lateral Join in PostgreSQL, one can write very complex logic using only the standard SQL language.

There are several parameters in PostgreSQL for controlling the function behavior; these parameters are applicable to the PL/pgSQL and SQL functions as well. For example, SECURITY DEFINER and SECURITY INVOKER define execution security context and privileges. A function planner parameters help the planner to generate execution plans. These parameters are COST, LEAKPROOF, and ROWS.

The dynamic SQL technique enables the developers to build SQL statements dynamically at runtime. One can create general purpose, flexible functions because the full text of an SQL statement may be unknown at the time of compilation. Dynamic SQL needs careful handling because it is exposed to SQL injection attacks.

8
PostgreSQL Security

Data protection and security are essential for the continuity of business. Data protection is not nice to have, but it is required by the legal system. Sensitive data, such as user information, email addresses, geographical addresses, and payment information, should be protected against any data breach. There are several other topics related to data security, such as data privacy, retention, and loss prevention.

There are several levels of data protection, often defined in the data protection policy and by the country's legal system. Data protection policy often defines data dissemination to other parties, users authorized to access the data, and so on. Data should be protected on different levels, including transferring and encrypting data on storage devices. Data security is a huge topic and often there are data security managers dedicated only to these tasks.

Authentication in PostgreSQL

Authentication answers the question, who is the user? PostgreSQL supports several authentication methods, including trust, ident, password, GSSAPI, SSPI, LDAP, PAM, and so on. To understand authentication, one needs to have the following information:

- Authentication is controlled via a `pg_hba.conf` file, where `hba` stands for host-based authentication.

- It is good to know the default initial authentication settings shipped with PostgreSQL distribution.

- The `pg_hba.conf` file is often located in the data directory, but it also can be specified in the `postgresql.conf` configuration file.

- When changing the authentication, one needs to send a SIGHUP signal, and this is done via several methods based on the PostgreSQL platform. Also note that the user who sends the signal should be a superuser or the postgres or a root system user on the Linux distribution; again, this depends on the platform.

```
psql -U postgres -c "SELECT pg_reload_conf();"

sudo service postgresql reload

sudo /etc/init.d/postgresql reload

sudo Kill -HUP <postgres process id>
```

- The order of pg_hba.conf records matters. The session connection is compared with pg_hba.conf records one by one until it is rejected or the end of the configuration file is reached.

- Finally, it is important to check the PostgreSQL log files to determine whether there are errors after configuration reload.

PostgreSQL pg_hba.conf

As in postgresql.conf, the pg_hba.conf file is composed of a set of records, lines can be commented using the hash sign, and spaces are ignored. The structure of the pg_hba.conf file record is as follows:

```
host_type database user [IP-address| address] [IP-mask] auth-method
[auth-options]
```

The host_type part of this query can be:

- **Local**: This is used in Linux systems to allow users to access PostgreSQL using socket connections

- **Host**: This is to allow connections from other hosts, either based on the address or IP address, using TCP/IP with and without SSL encryption

- **Hostssl**: This is similar to host, but the connection should be encrypted using SSL in this case

- **Hostnossl**: This is also similar to host, but the connection should not be encrypted in this case

The database part of the query is the name of the database that the user would like to connect to. For flexibility, one could also use a comma-separated list to specify several databases, or one could use all to indicate that the user can access all the databases in the database cluster. Also, the sameuser and samerole values can be used to indicate that the database name is the same as the username or the user is a member of a role with the same name as the database.

The user part of the query specifies the database user's name; again, the `all` value matches all users. The IP address, address, and IP subnet mask are used to identify the host where the user tries to connect from. The IP address can be specified using a CIDR or dot decimal notation. Finally, the password authentication methods can be trust md5, reject, and so on.

The following are some typical examples of configuring a PostgreSQL authentication:

- Any user on the PostgreSQL cluster can access any database using the UNIX domain socket, as shown in the following database table:

```
# TYPE     DATABASE     USER    ADDRESS    METHOD
Local      all     all        trust
```

- Any user on the PostgreSQL cluster can access any database using the local loopback IP address, as in this table:

```
# TYPE     DATABASE   USER   ADDRESS     METHOD
Host       all     all    127.0.0.1/32     trust
host       all     all    ::1/128      trust
```

- The following database table rejects all connections that come from `92.168.0.53` but accepts all the connections that come from the range, `192.168.0.1/24`:

```
# TYPE     DATABASE   USER   ADDRESS      METHOD
Host       all     all    92.168.0.53/32   reject
Host       all     all    92.168.0.1/24   trust
```

Listen addresses

The `listen_addresses` is defined in `postgresql-conf`. The PostgreSQL listen_ addresses connection setting is used to identify the list of IP addresses that the server should listen to from client applications. The `listen_ addresses` are comma-separated lists of host names or IP addresses. Changing this value requires a server restart. In addition to the preceding, one should note the following:

- The default value is localhost
- Giving an empty list means that the server should accept only Unix socket connection
- The value * indicates all

Let's test the listen address Unix socket connection by changing the `listen_addresses` to `''`, as follows:

```
#Change the listen address
psql -c "ALTER SYSTEM SET listen_addresses ='';"
# Restart the server
/etc/init.d/postgresql restart
# connect using host
psql -h localhost -c 'SELECT 1';
psql: could not connect to server: Connection refused
   Is the server running on host "localhost" (127.0.0.1) and accepting
   TCP/IP connections on port 5432?
# connect using UNIX domain socket
psql -c 'SELECT 1';
 ?column?
----------
        1
(1 row)
```

Authentication best practices

Authentication best practices depend on the whole infrastructure setup, the application's nature, the user's characteristics, data sensitivity, and so on. For example, the following setup is common for start-up companies: the database application, including the database server, is hosted on the same machine and only used from one physical location by intracompany users.

Often, database servers are isolated from the world using firewalls; in this case, one can use the md5 authentication method and limit the IP addresses so that the database server accepts connections within a certain range or set. Note that it is important not to use a superuser or database owner account to connect to the database because if this account were hacked, the whole database cluster would be exposed.

If the application server—business logic—and database server are not on the same machine, one can use a strong authentication method, such as LDAP and Kerberos. However, for small applications where the database server and application are on the same machine, the md5 authentication method and limiting the listen address to the localhost might be sufficient.

To authenticate an application, it is recommended to use only one user and try to reduce the maximum number of allowed connections using a connection pooling software to better tune PostgreSQL resources. Another level of security might be needed in the application business logic to distinguish different login users. For real world users, LDAP or Kerberos authentication is more desirable.

Furthermore, if the database server is accessed from the outer world, it is useful to encrypt sessions using SSL certificates to avoid packet sniffing.

Also, one should remember to secure database servers, which trust all localhost connections as anyone who accesses the localhost can access the database server. Finally, when using MD5, it is important also to secure it in the business logic level and add salt as there are dictionaries to crack MD5 hashes.

PostgreSQL default access privileges

By default, PostgreSQL users—also known as roles with login option—can access the public schema. Also, note that the default PostgreSQL authentication policy allows users to access all databases from the localhost using peer authentication on a Linux system. Also, a user can create objects in the public schema of any database he/she can access; for example, the user can create a function and execute it in the public schema. In addition to this, the user can alter some settings.

The user cannot access other user objects in the public schema or create databases and schemas. However, the user can sniff data about the database objects by querying the system catalog. Unprivileged users can get information about other users, table structure, table owner, some table statistics, and so on. The following example shows how the user test is able to get information about table a, which is owned by a postgres user:

```
test=> SELECT * FROM a;
ERROR:  permission denied for relation a
test=> SELECT current_user;
 current_user
--------------
 test
(1 row)
test=> SELECT tableowner FROM pg_tables WHERE tablename ='a';
 tableowner
------------
 postgres
```

```
(1 row)

test=> \d a
        Table "public.a"
 Column |  Type    | Modifiers
--------+---------+-----------
 num    | integer |

test=> \x
Expanded display is on.
test=>
test=> select * from pg_stat_user_tables ;
-[ RECORD 1 ]-----+------------------------------
relid             | 16386
schemaname        | public
relname           | a
seq_scan          | 0
seq_tup_read      | 0
idx_scan          |
idx_tup_fetch     |
n_tup_ins         | 201
n_tup_upd         | 0
n_tup_del         | 0
n_tup_hot_upd     | 0
n_live_tup        | 201
n_dead_tup        | 0
last_vacuum       |
last_autovacuum   |
last_analyze      | 2015-06-07 22:48:59.311121+02
last_autoanalyze  |
vacuum_count      | 0
autovacuum_count  | 0
analyze_count     | 3
autoanalyze_count | 0
test=> \x
Expanded display is off.
```

```
test=> SELECT * FROM pg_user;

 usename  | usesysid | usecreatedb | usesuper | usecatupd | userepl |
passwd  | valuntil | useconfig

----------+----------+-------------+----------+-----------+---------+----
------+----------+-----------
 postgres |       10 | t           | t        | t         | t       |
******** |          |
 test     |    16385 | f           | f        | f         | f       |
******** |          |
(2 rows)
```

Also, the user can access functions that are created in the public schema by other users as long as this function does not access objects that the user cannot access:

```
postgres=# SELECT current_user;


 current_user
--------------
 postgres
(1 row)
```

```
postgres=# CREATE OR REPLACE FUNCTION b ()  RETURNS text AS $$ SELECT
'Hello'::text $$ LANGUAGE sql ;
CREATE FUNCTION
postgres=# SET ROLE test;
SET
postgres=> SELECT * FROM b();
   b
-------
 Hello
(1 row)
```

For mistrusted languages, such as plpythonu, the user cannot create functions unless he/she is a superuser. If anyone who is not a superuser tries to create a function using C language or plpythonu, he/she will get the following error:

```
postgres=> CREATE FUNCTION min (a integer, b integer)
  RETURNS integer
AS $$
  if a < b:
    return a
```

```
  else:
    return b
$$ LANGUAGE plpythonu;
ERROR:  permission denied for language plpythonu
```

To prevent the user from accessing the public schema, the public schema privileges should be revoked, as follows:

```
test=# SELECT session_user;
 session_user
--------------
 postgres
(1 row)


test=# REVOKE ALL PRIVILEGES ON SCHEMA PUBLIC FROM public;
REVOKE
test=# set role test;
SET
test=> create table b();
ERROR:  no schema has been selected to create in
```

Note that the user test has explicit privileges on the public schema; the user inherits these privileges from the public role.

For views, the view owner cannot execute a view unless he/she has permission to access the base tables used in the view, as shown in the following example:

```
car_portal=# CREATE TABLE table1 AS SELECT 1 As f1;
SELECT * FROM view_table1;
SELECT 1
car_portal=# CREATE VIEW view_table1  AS SELECT f1 FROM table1;
CREATE VIEW
car_portal=# CREATE ROLE test_view_role;
CREATE ROLE
car_portal=# ALTER TABLE view_table1 OWNER TO test_view_role;
ALTER TABLE
car_portal=# SET ROLE test_view_role;
SET
car_portal=> SELECT * FROM view_table1;
ERROR:  permission denied for relation table1
```

Role system and proxy authentication

Often, when designing an application, a user is used to configure database connections and connection tools. Another level of security needs to be implemented to ensure that the user who uses the application is authorized to perform a certain task. This logic is often implemented in application business logic. Also, the database's role system can be used to partially implement this logic by delegating the authentication to another role after the connection is established or reused using the SET SESSION AUTHORIZATION user_name statement or SET ROLE command in a transaction block.

The SET role requires a role membership, while SET SESSION AUTHORISATION requires superuser privileges. Allowing an application to connect as a superuser is dangerous because the SET SESSION and SET ROLE commands can be reset using the RESET ROLE and RESET SESSION commands, respectively, allowing the application to gain superuser privileges.

To understand how the PostgreSQL role system can be used to implement authentication and authorization, we will use the role system in the car portal app. In the car portal application, several groups of users can be classified as web_app, public_user, registered_user , seller, and admin. The web_app user is used to configure business logic connection tools; the public user, registered_user, and seller are used to distinguish users. The public_user group can access only public information, such as advertisements, but cannot add ratings as registered users nor create advertisements as seller. Admin is a superrole to manage all of the application's content, such as filtering out spams and deleting the users that do not adhere to the website's policies. When the car web portal application connects to the database, the web_app user is used. After this, car_portal invokes the SET ROLE command based on the user class. This authentication method is known as proxy authentication.

The following examples demonstrate how a role system can be used to implement proxy authentication. The first step is to create roles and assign role memberships and privileges:

```
CREATE ROLE web_app LOGIN NOINHERIT;
CREATE ROLE public_user NOLOGIN;
GRANT SELECT ON car_portal_app.advertisement_picture, car_portal_app.
advertisement_rating , car_portal_app.advertisement TO public_user;
GRANT public_user TO web_app;
GRANT USAGE ON SCHEMA car_portal_app TO web_app, public_user;
```

The NOINHERIT option for the web_app user does not allow the user to inherit the permissions of role membership; however, web_app can change the role to public user, as in the following example:

```
$ psql -h localhost -U web_app -d car_portal
car_portal=> SELECT session_user, current_user;
 session_user | current_user
--------------+--------------
 web_app      | web_app
(1 row)


car_portal=> SELECT * FROM car_portal_app.advertisement;
ERROR:  permission denied for relation advertisement
car_portal=> SET ROLE public_user;
SET
car_portal=> SELECT * FROM car_portal_app.advertisement;
 advertisement_id | advertisement_date | car_id | seller_account_id
------------------+--------------------+--------+-------------------
(0 rows)


car_portal=> SELECT session_user, current_user;
 session_user | current_user
--------------+--------------
 web_app      | public_user
(1 row)
```

PostgreSQL security levels

PostgreSQL has different security levels defined on PostgreSQL objects, including tablespace, database, schema, table, foreign data wrapper, sequence, domain, language, and large object. One can have a peek into different privileges by running the \h meta command in psql, as follows:

```
car_portal=> \h GRANT
Command:     GRANT
Description: define access privileges
Syntax:
```

```
GRANT { { SELECT | INSERT | UPDATE | DELETE | TRUNCATE | REFERENCES |
TRIGGER }
    [, ...] | ALL [ PRIVILEGES ] }
    ON { [ TABLE ] table_name [, ...]
          | ALL TABLES IN SCHEMA schema_name [, ...] }
    TO { [ GROUP ] role_name | PUBLIC } [, ...] [ WITH
    GRANT OPTION ]
...
```

Database security level

To disallow users from connecting to the database by default, one needs to revoke the default database permissions from public, as follows:

```
$ psql -h localhost -U postgres -d car_portal
car_portal=# REVOKE ALL ON DATABASE car_portal FROM public;
REVOKE
car_portal=# \q


$ psql -h localhost -U web_app -d car_portal
psql: FATAL:  permission denied for database "car_portal"
DETAIL:  User does not have CONNECT privilege.
```

To allow the user to connect to the database, the connect permissions should be granted explicitly, as follows:

```
$ psql -h localhost -U postgres -d car_portal
car_portal=# GRANT CONNECT ON DATABASE car_portal TO web_app;
GRANT
car_portal=# \q


$ psql -h localhost -U web_app -d car_portal
car_portal-> \l car_portal

                                                        List of databases
     Name    |     Owner      |  Encoding  |            Collate             |
Ctype        |                |    Access privileges
------------+----------------+----------+----------------------------+---
--------------------------+----------------------------------
```

```
 car_portal | car_portal_app | UTF8       | English_United States.1252 |
English_United States.1252 | car_portal_app=CTc/car_portal_app+
           |                |            |                            |
| web_app=c/car_portal_app
(1 row)
```

One also could revoke the default permissions from template databases to ensure that all newly created databases don't allow users to connect by default.

If the database permissions are empty when using the \l meta command, this indicates that the database has the default permissions; execute the following query:

```
$ psql -h localhost -U postgres -d car_portal


car_portal=# CREATE DATABASE test;
CREATE DATABASE
car_portal=# \l test
                                    List of databases
 Name  |  Owner   | Encoding |              Collate             |
Ctype             | Access privileges
-------+----------+----------+----------------------------------+--------------
---------------+-------------------
 test | postgres | UTF8      | English_United Kingdom.1252 | English_
United Kingdom.1252 |
(1 row)
```

Schema security level

The Grant synopsis for schema is as follows:

```
GRANT { { CREATE | USAGE } [, ...] | ALL [ PRIVILEGES ] }
    ON SCHEMA schema_name [, ...]
    TO { [ GROUP ] role_name | PUBLIC } [, ...] [ WITH
    GRANT OPTION ]
```

To allow a user access to a certain schema, the usage permissions should be granted, as seen in the preceding and following examples:

```
GRANT USAGE ON SCHEMA car_portal_app TO web_app, public_user;
```

Table-level security

The table permissions are INSERT, UPDATE, DELETE, TRIGGER, REFERENCE, and TRUNCATE. Also, one could use the keyword ALL to grant all privileges at once, as follows:

```
GRANT ALL ON <table_name> TO <role>;
```

Apart from this, one could use a comma-separated list for both tables and roles or even grant permissions on all relations in a schema to a certain role.

Column-level security

PostgresSQL allows permissions to be defined on the column level. To explore this feature, let's create a table and role, as follows:

```
car_portal=# CREATE TABLE test_column_acl AS SELECT * FROM (values (1,2),
(3,4)) as n(f1, f2);
SELECT 2
car_portal=# CREATE ROLE test_column_acl;
CREATE ROLE
car_portal=# GRANT SELECT (f1) ON test_column_acl TO test_column_acl;
GRANT


--We have revoked default permission on public in previous examples
car_portal=# GRANT USAGE ON SCHEMA public TO test_column_acl;
GRANT
car_portal=# SET ROLE test_column_acl;
SET
car_portal=> SELECT * FROM public.test_column_acl;
ERROR:  permission denied for relation test_column_acl
car_portal=> SELECT f1 FROM public.test_column_acl;
 f1
----
  1
  3
(2 rows)
car_portal=> \x
Expanded display is on.
```

```
car_portal=> \dp public.test_column_acl
Access privileges
-[ RECORD 1 ]------------+----------------------------
Schema                   | public
Name                     | test_column_acl
Type                     | table
Access privileges        |
Column access privileges | f1:
                         |   test_column_acl=r/postgres
```

Row-level security

Currently, row-level security is not supported by postgres; however, one could use views to define row-level security on data. Row-level security will be supported in the upcoming version of PostgreSQL 9.5.

Encrypting data

By default, PostgreSQL internally encrypts sensitive data, such as roles' passwords. However, database users can also encrypt and decrypt sensitive data using the `pgcrypto` extension.

PostgreSQL role password encryption

When creating a role with password and login options, one can see the role's details in the `pg_shadow` catalog relation. Note that it is not recommended to use the following format to create the password because the statement can appear in `pg_stat_activity` or the server logs:

```
CREATE ROLE <role_name> WITH LOGIN PASWWORD 'role_password';
```

The passwords in `pg_catalog` are encrypted with a slat by default, as shown in the following example. Note how `passwd` for the a and b roles are different even though they have the same password:

```
CREATE ROLE a WITH LOGIN PASWWORD 'a';
CREATE ROLE b WITH LOGIN PASWWORD 'a';
SELECT usename, passwd FROM pg_shadow WHERE usename IN ('a','b');
 usename |                 passwd
```

```
---------+------------------------------------
 b       | md5187ef4436122d1cc2f40dc2b92f0eba0
 a       | md54124bc0a9335c27f086f24ba207a4912
(2 rows)
```

The role password is resent when a role is rested, as follows:

```
ALTER ROLE a RENAME TO x;
NOTICE:  MD5 password cleared because of role rename
ALTER ROLE
```

When creating a user with a password, it is recommended to use the \password psql meta command because it ensures that the password does not appear in clear text form in the psql history command, server log files, or elsewhere. To change the postgres role password, one needs to log in as postgres and then invoke this command, as follows:

```
$ psql -h localhost -U postgres
postgres=# \password
Enter new password:
Enter it again:
postgres=#
```

pgcrypto

The pgcrypto extension provides a cryptographic functionality. Data encryption and decryption consume hardware resources, so it is important to have a balance between data sensitivity and decryption complexity. There are two kinds of data encryption, as follows:

- One-way data encryption uses a function to generate a hash, which cannot be reversed. The resulted encrypted text has often a fixed length; for example, MD5 encryption generates 16 bytes of hashes. A good hash function should be quick to compute and not produce the same hash for a different input.
- Two-way data encryption allows the data to be encrypted and decrypted.

Pgcrypto comes with functions to support one-way and two-way encryption. It supports several hashing algorithms. Pgcrypto can be installed using the CREATE EXTENSION command, as follows:

```
CREATE EXTENSION pgcrypto;
```

One-way encryption

In one-way encryption, retrieving data in a clear text form is not important. The encrypted text (digest) is used to verify that the user knows the secret text. One-way encryption is often used to store passwords. PostgreSQL supports out-of-the-box MD5 encryption; however, as MD5 can be cracked easily, one could use MD5 with salt, as seen in the preceding pg_shadow example.

The common scenario of validating a password is comparing the generated MD5 digest with the stored one, as follows:

```
CREATE TABLE account (id INT, password text);

INSERT INTO account VALUES (1, md5('my password'));

SELECT (md5('my password') = password) AS authenticated FROM account;

---output
 authenticated

---------------

 t

(1 row)
```

Pgcrypto provides two functions to encrypt the password. These functions are crypt and gen_salt; also, the pgcrypto extension relieves the user from maintaining the salt. Crypt and gen_salt can be used almost in the same way as MD5 to store the password, as follows:

```
truncate account;

INSERT INTO account VALUES (1, crypt ('my password', gen_salt('md5'))),
(2, crypt ('my password', gen_salt('md5')));

SELECT * FROM account;
 id |          password
----+-----------------------------------
  1 | $1$XoZUm6GT$AnqHLYDuxQs8qLAQxlc6r/
  2 | $1$dZp2EIKk$v48D/SbgKhCMYABHreIKF1
(2 rows)

SELECT crypt('my password', '$1$XoZUm6GT$AnqHLYDuxQs8qLAQxlc6r/') =
'$1$XoZUm6GT$AnqHLYDuxQs8qLAQxlc6r/' AS authenticated  FROM account WHERE
id = 1 ;
 authenticated

---------------

 t

(1 row)
```

Note how the password differs due to a different generated salt. Also, note how the salt does not need to be maintained. Also, one could have a stronger password by tuning the salt generation. For example, one could use blowfish hashing and specify the iteration count. Note that the more the iteration counts, the slower the decryption, and more time is subsequently required to break it, as shown in the example:

```
car_portal=# \timing
Timing is on.
car_portal=# SELECT crypt('my password', gen_salt('bf',4));
                            crypt
-------------------------------------------------------------
 $2a$04$GuQUIr.JmnCypsu49CrZseQAsFKzmWcfmfBrfRRU2JJ.agqv1RcEy
(1 row)


Time: 2.060 ms
car_portal=# SELECT crypt('my password', gen_salt('bf',8));
                            crypt
-------------------------------------------------------------
 $2a$08$955AL.pjCUScYupcVNIQKeOs6j.uC3v0HOE2c3aezQQhOJi8zMLRK
(1 row)


Time: 25.478 ms
car_portal=# SELECT crypt('my password', gen_salt('bf',12));
                            crypt
-------------------------------------------------------------
 $2a$12$ejO0flBvlUv9pJ/7SNneT.DYn6W7oPSKiWUcTkRLLHzTMjjI37Lle
(1 row)


Time: 420.496 ms
car_portal=# SELECT crypt('my password', gen_salt('bf',16));
                            crypt
-------------------------------------------------------------
 $2a$16$gWTTGf45/tqmGaEHVmZHD.RX/Vmjrm.3dA4S0Edhu6oo7Ei9gQ6r2
(1 row)


Time: 6598.780 ms
```

```
car_portal=# SELECT crypt('my password', '$2a$16$gWTTGf45/tqmGaEHVmZHD.
RX/Vmjrm.3dA4SOEdhu6oo7Ei9gQ6r2');
                                crypt
---------------------------------------------------------------
 $2a$16$gWTTGf45/tqmGaEHVmZHD.RX/Vmjrm.3dA4SOEdhu6oo7Ei9gQ6r2
(1 row)
```

Two-way encryption

Two-way encryption is used to store sensitive information, such as payment information. Pgcrypto provides two functions—mainly encrypt and decrypt—as shown in the following script:

```
car_portal=# \df encrypt
                        List of functions
 Schema |  Name   | Result data type | Argument data types |  Type
--------+---------+------------------+---------------------+--------
 public | encrypt | bytea            | bytea, bytea, text  | normal
(1 row)


car_portal=# \df decrypt
                        List of functions
 Schema |  Name   | Result data type | Argument data types |  Type
--------+---------+------------------+---------------------+--------
 public | decrypt | bytea            | bytea, bytea, text  | normal
(1 row)
```

The encrypt and decrypt functions require three arguments: the data to encrypt, the key, and the encryption algorithm. The following example shows how to encrypt and decrypt the string Hello world using the aes encryption algorithm:

```
car_portal=# SELECT encrypt ('Hello World', 'my key', 'aes');
             encrypt
------------------------------------
 \xe3d6d1ddea318dbf88e34421fd095727
(1 row)
car_portal=# SELECT decrypt ('\xe3d6d1ddea318dbf88e34421fd095727', 'my
key' , 'aes');
            decrypt
```

```
---------------------------
 \x48656c6c6f20576f726c64
(1 row)
car_portal=# SELECT convert_from('\x48656c6c6f20576f726c64', 'utf-8');
 convert_from
 -------------
 Hello World
(1 row)
```

The preceding form of encryption has some limitations; for example, the statement can appear in `pg_stat_activity` or in the database server log, and thus, one could get the key.

Two-way encryption can be achieved in two ways: symmetric and asymmetric encryption. The preceding example shows how symmetric encryption works, where there is a key used to encrypt and decrypt data. Asymmetric encryption uses public and private keys; the public key is used to encrypt the data, and the private key used to decrypt it. Asymmetric encryption is more secure than symmetric encryption but harder to set up. To set up asymmetric encryption and decryption, one needs to generate a public key via the `gpg` tool. The first step in generating the key is to execute the following command. Note that the `gpg` command asks for a passphrase; in this example, the passphrase should not be provided:

```
gpg --gen-key
```

Now, to extract the public and private keys, one could execute the following commands:

```
# gpg --list-secret-key
/root/.gnupg/secring.gpg
---------------------------
sec    2048R/2C914A6D 2015-06-25
uid                    Salahaldin Juba <example@mial.com>
ssb    2048R/56C8FA64 2015-06-25
# gpg -a --export 2C914A6D > /var/lib/postgresql/9.4/main/public.key
# gpg -a --export-secret-key 56C8FA64 > /var/lib/postgresql/9.4/main/
secret.key# chown postgres:postgres /var/lib/postgresql/9.4/main/public.
key
#chown postgres:postgres /var/lib/postgresql/9.4/main/secret.key
```

The gpg option `--list-secret-key` is used to determine the key IDs, and the options `--export-secret-key` and `--export` are used to export the public and the private keys, respectively. The `-a` option is used to dump the keys in copy and paste formats; however, on the PostgreSQL backend, we need to run the `dearmor` function. Also, the keys were moved to the database cluster folder for convenience purposes to use the `pg_read_file` function. Finally, it is recommended to change the keys' ownership to postgres to protect the files on the hard disk.

After the generation of the keys, one could create a wrapper around `pgp_pub_encrypt` and `pgp_pub_decrypt` to hide the location of the keys, as follows:

```
CREATE OR REPLACE FUNCTION encrypt (text) RETURNS bytea AS
$$
BEGIN
  RETURN pgp_pub_encrypt($1, dearmor(pg_read_file('public.key')));
END;
$$ Language plpgsql;


CREATE OR REPLACE FUNCTION decrypt (bytea) RETURNS text AS
$$
BEGIN
  RETURN  pgp_pub_decrypt($1, dearmor(pg_read_file('secret.key')));
END;
$$ Language plpgsql;
test=# SELECT decrypt(encrypt('hello'));
 decrypt
---------
 hello
(1 row)
```

Summary

Securing data against a breach is a mandatory task. Data security can be breached through different techniques. A database user can reuse the default database privileges to gain information about other users, execute certain user functions, or monitor `pg_stat_activity`. Also, some data can be sniffed using `tcpdump`; so, one should use SSL connections to secure the network traffic. In this chapter, PostgreSQL security is tackled from the authorization, authentication, and data encryption aspects; however, one also should protect the code against SQL injection and other known security issues, such as function cost, and view the security barrier as shown in the previous chapters.

The next chapter will focus on the PostgreSQL system catalog and introduce several recipes to maintain the database. The recipes will be used to extract potential problems in the database, such as missing indexes and introduce the solutions to tackle these problems.

9
The PostgreSQL System Catalog and System Administration Functions

The PostgreSQL system catalog and system administration functions can aid both developers and administrators to keep the database clean and performant. System catalogs can be used to automate several tasks, such as finding tables without indexes, finding dependencies between database objects, and extracting information about the database through health checks, such as table bloats, database size, locks, and so on. Information extracted from the system catalog can be employed in monitoring solutions such as Nagios and in dynamic SQL. This chapter will be formatted a little bit differently and follow a cookbook approach.

The system catalog

PostgreSQL describes all database objects using the meta information stored in database relations. These relations hold information about tables, views, functions, indexes, **foreign data wrappers (FDWs)**, triggers, constraints, rules, users, groups, and so on. This information is stored in the pg_catalog schema, and to make it more human readable, PostgreSQL also provides the information_schema schema, where the meta information is wrapped and organized in views.

In the psql client, one can see exactly what is happening behind the scene when a certain meta command is executed, such as \z, by enabling ECHO_HIDDEN. The ECHO_HIDDEN or -E switch allow users to study the internals of PostgreSQL. You need to run the following command:

```
car_portal=# \set ECHO_HIDDEN
car_portal=# \z car_portal_app.car
********* QUERY **********
SELECT n.nspname as "Schema",
  c.relname as "Name",
  CASE c.relkind WHEN 'r' THEN 'table' WHEN 'v' THEN
  'view' WHEN 'm' THEN 'materialized view' WHEN 'S' THEN
  'sequence' WHEN 'f' THEN 'foreign table' END as
  "Type",
  pg_catalog.array_to_string(c.relacl, E'\n') AS "Access
  privileges",
  pg_catalog.array_to_string(ARRAY(
    SELECT attname || E':\n  ' ||
    pg_catalog.array_to_string(attacl, E'\n  ')
    FROM pg_catalog.pg_attribute a
    WHERE attrelid = c.oid AND NOT attisdropped AND
    attacl IS NOT NULL
  ), E'\n') AS "Column access privileges"
FROM pg_catalog.pg_class c
    LEFT JOIN pg_catalog.pg_namespace n ON n.oid =
    c.relnamespace
WHERE c.relkind IN ('r', 'v', 'm', 'S', 'f')
  AND c.relname ~ '^(car)$'
  AND n.nspname ~ '^(car_portal_app)$'
ORDER BY 1, 2;
**************************


                        Access privileges
     Schema      | Name | Type  | Access privileges | Column access
privileges
----------------+------+-------+-------------------+--------------------
-----
 car_portal_app | car  | table |                   |
(1 row)
```

As seen in the preceding example, when the \z meta command is used, the query is sent to the database server backend. In addition to ECHO_HIDDEN, one can have a peek at the information_schema and pg_catalog views, as follows:

```
SELECT * FROM information_schema.views where table_schema IN ('pg_
catlog', 'information_schema');
```

The pg_catalog and information_schema views contain hundreds of views, tables, and administration functions; for this reason, only some of the common and heavily used catalog tables will be described.

The pg_class table is one of the main tables in pg_cataolg; it stores information about various relation types, as seen in the following list:

- Tables
- Indexes
- Views
- Sequences
- Materialized views
- Composite types
- TOAST tables

The relkind attribute in pg_class specifies the relation type. The following characters are used to identify relations:

Characters	Tables
r	Relations
v	Views
m	Materialized views
f	Foreign tables
t	Toast tables
i	Indexes
c	Composite type

As this table is used to describe all relations, some columns are meaningless for some relation types.

One could think of **The Oversized-Attribute Storage Technique (TOAST)** as a vertical partitioning strategy. PostgreSQL does not allow tuples to span multiple pages where the page size is often 8 KB; therefore, PostgreSQL stores, breaks, and compresses large objects into several chunks and stores them in other tables called TOAST tables.

The relations are identified by object identifiers. These identifiers are used as primary keys in the `pg_catalog` schema, so it is important to know how to convert **object identifiers (OID)** into text to get the relation name. Also, note that the OIDs have types; for example, the `regcalss` type is used to identify all relations stored in `pg_class`, while the `regprocedure` type is used to identify functions. The following example shows how to convert a table name to OID and vice versa:

```
car_portal=# SELECT 'car_portal_app.car'::regclass::oid;
  oid
-------
 24807
(1 row)


car_portal=# SELECT 24807::regclass::text;
      text
--------------------
 car_portal_app.car
(1 row)
```

Another approach is to use `pg_class` and `pg_namespace` to get the OID, as follows:

```
car_portal=# SELECT c.oid FROM pg_class c join pg_namespace n ON
(c.relnamespace = n.oid) WHERE relname ='car' AND nspname ='car_portal_
app';
  oid
-------
 24807
(1 row)
```

Another important table is `pg_attribute`; this table stores information about the table and other `pg_class` object columns. The `pg_index` table, as the name suggests, stores information about indexes. In addition to these, `pg_depend` and `pg_rewrite` are used to store information about dependent objects and rewrite rules for tables and views. The complete list of catalog tables can be found in the PostgreSQL online documentation.

Another important set of tables and views is `pg_stat<*>`; these tables provide statistics about tables, indexes, columns, sequences, and so on. Information stored in these tables is highly valuable to debug performance issues and usage patterns. The following query shows the statistics of the tables and views:

```
SELECT relname, case relkind when 'r' then 'table'  WHEN 'v' THEN 'VIEW'
END as type FROM pg_class WHERE relname like 'pg_sta%' AND relkind IN
('r','v');
```

The following sections show some recipes that are often used in PostgreSQL. Some of these recipes might be used on a daily basis: such as `SELECT pg_reload_conf()`, which is used to reload the database cluster after amending `pg_hba.conf` or `postgresql.conf`, and `SELECT pg_terminate_backend(pid)`, which is used to kill a certain process.

Getting the database cluster and client tools version

The PostgreSQL version allows the developer to know the supported features and helps them write compatible SQL queries for different versions. For example, the process ID attribute name in the `pg_stat_activity` view in PostgreSQL versions older than 9.2 is `procpid`; in PostgreSQL version 9.2, this attribute name is `pid`.

Getting ready

Getting the database and build version right is important because it allows the developer to know the supported features and compatibility between client tools and the backend version.

How to do it...

The `version()` function, as shown in the following query, shows the version information as well as build system:

```
car_portal=# SELECT version ();
                          version
----------------------------------------------------------------
 PostgreSQL 9.4.1, compiled by Visual C++ build 1800, 64-bit
(1  row)
```

There's more...

It is also important to check the client tools' version, whether it is `pg_restore`, `pg_dumpall` or psql, in order to check its compatibility with the server. This can be done as follows:

```
pg_dump --version
pg_dump (PostgreSQL) 9.3.5
```

The `pg_dump` utility generates dumps that can be restored on newer versions of PostgreSQL. Also, `pg_dump` can dump data from PostgreSQL versions older than its own version but not for a PostgreSQL version newer than its own version, as shown in the following query:

```
$ pg_dump -h localhost -U postgres -d car_portal > car_portal.sql
pg_dump: server version: 9.4.1; pg_dump version: 9.3.5
pg_dump: aborting because of server version mismatch
```

Terminating and canceling user sessions

Database administrators often need to kill server processes for various reasons. For example, in certain scenarios, very slow queries running on the slave or master, which are configured using streaming replication, can break the replication.

Getting ready

It is important to terminate some database connections and processes in the case of dead locks, in case the maximum number of connections is exceeded, as well as for maintenance purposes, such as dropping the database as one cannot drop the database if someone is connected to it.

How to do it...

PostgreSQL provides the `pg_terminate_backend(pid)` and `pg_cancel_backend(pid)` functions, while `pg_cancel_backend` only cancels the current query and `pg_terminate_backend` kills the entire connection. The following query terminates all connections to the current database except the session connection:

```
SELECT pg_terminate_backend(pid) FROM pg_stat_activity WHERE datname =
current_database() AND pid <> pg_backend_pid();
```

How it works...

The `pg_cancel_backend` function cancels the current query, but the application may run the same query again. The `pg_terminate_backend` function terminates the connection, and this also can be done via the kill Linux command. However, the kill command may be dangerous if one kills the postgres server process instead on the connection process.

There's more...

When combining `pg_stat_activity` and `pg_terminate_backend`, one can achieve greater flexibility. For example, in streaming replication, one can detect queries that take a lot of time on the slaves and thus cause a replication lag. Also, if a certain application is not configured properly and has a big number of idle connections, one can kill them to free memory and allow other clients to connect to the database.

Finally, if one is not able to drop a certain database because clients try to connect to it, one can execute the following query, which disallows users from connecting to the database and then kills the connections:

```
UPDATE pg_database set datallowconn = 'false' WHERE datname = 'database
to drop';
--- now kill the connections
```

Setting and getting database cluster settings

The PostgreSQL configuration settings control several aspects of the PostgreSQL cluster. For the administration aspect, one can define the statement time out, number of allowed connections, transaction type—read only or read/write—, and so on. From the development point of view, these settings can help a developer optimize queries.

Getting ready

The following recipe shows how to get and set a certain configuration value.

How to do it…

Getting a value can be done in several ways, such as selecting the value from the `pg_settings` catalog view, browsing the `postgresql.conf` file, or using the following function and statement:

```
car_portal=# SELECT current_setting('work_mem');
 current_setting
-----------------
 4MB
(1 row)
```

```
car_portal=# show work_mem;
 work_mem
----------
 4MB
(1  row)
```

In order to change a certain configuration value, one could use the `set_config(settin_name, setting_value, scope)` function, as follows:

```
car_portal=# SELECT set_config('work_mem', '8 MB', true); -- true means
only current transaction is affected
 set_config
------------
 8MB
(1 row)
```

If one wants to use the preceding function to set a certain value for the whole session, the `true` value should be replaced with `false`.

Also, note that the `set_config` function can raise an error if the setting cannot be set, as follows:

```
car_portal=# SELECT set_config('shared_buffers', '1 GB', false);
ERROR:  parameter "shared_buffers" cannot be changed without restarting
the server
```

There's more...

The ALTER SYSTEM command is used to change PostgreSQL configuration parameters. The synopsis for ALTER SYSTEM is:

```
ALTER SYSTEM SET configuration_parameter { TO | = } { value | 'value' |
DEFAULT }
```

```
ALTER SYSTEM RESET configuration_parameter
ALTER SYSTEM RESET ALL
```

In case the setting value requires a system reload or restart, the setting will take effect after the system reload or restart, respectively. The ALTER SYSTEM command requires superuser privileges.

Finally, browsing the postgresql.conf file is a bit tricky due to the big number of postgres settings. Also, most settings have the default boot values; therefore, getting the server configuration settings that are not assigned the default values in postresql.conf can be easily done, as follows:

```
car_portal=# SELECT name, current_setting(name), source FROM pg_settings
WHERE source IN ('configuration file');
```

name	current_setting	source
DateStyle	ISO, DMY	configuration file
default_text_search_config	pg_catalog.english	configuration file

Getting the database and database object size

Managing disk space and assigning table spaces to tables as well as databases requires knowledge about the size of the database and database objects. When performing a logical restore, one could get information about the progress by comparing the original database size and the one which is being restored. Finally, the database object size often gives information about bloats.

Getting ready

Getting the database size is an important administration task because it allows the administrator to put migration plans and handle common maintenance issues, such as out-of-space and bloat issues.

How to do it...

To get the database size, one can get the `oid` database from the `pg_database` table and run the Linux command, `du -h /data_directory/base/oid`, where `data_directory` is the database cluster folder specified in the `postgresql.conf` configuration file. In this regard, a quick look at the PostgreSQL cluster folders is quite useful. For example, to determine the creation date of a certain database, one could have a look at the `PG_VERSION` file creation date located in the database directory.

In addition to this, PostgreSQL provides the `pg_database_size` function to get the database size and the `pg_size_pretty` function to display the size in a human readable form, as follows:

```
car_portal=# SELECT pg_database.datname, pg_size_pretty(pg_database_
size(pg_database.datname)) AS size FROM pg_database;
   datname   |   size
-------------+---------
 template1   | 6417 kB
 template0   | 6409 kB
 postgres    | 6540 kB
 test        | 6532 kB
 car_portal  | 29 MB
(1  rows)
```

There's more...

One can get the table size, including indexes and toast tables, using the `pg_totoal_relation_size` function. If one is interested only in the table size, one can use the `pg_relation_size` function. This information helps manage table growth as well as table spaces. Take a look at the following query:

```
car_portal=# SELECT tablename, pg_size_pretty(pg_total_relation_size(sch
emaname||'.'||tablename)) FROM pg_tables WHERE schemaname = 'car_portal_
app' LIMIT 2;
```

```
        tablename        | pg_size_pretty
-------------------------+----------------
 advertisement_rating    | 16 kB
 log                     | 48 kB
(1  rows)
```

Finally, to get the index size, one could use the `pg_relation_size` function, as follows:

```
car_portal=# SELECT indexrelid::regclass,  pg_size_pretty(pg_
relation_size(indexrelid::regclass))  FROM pg_index WHERE
indexrelid::regclass::text like 'car_portal_app.%' limit 2;
                              indexrelid                                |
pg_size_pretty
-----------------------------------------------------------------------+--
--------------
 car_portal_app.account_email_key                                      |
16 kB
 car_portal_app.account_history_account_id_search_key_search_date_key  |
8192 bytes
(1  rows)
```

Cleaning up the database

Often, a database can contain several unused objects or very old data. Cleaning up these objects helps administrators perform a backup of images more quickly. From the development point of view, unused objects are similar to quiet noise because they affect the refactoring process.

Getting ready

In database applications, one needs to keep the database clean as database objects might hinder quick development due to the objects' dependencies. To clean the database, one needs to identify the unused database objects, including tables, views, indexes, and functions.

A recipe for bloated tables and indexes will not be introduced here; you can take a look at the bucardo `check_postgres` Nagios plugin code at `https://bucardo.org/wiki/Check_postgres` to understand how bloats in tables and indexes can be calculated.

How to do it…

Table statistics, such as the number of live rows, index scans, and sequential scans, can help identify empty and unused tables. Note that the following queries are based on statistics, so the result needs to be validated. The `pg_stat_user_tables` function provides this information, and the following query shows only two empty tables:

```
car_portal=# SELECT relname FROM pg_stat_user_tables WHERE n_live_tup= 0
limit 2;
        relname
----------------------

 logged_actions

 advertisement_picture

(1  rows)
```

To find the empty columns, one can have a look at the `null_fraction` attribute of the `pg_stats` table, as follows:

```
car_portal=# SELECT schemaname, tablename, attname FROM pg_stats WHERE
null_frac= 1 and schemaname NOT IN ('pg_catalog', 'information_schema')
limit 1;
   schemaname    | tablename | attname
-----------------+-----------+---------

 car_portal_app | log       | old_row

(1 row)
```

To find the useless indexes, two techniques can be applied: the first technique is to determine whether an index is duplicated or overlapped with another index, and the second technique is to assess whether the index is used based on the index statistics.

The following query can be used to assess whether an index is used excluding constraint indexes — the unique constraints and primary keys — based on the catalog statistics:

```
SELECT schemaname, relname, indexrelname FROM pg_stat_user_indexes s
JOIN pg_index i ON s.indexrelid = i.indexrelid WHERE idx_scan=0 AND NOT
indisunique AND NOT indisprimary;
```

Overlapping index attributes can be used to identify duplicate indexes, as shown in the following example:

```
WITH index_info AS

(SELECT pg_get_indexdef(indexrelid) AS index_def, indexrelid::regclass
index_name , indrelid::regclass table_name, array_agg(attname) AS index_
att
```

```
FROM

  pg_index i JOIN

  pg_attribute a ON i.indexrelid = a.attrelid

GROUP BY pg_get_indexdef(indexrelid), indrelid,  indexrelid

)

SELECT DISTINCT

  CASE WHEN a.index_name > b.index_name THEN a.index_def
  ELSE b.index_def END AS index_def,

  CASE WHEN a.index_name > b.index_name THEN
  a.index_name ELSE b.index_name END AS index_name,

  CASE WHEN a.index_name > b.index_name THEN b.index_def
  ELSE a.index_def END AS overlap_index_def,

  CASE WHEN a.index_name > b.index_name THEN b.index_def
  ELSE a.index_def END AS overlap_index_name,

  a.table_name

FROM

  index_info a INNER JOIN index_info b ON (a.index_name != b.index_name
AND a.table_name = b.table_name AND a.index_att && b.index_att );
```

There's more...

Cleaning up unused views and functions is a little bit tricky. By default, PostgreSQL collects statistics about indexes and tables but not functions. To enable statistics collection on functions, the `track_functions` setting needs to be enabled. The statistics on functions can be found in the `pg_stat_user_functions` table.

For views, there are no statistics collected unless the views are materialized. In order to assess whether a view is used, we need to do this manually. This can be done by rewriting the view and joining it with a function with a certain side effect, such as updating a table and increasing the number of times the view is accessed or raising a certain log message. To test this technique, let's write a simple function that raises a log, as follows:

```
CREATE OR REPLACE FUNCTION monitor_view_usage (view_name TEXT) RETURNS
BOOLEAN AS $$

BEGIN

  RAISE LOG 'The view % is used on % by % ', view_name,
  current_time, session_user;

  RETURN TRUE;

END;

$$
```

```
LANGUAGE plpgsql
```

```
cost .001;
```

Now, let's assume that we want to drop the following view; however, there is uncertainty regarding whether an application depends on it:

```
CREATE OR REPLACE VIEW sport_car AS
SELECT car_id, number_of_owners,regestration_number
FROM car_portal_app.car
WHERE number_of_doors = 3;
```

To ensure that the view is not used, the view should be rewritten as follows, where the `monitor_view_usage` function is used, and the log files should be monitored for a certain period of time. The following query can help:

```
CREATE OR REPLACE VIEW sport_car AS SELECT car_id, number_of_owners,
regestration_number
FROM car_portal_app.car CROSS JOIN monitor_view_usage ('sport_car')
WHERE number_of_doors = 3;
```

If the view is used, an entry in the log file should appear, as follows:

```
2015-06-03 17:55:04 CEST LOG:  The view sport_car is used on
17:55:04.571+02 by postgres.
```

Cleaning up data in the database

Cleaning up data is an important topic; often, the data life cycle is not defined when creating a database application. This leads to tons of outdated data. Unclean data hinders several processes, such as database refactoring. Also, it can have a side effect on all processes in the company, such as wrong report results, billing issues, unauthorized access, and so on.

Getting ready

Several recipes were introduced to determine unused objects, but this is not all. The data itself should be cleaned, and the data life cycle should be defined.

For unclean data, there are several scenarios; however, let's focus here only on duplicated rows due to the missing unique and primary key constraints.

How to do it...

The first step is to identify the tables that do not have unique and primary key constraints. This is quite easy using the information schema, as follows:

```
SELECT table_catalog, table_schema, table_name
FROM
    information_schema.tables
WHERE
    table_schema NOT IN ('information_schema',
    'pg_catalog')
EXCEPT
SELECT
    table_catalog, table_schema, table_name
FROM
    information_schema.table_constraints
WHERE
    constraint_type IN ('PRIMARY KEY', 'UNIQUE') AND
    table_schema NOT IN ('information_schema', 'pg_catalog');
```

The second step is to identify the tables that really contain duplicates; this can be performed by aggregating the data on the table. To check this, let's create a table with some duplicates in it, as follows:

```
CREATE TABLE duplicate AS SELECT (random () * 9  + 1)::INT as f1 ,
(random () * 9 + 1)::INT as f2 FROM generate_series (1,20);


SELECT count(*), f1, f2 FROM duplicate GROUP BY f1, f2 having count(*) >
1 limit 3;
 count | f1 | f2
-------+----+----
     3 |  7 |  7
     2 |  7 |  2
     2 |  7 |  6
(3 rows)
```

The tricky part is to delete the duplicates as the rows are identical. To delete duplicates, a certain row needs to be marked to stay, and the rest need to be deleted. This can be achieved using the `ctid` column. In PostgreSQL, each row has a header, and the `ctid` column is the physical location of the row version within the table. Thus, the `ctid` column can be used as a row identifier temporarily because this identifier may change after running maintenance commands, such as CLUSTER.

To delete the duplicate, one can perform the following query:

```
with should_not_delete as (
    SELECT min(ctid) FROM duplicate group by f1, f2
) DELETE FROM duplicate WHERE ctid NOT IN (SELECT min FROM should_not_
delete);
```

There's more...

There are several other approaches to clean up duplicate rows. For example, one can use the CREATE TABLE and SELECT DISTINCT statements to create a table with a unique set of rows. Then, one can drop the original table and rename the created table after the original table, as shown in the following example:

```
CREATE TABLE <tmp> AS SELECT DISTINCT * FROM <orig_tbl>;
DROP TABLE <orig_tbl>;
ALTER TABLE <tmp> RENAME TO <orig_tbl>;
```

Note that this approach might be faster than the approach represented in the preceding example; however, this technique may not work if there are other objects depending on the table that needs to be dropped, such as views, indexes, and so on.

If the table that contains duplicate records has a primary key, one can drop the table using the DELETE...USING statement, as follows:

```
DELETE FROM dup_table a USING dup_table b
WHERE a.tt1 = b.tt1 AND ... AND b.attn= b.attn
AND a.pk < p.pk.
```

The list of attributes, `att1,..., attn`, is used to join the table with itself, and the primary key indicated in the code as `pk` is used to specify the record that needs to be deleted. Note that this approach is often faster than the first approach as it does not require aggregation.

Managing database locks

Lock management is essential in a production environment and should be monitored closely. There are several types of locks, such as deadlocks, advisory locks, and table locks. For tables, there are several lock modes; the only mode that blocks SELECT statements is ACCESS EXCLUSIVE. Access to the exclusive mode can be acquired through statements that alter the table's physical structure, such as ALTER, DROP, TRUNCATE, VACUUM FULL, CLUSTER, and REINDEX and finally using the LOCK command in the ACCESS EXCLUSIVE mode.

The table's looks might cause some queries to wait until the lock is lifted, depending on the lock mode and the query type. Also, some queries may wait for a long time due to keeping the transaction uncommitted or the connection idle in transaction.

In the case of idle in-transaction queries, one could detect the locks using the pg_stat_activity and pg_lock tables, as follows:

```
SELECT
    lock1.pid as locked_pid,
    stat1.usename as locked_user,
    stat1.query as locked_statement,
    stat1.state as state,
    stat2.query as locking_statement,
    stat2.state as state,
    now() - stat1.query_start as locking_duration,
    lock2.pid as locking_pid,
    stat2.usename as locking_user
FROM pg_catalog.pg_locks lock1
    JOIN pg_catalog.pg_stat_activity stat1 on lock1.pid = stat1.pid
    JOIN pg_catalog.pg_locks lock2 on
    (lock1.locktype,lock1.database,lock1.relation,
    lock1.page,lock1.tuple,lock1.virtualxid,
    lock1.transactionid,lock1.classid,lock1.objid,
    lock1.objsubid) IS NOT DISTINCT FROM
        (lock2.locktype,lock2.DATABASE,
        lock2.relation,lock2.page,
        lock2.tuple,lock2.virtualxid,
        lock2.transactionid,lock2.classid,
        lock2.objid,lock2.objsubid)
    JOIN pg_catalog.pg_stat_activity stat2 on lock2.pid
    = stat2.pid
WHERE NOT lock1.granted AND lock2.granted;
```

To test the query, let's open three sessions to create locks on the car table. In the first session, let's lock the table, as follows:

```
car_portal=# BEGIN;
BEGIN
car_portal=# LOCK TABLE car_portal_app.car IN ACCESS EXCLUSIVE MODE;
LOCK TABLE
car_portal=#
```

In the second session, let's try to delete all entries from the car table, as follows:

```
car_portal=# DELETE FROM car; -- this will wait until the lock is removed
```

In the third session, when executing the query that finds the locks, one should get a result as follows:

```
car_portal=# \x
Expanded display is on.
car_portal=# SELECT
lock1.pid as locked_pid, ...;


-[ RECORD 1 ]-----+-------------------------------------------
locked_pid        | 8536
locked_user       | postgres
locked_statement  | DELETE FROM car;
state             | active
locking_statement | LOCK TABLE CAR IN ACCESS EXCLUSIVE MODE;
                  |
state             | idle in transaction
locking_duration  | 00:01:02.378
locking_pid       | 11884
locking_user      | postgres
```

Adding missing indexes on foreign keys and altering the default statistic

High performance in PostgreSQL can be achieved by having optimal execution plans and proper indexes. Execution plans depend on the statistics gathered from the tables; fortunately, in postgres, one can control the behavior of the statistic collection.

Getting ready

For a developer, it is important to get good performance. When handling foreign keys, there are two recommendations to increase the performance, which are as follows:

- **Always index foreign keys**: Indexing a table on a foreign key allows PostgreSQL to fetch data from the table using an index scan.

- Increase the column statistic target on foreign keys: This is also applicable to all predicates because it allows PostgreSQL to have a better estimation of the number of rows. The default statistic target is 100, and the maximum is 10,000. Increasing the statistics target makes the ANALYZE command slower.

How to do it...

Both of the preceding approaches require identifying foreign keys. The pg_catalog. pg_constraint function can be used to look up table constraints. To get all foreign key constrains, one can simply run the following query:

```
SELECT * FROM pg_constraint WHERE contype = 'f';
```

Also, from the previous examples, we can see how to get overlapping indexes; one can combine information from both tables to get foreign keys that do not have indexes, as follows:

```
SELECT conrelid::regclass,conname,reltuples::bigint,indkey,conkey ,CASE
WHEN conkey && string_to_array(indkey::text, ' ')::SMALLINT[] THEN FALSE
ELSE TRUE END as might_require_index

  FROM pg_constraint JOIN pg_class ON (conrelid = pg_class.oid) JOIN
  pg_index ON indrelid = conrelid WHERE contype = 'f'
```

Note that if `indkey` overlaps with `conkey`, we might not need to add an index; however, this should be validated by the usage pattern and how the rows are selected. Also, in the preceding example, the number of reltuples is selected as this is an important factor to decide index creation because performing sequential scans on big tables is quite costly. After the identification of foreign keys, one can use the `CREATE INDEX` command and `ALTER TABLE` to create indexes and alter default statistics, respectively.

Getting the views dependency tree

When refactoring a certain view, such as adding a new column or changing the column type, one needs to refactor all the views that depend on this particular view. Unfortunately, PostgreSQL does not provide the means to create a logical dump of dependent object.

Getting ready

PostgreSQL provides `pg_dump` to dump a certain database or a specific set of objects in a database. Also, in development, it is recommended to keep the code in a GIT repository.

Unfortunately, often the SQL code for legacy applications is not maintained in the version control system. In this case, if there is requirement to change a certain view definition or even a column type, it is necessary to identify the affected views, dump them, and then restore them.

How to do it...

The first step is to identify the views to be dropped and restored. Depending on the task, one can write different scripts; a common pattern is to drop the views depending on a certain view, table, or table column. The base `pg_catalog` tables, `pg_depend` and `pg_rewrite`, store the dependency information and view rewriting rules; more human readable information can be found in `information_schema.view_table_usage`.

Let's assume that there are several views that depend on each other, as shown in the following figure, and the base view a needs to be refactored, which means dropped and created:

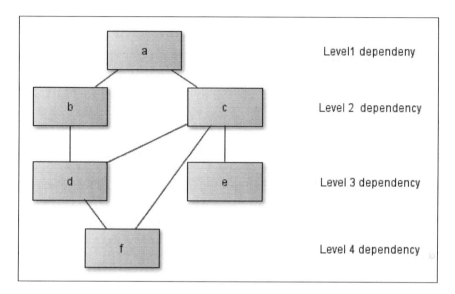

To generate this tree of dependency, one can execute the following queries:

```
CREATE VIEW a AS SELECT 1 FROM car;

CREATE VIEW b AS SELECT 1 FROM a;

CREATE VIEW c AS SELECT 1 FROM a;

CREATE VIEW d AS SELECT 1 FROM b,c;

CREATE VIEW e AS SELECT 1 FROM c;

CREATE VIEW f AS SELECT 1 FROM d,c;
```

To get the views and find out how they depend on each other in the preceding queries, the following query can be used:

```
SELECT view_schema,view_name parent, table_schema, table_name   FROM
information_schema.view_table_usage WHERE view_name LIKE '_' order by
view_name;
 view_schema | parent | table_schema | table_name
-------------+--------+--------------+------------
 public      | a      | public       | car
```

public	b	public	a
public	c	public	a
public	d	public	c
public	d	public	b
public	e	public	c
public	f	public	c
public	f	public	d

(8 rows)

Now, to solve the dependency tree, a recursive query will be used, as follows:

```
CREATE OR REPLACE FUNCTION get_dependency (schema_name text, view_name
text) RETURNS TABLE (schema_name text, view_name text, level int) AS $$
WITH RECURSIVE view_tree(parent_schema, parent_view, child_schema, child_
view, level) as
(
  SELECT
  parent.view_schema,
  parent.view_name ,
  parent.table_schema,
  parent.table_name,
  1
  FROM
  information_schema.view_table_usage parent
  WHERE
  parent.view_schema = $1 AND
  parent.view_name = $2
  UNION ALL
  SELECT
  child.view_schema,
  child.view_name,
  child.table_schema,
  child.table_name,
  parent.level + 1
  FROM
```

```
    view_tree parent JOIN
    information_schema.view_table_usage child ON
    child.table_schema = parent.parent_schema AND
    child.table_name = parent.parent_view
)
SELECT DISTINCT
    parent_schema,
    parent_view,
    level
FROM
    (SELECT
        parent_schema,
        parent_view,
        max (level) OVER (PARTITION BY parent_schema,
        parent_view) as max_level,
        level
    FROM
        view_tree) AS FOO
WHERE level = max_level;
$$
LANGUAGE SQL;
```

In the preceding query, the inner part of the query is used to calculate dependency levels, while the outer part of the query is used to eliminate duplicates. The following shows the dependencies for view a in the right order:

```
car_portal=# SELECT * FROM get_dependency ('public', 'a') ORDER BY Level;
 schema_name | view_name | level
-------------+-----------+-------
 public      | a         |   1
 public      | b         |   2
 public      | c         |   2
 public      | d         |   3
 public      | e         |   3
 public      | f         |   4
(6 rows)
```

There's more…

To dump the view's definition, one can use `pg_dump` with the -t option, which is used to dump a certain relation. So, to dump the views in the previous example, one can use the following trick:

```
pg_dump -s $(psql -t car_portal -c "SELECT string_agg (' -t ' || quote_
ident(schema_name)||'.'||quote_ident(view_name), ' ' ORDER BY level )
FROM get_dependency ('public'::text, 'a'::text)" ) -d  car_portal>/tmp/
dump.sql
```

The psql uses the -t option to return tuples, and the string aggregate function is used to generate the list of views that need to be dumped based on the level order. So, the inner psql query gives the following output:

```
-t public.a  -t public.b  -t public.c  -t public.d  -t public.e  -t
public.f
```

Summary

In addition to the PostgreSQL catalog, there are several tools and extensions that provide monitoring information, such as `pg_stat_statements`, which shows statistics about the queries executed in the database server, and `pg_buffercache`, which is used to get deeper insight into caching.

The PostgreSQL catalog contains meta information about PostgreSQL databases and objects. This information can be retrieved and manipulated using SQL statements. However, it is not recommended to manipulate the data directly in a catalog schema. Also, a more user friendly version of this meta information can be found in the `information_schema` schema.

- PostgreSQL provides a huge set of administration functions to get information from the database cluster and also to configure its behavior. Some database administration functions can be used to control the database system's behavior.

- One should keep an eye on the `pg_stat_activity` function to determine the unclosed connections.

- The `pg_stat_activity` and `pg_locks` functions can be used to find out locks in the database.

- Statistic tables and views are useful in determining performance bottlenecks as well as cleaning the database. It enables developers to monitor different aspects of the database, such as unused objects, duplicated data, as well as missing indexes and unique constraints.

- Knowing the database internal structure, table structure, and row structure is useful in understanding the database's behavior and in solving several problems. The `ctid` column can be used to clean duplicate data.

- Some of the functions and catalog tables shown in this chapter, such as the `current_setting` function, will be used in the next chapter — *Chapter 10, Optimizing Database Performance* — to show the effects of different settings on different execution plans.

10

Optimizing Database Performance

There are several aspects of tuning database performance, such as hardware configuration, network setting, database configuration, rewriting of SQL queries, maintenance of indexes, and so on. In this chapter, we will focus only on basic configuration and query rewriting.

Generally speaking, tuning database performance requires knowledge about the system's nature; for example, we need to know whether the database system can be used for **online analytical processing (OLAP)** or **online transactional processing (OLTP)**. The database system may be IO or CPU bound; these define the whole database cluster setup, such as the number of CPUs, CPU power, RAID setup, amount of RAM, and the database's cluster configuration. After the database server is configured, one could use benchmark framework, such as `pgbench`, to calculate the number of transactions per second (TPS) for the database server setup.

The second step in optimizing database performance is carried out after the system is up and running and often periodically. In this state, one could set up a monitoring system, such as a `pgbadger` monitoring tool, PostgreSQL load analyzer (PoWA), and `pg_stat_` statements, to find the bottlenecks and the slow queries.

To optimize a slow query, it should be analyzed first. If the query is poorly written, rewriting it might be enough. Otherwise, missing indexes can be created, server configuration settings can be amended, the physical structure can be refactored, and so on.

PostgreSQL configuration tuning

PostgreSQL's default configuration values are not suitable for the production environment; several default values are often undersized.

 In developing PostgreSQL applications, it is a good idea to have a test system that is configured very closely to a production environment to get accurate performance measures.

In any PostgreSQL environment, the following configuration should be reviewed.

Maximum number of connections

The maximum number of connections is an important parameter in configuring a database. Each client connection consumes memory, thus affecting also the total amount of memory that can be allocated for other purposes. The `max_connections` configuration parameter's default value is `100`; lowering this value allows the database administrator to increase the `work_mem` setting.

In general, it is good practice to use connection pooling software to reduce the amount of used memory and increase performance, as killing and establishing a connection wastes time. There are a lot of connection-pooling tools, and the most mature ones are:

- Pgbouncer
- Pgpool-II

Also, one could use connection pooling on the business level, such as the Java connection-pooling API and C3P0.

Memory settings

There are several settings to control memory consumption and the way memory is consumed, and these settings are:

- **Shared buffers (shared_buffers)**: The default value for shared buffers is 32 MB; however, it is recommended to set it around 25 percent of the total memory, but not more than 8 GB on Linux systems and 512 MB on windows system. Sometimes, increasing `shared_buffers` to a very high value leads to an increase in performance because the database can be cached completely in the RAM. However, the drawback of increasing this value too much is that one can't allocate memory for CPU operations such as sorting and hashing.

- **Working memory (work_mem)**: The default value is 1 MB; for CPU-bound operations, it is important to increase this value. The work_mem setting is linked with the number of connections, so the total amount of RAM used equals the number of connections multiplied by work_mem. Working memory is used to sort and hash, so it affects the queries that use the ORDER BY, DISTINCT, UNION, and EXCEPT constructs. To test your working method, you could analyze a query that uses sort and take a look at whether the sort operation uses the memory or hard disk, as follows:

```
EXPLAIN ANALYZE SELECT n FROM generate_series(1,5) as foo(n) order
by n;

Sort  (cost=59.83..62.33 rows=1000 width=4) (actual
time=0.075..0.075 rows=5 loops=1)

  Sort Key: n

  Sort Method: quicksort  Memory: 25kB

  -> Function Scan on generate_series foo  (cost=0.00..10.00
rows=1000 width=4) (actual time=0.018..0.018 rows=5 loops=1)"

Total runtime: 0.100 ms
```

Hard disk settings

There are several hard disk settings that can boost IO performance; however, this boost comes with a penalty. For example, the fsync setting forces each transaction to be written to the hard disk after each commit. Turning this off will increase performance, especially for bulk upload operations. Also, a checkpoint_segment of small value might also lead to performance penalty in write-heavy systems; on the other hand, increasing the checkpoint_segments setting to a high value will increase recovery time.

In specific cases, such as bulk upload operations, performance can be increased by altering hard disk settings, changing the logging configuration to log minimal info, and finally disabling auto vacuuming; however, after the bulk operation is over, one should not forget to reset the server configurations and run the VACUUM ANALYZE command.

Planner-related settings

Effective cache size (`effective_cache_size`) should be set to an estimate of how much memory is available for disk caching in the operating system and within the database after taking into account what is used by the operating system and other applications. This value for a dedicated postgres server is around 50 percent to 70 percent of the total RAM. Also, one could play with a planner setting, such as `random_page_cost`, to favor index scan over sequential scans. The `random_page_cost` setting's default value is 4.0. In high-end SAN/NAS technologies, one could set this value to 3, and for SSD, one could use a random page cost of 1.5 to 2.5.

The preceding list of parameters is minimal; in reality, one needs to also configure the `logging`, `checkpoint`, `wal`, and `vacuum` settings. Also, note that some parameters cannot be changed easily on production systems because they require a system restart, such as `max_connections`, `shared_buffers`, `fsync`, and `checkpoint_segments`. In other cases, such as `work_mem`, it can be specified in the session, giving the developer the option of tuning queries that need specific `work_mem`.

Benchmarking is your friend

`pgbench` is a simple program used to execute a prepared set of SQL commands to calculate the average transaction rate (transactions per second). `pgbench` is an implementation of the **Transaction Processing Performance Council (TPC)** TPC-B standard. `pgbench` can also be customized with scripts. In general, when using a benching framework, one needs to set it up on a different client in order not to steal the RAM and CPU from the tested server. Also, one should run `pgbench` several times with different load scenarios and configuration settings.

Finally, in addition to `pgbench`, there are several open source implementations for different benchmarking standards, such as TPC-C and TPC-H.

The `pgbench` synopsis is as follows:

```
pgbench [options] dbname
```

The `-i` option is used to initialize the database with test tables, and the `-s` option determines the database scale factor, also known as the number of rows in each table. A default output of `Pgbench` using a default scale factor on a virtual machine with one CPU looks similar to the following:

```
$pgbench -i test_database
creating tables...
100000 of 100000 tuples (100%) done (elapsed 0.71 s, remaining 0.00 s).
vacuum...
```

```
set primary keys...

done.

$pgbench -c 4 -T 50 test_database

starting vacuum...end.

transaction type: TPC-B (sort of)

scaling factor: 1

query mode: simple

number of clients: 4

number of threads: 1

duration: 50 s

number of transactions actually processed: 5602

latency average: 35.702 ms

tps = 111.906044 (including connections establishing)

tps = 112.599272 (excluding connections establishing)
```

Finally, the pgbench manual pages (pgbench --help) explain the different query options.

Tuning PostgreSQL queries

PostgreSQL provides the means to figure out why a certain query is slow. PostgreSQL behind the scene analyzes the tables, collects statistics from them, and builds histograms using auto vacuuming. Auto vacuuming, in general, is used to recover disk space, update table statistics, and perform other maintenance tasks, such as preventing transaction ID wraparound. Table statistics allow PostgreSQL to pick up an execution plan at the least cost. The least cost is calculated by taking into account the IO and, naturally, CPU cost.

Also, PostgreSQL enables users to see the generated execution plan by providing the EXPLAIN command.

For beginners, it is extremely useful to write the same query in different ways and compare the results. For example, in some cases, the NOT IN construct can be converted to LEFT JOIN or NOT EXIST. Also, the IN construct can be rewritten using INNER JOIN as well as EXISTS. Writing the query in several ways teaches the developer when to use or avoid a certain construct and what the conditions that favor a certain construct are. In general, the NOT IN construct can sometimes cause performance issues because postgres cannot use indexes to evaluate the query.

Another important issue is to keep tracking the new SQL commands and features. The PostgreSQL development community is very active, and their contributions are often targeted to solving common issues. For example, the LATERAL JOIN construct, which was introduced in PostgreSQL 9.3, can be used to optimize certain GROUP BY and LIMIT scenarios.

The EXPLAIN command and execution plan

The first step in tuning PostgreSQL queries is to understand how to read the execution plans generated by the EXPLAIN command. The EXPLAIN command shows the execution plan of a statement and how data from the tables are scanned; for example, the table might be scanned using an index or sequential scan. Also, it shows how the tables are joined, the join method, and the estimated number of rows. The EXPLAIN command also has several options; the ANALYZE option, causes the statement to be executed and returns the actual time and number of rows. Finally, the EXPLAIN command can give insights into buffer's usage and caching. The synopsis for EXPLAIN command is as follows:

```
EXPLAIN [ ( option [, ...] ) ] statement
EXPLAIN [ ANALYZE ] [ VERBOSE ] statement


where option can be one of:

    ANALYZE [ boolean ]
    VERBOSE [ boolean ]
    COSTS [ boolean ]
    BUFFERS [ boolean ]
    TIMING [ boolean ]
    FORMAT { TEXT | XML | JSON | YAML }:
```

To understand EXPLAIN, let's have a look at the following example:

```
CREATE TABLE test_explain_1 (
  id INT PRIMARY KEY,
  name TEXT NOT NULL
);


INSERT INTO test_explain_1 SELECT n , md5 (random()::text) FROM generate_
series (1, 100000) AS foo(n);
-- To update table statistics
```

```
ANALYZE test_explain_1 ;
-- Get the execution plane
EXPLAIN SELECT * FROM test_explain_1;
-- Output
Seq Scan on test_explain_1  (cost=0.00..1834.00 rows=100000 width=37)
```

In the preceding example, a table was created and random data was generated and inserted into the table. The execution plan is only a one-node sequential scan on the `test_explain_1` table, as shown in the preceding code. The number of rows is estimated correctly as we analyzed the table after insert.

Auto vacuum is important to keep your database's statistics up to date. Certainly, wrong statistics mean nonoptimal execution plans. After database bulk operations, it is good to run the ANALYZE command to update the statistics. Also, one could control the data sampling performed by ANALYZE using ALTER TABLE ... ALTER COLUMN ...SET STATISTICS <integer>; this will allow a better estimation of rows.

The cost is an estimation of the effort required to execute the query. In the preceding example, the cost, 0.00, is the cost to retrieve the first row, while the cost, 1834.00, is the cost to retrieve all rows, which is calculated as follows:

$$\left(number\ of\ relation\ pages * seq\_page\_cost\right) + \left(number\ of\ rows * cpu\_tuple\_cost\right)$$

The number of relation pages and rows can be found in the `pg_class`, and `seq_page_cost` and `cpu_tuple_cost` are planner-related configuration settings. So, the cost 1.834 is calculated as shown in the following example:

```
SELECT relpages*current_setting('seq_page_cost')::numeric +
reltuples*current_setting('cpu_tuple_cost')::numeric as cost
FROM pg_class
WHERE relname='test_explain_1';
 cost
------
 1834
(1 row)
```

For the simple case of a sequential scan, it is almost straightforward to calculate the cost. However, when a query involves predicates' evaluation, grouping, ordering, and joining, cost estimation becomes complicated.

Finally, the width 37 is the average width of the tuple in bytes. This information can be found in the pg_stats table.

To really execute and get the cost in real time, one could use EXPLAIN (ANALYZE), as follows:

```
EXPLAIN (ANALYZE) SELECT * FROM test_explain_1 WHERE id >= 10 and id <
20;
                                                          QUERY PLAN
-----------------------------------------------------------------------
--------------------------------------------------------------
 Index Scan using test_explain_1_pkey on test_explain_1  (cost=0.29..8.47
rows=9 width=37) (actual time=0.008..0.011 rows=10 loops=1)
   Index Cond: ((id >= 10) AND (id < 20))
 Total runtime: 0.031 ms
(3 rows)
```

In the preceding query, the planner got a very close estimation, as compared to the real values: it estimated 9 rows instead of 10. Also, the planner-generated execution plan now uses an index scan. In the execution plan, one could also see other information such as the number of loops and actual time.

Note that the execution plan is two lines with different indentations now. One should read the execution plan bottom-up and from the most to least indented. This can be seen more clearly in the following example, which performs a self-join on test_explain_1, as follows:

```
car_portal=# EXPLAIN SELECT * FROM test_explain_1 a JOIN test_explain_1 b
ON (a.id = b.id) WHERE a.id < 100;
                                                          QUERY PLAN
-----------------------------------------------------------------------
----------------------------
 Nested Loop  (cost=0.58..694.89 rows=90 width=74)
   -> Index Scan using test_explain_1_pkey on test_explain_1 a
(cost=0.29..9.87 rows=90 width=37)
         Index Cond: (id < 100)
   -> Index Scan using test_explain_1_pkey on test_explain_1 b
(cost=0.29..7.60 rows=1 width=37)
         Index Cond: (id = a.id)
(5 rows)
```

The EXPLAIN (BUFFERS) option shows the effect of caching and whether the cache is configured properly. To take a look at the complete effect of caching, one needs to perform cold and hot testing. The following example shows this using three pages read from the buffers:

```
EXPLAIN (ANALYZE, BUFFERS) SELECT * FROM test_explain_1 WHERE id >= 10
and id < 20;

                                                            QUERY PLAN

--------------------------------------------------------------------
--------------------------------------------------------------

 Index Scan using test_explain_1_pkey on test_explain_1  (cost=0.29..8.47
rows=9 width=37) (actual time=0.008..0.010 rows=10 loops=1)

   Index Cond: ((id >= 10) AND (id < 20))

   Buffers: shared hit=3

 Total runtime: 0.026 ms

(4 rows)
```

Detecting problems in query plans

The EXPLAIN command can show why the query is slow, especially if the two options—BUFFER and ANALYZE—are used. There are some hints that enable us to decide whether the execution plan is good or not; these hints are as follows:

- **The estimated row number in comparison with the actual rows**: This is important because this parameter defines the method of the query's execution. There are two cases: the estimated number of rows may either be overestimated or underestimated. Wrong estimation affects the entire algorithm, which is used to fetch data from the hard disk, sort it, join it, and so on. In general, if the number of rows is overestimated, this affects performance, but not as much as if the number of rows is underestimated. For example, if one performs a nested loop join on very big tables, it will make the query very slow.

- **In-memory or in-disk sort operation**: When performing a sorting operation, such as DISTINCT, if there is enough memory, this operation will be performed in the RAM.

- **Buffer cache**: This shows how much of the data is cached and what the hit ratio is.

In order to show a wrong execution plan, let's confuse postgres by performing an operation on the column id, as follows:

```
EXPLAIN SELECT * FROM test_explain_1 WHERE upper(id::text)::int < 20;
                              QUERY PLAN
-------------------------------------------------------------------
 Seq Scan on test_explain_1   (cost=0.00..3334.00 rows=33333 width=37)
   Filter:  ((upper((id)::text))::integer < 20)
(2 rows)
```

In the previous case, postgres was not able to evaluate upper(id::text)::int < 20 properly. Also, it cannot use the index scan because there is no index matching the column expression. Note that the number of returned rows is extremely high, as compared to the real number as well. If this query were a subquery of another query, the error would be cascaded because it might be executed several times.

Finally, knowledge about different algorithms, such as the nested loop join, hash join, index scan, bitmap index scan, and so on, can be useful in detecting the root cause of performance degradation.

Common mistakes in writing queries

There are some common mistakes and bad practices that a developer may fall into, which are as follows.

Unnecessary operations

Some developers often use DISTINCT or do not know the difference between UNION, UNION ALL, EXCEPT, EXCEPT ALL, and so on. This causes slow queries, especially if the expected number of rows is high. For example, the following two queries are equivalent, but the one with DISTINCT is much slower:

```
\timing
car_portal=# SELECT * FROM test_explain_1;
Time: 71.258 ms
car_portal=# SELECT DISTINCT * FROM test_explain_1;
Time: 201.143 ms
```

Another common mistake is to use DISTINCT with UNION, as in the following query:

```
SELECT DISTINCT filed_list FROM table_1 UNION
SELECT DISTINCT filed_list FROM table_2
```

The UNION query would eliminate all duplicates, even if table_1 or table_2 have duplicates.

Another common mistake is to use order by in a view definition. If ORDER BY is used when selecting data from the view, it also introduces unnecessary sort operations, as in the following query:

```
CREATE OR REPLACE VIEW test_explain_1_VIEW AS SELECT * FROM test_explain_1;
EXPLAIN SELECT * FROM test_explain_1_view order by id ASC;
                                                      QUERY PLAN
------------------------------------------------------------------------
---------------------------

 Index Scan using test_explain_1_pkey on test_explain_1
(cost=0.29..3441.29 rows=100000 width=37)
(1 row)
```

```
# CREATE OR REPLACE VIEW test_explain_1_VIEW AS SELECT * FROM test_explain_1 ORDER BY id DESC;
# EXPLAIN SELECT * FROM test_explain_1_view order by id ASC;
                                                      QUERY PLAN
------------------------------------------------------------------------
-----------------------------------------

 Sort   (cost=15483.11..15733.11 rows=100000 width=37)
   Sort Key: test_explain_1.id
   ->  Index Scan Backward using test_explain_1_pkey on test_explain_1
(cost=0.29..3441.29 rows=100000 width=37)
(3 rows)
```

Note, in the preceding example, the cost difference between the two SELECT queries on different views.

Misplaced indexes

Missing indexes on column expressions causes a full table scan; the most common use case is to allow the user to perform operations on case-insensitive data, such as search and login. For example, one could log in using the login name in a case-sensitive way. This could be achieved using lower or upper case matching. To test this, let's create another table, as follows, as the md5 hashing only generates lower text:

```
CREATE OR REPLACE FUNCTION generate_random_text ( int  ) RETURNS TEXT AS
$$
SELECT string_agg(substr('0123456789abcdefghijklmnopqrstuvwxyzABCDEFGH
IJKLMNOPQRSTUVWXYZ', trunc(random() * 62)::integer + 1, 1), '')   FROM
generate_series(1, $1)
$$
LANGUAGE SQL;


CREATE TABLE login as SELECT n, generate_random_text(8) as login_name
FROM generate_series(1, 1000) as foo(n);
CREATE INDEX ON login(login_name);
VACUUM ANALYZE login;
```

The generate_random_text(n) function is used to generate random text of length n. Let's assume that we want to check whether an entry exists in table one; we could do this as follows:

```
EXPLAIN SELECT * FROM login WHERE login_name = 'jxaG6gjJ';
Index Scan using login_login_name_idx on login  (cost=0.28..8.29 rows=1
width=13)
   Index Cond: (login_name = 'jxaG6gjJ'::text)
```

As seen in the preceding example, an index scan is used as there is an index on login_name.

Using functions on constant arguments also causes the index to be used if this function is not volatile as the optimizer evaluates the function as follows:

```
EXPLAIN SELECT * FROM login WHERE login_name = lower('jxaG6gjJ');
Index Scan using login_login_name_idx on login  (cost=0.28..8.29 rows=1
width=13)
   Index Cond: (login_name = 'jxag6gjj'::text)
```

Using functions on columns, as stated in the preceding example, causes a sequential scan, as shown in the following query:

```
EXPLAIN SELECT * FROM login WHERE lower(login_name) = lower('jxaG6gjJ');
"Seq Scan on login  (cost=0.00..21.00 rows=5 width=13)"
"  Filter: (lower(login_name) = 'jxag6gjj'::text)"
```

Note that here, the number of rows returned is also five as the optimizer cannot evaluate the predict correctly. To solve this issue, simply add an index, as follows:

```
CREATE INDEX ON login(lower(login_name));
EXPLAIN SELECT * FROM login WHERE lower(login_name) = lower('jxaG6gjJ');
Index Scan using login_lower_idx on login  (cost=0.28..8.29 rows=1
width=13)"
  Index Cond: (lower(login_name) = 'jxag6gjj'::text)
```

Also, text indexing is governed by the access pattern. In general, there are two ways to index text: the first approach is to use an index with opclass, which allows anchored text search, and the second approach is to use tsquery and tsvector. In the `test_explain_1` table, one could create an opclass index, as follows:

```
SELECT * FROM test_explain_1 WHERE name like 'a%';
Time: 19.565 ms
CREATE INDEX on test_explain_1 (name text_pattern_ops);
SELECT * FROM test_explain_1 WHERE name like 'a%';
Time: 7.860 ms
EXPLAIN SELECT * FROM test_explain_1 WHERE name like 'a%';
                                    QUERY PLAN
-------------------------------------------------------------------------
------------------
 Bitmap Heap Scan on test_explain_1  (cost=281.22..1204.00 rows=7071
width=37)
   Filter: (name ~~ 'a%'::text)
   -> Bitmap Index Scan on test_explain_1_name_idx  (cost=0.00..279.45
rows=7103 width=0)
        Index Cond: ((name ~>=~ 'a'::text) AND (name ~<~ 'b'::text))
(4 rows)
```

Note the execution plan after creating the index; an index scan was used instead of a sequential scan, and performance increased.

Unnecessary table or index scans

Often, one can see queries that cause several table scans if one uses a select statement in a select list or the query is not well written. For example, let's assume that there is a query to get the count of bad and good ranking as per a certain advertisement, which is written as follows:

```
SELECT
(SELECT count(*) FROM car_portal_app.advertisement_rating WHERE rank = 1
AND advertisement_rating_id = 1) AS good,
(SELECT COUNT(*) FROM car_portal_app.advertisement_rating WHERE rank = 5
AND advertisement_rating_id = 1) AS bad;
```

This query caused the same index to be scanned twice, as shown in the execution plan. Take a look at the following query:

```
Result  (cost=16.36..16.38 rows=1 width=0)

  InitPlan 1 (returns $0)

    ->  Aggregate   (cost=8.17..8.18 rows=1 width=0)

          ->  Index Scan using
          advertisement_rating_pkey on
          advertisement_rating  (cost=0.15..8.17 rows=1
          width=0)

                Index Cond: (advertisement_rating_id =
      1)

                Filter: (rank = 1)

  InitPlan 2 (returns $1)

    ->  Aggregate   (cost=8.17..8.18 rows=1 width=0)

          ->  Index Scan using
          advertisement_rating_pkey on
          advertisement_rating advertisement_rating_1
            (cost=0.15..8.17 rows=1 width=0)

                Index Cond: (advertisement_rating_id =
      1)

                Filter: (rank = 5)
```

The preceding query could be written using COUNT FILTER or COUNT CASE expression END, as follows:

```
SELECT count(*) FILTER (WHERE rank=5) as bad, count(*) FILTER (WHERE
rank=1) as good FROM car_portal_app.advertisement_rating WHERE
advertisement_rating_id = 1;
```

Using correlated nested queries

Correlated nested queries can cause performance issues because the subquery is executed within a loop; for example, the following query is not optimal:

```
CREATE TABLE test_explain_2 AS SELECT n as id, md5(n::text) as name FROM
generate_series(1, 1000) as foo(n);
```

```
SELECT 1000
```

Time: 14.161 ms

```
SELECT * FROM test_explain_1 WHERE EXISTS (SELECT 1 FROM test_explain_2
WHERE id = id);
```

Time: 78.533 ms

The preceding query could be written using the INNER JOIN or IN construct, as follows:

```
# SELECT test_explain_1.* FROM test_explain_1 INNER JOIN  test_explain_2
USING (id);
```

Time: 2.111 ms

```
SELECT * FROM test_explain_1 WHERE id IN (SELECT id FROM test_explain_2);
```

Time: 2.143 ms

Using CTE when not mandatory

Common table expressions (**CTEs**) are an amazing feature; they allow the developer to write very complex logic. Also, a CTE can be used in several places to optimize performance. However, using a CTE may be problematic in the case of predicate push down as PostgreSQL does not optimize beyond CTE boundaries; each CTE runs in isolation. To understand this limitation, let's have a look at the following two dummy-equivalent examples and note the difference between their performance:

```
car_portal=# With test_explain AS (SELECT * FROM test_explain_1) SELECT *
FROM test_explain WHERE id = 4;
 id |                name
----+----------------------------------
  4 | aa0cca507bdb343206f579cab2a46169
(1 row)
```

```
Time: 82.280 ms
SELECT * FROM (SELECT * FROM test_explain_1) as foo WHERE id = 4;
 id |                name
```

```
----+----------------------------------
  4 |  aa0cca507bdb343206f579cab2a46169
(1 row)
Time: 0.643 ms
```

Using the PL/pgSQL procedural language consideration

PL/pgSQL language caching is an amazing tool to increase performance; however, if the developer is not careful, it may lead to a bad execution of plans. For example, let's assume that we want to wrap the following query in a function:

```
SELECT * FROM test_explain_1 WHERE id <= <predicate>;
```

In this example, we should not use caching as the execution plan might differ depending on the predicate value. For example, if we use the value 1 as predicate, postgres will perform an index scan. However, if we use the predicate 90,000, postgres will most probably use an sequential scan. Due to this caching, the execution of this query is wrong. However, consider that the preceding select statement is as follows:

```
SELECT * FROM test_explain_1 WHERE id = <predicate>;
```

In this case it is better to cache it as the execution plan is the same for all the predicates due to the index on the id column.

Also, exception handling in PL/pgSQL is quite expensive, so one should be careful while using this feature.

Cross column correlation

Cross column correlation can cause a wrong estimation of the number of rows as PostgreSQL assumes that each column is independent of other columns. In reality, there are a lot of examples where this is not true. For example, one could find patterns where the first and last names in certain cultures are correlated. Another example is the country and language preference of the users. To understand cross column correlation, let's create a table called users, as follows:

```
CREATE TABLE users (
    id serial primary key,
    name text,
    country text,
```

```
    language text
);
```

```
INSERT INTO users(name, country, language) SELECT generate_random_
text(8), 'Germany', 'German' FROM generate_series(1, 10);
```

```
INSERT INTO users(name, country, language) SELECT generate_random_
text(8), 'USA', 'English' FROM generate_series(1, 10);
```

```
VACUUM ANALYZE users;
```

If one wants to get users whose language is German and country is Germany, he/ she will end up with a wrong estimation of rows as both columns are correlated, as follows:

```
EXPLAIN SELECT * FROM users WHERE country = 'Germany' and language
='German';
```

```
Seq Scan on users   (cost=0.00..1.30 rows=5 width=26)
    Filter: ((country = 'Germany'::text) AND (language = 'German'::text))
```

Note that the number of estimated rows is five, which is calculated as follows:

*Estimated number of rows = Total_number_of_rows * selectivity of country * selectivity of language*

*Estimated number of rows = 20 *.5 * .5 = 5*

A simple solution to correct the number of rows is to change the physical design of the table and combine both fields in one, as follows:

```
CREATE TABLE   user_2 (
    id serial,
    name text,
    user_info jsonb
);
```

```
INSERT INTO user_2(name,  user_info) SELECT generate_random_text(8),
'{"country":"Germany", "language":"German"}'  FROM generate_series(1,
10);
```

```
INSERT INTO user_2(name,  user_info) SELECT generate_random_text(8),
'{"country":"USA", "language":"English"}'  FROM generate_series(1, 10);
```

```
VACUUM ANALYZE user_2;
```

In the preceding example, jsonb is used to wrap the country and language; the explain plan gives the correct estimation of the number of rows, as follows:

```
EXPLAIN SELECT * FROM user_2 WHERE user_info = '{"country":"USA",
"language":"English"}';

Seq Scan on user_2  (cost=0.00..1.25 rows=10 width=60)

  Filter: (user_info = '{"country": "USA", "language":
"English"}'::jsonb)
```

Table partitioning

Table partitioning is used to increase performance by physically arranging data in the hard disk based on a certain grouping criteria. There are two techniques for table partitioning:

- **Vertical table partitioning**: The table is divided into several tables in order to decrease the row size. This allows a faster sequential scan on divided tables as a relation page holds more rows. To explain, let's assume that we want to store pictures for each seller in the database to be used as their respective logos. One could model this by adding a column of the bytea or blob type. The other approach is to have another table reference the sellers table, as follows:

```
CREATE TABLE car_portal_app.seller_logo (

   seller_id INT PRIMARY KEY REFERENCES car_portal_app.seller_
account (seller_account_id),

   logo bytea NOT NULL

);
```

- **Horizontal table partitioning**: This is used to decrease the whole table size by splitting the rows over multiple tables; it is supported by table inheritance and constraint exclusion.

In horizontal table partitioning, the parent table is often a proxy, while the child tables are used to store actual data. Table inheritance can be used to implement horizontal table partitioning, whereas constraint exclusion is used to optimize performance by only accessing the child tables that contain required data when performing a query. In general, when one wants to create table partitioning, he/she needs to do the following:

- Create a parent table, which will act as proxy
- Create child tables, where data will be saved

- Create a trigger or rules on the master table to correctly save data in child tables based on partition criteria
- Create check constraints in child tables to speed up the process of querying data

To understand table partitioning and constraint exclusion, let's assume that we have a `log` table where each entry has `log_type`, as follows:

```
CREATE TABLE log (
  log_id SERIAL PRIMARY KEY,
  log_information JSONB,
  log_type CHAR(1)
);
```

Also, let's assume that we want to partition the `log` table based on `log_type` using this naming convention: `log_u` for update, `log_d` for delete, and `log_i` for insert. The child tables can be created as follows:

```
CREATE TABLE log_u ( CHECK ( log_type = 'u') ) INHERITS (log);
CREATE TABLE log_i ( CHECK ( log_type = 'i') ) INHERITS (log);
CREATE TABLE log_d ( CHECK ( log_type = 'd') ) INHERITS (log);
```

To store data in a child table, a trigger on the log table should be created, as follows:

```
CREATE OR REPLACE FUNCTION log_insert() RETURNS TRIGGER AS $$
BEGIN
    IF ( NEW.log_type = 'u' ) THEN
        INSERT INTO log_u VALUES (NEW.*);
    ELSIF ( NEW.log_type = 'i' ) THEN
        INSERT INTO log_i VALUES (NEW.*);
     ELSIF ( NEW.log_type = 'd' ) THEN
        INSERT INTO log_d VALUES (NEW.*);
    ELSE
        RAISE EXCEPTION 'Unknown log type';
    END IF;

    RETURN NULL;
END;
$$ LANGUAGE plpgsql;
```

```
CREATE TRIGGER log_insert
    BEFORE INSERT ON log
    FOR EACH ROW EXECUTE PROCEDURE log_insert();
```

Note that the trigger execution time is before, and it returns NULL; thus, no rows are inserted on the master table, and the message INSERT 0 0 is shown. This causes some ORM, such as hibernate, to not function properly because when data is inserted or updated, the right number of affected rows is not returned. One can overcome this limitation using rules.

To test the table partitioning, let's insert three records with different types, as follows:

```
car_portal=# INSERT INTO log (log_information, log_type) VALUES
('{"query": "SELECT 1", "user":"x" }', 'i');

INSERT 0 0

car_portal=# INSERT INTO  log (log_information, log_type) VALUES
('{"query": "UPDATE ...", "user":"x" }', 'u');

INSERT 0 0

car_portal=# INSERT INTO  log (log_information, log_type) VALUES
('{"query": "DELETE ...", "user":"x" }', 'd');

INSERT 0 0 car_portal=# VACUUM ANALYSE LOG;

VACUUM
```

To test the constraint exclusion, let's check the execution plan of selecting from the log table all entries with log_type='i', is as follows:

```
car_portal=# EXPLAIN SELECT * FROM log WHERE log_type='i';
                          QUERY PLAN
------------------------------------------------------------
 Append  (cost=0.00..1.01 rows=2 width=44)
   ->  Seq Scan on log  (cost=0.00..0.00 rows=1 width=44)
         Filter: (log_type = 'i'::bpchar)
   ->  Seq Scan on log_i  (cost=0.00..1.01 rows=1 width=45)
         Filter: (log_type = 'i'::bpchar)
(5 rows)
```

Note in the preceding execution plan that two tables are scanned: the parent and child tables with the name log_i. This is the expected behavior of constraint exclusion as check constraint CHECK (log_type = 'i') matches the log_type='i' predicate in a select statement.

Constraint exclusion limitations

Sometimes, constraint exclusion fails to kick in, leading to very slow queries. There are limitations on constraint exclusion, which are as follows:

- The constraint exclusion setting can be disabled
- Constraint exclusion works only on range and equality expressions
- Constraint exclusion does not work if the `where` expression is not written in the equality or range manner

Let's assume that we want to partition a table based on text pattern, such as "pattern `LIKE 'a%'`". This can be achieved by rewriting the `LIKE` construct using range equality such as `pattern >= 'a '` and `pattern < 'b'`. So, instead of having a check constraint on a child table using the `LIKE` construct, one should have it based on ranges. Also, if a user performs a select statement using the `LIKE` construct, constraint exclusion will not work.

Summary

There are several aspects of tuning the performance of PostgreSQL. These aspects are related to hardware configuration, network settings, and PostgreSQL configuration. PostgreSQL is often shipped with a configuration that is not suitable for production. Due to this, one should at least configure the PostgreSQL buffer setting, RAM settings, number of connections, and logging. Note that several PostgreSQL settings are correlated, such as the RAM settings and number of connections. In addition to this, one should take great care with settings that require a server restart because these are difficult to change in the production environment.

Often, PostgreSQL produces a good execution plan if the physical structure of a database is normalized and the query is written properly. However, this is not always the case. To overcome performance issues, PostgreSQL provides the `EXPLAIN` utility command, which can be used to generate execution plans. The `EXPLAIN` command has several options, such as `ANALYZE` and `BUFFERS`. Also, one should know the limitations of PostgreSQL in order to write good queries, such as cross column statistics, CTE execution boundaries, and PL/pgSQL features. In addition to these, one should know the exact difference between different SQL statements and how they are executed, such as `UNION`, `UNION ALL`, `DISTINCT`, and so on. Furthermore, one should learn how to rewrite the same query in different ways and compare the performance of each.

Finally, PostgreSQL has many features to boost performance, such as constraint exclusion and techniques of table partitioning—mainly horizontal and vertical partitioning. Add to this many external tools to handle caching as well as connection pooling.

11
Beyond Conventional Data types

PostgreSQL can handle rich data types due to its powerful extensions. Data that does not fit the relational model inherently, such as semistructured data, can be stored and manipulated, either using out-of-the-box data types or extensions. Also, the PostgreSQL community focuses not only on enhancing relational database features, but also on supporting rich data types, such as arrays, XMLs, hash stores, and JSON documents. The focus shift is a result of embracing changes in the software development process' life cycle, such as agile development methods, and supporting unknown and rapid software requirements.

Nonconventional data types allow PostgreSQL to store different data types such as geographical, binary, as well as schema-less data, such as JSON documents and hash stores. PostgreSQL supports some of these data types out of the box, including JSON, JSONB, XML, array, bytea, and BLOB. More data types are available via extensions such as hstore and PostGIS.

JSON, JSONB, and hstore allow PostgreSQL to handle schema-less models, which in turn allow developers to make real-time adjustments to data in an automatic and transparent way. Using JSON, JSONB, and hash store allows developer to change the data structure without changing the table structure using the ALTER command. Also, it allows them to have a flexible data model without using the **entity-attribute-value (EAV)** model, which is difficult to handle in the relational model. However, developers should take care of handling data integrity in the business logic to ensure that the data is clean and error-free.

In this chapter, arrays, hstore, XML, and JSON data types will be introduced. However, it would be nice to have a look at the PostGIS extension, knowing that PostGIS supports raster and vector formats and provides very rich functions to manipulate data.

PostgreSQL arrays

Multidimensional arrays are supported; here, the array type can be a base, enum, or composite type. Array elements should have only one data type. PostgreSQL arrays allow duplicate values as well as null values. The following example shows how to initialize a one-dimensional array and get the first element:

```
SELECT ('{red, green, blue}'::text[])[1] as red ;

red

-----

 red

(1 row)
```

The array length, by default, is not bound to a certain value, but this can also be specified when using arrays to define a relation. By default, an array index, as shown in the preceding example, starts from index one; however, this behavior can be changed by defining the dimension when initializing the array, as follows:

```
car_portal=# SELECT '[0:1]={1,2}'::INT[];

     int4

-------------

 [0:1]={1,2}

(1 row)


car_portal=# SELECT ('[0:1]={1,2}'::INT[])[0];

 int4

------

    1

(1 row)


car_portal=# SELECT ('[0:1]={1,2}'::INT[])[1];

 int4

------

    2

(1 row)
```

Arrays can be initialized using the { } construct. Another way to initialize an array is as follows:

```
SELECT array['red','green','blue'] AS primary_colors;
```

PostgreSQL provides many functions to manipulate arrays, such as `array_remove` to remove a certain element. The following are some of the function arrays:

```
SELECT
    array_ndims(two_dim_array) AS "Number of dimensions",
    array_dims(two_dim_array) AS "Dimensions index range",
    array_length(two_dim_array, 1) AS "The array length of 1st
    dimension",
    cardinality(two_dim_array) AS "Number of elements",
    two_dim_array[1][1] AS "The first element"
FROM
    (VALUES ('{{red,green,blue}, {red,green,blue}}'::text[][])) AS foo(two_
dim_array);
```

```
-[ RECORD 1 ]--------------------+----------
Number of dimensions             | 2
Dimensions index range           | [1:2][1:3]
The array length of 1st dimension | 2
Number of elements               | 6
The first element                | red
```

A very common use case of arrays is to model multivalued attributes. For example, a dress can have more than one color, and a newspaper article can have several tags. Another use case is to model a hash store. This is achieved by having two arrays— one with the keys and another with the values—and the array index is used to associate the key with the value. For example, `pg_stats` uses this approach to store information about the common values' histogram. The `most_common_vals` and the `most_common_freqs` columns are used to list the most common values in a certain column and the frequencies of these most common values, respectively, as shown in the following example:

```
car_portal=# SELECT * FROM pg_stats WHERE array_length(most_common_
vals,1) < 10 AND schemaname NOT IN ('pg_catalog','information_schema')
LIMIT 1;
```

```
-[ RECORD 1 ]----------+-----------------------------------------------
----------------------------------------
schemaname             | public
tablename              | duplicate
attname                | f2
inherited              | f
null_frac              | 0
avg_width              | 4
n_distinct             | -0.263158
most_common_vals       | {4,3,9,8,2,5,6,7,10}
most_common_freqs      | {0.184211,0.157895,0.131579,0.105263,0.0789474,0
.0789474,0.0789474,0.0789474,0.0789474}
histogram_bounds       |
correlation            | -0.0405953
most_common_elems      |
most_common_elem_freqs |
elem_count_histogram   |
```

Another use case of arrays is to store scientific information. Note that there are dedicated databases designed specifically to store and manipulate arrays, such as SciDB.

Also, arrays can be used to facilitate coding and in performing some SQL tricks, such as passing several arguments to the function using the VARIADIC array option or performing loops using the generate_series function. This allows the developers to perform complex tasks without using the PL/pgSQL language. For example, let's assume that we want to have at least one column as not null out of several columns. This, in reality, can be used to check for disjoint attributes or model inheritance. For example, let's assume we have a table called vehicle that contains a vehicle's common attributes. Also, let's assume that we have several types of vehicles, such as trucks, cars, sport cars, and so on. One could model this by having several columns referencing the car, truck, and sport car tables. To understand how one can use the VARIADIC function, let's model the vehicle inheritance example, as follows:

```
CREATE OR REPLACE FUNCTION null_count (VARIADIC arr int[]) RETURNS INT AS
$$
  SELECT count(CASE WHEN m IS NOT NULL THEN 1 ELSE NULL END)::int FROM
unnest($1) m(n)
$$ LANGUAGE SQL
```

To use the preceding function, one needs to add a check to the table, as follows:

```
CREATE TABLE car (
  car_id SERIAL PRIMARY KEY,
  car_number_of_doors INT DEFAULT 5
)


CREATE TABLE bus (
  bus_id SERIAL PRIMARY KEY,
  bus_number_of_passengers INT DEFAULT 50
)


CREATE TABLE vehicle (
  vehicle_id SERIAL PRIMARY KEY,
  registration_number TEXT,
  car_id INT REFERENCES car(car_id),
  bus_id INT REFERENCES bus(bus_id),
  CHECK (null_count(car_id, bus_id) = 1)

)
INSERT INTO CAR VALUES (1, 5);
INSERT INTO BUS VALUES (1, 25);
```

To test the function, let's execute some insert commands, as follows:

```
postgres=# INSERT INTO CAR VALUES (1, 5);
INSERT 0 1
postgres=# INSERT INTO BUS VALUES (1, 25);
INSERT 0 1
postgres=#
postgres=# INSERT INTO vehicle VALUES (default, 'a234', null, null);
ERROR:  new row for relation "vehicle" violates check constraint
"vehicle_check"
DETAIL:  Failing row contains (5, a234, null, null).
postgres=# INSERT INTO vehicle VALUES (default, 'a234', 1, 1);
ERROR:  new row for relation "vehicle" violates check constraint
"vehicle_check"
DETAIL:  Failing row contains (6, a234, 1, 1).
```

```
postgres=# INSERT INTO vehicle VALUES (default, 'a234', null, 1);
INSERT 0 1
postgres=# INSERT INTO vehicle VALUES (default, 'a234', 1, null);
INSERT 0 1
```

Note that to call the `null_count` function, we need to add `VARIADIC` to the function's argument, as follows:

```
postgres=# SELECT * FROM null_count(VARIADIC ARRAY [null, 1]);
 null_count
------------
          1
(1 row)
```

Another trick is to generate the substring of a text; this comes in handy when one would like to get the longest prefix match. The longest prefix match is very important in areas such as telecommunication as some mobile operator or telephone companies can rent a range of numbers to another operator. Longest prefix matching is used to determine the network. The following example shows how we can achieve this:

```
.  CREATE TABLE prefix (
   network TEXT,
   prefix_code TEXT NOT NULL
);
CREATE INDEX ON prefix(prefix_code);


INSERT INTO prefix VALUES ('Palestine Jawwal', 97059), ('Palestine
Jawwal',970599), ('Palestine watania',970597);


CREATE OR REPLACE FUNCTION prefixes(TEXT) RETURNS  TEXT[] AS
$$
   SELECT ARRAY(SELECT substring($1,1,i) FROM generate_series(1,
length($1)) g(i))::TEXT[];
$$ LANGUAGE SQL IMMUTABLE;
```

The index on the prefix code will be used to perform an index scan on the table prefix. The function prefixes will return an array with the prefix substring. To test whether longest prefix matching worked, let's get the longest prefix for the number 97059973456789 through the following code:

```
postgres=# SELECT * FROM prefix WHERE prefix_code = any
(prefixes('97059973456789')) ORDER BY length(prefix_code) DESC limit 1;

     network       | prefix_code
-------------------+-------------
 Palestine Jawwal  | 970599
```

One can use arrays for several purposes; for example, prior to the introduction of window functions in PostgreSQL version 8.4, arrays and the generate_series function were used to mimic the row_number function.

Common functions of arrays and their operators

Array operators are similar to other data type operators. For example, the = sign is used for equality comparison, and the || operator is used for concatenation. Also, in the previous chapters, we saw some operators similar to &&, which returns true if the arrays are overlapping. Finally, the @> and <@ operators are used if an array contains or is contained by another array, respectively.

The unnest function is used to return a set of elements from an array. This is quite useful when one would like to use set operations on arrays, such as distinct, order by, intersect, union, and so on. The following example is used to remove the duplicates and sort the array in an ascending order:

```
car_portal=# SELECT array(SELECT DISTINCT unnest (array [1,1,1,2,3,3])
ORDER BY 1);
  array
---------
 {1,2,3}
(1 row)
```

In the preceding example, the result of the unnest function is sorted and duplicates are removed using ORDER BY and DISTINCT, respectively. The () function array is used to construct the array from a set, as follows:

```
car_portal=# SELECT array (VALUES (1),(2));
 array
-------
 {1,2}
(1 row)
```

The array ANY function is similar to the SQL IN () construct and is used to compare containment, as shown in the following example:

```
car_portal=# SELECT 1 in (1,2,3), 1 = ANY ('{1,2,3}'::INT[]);
 ?column? | ?column?
----------+----------
 t        | t
(1 row)
```

Modifying and accessing arrays

An array element can be accessed via an index; if the array does not contain an element for this index, the NULL value is returned, as shown in the following example:

```
CREATE TABLE car(
  id SERIAL PRIMARY KEY,
  color text []
);


INSERT INTO car(color) VALUES ('{red, green}'::text[]);
INSERT INTO car(color) VALUES ('{red}'::text[]);
car_portal=# SELECT color [3] IS NOT DISTINCT FROM null FROM car;
 ?column?
----------
 t
 t
(2 rows)
```

Also, an array can be sliced by providing a lower and upper bound, as follows:

```
car_portal=# SELECT color [1:2] FROM car;
    color
-------------
 {red,green}
 {red}
(2 rows)
```

When updating an array, one could completely replace the array, amend a slice value, amend an element value, or append the array using the | | concatenation operator, as follows:

```
--- append array using concatenation
car_portal=# SELECT ARRAY ['red', 'green'] || '{blue}'::text[] AS concat_
array;
    concat_array
-----------------
 {red,green,blue}
(1 row)
--- update slice
car_portal=# UPDATE car set color[1:2] = '{black, white}';
UPDATE 2
car_portal=# SELECT * FROM car;
 id |     color
----+---------------
  4 | {black,white}
  3 | {black,white}
(2 rows)
```

The remove function array can be used to remove all the elements that are equal to a certain value, as follows:

```
car_portal=# SELECT array_remove ('{Hello, Hello, World}'::TEXT[],
'Hello');
 array_remove
-------------
 {World}
(1 row)
```

To remove a certain value based on an index, one can use the WITH ORDINALITY clause. So, let's assume that we want to remove the first element of an array; this can be achieved as follows:

```
car_portal=# SELECT ARRAY(SELECT unnest FROM unnest ('{Hello, Hello,
World}'::TEXT[]) WITH ordinality WHERE ordinality <> 1);
     array
---------------
 {Hello,World}
(1 row)
```

Indexing arrays in PostgreSQL

The GIN index can be used to index arrays; standard PostgreSQL distributions have the GIN operator class for one-dimensional arrays. The GIN index is supported for the following operators: contains "@>", is contained by "<@", overlapping "&&", and equality "=" operators. Take a look at the following code:

```
CREATE INDEX ON car USING GIN (color);
--- to force index, sequential scan is disabled
SET enable_seqscan TO off;


EXPLAIN SELECT * FROM car WHERE '{red}'::text[] && color;
--- Result
Bitmap Heap Scan on car  (cost=8.00..12.01 rows=1 width=36)
  Recheck Cond: ('{red}'::text[] && color)
  -> Bitmap Index Scan on car_color_idx  (cost=0.00..8.00 rows=1
  width=0)
        Index Cond: ('{red}'::text[] && color)
```

Hash store

A hash store, key value store, or associative array is a famous data structure among modern programing languages such as Java, Python, and Node.js. Also, there are dedicated database frameworks to handle this kind of data, such as the redis database.

PostgreSQL has supported hash store—hstore—since the PostgreSQL version 9.0. The hstore extension allows developers to leverage the best in different worlds. It increases the developer's agility without sacrificing the powerful features of PostgreSQL. Also, hstore allows the developer to model semistructured data and sparse arrays in a relational model.

To create the hstore, one simply needs to execute the following command:

```
CREATE EXTENSION hstore;
```

The textual representation of hstore includes zero or higher key=> value, followed by a comma. An example of the hstore data type is as follows:

```
car_portal=# SELECT 'tires=>"winter tires", seat=>leather'::hstore;
                hstore
-------------------------------------------
 "seat"=>"leather", "tires"=>"winter tires"
(1 row)
```

One could also generate a single value hstore using the hstore(key, value) function:

```
car_portal=# SELECT hstore('´Hello', 'World');
      hstore
-------------------
 "´Hello"=>"World"
(1 row)
```

Note that in hstore, the keys are unique, as shown in the following example:

```
car_portal=# SELECT 'a=>1, a=>2'::hstore;
  hstore
----------
 "a"=>"1"
(1 row)
```

In the car web portal, let's assume that the developer wants to support several other attributes, such as air bags, air conditioning, power steering, and so on. The developer, in the traditional relational model, should alter the table structure and add new columns. Thanks to hstore, the developer can store this information using the key value store without having to keep altering the table structure, as follows:

```
ALTER TABLE car_portal_app.car ADD COLUMN features hstore;
```

One limitation of the hstore is that it is not a full document store, so it is difficult to represent nested objects in an hstore. One advantage of an hstore is that it can be indexed using the GIN and GiST indexes.

Modifying and accessing an hstore

The -> operator is used to get a value for a certain key. To append an hstore, the || concatenation operator can be used. Furthermore, the minus sign (-) is used to delete a key value pair. To update an hstore, the hstore can be concatenated with another hstore that contains the updated value. The following example shows how hstore keys can be inserted, updated, and deleted:

```
CREATE TABLE car_test_hstore (
  car_id INT PRIMARY KEY,
  features hstore
);


INSERT INTO car_test_hstore(car_id, features) VALUES (1,
'Engine=>Diesel'::hstore);


-- To add a new key
UPDATE car_test_hstore SET features = features || hstore ('Seat',
'Lethear') WHERE car_id = 1;
-- To update a key, this is similar to add a key
UPDATE car_test_hstore SET features = features || hstore ('Engine',
'Petrol') WHERE car_id = 1;
-- To delete a key
UPDATE car_test_hstore SET features = features - 'Seat'::TEXT WHERE car_
id = 1;


SELECT * FROM car_test_hstore WHERE car_id = 1;
--- Result
car_id |        features
--------+--------------------
     1 | "Engine"=>"Petrol"
(1 row)
```

The hstore data type is very rich in functions and operators; there are several operators to compare hstore content. For example, the ?, ?&, and ?| operators can be used to check whether hstore contains a key, set of keys, or any of the specified keys, respectively. Also, an hstore can be cast to arrays, sets, and JSON documents.

As an hstore data type can be cast to a set using each (hstore) function, one can use all the relational algebra set operators on an hstore, such as DISTINCT, GROUP BY, and ORDER BY.

The following example shows how to get distinct hstore keys; this could be used to validate hstore keys:

```
TRUNCATE  Table car_test_hstore;

INSERT INTO car_test_hstore(car_id, features) VALUES (1,
'Engine=>Diesel'::hstore);

INSERT INTO car_test_hstore(car_id, features) VALUES (2, 'engine=>Petrol,
seat=>lether'::hstore);

car_portal=# SELECT DISTINCT (each(features)).key  FROM car_test_hstore;
  key
--------
 Engine

 seat

 engine
(3 rows)
```

Indexing an hstore in PostgreSQL

An hstore data type can be indexed using the GIN and GiST indexes, and picking the right index type depends on several factors, such as the number of rows in the table, available space, index search and update performance, the queries' pattern, and so on.

In general, GIN index lookups are three times fasters than GiST, but the former are more expensive to build and update and require more space. To properly pick up the right index, it is good to perform a benchmarking.

The following example shows the effect of using the GIN index in retrieving a record that has a certain key. The ? operator returns `true` if `hstore` contains a key:

```
CREATE INDEX ON car_test_hstore USING GIN (features);

SET enable_seqscan to off;
EXPLAIN SELECT car_id, features->'Engine'  FROM car_test_hstore WHERE
features ? 'Engine';
                                          QUERY PLAN
----------------------------------------------------------------------
--------------------

 Bitmap Heap Scan on car_test_hstore  (cost=8.00..12.02 rows=1 width=36)

   Recheck Cond: (features ? 'Engine'::text)

   -> Bitmap Index Scan on car_test_hstore_features_idx1
(cost=0.00..8.00 rows=1 width=0)

        Index Cond: (features ? 'Engine'::text)

(4 rows)
```

Certainly, if an operator is not supported by the GIN index, such as the -> operator, one can still use the B-tree index as follows:

```
CREATE INDEX ON car_test_hstore((features->'Engine'));

SET enable_seqscan to off;

EXPLAIN SELECT car_id, features->'Engine'  FROM car_test_hstore WHERE
features->'Engine'= 'Diesel';
                                          QUERY PLAN
----------------------------------------------------------------------
-----------------------

 Index Scan using car_test_hstore_expr_idx on car_test_hstore
(cost=0.13..8.15 rows=1 width=36)

   Index Cond: ((features -> 'Engine'::text) =
   'Diesel'::text)

(2 rows)
```

The PostgreSQL JSON data type

JSON is a universal data structure that is human and machine readable. JSON is supported by almost all modern programming languages, embraced as a data interchange format, and heavily used in restful web services.

JSON and XML

XML and JSON are both used to define the data structure of exchanged documents. JSON grammar is simpler than that of XML, and JSON documents are more compact. JSON is easier to read and write. On the other hand, XML can have a defined data structure enforced by the **XML schema definition (XSD)** schema. Both JSON and XML have different usages as exchange formats; based on personal experience, JSON is often used within the organization itself or with web services and mobile applications due to its simplicity, while XML is used to define highly structured documents and formats to guarantee interoperability with data exchange between different organizations. For example, several **Open Geospatial Consortium (OGC)** standards, such as web map services, use XML as an exchange format with a defined XSD schema.

The JSON data type

PostgreSQL supports two JSON data type, mainly JSON and JSONB, both of which are implementations of RFC 7159. Both types can be used to enforce JSON rules. Both types are almost identical; however `jsonb` is more efficient as it stores JSON documents in a binary format and also supports indexes. When using JSON, it is preferable to have UTF8 as the database encoding to ensure that the JSON type conforms to RFC 7159 standards. On one hand, when storing data as a JSON document, the JSON object is stored in a textual format. On the other hand, when storing a JSON object as JSONB, the JSON primitive data types mainly string, Boolean, and number will be mapped to text, Boolean and numeric respectively.

Modifying and accessing JSON types

When casting text as a `json` type, the text is stored and rendered without any processing; so, it will preserve the white space, numeric formatting, and elements' order details. JSONB does not preserve these details, as shown in the following example:

```
CREATE TABLE test_json(
  doc json
);
CREATE TABLE test_jsonb (
  doc jsonb
);
```

```
INSERT INTO test_json  VALUES ('{"car_id":1,        "model":"BMW"}'::json),
   ('{"name":"some name", "name":"some name"}'::json);
INSERT INTO test_jsonb  VALUES ('{"car_id":1,
"model":"BMW"}'::jsonb),
   ('{"name":"some name", "name":"some name"}'::jsonb);
SELECT * FROM test_json;
                       doc
-------------------------------------------
 {"car_id":1,        "model":"BMW"}
 {"name":"some name", "name":"some name"}
(2 rows)


SELECT * FROM test_jsonb;
               doc
--------------------------------
 {"model": "BMW", "car_id": 1}
 {"name": "some name"}
(2 rows)
```

The JSON objects can contain other nested JSON objects, arrays, nested arrays, arrays of JSON objects, and so on. JSON arrays and objects can be nested arbitrarily, allowing the developer to construct complex JSON documents. The array elements in JSON documents can be of different types. The following example shows how to construct an account with name as text value, address as JSON object, and rank as an array:

```
INSERT INTO test_jsonb VALUES ('{"name":"John", "Address":{"Street":"Some
street", "city":"Some city"}, "rank":[5,3,4,5,2,3,4,5]}'::JSONB);
INSERT 0 1
```

One could get the JSON object field as a JSON object or as text. Also, JSON fields can be retrieved using the index or the fieldname. The following table summarizes the JSON retrieval operators:

Return type		
JSON	**Text**	**Description**
->	->>	This returns a JSON field either using the field index or field name
#>	#>>	This returns a JSON field defined by a specified path

To get the `Address` and `city` from the JSON object created before, one could use two methods as follows (note that the field names of JSON objects are case sensitive):

```
SELECT doc->'Address'->>'city', doc#>>'{Address, city}' FROM test_jsonb
WHERE doc->>'name' = 'John';
 ?column?  | ?column?
-----------+-----------
 Some city | Some city
(1 row)
```

Currently, there is no way to update and delete a single field in the JSON object; however, one could work around this by deconstructing and constructing the JSON object. This can be done by converting the JSON object to a key value set using the `json_each` and `jsonb_each` functions. The following example shows how to decompose the JSON object in the previous example:

```
WITH RECURSIVE json_get(key, value, parent) AS(

SELECT (jsonb_each(doc)).* , 'null'::text  FROM test_jsonb WHERE doc-
>>'name' = 'John'

UNION ALL

SELECT (jsonb_each(value)).*, key FROM json_get WHERE jsonb_typeof(value)
= 'object')

SELECT * FROM json_get;
   key    |                          value                          | parent
----------+---------------------------------------------------------+---------
 name     | "John"                                                  | null
 rank     | [5, 3, 4, 5, 2, 3, 4, 5]                                | null
 Address  | {"city": "Some city", "Street": "Some street"}          | null
 city     | "Some city"                                             | Address
 Street   | "Some street"                                           | Address
(5 rows)
```

Another simpler approach is to convert the JSON object to text, then use regular expressions to replace or delete an element, and finally cast the text to JSON again. To delete the rank from the account object, one can do the following:

```
SELECT (regexp_replace(doc::text, '"rank":(.*)],',''))::jsonb FROM test_
jsonb WHERE doc->>'name' = 'John';
                               regexp_replace
-----------------------------------------------------------------------------
----
```

```
{"name": "John", "Address": {"city": "Some city", "Street": "Some
street"}}
```

(1 row)

A third option to manipulate JSON objects is to use a procedural language, such as PL/Python, or manipulate the JSON object in the business logic.

Indexing a JSON data type

JSONB documents can be indexed using the GIN index, and the index can be used for the following operators:

- @>: Does the left JSON value contain the right value?
- ?: Does the key string exist in the JSON doc?
- ?&: Do any of the elements in the text array exist in the JSON doc?
- ?|: Do all the keys/elements in the text array exist in the JSON doc?

To see the effect of indexing on the test_jsonb table, let's create an index and disable sequential scan, as follows:

```
CREATE INDEX ON test_jsonb USING GIN (doc);

SET enable_seqscan = off;

EXPLAIN SELECT * FROM test_jsonb WHERE doc @> '{"name":"John"}';

--- Result
                              QUERY PLAN
----------------------------------------------------------------------
---------
 Bitmap Heap Scan on test_jsonb  (cost=12.00..16.01 rows=1 width=32)
   Recheck Cond: (doc @> '{"name": "John"}'::jsonb)
   ->  Bitmap Index Scan on test_jsonb_doc_idx  (cost=0.00..12.00 rows=1
width=0)
         Index Cond: (doc @> '{"name": "John"}'::jsonb)
 (4 rows)
```

The PostgreSQL RESTful API with JSON

It is convenient to provide an interface to share commonly used data by several applications via a restful API. Let's assume we have a table that is used by several applications; one way to make these applications aware of this table is to create a **data access object (DAO)** for this table, wrap it in a library, and then reuse this library in these applications. This approach has some disadvantages, such as resolving library dependency and mismatching library versions. Also, deploying new versions of a library requires a lot of effort because applications using this library need to be compiled, tested, and deployed.

The advantage of providing a RESTful API interface for the PostgreSQL database is to allow easy access to data. Also, it allows the developer to utilize micro service architecture, which leads to better agility.

There are several open source frameworks to set up a RESTful API interface for PostgreSQL. To set up a complete CRUD API using Nginx, one can use the Nginx PostgreSQL upstream module—`ngx_postgres`—which is very easy to use and well supported. Unfortunately, it is not available as a Debian package, which means that one needs to compile Nginx and install it manually.

In the following example, a RESTful API to retrieve data is presented using Nginx and memcached, assuming that the data can fit completely in the memory. PostgreSQL pushes data to the memcached server, and Nginx pulls the data from the memcached server. Memcached is used to cache data and as an intermediary layer between postgres and Nginx.

As memcached uses the key/value data structure, one needs to identify the key to get data. Nginx uses the URI and passed arguments to map a certain request to a memcached value. In the following example, RESTful API best practices are not covered, and this is only for a technical demonstration. Also, in a production environment, one could combine caching and the PostgreSQL Nginx upstream module—`ngx_postgres`—to achieve a highly performant CRUD system. By combining memcached and `ngx_postgres`, one could get rid of the limitation of RAM size.

In order to push data to a memcached server, the PostgreSQL `pg_memcache` module is required. Take a look at the following code:

```
apt-get install postgresql-9.4-pgmemcache
psql -d template1 -c "CREATE EXTENSION pgmemcache"
```

To install the Nginx and memcached server on Linux, one can execute the following commands:

```
apt-get install nginx
apt-get install memcached
```

Also, to add the memcached server permanently to the PostgreSQL server, one can add the following custom variable in the customized options settings block in the `postgresql.conf` file:

```
$echo "pgmemcache.default_servers = 'localhost'">>/etc/postgresql/9.4/
main/postgresql.conf
$/etc/init.d/postgresql reload
```

To test the `memcached` and `pgmemcache` extensions, one can use the `memcached_add(key,value)` and `memcached_get(key)` functions to populate and retrieve a factionary memcached value, as follows:

```
template1=# SELECT memcache_add('/1', 'hello');
 memcache_add
--------------
 t
(1 row)


template1=# SELECT memcache_get('/1');
 memcache_get
--------------
 hello
(1 row)
```

In order to allow Nginx to access memcached, the memcached server needs to be configured, and the Nginx server configuration needs to be reloaded in order for the configuration to take effect. The following is a minimal Nginx configuration file — `nginx.conf` — to allow access to the memcached server. Note that in Ubuntu, the Nginx configuration file is located under `/etc/nginx/nginx.conf`:

```
user www-data;
worker_processes 4;
pid /run/nginx.pid;
events {
        worker_connections 800;
}
```

```
http {

    server {

        location / {

            set $memcached_key "$uri";

            memcached_pass 127.0.0.1:11211;

            default_type application/json;

            add_header x-header-memcached true;

        }


    }

}
```

In the preceding example, the Nginx web server is used to serve the responses from the memcached server defined by the memcached_pass variable. The response from memcached is obtained by the key, which is the **uniform resource identifier (URI)**. The default response type is JSON. Finally, the x-header-memcached header is set to true to enable troubleshooting.

To test the Nginx server setting, let's retrieve the value of the /1 key generated by the pgmemcache PostgreSQL extension, as follows:

```
$curl -I -X GET http://127.0.0.1/1

HTTP/1.1 200 OK

Server: nginx/1.4.6 (Ubuntu)

Date: Wed, 22 Jul 2015 14:50:26 GMT

Content-Type: application/json

Content-Length: 5

Connection: keep-alive

x-header-memcached: true
```

Note that the server responded successfully to the request, the response type is marked as JSON, and the response is obtained by memcached as shown by the header.

Let's assume that we want to have a restful web service to present user account information, including the account ID, first name, last name, and e-mail from the account table. The row_to_json () function can be used to construct a JSON document from a relational row, as follows:

```
car_portal=> SELECT row_to_json (row(account_id,first_name, last_name,
email)) FROM car_portal_app.account LIMIT 1;
                        row_to_json
```

```
----------------------------------------------------------------
 {"f1":1,"f2":"James","f3":"Butt","f4":"jbutt@gmail.com"}

(1 row)


car_portal=> SELECT row_to_json (account) FROM car_portal_app.account
LIMIT 1;

                                                           row_to_json
-----------------------------------------------------------------------
------------------------------------------------------------
 {"account_id":1,"first_name":"James","last_name":"Butt","email":"jbutt@
gmail.com","password":"1b9ef408e82e38346e6ebebf2dcc5ece"}

(1 row)
```

In the preceding example, the usage of the row(account_id, first_name, last_name, email) construct caused the row_to_json function to be unable to determine the attribute names, and the names were replaced with f1, f2, and so on. To work around this, one needs to give a name to the row. This can be done in several ways, such as using subqueries or giving an alias to the result; the following example shows one way to resolve the issue by specifying aliases using CTE:

```
 car_portal=> WITH account_info(account_id, first_name, last_name, email)
AS (

SELECT account_id,first_name, last_name, email FROM car_portal_app.
account LIMIT 1

) SELECT row_to_json(account_info) FROM account_info;
                                     row_to_json
-----------------------------------------------------------------------
--------------
 {"account_id":1,"first_name":"James","last_name":"Butt","email":"jbutt@
gmail.com"}

(1 row)
```

To generate entries for the account table using account_id—the primary key—as the hash key, one can use the following:

```
SELECT memcache_add('/'||account_id, (SELECT row_to_json(foo) FROM
(SELECT account_id, first_name,last_name, email ) AS FOO )::text)  FROM
car_portal_app.account;
```

Note that at this point, one can access data from the Nginx server. To test this, let's get the JSON representation for the account with `account_id` equaling 1, as follows:

```
$curl -sD - -o -X GET http://127.0.0.1/1
HTTP/1.1 200 OK
Server: nginx/1.4.6 (Ubuntu)
Date: Fri, 24 Jul 2015 16:38:13 GMT
Content-Type: application/json
Content-Length: 82
Connection: keep-alive
x-header-memcached: true


{"account_id":1,"first_name":"James","last_name":"Butt","email":"jbutt@
gmail.com"}
```

To ensure that the account table data is consistent with the memcached server data, one can add a trigger to reflect the changes performed on the table on memcached. Also, one needs to be careful with handling transaction rollbacks and come with the appropriate caching strategy to decrease data inconsistency between the cache and database system. The following example shows the effect of a rollback on memcached data:

```
car_portal=# BEGIN;
BEGIN
car_portal=# SELECT memcache_add('is_transactional?', 'No');
 memcache_add
--------------
 t
(1 row)


car_portal=# Rollback;
ROLLBACK
car_portal=# SELECT memcache_get('is_transactional?');
 memcache_get
--------------
 No
(1 row)
```

A PostgreSQL full text search

PostgreSQL provides a full text search capability, which is used to overcome SQL pattern matching operators, including LIKE and ILIKE, boosting the performance of the text search. For example, even though an index on text using the text_pattern_op class is supported, this index cannot be used to match a nonanchored text search. To explain this limitation, let's create the following table:

```
CREATE TABLE document(
  document_id serial primary key,
  document_body text
);


CREATE INDEX on document (document_body text_pattern_ops);


INSERT INTO document VALUES (default, 'Can not use text_pattern_op class
to search for non-anchored text');
```

To test the index with anchored and nonanchored text search, let's disable sequential scan and generate execution plans as shown in the following example:

```
car_portal=# EXPLAIN SELECT * FROM document WHERE document_body like
'Can%text_pattern';
                                    QUERY PLAN
--------------------------------------------------------------------------
--------------------
 Bitmap Heap Scan on document  (cost=4.21..13.68 rows=1 width=36)
   Filter: (document_body ~~ 'Can%text_pattern'::text)
   ->  Bitmap Index Scan on document_document_body_idx  (cost=0.00..4.21
rows=6 width=0)
        Index Cond: ((document_body ~>=~ 'Can'::text) AND (document_body
~<~ 'Cao'::text))
(4 rows)


car_portal=# EXPLAIN SELECT * FROM document WHERE document_body like
'%text_pattern';
                                    QUERY PLAN
--------------------------------------------------------------------------
----
 Seq Scan on document  (cost=10000000000.00..10000000025.38 rows=1
width=36)
```

```
        Filter: (document_body ~~ '%text_pattern'::text)
(2 rows)
```

Note that for nonanchored text, as in `%text_pattern`, the index is not used.

Another issue with the traditional LIKE and ILIKE operators is the ranking based on similarity and natural language linguistic support. The LIKE and ILIKE operators always evaluate a Boolean value: either as TRUE or as FALSE.

In addition to ranking nonanchored text search support, PostgreSQL full text search provides many other features. Full text search supports dictionaries, so it can supports language, such as synonyms.

The tsquery and tsvector data types

Full text search is based on the `tsvector` and `tsquery` data types; here, `tsvector` represents a document in a normalized state.

The tsvector data type

The `tsvector` data type is a sorted list of distinct lexemes. Duplicate elimination and sorting is done during input, as follows:

```
SELECT 'A wise man always has something to say, whereas a fool always
needs to say something'::tsvector;
                                                tsvector
-------------------------------------------------------------------------
-------------------
 'A' 'a' 'always' 'fool' 'has' 'man' 'needs' 'say' 'say,' 'something'
'to' 'whereas' 'wise'
(1 row)
```

Casting a text to `tsvector` does not normalize the document completely due to the lack of linguistic rules. To normalize the preceding example, one can use the `to_tsvector()` function to normalize the text properly, as follows:

```
SELECT to_tsvector('english', 'A wise man always has something to say,
whereas a fool always needs to say something');
                                    to_tsvector
-------------------------------------------------------------------------
--------------
 'alway':4,12 'fool':11 'man':3 'need':13 'say':8,15 'someth':6,16
'wherea':9 'wise':2
(1 row)
```

As shown in the preceding example, the `to_tsvector` function stripped some letters, such as `s` from `alway`, and also generated the integer position of lexemes, which can be used for proximity ranking.

The tsquery data type

The `tsquery` data type is used to search for certain lexemes. Lexemes can be combined with the `&` (AND), `|` (OR), and `!` (NOT) operators. Note that the NOT operator has the highest precedence, followed by AND and then OR. Also, parentheses can be used to group lexemes and operators to force a certain order.

The following example shows how we can search for certain lexemes using `tsquery`, `tsvector`, and the match operator (`@@`):

```
car_portal=# SELECT 'A wise man always has something to say, whereas a
fool always needs to say something'::tsvector @@ 'wise'::tsquery;
 ?column?
----------
 t
(1 row)
```

The `tsquery` also has the `to_tsquery` function to convert text to lexemes, as shown here:

```
car_portal=# SELECT to_tsquery('english', 'wise & man');
   to_tsquery
----------------
 'wise' & 'man'
(1 row)
```

Pattern matching

There are several factors affecting the result of pattern matching, including:

- Text normalization
- Dictionary
- Ranking

If the text is not normalized, text search might not return the expected result. The following examples show how pattern matching can fail with unnormalized text:

```
car_portal=# SELECT 'elephants'::tsvector @@ 'elephant';
 ?column?
----------
 f
(1 row)
```

In the preceding query, casting `elephants` to `tsvector` and the implicit casting of `elephant` to the query does not generate normalized lexemes due to missing information about the dictionary.

To add dictionary information, `to_tsvector` and `to_tsquery` can be used as follows:

```
car_portal=# SELECT to_tsvector('english', 'elephants') @@ to_
tsquery('english', 'elephant');
 ?column?
----------
 t
(1 row)
```

```
car_portal=# SELECT to_tsvector('simple', 'elephants') @@ to_
tsquery('simple', 'elephant');
 ?column?
----------
 f
(1 row)
```

Full text search supports pattern matching based on ranks. The `tsvector` lexemes can be marked with the labels, A, B, C, and D; where D is the default and A has the highest rank. The `setweight` function can be used to assign weight to `tsvector` explicitly, as follows:

```
SELECT setweight(to_tsvector('english', 'elephants'),'A') ||
setweight(to_tsvector('english', 'dolphin'),'b');
         ?column?
-------------------------
 'dolphin':2B 'eleph':1A
(1 row)
```

For ranking, there are two functions: `ts_rank` and `ts_rank_cd`. The `ts_rank` function is used for standard ranking, while `ts_rank_cd` is used for the cover density ranking technique. The following example shows the result of `ts_rank_cd` when used to search `eleph` and `dolphin`, respectively:

```
car_portal=# SELECT ts_rank_cd (setweight(to_tsvector('english',
'elephants'),'A') || setweight(to_tsvector('english', 'dolphin'),'B'),
'eleph' );
 ts_rank_cd
------------
          1
(1 row)


car_portal=# SELECT ts_rank_cd (setweight(to_tsvector('english',
'elephants'),'A') || setweight(to_tsvector('english', 'dolphin'),'B'),
'dolphin' );
 ts_rank_cd
------------
        0.4
(1 row)
```

Ranking is often used to enhance, filter out, and order the result of pattern matching. In real-life scenarios, different document sections can have different weights; for example, when searching for a movie, the highest weight could be given to the movie title and main character, and less weight could be given to the summary of the movie plot.

Full text search indexing

GiST can be used to index `tsvector` and `tsquery`, while GIN can be used to index `tsvector` only.

The GiST index is lossy and can return false matches, so PostgreSQL automatically rechecks the returned result and filtered out false matches. False matches can reduce performance due to the records' random access cost. The GIN index stores only the lexemes of `tsvector` and not the weight labels; due to this, the GIN index could be considered also lossy if weights are involved in the query.

The performance of the GIN and GiST indexes depends on the number of unique words, so it is recommended to use dictionaries to reduce the total number of unique words. The GIN index is faster to search and slower to build and requires more space than GiST. The `maintenance_work_mem` function can improve the GIN index's build time, but this does not work for the GiST index.

Summary

PostgreSQL is very rich in built-in data types and external extensions. It can be extended easily using the C and C++ languages. In fact, PostgreSQL provides an extension-building infrastructure called PGXS so that extensions can be built against an installed server. Some PostgreSQL extensions, such as PostGIS, require complete chapters to discuss.

PostgreSQL provides a very rich set of data types, such as XML, hstore, JSON, array, and so on. These data types can be used to ease the developer's life by not reinventing the wheel and utilizing the very rich set of functions and operators. Also, several PostgreSQL data types, such as hstore and JSON, can increase the developer's agility because the database's physical design is not amended frequently.

PostgreSQL arrays are very mature; they have a rich set of operators and function. PostgreSQL can handle multidimensional arrays with different base types. Arrays are useful in modeling multivalued attributes as well as in performing several tasks that are difficult to achieve using only the pure relational model.

Hash store is supported in PostgreSQL since version 9.0; it allows the developer to store key values in the data structure. Hash store is very useful in modeling semistructured data as well as in increasing the developer's agility.

Both JSON as well as XML documents are supported, allowing PostgreSQL to support different document exchange formats. PostgreSQL provides several JSON functions to convert rows to JSON and vice versa. This allows PostgreSQL to server also RESTful web services easily.

PostgreSQL also supports full text search. Full text search solves several problems related to language linguistics as well as nonanchored text search performance and enhances end user experience and satisfaction.

12
Testing

Software testing is the process of analyzing program components, programs, and systems with the intention of finding errors in them, and for determining or checking their technical limits and requirements.

The database is a specific system that requires special approaches for testing. This is because the behavior of database software components (views, stored procedures, or functions) depends not only on their code but also on the data; in many cases, it is not possible to just repeat the same function calls to get the same results.

That's why one should use specific techniques for testing database modules. PostgreSQL provides some features for helping developers and testers to do that.

In software architecture, the database usually lies at the lowest level. Business software processes the data, and the data is modeled and stored in the database. This is the reason why, in most cases, changes in the database schema affect many other software components.

This topic is closely related to database development and refactoring. Database objects are often accessed by several different systems, and when one of them is changed, the others can also be affected. Moreover, the database structure can be changed without changing the code of the software using the database, and the developer should be sure that the application would still work with the new data structure.

In this chapter, some methods of testing database objects are discussed. They can be applied when implementing changes in the data structure of complex systems, and when developing database interfaces.

Unit testing

Unit testing is a process in software development that makes it possible to check for errors in the various components or modules of software. In databases, those components are stored procedures, functions, triggers, and so on. A view definition, or even a code of queries that applications use, can be an object for unit testing.

The idea behind unit testing is that for every module of the software system, like class or function, there is a set of tests that invokes that module with a certain input data, and checks if the outcome of the invocation matches the expected result. When a module being tested needs to interact with other systems, those systems can be emulated by the test framework so that the interaction can also be tested.

The set of tests should be big enough to cover as much of the source code of the tested module as possible. This can be achieved when the tests imply invocation of the tested code with all possible logical combinations of values of input parameters. If the tested module is supposed to be able to react on invalid data, the tests should include that as well. The execution of those tests should be automated, which makes it possible to run the tests each time a new release of the tested module is developed.

All this makes it possible to change the software, and then quickly check whether the new version still satisfies the old requirements. This approach is called regression testing. Additionally, there is a software development technique called test-driven development. It implies writing tests that reflect the requirements of a software component first, and then developing code which satisfies the tests.

Unit testing in databases

The particularity of database unit tests is that not only the parameters of a function but also the data, which is stored in database tables, can be both the input and the outcome of the module being tested. Moreover, the execution of one test could influence the following tests due to the changes it makes to the data, so it might be necessary to execute the tests in a specific order.

Therefore, the testing framework should be able to insert data into the database, run tests, and then analyze the new data. Furthermore, the testing framework could also be required to manage the transactions in which the tests are executed. The easiest way to do all of that is by writing the tests as SQL scripts. In many cases, it is convenient to wrap them into stored procedures (functions in case of PostgreSQL). These procedures can be put in the same database where the components being tested were created.

Testing functions can take test cases from a table iterating through its records. There could be many testing functions, and one separate function that executes them one by one and then formats the result protocol.

Let's create a simple example. Suppose there is a table in the database and a function performing an action on the data in the table:

```
CREATE TABLE counter_table(counter int);
CREATE FUNCTION increment_counter() RETURNS void AS
$$
BEGIN
  INSERT INTO counter_table SELECT count(*) FROM
  counter_table;
END;
$$
LANGUAGE plpgsql;
```

The table contains only one integer field. The function counts the number of records in the table, and inserts that number in the same table. So, subsequent calls of the function will cause insertion of the numbers 0, 1, 2, and so on into the table. This functionality is an object for testing. So, the test function can be the following:

```
CREATE FUNCTION test_increment() RETURNS boolean AS
$$
DECLARE
  c int; m int;
BEGIN
  RAISE NOTICE '1..2';
  -- Separate test scenario from testing environment
  BEGIN
    -- Test 1. Call increment function
    BEGIN
      PERFORM increment_counter();
      RAISE NOTICE 'ok 1 - Call increment function';
    EXCEPTION WHEN OTHERS THEN
      RAISE NOTICE 'not ok 1 - Call increment function';
    END;
    -- Test 2. Test results
    BEGIN
      SELECT COUNT(*), MAX(counter) INTO c, m
        FROM counter_table;
      IF NOT (c = 1 AND m = 0) THEN
        RAISE EXCEPTION 'Test 2: wrong values in output
        data';
      END IF;
```

```
        RAISE NOTICE 'ok 2 - Check first record';
      EXCEPTION WHEN OTHERS THEN
        RAISE NOTICE 'not ok 2 - Check first record';
      END;
      -- Rollback changes made by the test
      RAISE EXCEPTION 'Rollback test data';
    EXCEPTION
      WHEN raise_exception THEN RETURN true;
      WHEN OTHERS THEN RETURN false;
    END;
  END;
$$
LANGUAGE plpgsql;
```

The preceding test function works in the following way:

- The whole test scenario is executed in its own BEGIN-EXCEPTION-END block. It isolates the test from the transaction that has executed the test, and makes it possible to run another test afterwards, which could use the same data structures.

- Each test in the test scenario is also executed in its own BEGIN-EXCEPTION-END block. This makes it possible to continue testing even if one of the tests fails.

- The first test runs the increment_counter() function. The test is considered successful if the function is called without any error. The test is considered unsuccessful if an exception of any kind occurs.

- The second test selects the data from the table, and checks if it matches the expected values. If the data is wrong, or if the select statement fails for any reason, the test fails.

- The result of testing is reported to the console by the RAISE NOTICE commands. The output format follows the **Test Anything Protocol (TAP)** specification, and can be processed by a test harness (external testing framework), like Jenkins.

If we run the preceding test function, we will get the following protocol:

```
username=# SELECT test_increment();
NOTICE:  1..2
NOTICE:  ok 1 - Call increment function
NOTICE:  ok 2 - Check first record
 test_increment
----------------
 t
(1 row)
```

The test is successful!

Suppose the requirements have been changed, and now it is necessary to add another field in the table to record the time when a value was inserted:

```
username=# ALTER TABLE counter_table ADD insert_time timestamp with
time zone NOT NULL;
```

After the change of the data structure, one should run the test again to see if the function still works:

```
username=# SELECT test_increment();
NOTICE:   1..2
NOTICE:   not ok 1 - Call increment function
NOTICE:   not ok 2 - Check first record
 test_increment
----------------
 t
(1 row)
```

The test fails. That happens because the `increment_counter()` function does not know about the other field, and it should also be changed:

```
CREATE OR REPLACE FUNCTION increment_counter() RETURNS void AS
$$
BEGIN
   INSERT INTO counter_table SELECT count(*), now() FROM counter_table;
END;
$$
LANGUAGE plpgsql;
```

And now, if the testing function is called again, it will succeed:

```
username=# SELECT test_increment();
NOTICE:   1..2
NOTICE:   ok 1 - Call increment function
NOTICE:   ok 2 - Check first record
 test_increment
----------------
 t
(1 row)
```

The preceding test function is not perfect. First, it does not check if the function `increment_counter()` actually counts the records. The test will succeed even if the function `increment_counter()` just inserts the constant value of zero in the database. To fix that, the test function should run the test twice, and check the new data.

Secondly, if the test fails, it would be good to know the exact reason for the failure. The testing function can get that information from PostgreSQL using the GET STACKED DIAGNOSTICS command, and show it with RAISE NOTICE.

The current and the improved versions of the code are available in the addendum, in the files unit_test_short.sql and unit_test_full.sql.

It is a very good practice to have unit tests for the database components in complicated software systems. This is because, in many cases, the database is a component that is shared among many software modules. And any development in the database on behalf of one of those modules can cause the other modules to break. In many cases, the system by which the database object is being used and the way in which it is being used is not clear. That's why it is essential to have unit tests that emulate the usage of the database by each of the external systems. And when developers work on changes to the data structure, those tests should be executed to check if the systems can work with the new structure.

The tests could be run in a newly created testing environment. In that case, the install script should include some code for creating testing data and some necessary data like the commonly used lookup tables. Additionally, the test environment could be based on a clone of the production database. The test script should also contain some cleanup code.

Unit test frameworks

The preceding example has some more drawbacks. For example, if the function being tested raises warnings or notices, they will spoil the test protocol. Moreover, it implies that the testing function is not written very well. For example: the test ID and description are repeated, the BEGIN-END blocks are bulky, and the developer of the test function did not take care about formatting the result protocol. All these tasks could be automated by using any of the unit test frameworks.

There is no unit test framework that comes out of the box with PostgreSQL, but there are several of them available from the community.

The most commonly used one is *pgTAP* (http://pgtap.org/). One can download it from GitHub, and install in the test database. The installation is quite easy and described well in the documentation.

The tests are written as SQL scripts, and they can be run in batches by the utility called pg_prove, which is provided with pgTAP. There is also a way to write tests as stored functions using plpgsql.

The pgTAP framework provides the user with a set of helper functions that are used to wrap the testing code. They also write the results into a temporary table, which is used later to generate the testing protocol. For example, the `ok()` function reports a successful test if its argument is true, and a failed test, if not. The `has_relation()` function checks the database if the specified relation exists. There are about a hundred of those functions.

The test scenario that was described in the preceding section can be implemented in the following script using pgTAP:

```
-- Isolate test scenario in its own transaction
BEGIN;
-- report 2 tests will be run
SELECT plan(2);
-- Test 1. Call increment function
SELECT lives_ok('SELECT increment_counter()','Call increment
function');
-- Test 2. Test results
SELECT is( (SELECT ARRAY [COUNT(*), MAX(counter)]::text FROM counter_
table), ARRAY [1, 0]::text,'Check first record');
-- Report finish
SELECT finish();
-- Rollback changes made by the test
ROLLBACK;
```

And the result of execution of the script:

```
1..2
ok 1 - Call increment function
ok 2 - Check first record
```

There are several other unit test frameworks that are not as popular:

`plpgunit`: The tests are written as functions in `plpgsql`. They use the provided helper functions to perform tests like `assert.is_equal()`, which checks if two arguments are equal. The helper functions format the results of testing and display them on the console. A managing function, `unit_tests.begin()`, runs all the testing functions, logs their output into a table, and formats the results protocol.

The advantage of `plpgunit` is its simplicity — it is very lightweight and easy to install, there is only one SQL script that you needs to run to get the framework in their database.

The `plpgunit framework` is available in GitHub at `https://github.com/mixerp/plpgunit`.

Another unit test framework that is available is the `dklab_pgunit`. The general idea is similar to `plpgunit`; the tests are `plpgsql` functions, which are executed by another managing function. The main difference is that this framework can optimize the process of running the tests when several of them use the same set up procedure. That procedure will be executed only once, and then several tests will use the same results. The biggest advantage of this framework is that it can be used not only on an empty, just-created test database but also on an image of the production database, which can be quite heavy.

Unfortunately, the project seems to be abandoned since 2008. The `dklab_pgunit` framework can be found at `http://en.dklab.ru/lib/dklab_pgunit/`.

Schema difference

When one works on a new version of the database schema for an application, sometimes, it is necessary to understand the difference between the old and new structure. This information is used in release notes, and it can also be analyzed to check if the changes might have any undesired impact on other applications.

The differences can be found using conventional command-line utilities.

For example, suppose one changed the structure of the car portal database, which is used as a sample database in this book. The script to create the database is in the addendum. To learn how to create a database and how to use the psql console and other PostgreSQL utilities, please refer to the previous chapters.

First, let's create another database which will contain the updated schema:

```
user@host:~$ createdb car_portal_new -T car_portal -O car_portal_app
```

Now there are two identical databases. Then, deploy the changes in the schema to the new database:

```
user@host:~$ psql car_portal_new
psql (9.4.0)
Type "help" for help.
car_portal_new=# ALTER TABLE car_portal_app.car ADD insert_date
timestamp with time zone DEFAULT now();
```

Now the structure of those two databases is different. To find the difference, let's dump the schema into the files:

```
user@host:~$ pg_dump -s car_portal > old_db.sql
user@host:~$ pg_dump -s car_portal_new > new_db.sql
```

Now, one can use any utility to compare the two text files. For example, the Linux `diff` utility will return the following output (the output is truncated):

```
user@host:~$ diff -U 7 old_db.sql new_db.sql
--- old_db.sql   2015-01-24 13:46:20.608109000 -0500
+++ new_db.sql   2015-01-24 13:46:28.312109000 -0500
@@ -251,15 +251,16 @@
 CREATE TABLE car (
     car_id integer NOT NULL,
     number_of_owners integer NOT NULL,
     registration_number text NOT NULL,
     manufacture_year integer NOT NULL,
     number_of_doors integer DEFAULT 5 NOT NULL,
     car_model_id integer,
-    mileage integer NOT NULL
+    mileage integer NOT NULL,
+    insert_date timestamp with time zone DEFAULT now()
 );
```

In Windows, similar results can be achieved using the `fc` command:

```
C:\dbdumps> fc old_db.sql new_db.sql
Comparing files old_db.sql and NEW_DB.SQL
***** old_db.sql
    car_model_id integer,
    mileage integer NOT NULL
);
***** NEW_DB.SQL
    car_model_id integer,
    mileage integer NOT NULL,
    insert_date timestamp with time zone DEFAULT now()
);
*****
```

From both the outputs it is visible that one line was changed, and another line was added to the script.

Alternatively, this file comparison can be done using any of the commonly used text editors, like `vim` or Notepad++.

In many cases, it is not enough to just see the difference in the schema. It could also be necessary to synchronize the schema of the two databases. There are some commercial products that can do that, like EMS DB Comparer for PostgreSQL.

Moreover, there are many open source projects. For example, `apgdiff`, which is written in Java and available at `http://www.apgdiff.com/index.php`.

The output of `apgdiff` will be:

```
user@host:~$ java -jar apgdiff-2.4.jar old_db.sql new_db.sql

SET search_path = car_portal_app, pg_catalog;

ALTER TABLE car
        ADD COLUMN insert_date timestamp with time zone DEFAULT
        now();
```

It is an SQL script that can be used to migrate from the old data structure to the new one.

The interfaces test

When a big database is shared by many applications, it is sometimes hard to understand who is using what, and what would happen if the database schema changes. In that case, it makes sense to build the whole system using layered architecture. The physical data structure is located at the bottom-most layer. Applications do not access it directly.

Moving upwards from the bottom, the second last layer contains structures that abstract logical entities from their physical implementation. These structures play the role of data abstraction interfaces. There are several ways to implement them. They can be created in the database as functions. In that case, applications will work with the data by invoking them. Another approach is by using updatable views. In that case, applications can access the logical entities with conventional SQL statements. Additionally, this interface can be implemented outside the database as a lightweight service processing the requests of high level systems, performing queries, and making changes to the database. Each approach has its own set of benefits and drawbacks.

At the top are the applications that implement business logic. They do not care about the physical structure of the data, and interact with the database through data abstraction interfaces.

This approach reduces the number of agents that access the physical data structures, and is clearly able to show how the database is used or can be used. The database documentation contains the specification of those interfaces. So the database developer, when working on refactoring the database schema, should only make sure that the interfaces follow the specification, and until they do, the rest of the database is "free to change".

The existence of these interfaces makes its easier to develop unit tests: it is clear what to test and how, since the specification is given.

Data difference

The easiest way to create a database abstraction interface is by using views to access the data. In this case, if one wants to change the table structure, it can be done without changing the code of the external applications: the only thing necessary is updating the definitions of the interface views. However, it is important to check if the new view returns the same data as the old one.

The situation is the easiest when it is possible to implement a view in the same database. One just needs to create a copy of the production database in the test environment, or prepare a test database containing all possible combinations of the attributes of the business entities. Then the new version of the view can be deployed with a different name. The following query can then be used to see if the new view returns the same data:

```
WITH n AS (SELECT * FROM new_view),
o AS (SELECT * FROM old_view)
SELECT 'new', * FROM
   (SELECT * FROM n EXCEPT ALL SELECT * FROM o) a
UNION ALL
SELECT 'old', * FROM
   (SELECT * FROM o EXCEPT ALL SELECT * FROM n) b;
```

new_view and old_view refer to the names of the respective relations. The query returns no rows if both the views return the same result.

However, this works only when both views are in the same database, and the old view works as it worked before the refactoring. In case the structure of underlying tables changes, the old view cannot work as it did before, and the comparison in that case is not applicable. This problem can be solved by creating a temporary table from the data returned by the old view before refactoring, and then comparing that temporary table with the new view.

This can also be done by comparing the data from different databases: the old one before refactoring and the new one. One can use external tools to do so. For example, data from both the databases can be dumped into files using psql, and then those files can be compared using diff (this will work only if the rows have the same order). There are some commercial tools as well, which provide this functionality.

Another approach is connecting two databases, making queries, and making the comparison inside the database. This might seem complicated, but in fact, it is the fastest and most reliable way. There are a couple of methods to connect two databases: through the extensions dblink (database link) or postgres_fdw (foreign data wrapper).

Using the dblink extension may seem easier than using postgres_fdw, and it allows performing different queries for different objects. However, this technology is older, it uses a syntax that is not standard-compliant, and has performance issues, especially when big tables or views are queried.

On the other hand, postgres_fdw requires creating an object in the local database for each object in the remote database that is going to be accessed, which is not that convenient. However, that makes it easy to use the remote tables together with the local tables in queries, and it is faster.

In the example in the previous section, another database was created from the original database car_portal, and another field was added to the table car_portal_app.car. Let's try to find out if that operation caused changes in the data.

First, connect to the new database as a super user:

```
user@host:~$ psql -h localhost -U postgres car_portal_new
psql (9.4.0)
Type "help" for help.
car_portal_new=#
```

Then create an extension for foreign data wrapper. The binaries for the extension are included in the PostgreSQL server package.

```
car_portal_new=# CREATE EXTENSION postgres_fdw ;
```

Once the extension has been created, create a server object and a user mapping:

```
car_portal_new=# CREATE SERVER car_portal_original FOREIGN DATA
WRAPPER postgres_fdw OPTIONS (host 'localhost', dbname 'car_portal');
car_portal_new=# CREATE USER MAPPING FOR CURRENT_USER SERVER car_
portal_original;
```

As the last step, create a foreign table:

```
car_portal_new=# CREATE FOREIGN TABLE car_portal_app.car_orignal (car_
id int, number_of_owners int, registration_number text, manufacture_
year int, number_of_doors int, car_model_id int, mileage int) SERVER
car_portal_original OPTIONS (table_name 'car');
car_portal_new=# SELECT * FROM car_portal_app.car_orignal ;
car_id | number_of_owners | registration_number | manufacture_year |
number_of_doors | car_model_id | mileage
--------+------------------+---------------------+------------------+-
----------------+--------------+---------
     1 |                3 | MUWH4675            |             2008 |
5 |           65 |   67756
     2 |                1 | VSVW4565            |             2014 |
3 |           61 |    6616
     3 |                1 | BKUN9615            |             2014 |
5 |           19 |   48221
...
(229 rows)
```

Now the table is ready, and it can be queried. To compare the data, the same query can be used as an example for the old and new views:

```
WITH n AS
(SELECT car_id, number_of_owners, registration_number,
   manufacture_year, number_of_doors, car_model_id,
   mileage
 FROM car_portal_app.car),
o AS (SELECT * FROM car_portal_app.car_orignal)
SELECT 'new', * FROM
  (SELECT * FROM n EXCEPT ALL SELECT * FROM o) a
UNION ALL
SELECT 'old', * FROM
  (SELECT * FROM o EXCEPT ALL SELECT * FROM n) b;
?column? | car_id | number_of_owners | registration_number |
manufacture_year | number_of_doors | car_model_id | mileage
----------+--------+------------------+---------------------+---------
---------+------------------+--------------+---------
(0 rows)
```

The result is zero rows, which means the data in both the tables is the same.

PostgreSQL benchmarks

An important question regarding a database system is: how fast is it? How many transactions can it handle per second, or how much time a particular query takes to execute? The topic on the performance of a database has been covered in *Chapter 10, Optimizing Database Performance*. Here, we will only discuss the task of measuring it.

The Psql meta-command \timing is used to measure the time of execution of a particular SQL command. Once timing is enabled, psql shows the time of execution for each command:

```
car_portal-# \timing
Timing is on.
car_portal=# SELECT count(*) FROM car_portal_app.car;
 count
-------
   229
(1 row)
Time: 19.492 ms
```

Usually, that is enough to understand which query is faster. However, one cannot rely on that timing when it comes to estimating the number requests the server can handle per second. This is because the time for a single query depends on many random factors: the current load of the server, the state of the cache, and so on.

PostgreSQL provides a special utility that connects to the server and runs a test script many times. It is called pgbench. By default, pgbench creates its own small database and executes a sample SQL script on it, which is quite similar to what a typical OLTP application usually does. This is already enough to understand how powerful the database server is, and how changes to the configuration parameters affect the performance.

To get more specific results, one should prepare a test database that has a size comparable to the database in production. A test script, which contains the same or similar queries that the production system performs, should also be prepared.

For example, it is assumed that the car portal database is used by a web application. The typical usage scenario is querying the car table to get the number of records, and then querying it again to retrieve the first 20 records, which fit into a page on the screen. The following is the test script:

```
SELECT count(*) FROM car_portal_app.car;
SELECT * FROM car_portal_app.car INNER JOIN car_portal_app.car_model
USING (car_model_id) ORDER BY car_id LIMIT 20;
```

It is saved in a file called `test.sql`, which will be used by `pgbench`.

It is necessary to initialize the sample data for `pgbench`:

```
user@host:~$ pgbench -i car_portal
NOTICE:   table "pgbench_history" does not exist, skipping
NOTICE:   table "pgbench_tellers" does not exist, skipping
NOTICE:   table "pgbench_accounts" does not exist, skipping
NOTICE:   table "pgbench_branches" does not exist, skipping
creating tables...
100000 of 100000 tuples (100%) done (elapsed 0.17 s, remaining 0.00
s).
vacuum...
set primary keys...
done.
```

And now the test can be started, as follows:

```
user@host:~$ pgbench -f test.sql -T 60 car_portal
starting vacuum...end.
transaction type: Custom query
scaling factor: 1
query mode: simple
number of clients: 1
number of threads: 1
duration: 60 s
number of transactions actually processed: 137249
latency average: 0.437 ms
tps = 2287.475213 (including connections establishing)
tps = 2287.600382 (excluding connections establishing)
```

As one can see, the performance is more than two thousand transactions per second, which is more than enough for a small car portal application. However, `pgbench` was running on the same machine as the database server, and they shared the same CPU. To get more realistic statistics, `pgbench` should be started on the machine where the application server is installed, and the number of connections in use should match the configuration of the application server. Usually, for such simple queries, the network connection and transmit times play a bigger role than database processing.

`pgbench` allows a user to specify the number of connections it establishes to the database server. Moreover, it provides a functionality to generate random queries to the database. So, it can be quite useful for assessing database performance and for tuning database server configurations.

Summary

In this chapter, we covered some aspects of software testing and the way in which it can be applied to databases.

Unit testing techniques can be used in databases, which is good practice. However, database unit testing has its own specificities. First, the objects for unit testing are not only program modules, like functions, but also views, triggers, and the data itself. Secondly, the data in the database sometimes defines the behavior of the modules being tested. That makes database unit testing different from testing other kinds of software.

Unit tests for databases could be written as SQL scripts or stored functions in the database. There are several frameworks that help in writing unit tests and in processing the results of testing.

Another aspect of testing the database software is comparing data in the same database or between databases. This can be done via SQL queries, and sometimes, it requires establishing connections between databases. Connections between databases can be established via `dblinks` or foreign data wrapper objects.

Database schemas can be compared quite simply by using command-line tools provided with PostgreSQL and operating systems. Additionally, there are open source and commercial software products that do that too.

`pgbench` is a utility that can be used to assess the performance of a database system.

13

PostgreSQL JDBC

Java Database Connectivity (JDBC) is an API that a user allows to connect to a database from within a Java application in a standardized way. The API is independent of a specific database vendor, and allows creation of applications that can easily be adapted for use with different databases.

This chapter describes the way to use JDBC for connecting to a database, and using a PostgreSQL database from within a Java application.

After discussing how to install and initialize the PostgreSQL JDBC driver and opening a connection to a database, the fundamental concepts and features of the JDBC API will be explained.

This chapter covers executing the basic SQL statements introduced in *Chapter 5, SQL Language*, from within Java code and handling the results returned from a query.

Later in this chapter, the reader will learn how to call stored procedures, and how to access their results.

For this chapter, it is assumed that the reader has a basic knowledge of Java and the usage of one of the common IDEs like Eclipse or Netbeans.

Introduction to JDBC

JDBC is a database-independent **application programming interface (API)** for enabling the interaction between Java applications and a database. It was specified by the Oracle Corporation, and was first released with Sun JDK 1.1 in 1997.

JDBC does not implement any database-specific instructions by itself, but provides a common framework of interfaces against which the database vendors can implement a driver for a specific database. This enables a Java developer to write code that can be used to connect to any database that provides a JDBC driver without changing the implementation.

JDBC can be divided into four core components:

- **JDBC driver**: A collection of Java database-specific Java classes that implement the interfaces defined in JDBC

- **Connections**: Each connection object holds one connection to a database, and is responsible for all the communication with the database

- **Statements**: Statements and their subtypes are used to execute queries and updates on a database

- **ResultSets**: Queries on a database return a `ResultSet` that holds the returned data of a query and meta information about the queried table

Connecting to a PostgreSQL database

In order to interact with the database, it is necessary to install the correct driver, and to open a connection to the database.

Installing the driver

The first step before writing the source code is to install a version of the JDBC PostgreSQL driver that is compatible with both: the used JDK version and the version of the database server.

The webpage at the hyperlink `http://jdbc.postgresql.org/download.html` shows the driver that is compatible with the used versions of PostgreSQL and JDK.

The driver can either be downloaded as a `.jar` file, and then manually added to the class-path. Or, if a build tool like Maven or Gradle is used, it can be downloaded and installed automatically by adding the resource to the build-script accordingly. A link to the Maven Repository where the resource definitions can be looked up is provided on the driver download page.

 This chapter refers to the JDBC4 specifications as implemented in version 9.3-1102 JDBC 41 of the PostgreSQL driver. Some examples might not work with the earlier versions of PostgreSQL JDK or the JDBC driver.

Initializing the driver

Before connecting to a database, the JDBC driver must be loaded and initialized.

Prior to JDBC 4.0, it was necessary to load the driver class by calling `Class.forName("org.postgresql.Driver")` once before using it. This loads the driver into memory, and it registers itself with JDBC.

Since JDBC 4.0, it is also possible to pass the JDBC driver class as an argument to the JVM when the application is started:

```
java -Djdbc.drivers=org.postgresql.Driver carportal.MainClass
```

This causes the JVM to load the driver during its initialization process, and provides an even more flexible method to use the existing code with different JDBC implementations.

Obtaining a connection

A Java class that uses JDBC needs to import the `java.sql` package:

```
import java.sql.*;
```

It should not use the packages from the `org.postgresql` package unless the PostgreSQL extensions to the JDBC are used. This keeps the code portable to other database vendors.

After importing the `java.sql` package, a connection to a database can be obtained from the `DriverManager` class by calling one of its `getConnection` methods:

- `DriverManager.getConnection(String url)`
- `DriverManager.getConnection(String url, String username, String password)`
- `DriverManager.getConnection(String url, Properties properties)`

All three methods return a `java.sql.Connection` object, which can subsequently be used to interact with the database.

The parameter `url` in all these methods specifies how the driver will connect to the database, and can be in one of these formats:

- `jdbc:postgresql:<databaseName>`
- `jdbc:postgresql://<host>/<databaseName>`
- `jdbc:postgresql://<host>:<port>/<databaseName>`

Using a URL without a host and port will create a connection to a PostgreSQL server running on the local computer (localhost) and listening on the PostgreSQL standard port (5432).

If the database server runs on a remote host or uses a non-standard port number, these parameters have to be added to the connection URL. The host can be given either as the host name or the IP address.

The IPv6 addresses must be enclosed in square brackets:

```
jdbc:postgresql://[::1]:5432/carportal
```

If the database server requires additional parameters to be set when opening a connection, these can be specified by using the last two getConnection methods listed earlier. The most common case will be that a database requires a username and password.

Other parameters might be setting the protocol version or enabling the SSL support. These parameters can be passed as name/value pairs stored in a java.util. Properties object.

A complete list of connection parameters can be found in the documentation of the JDBC driver. For the PostgreSQL driver version used in this chapter, the documentation can be found at http://jdbc.postgresql.org/documentation/93/connect.html#connection-parameters.

After usage, the connection should be closed again to free the resources:

```
Connection connection = null;
String url = "jdbc:postgresql:carportal";
try{
  connection = DriverManager.getConnection(url);
}
finally{
  if(connection!=null){
    connection.close();
  }
}
```

Since the `Connection` interface extends `java.lang.AutoCloseable`, using a try-with-resources block is a more convenient way of closing the connection after usage:

```
String url = "jdbc:postgresql:carportal";
try(Connection connection = DriverManager.getConnection(url))
{
  // use the connection here
}
```

Now the JVM will automatically close the connection when the try-block is exited.

Error handling

Most methods that interact with a database can throw an `SQLException`. The `SQLException` interface defines the following methods to retrieve the details about the cause of the error that has occurred:

- `String getMessage()`: This returns a textual description of the error.

- `String getSQLState()`: This returns a five-character long alphanumeric code.

- `int getErrorCode()`: This may return a vendor-specific error code if implemented by the driver. In most cases, this will be the error code returned by the database server.

- `Throwable getCause()`: If `SQLException` was caused by an instance of throwable being thrown, then throwable is returned.

- `SQLException getNextException()`: If more than one error occurred, the associated `SQLExceptions` can be iterated by sequentially calling this method until null is returned.

SQLWarnings

`SQLWarnings` is a subclass of `SQLException` that provides information about the database access warnings.

`SQLWarnings` are not thrown, but can be retrieved by calling the `getWarnings` method on objects of the types `Connection`, `Statement`, or `ResultSet`. If more than one warning was raised, they can be iterated the same same way as `SQLException` by calling the `getNextWarning` method on the `SQLWarnings` objects.

Upon execution of a statement, all the present warnings will be cleared.

Issuing a query and processing the results

Queries can be executed using two different kinds of statements. Simple queries can be executed using static statements, while prepared statements allow the changing of parameters before execution.

Static statements

To execute a static SQL statement, a `Statement` object has to be obtained from the `Connection` object first:

```
Statement statement = connection.createStatement();
```

The `Statement` can then be used to execute queries or updates on the target database.

As with the connection, it is good practice to close a statement as soon as it stops being used. If the statement is not closed, it will be closed implicitly when the underlying connection is closed.

The following example shows the way to get data from a table using the `executeQuery` method:

```
ResultSet resultSet = statement.executeQuery(
        "SELECT account_id, first_name, last_name FROM account");
```

The method returns a `ResultSet`, which will be introduced later in this chapter.

To insert, update, or delete rows, the `executeUpdate` method can be used:

```
int rowCount = statement.executeUpdate("DELETE FROM account");
```

The returned integer value states the number of rows that were affected by the update or delete operation.

If a table has columns that are configured to auto-generate keys, like `account_id` in the account table introduced in *Chapter 3, PostgreSQL Basic Building Blocks*, it is useful to be able to obtain the keys of a newly inserted row for referencing that row later.

Therefore, JDBC contains variations of the `executeUpdate` method that accept an array of either the names of the key columns or their indexes in the target table as an additional parameter. To configure the statement to return the `account_id` of a newly inserted account, the `executeUpdate` method can be called like this:

```
String sql = "INSERT INTO account (first_name, last_name, email,
password)                    VALUES ('John', 'Doe', 'john@doe.com',
'youDontKnow')";
statement.executeUpdate(sql, new String[]{"account_id"});
```

Or, assuming that `account_id` is the first column in the target table, the `executeUpdate` method can be called as follows:

```
statement.executeUpdate(sql, new int[]{1});
```

 In JDBC, indexes are one-based, rather than zero-based.

The generated indexes can then be obtained by calling `getGeneratedKeys` after inserting new data:

```
ResultSet newKeys = statement.getGeneratedKeys();
if(newKeys.next()){
   int newAccountID = newKeys.getInt("account_id");
}
```

For operations that do not insert new rows, or a target table that does not contain columns with auto-generated keys, the additional parameter is ignored, and the `ResultSet` returned by `getGeneratedKeys` will be empty.

PreparedStatements

In many applications, an SQL statement is executed multiple times with different parameters. It is not efficient to construct the query-string over and over again and execute it using a `Statement`. In these cases, a `PreparedStatement` should be used.

A `PreparedStatement` extends the `Statement` interface, and contains a precompiled SQL statement. It can be used to efficiently execute the statement multiple times with different parameters.

A `PreparedStatement` is initialized with a query string, just like a fixed `Statement`, but allows the usage of question marks as place holders for parameters that can be set later.

JDBC provides setter methods for different data types to assign a value to a parameter.

In the following example, the PreparedStatement is used to change the password of an account with the account_id as 42. It can be reused to do the same with different accounts by simply changing the parameters using the different setter methods and then calling executeUpdate. Moreover, the setter methods take care of any necessary formatting, such as putting quotes around strings:

```
PreparedStatement statement = connection.prepareStatement(
                "UPDATE account SET password=? WHERE account_id=?");
statement.setString(1, "myNewPassword");
statement.setInt(2, 42);
int changedRows = statement.executeUpdate();
```

Before executing a PreparedStatement, all parameters must have a value assigned to them. If this is not the case, an SQLException will be thrown.

Once assigned, the parameters retain their values between executions. If necessary, they can be unset by calling clearParameters on PreparedStatement.

JDBC provides a dedicated setNull method to assign a null value to a column. Passing null to one of the other setter methods will usually throw a NullPointerException. In the preceding example, setting the password column to null could be done by calling:

```
statement.setNull("password");
```

Or, alternatively, you can call:

```
statement.setNull(1);
```

Like the Statement class, PreparedStatement also offers a method to query data from the target table. Again, a ResultSet is returned:

```
PreparedStatement statement = connection.prepareStatement(
                        "SELECT * from account where account_id
= ?");
statement.setInt(1, 42);
ResultSet result = statement.executeQuery();
```

Using a ResultSet

In SQL, a result set is defined as a set of rows returned by a query as well as metadata about the structure of the queried table.

In JDBC, the methods that query data from a table are defined to return an object of the type ResultSet.

A ResultSet is always tied to the Statement object that created it. Moreover, there can be only one ResultSet per Statement. If a Statement is closed or re-executed, an existing ResultSet will be closed too.

Navigating through a ResultSet

In order to navigate through the results, the ResultSet contains a cursor, which initially points before the first returned row. Therefore, it is necessary to position it on the first row before getting data from the ResultSet by calling the next method.

The next method moves the cursor forward by one row. It returns true if such a row exists, and false otherwise. Therefore, the next method can be conveniently used to iterate through a ResultSet using a while loop:

```
ResultSet result = statement.executeQuery(
                          "select account_id, last_name from
account");
while(result.next())
{
  //get row data
}
```

The JDBC API also defines a set of methods to query the current position of the cursor:

- int getRow(): This returns the row number of the cursor position, or 0 if the cursor is not positioned on any row

- boolean isAfterLast(): This returns true if the cursor is positioned after the last row

- boolean isBeforeFirst(): This returns true if the cursor is positioned before the first row

- boolean ifFirst(): This returns true if the cursor is positioned on the first row

- boolean isLast(): This returns true if the cursor is positioned on the last row

Reading row data

To get data from a row, the JDBC API provides several getter methods, such as `getInt` or `getString`, which convert the SQL data types to the matching Java types. It also offers the `getObject` method, which returns data as a Java object without casting it to a specific type. This can be useful if the type of a column is not known in the context of the Java code.

All getter methods accept either a column index or a column name as argument.

To get the first and last name of an account, the body of the while loop in the previous example might contain statements like these:

```
int accountId = result.getInt(1);
String lastName = result.getString("last_name");
```

While using the index is generally more efficient, using the column name makes the code more readable, and prevents errors in case the number or order of columns is changed in the query or table definition.

It is also possible to find the index of a column by its name using the `findColumn` method:

```
int columnIndex = result.findColumn(columnName);
```

Handling null values

Some SQL data types are mapped to primitive data types like `int` or `boolean` in Java. As these primitive types can't hold null values, they will be set to their default value (for example, 0 for numeric values or false for boolean) if the value of the column in the database is null.

However, it is possible to check for null values using the `wasNull` method after invoking one of the getter methods:

```
Integer n = result.getInt(1);
if(result.wasNull())
{
  n = null;
}
```

This could, for example, be used to wrap primitives in their object-type wrapper classes to achieve the same behavior along all data types.

Scrollable and updateable ResultSets

By default, a `ResultSet` can only be navigated forward and is read-only. Moreover, it does not reflect the changes on the underlying data. To change this behavior, the `createStatement` and `prepareStatement` methods can be called with additional parameters specifying the type and concurrency of the `ResultSets`:

```
connection.createStatement(type, concurrency);
connection.prepareStatement(sql, type, concurrency);
```

Possible values for `type` are:

- `ResultSet.TYPE_FORWARD_ONLY`: The cursor may only move forward, which is the default setting

- `ResultSet.TYPE_SCROLL_INSENSITIVE`: The cursor may move in both directions, but the `ResultSet` does not reflect the changes made to it

- `ResultSet.TYPE_SCROLL_SENSITIVE`: The cursor may move in both directions, and `ResultSet` will reflect the changes that are made to its data

Setting a `ResultSet` to `TYPE_SCROLL_SENSITIVE` does not mean that it will reflect changes in the database; it reflects only the changes made to the data stored in the `ResultSet` itself. To pick up the changes made in the current row in the database, `refreshRow` has to be called.

Values for concurrency, which configure a read-only or an updateable `ResultSet`, can be the following:

- `ResultSet.CONCUR_READ_ONLY` (default)

- `ResultSet.CONCUR_UPDATABLE`

Navigating through a ResultSet

In addition to moving forward by calling next, a scrollable `ResultSet` allows backwards navigation and positioning the cursor at a specific row:

- `boolean previous()`: Moves the cursor to the previous row. Returns true if such a row exists. Otherwise, the cursor is positioned before the first row, and false is returned.

- `boolean absolute(int rowNumber)`: Positions the cursor at the given row, and returns true if such a row exists.

- `boolean relative(int numberOfRows)`: Moves the cursor forward or backwards by the given number of rows. Returns true if the new position is within the `ResultSet`. Otherwise, the cursor is positioned before the first or after the last row, and false is returned.

- `boolean aferLast()`: Positions the cursor after the last row.
- `boolean beforeFirst()`: Positions the cursor before the first row.
- `boolean first()`: Positions the cursor on the first row.
- `boolean last()`: Positions the cursor on the last row.

 The preceding methods can't be used on a `TYPE_FORWARD_ONLY` ResultSet. Doing so will raise an `SQLException`.

Both the absolute and relative methods also accept negative values. While the relative method will move the cursor backwards in such a case, the `absolute` method will handle the value as a position with respect to the end of the `ResultSet`. Calling `absolute(-1)` would, for example, have the same result as a call of the method last.

Changing the data in a ResultSet

To update the current row in an updateable `ResultSet`, JDBC provides update methods similar to the getter and setter methods. After changing the fields in a `ResultSet`, updateRow must be called to make the changes persistent.

Instead of updating a row, it can also be inserted as a new set of data by calling insertRow, or deleted by calling deleteRow.

To navigate a ResultSet in the reverse order, and to change a column of the current row, one can do something like the following:

```
PreparedStatement statement = connection.prepareStatement(
"select * from account",
ResultSet.TYPE_SCROLL_INSENSITIVE,
ResultSet.CONCUR_UPDATABLE);
ResultSet result = statement.executeQuery();
result.afterLast();
while(result.previous())
{
  int accountID = result.getInt("account_id");
  String email = getNewEmailAddress(accountID);
  result.updateString("email", email);
  result.updateRow();

}
```

The example assumes that there exists a method with the name `getNewEmailAddress` that queries and returns a new e-mail address for a given account ID.

Using cursors

By default, a `ResultSet` will contain the complete result of a query. When working with large datasets, this behavior might be inefficient, and can be changed by using a cursor.

A cursor is a control structure that points to one row in a set of rows. It can be used to navigate a set of rows similar to an iterator in Java or other object-oriented languages.

To use a cursor, auto-commit must first be turned off for the used connection:

```
connection.setAutoCommit(false);
```

Then, after creating a statement, the fetch size can be set:

```
statement.setFetchSize(10);
ResultSet result = statement.executeQuery(
"select * from account");
while(result.next())
{
  //read row data
}

statement.setFetchSize(0);
connection.setAutoCommit(true);
```

Now, the JDBC driver will no longer load the complete result into the `ResultSet`, but fetch the next ten rows whenever needed.

Setting the fetch size to 0 will restore the original behavior of loading the complete result.

Also, auto-commit should be turned on again after using the cursor.

Getting information about the table structure

In some cases, the structure of a table is not known at the time of implementation, or it is intended to keep the code independent of a table structure.

In such cases, a `ResultSetMetaData` object can be retrieved from `ResultSet` to query the structural information of a table at runtime.

The following example shows how to get some basic information about a table's columns:

```
ResultSet result = statement.executeQuery("select * from account");
ResultSetMetaData metaData = result.getMetaData();

int columnCount = metaData.getColumnCount();
for(int c=1;c<=columnCount; c++)
{
   String columnName = metaData.getColumnName(c);

   int columnType = metaData.getColumnType(c);
   String columnClass = metaData.getColumnClassName(c);
   String columnTypeName = metaData.getColumnTypeName(c);
}
```

In the preceding example, different methods are used to gather information about the type of column.

The method `getColumnType` returns an integer value that matches one of the constants defined in `java.sql.Types`. This can be used when calling the `setObject` method on a `PreparedStatement`.

The `String` returned by `getColumnClassName` represents the fully qualified name of the underlying class of the object that would be returned by the `ResultSet` `getObject` method.

In the last command, `getColumnTypeName` returns the type-name of a column on the database side.

Other than getting column-type information, the `ResultSetMetaData` interface provides further methods to get information about a column like `isAutoIncrement` or `isNullable`, which can be looked up in the API's documentation.

Function handling

For calling stored procedures, JDBC provides the `CallableStatement` interface, which extends `PreparedStatement`. The API defines two escape syntaxes, which can be used to call a function on the database:

- `{? = call <procedure-name>[(?, ?, …)]}`
- `{call <procedure-name>[(?, ?, …)]}`

The first form includes a return parameter, while the second one does not. The list of parameters passed to the function can contain both input and output parameters. If a function does not expect any parameters, it can be left out completely.

Examples of function handling are as follows:

- `{? = call random}`: A call to a function without parameters
- `{call setval(?, ?)}`: A call without a return parameter
- `{? = call substring(?, ?, ?)}`: A call with the return parameter and the function parameter list

Calling a stored function

To execute a function from Java code, the first step is to get a `CallableStatement` from the open connection as follows:

```
CallableStatement statement =
                                connection.prepareCall("{? = call
substring(?, ?, ?)}");
```

The preceding example prepares a call of the `substring` function. Please note that the `CallableStatement` interface does not support functions that use keywords (for example, `substring('abcd' from 1 for 3)`), but only supports the regular function invocation syntax using a list of parameters. PostgreSQL does provide wrappers for such functions that accept parameter lists.

After preparing the `CallableStatement`, all output parameters must first be registered with their position and type:

```
statement.registerOutParameter(1, Type.VARCHAR);
```

Then, a value can be assigned to the input and output parameters using the setter methods defined in the `PreparedStatement` interface:

```
statement.setString(2, "function call example");
statement.setInt(3, 10);
statement.setInt(4, 4);
```

Finally, the function call can be executed, and its output parameter can be fetched using one of the getter methods defined in the `CallableStatement` interface:

```
statement.execute();
String substring = statement.getString(1);
System.out.println(substring);
statement.close();
```

The preceding example gets the substring of "function call example" starting at position 10 and with a length of four characters (which is "call"), and prints it to the screen.

Getting a ResultSet from a stored function

Stored functions can return more than one result. They can do this by either returning a set of some data type (SETOF) or by returning a `refcursor`. The way a function is called differs depending on which return method is used.

Getting a ResultSet from a function returning SETOF

Functions that return a set of values, such as the built-in `unnest` function, should be called from a `Statement` or `PreparedStatement` rather than from `CallableStatement`. Calling such a function is done just like executing a normal SELECT statement:

```
ResultSet result =
                    statement.executeQuery("SELECT * FROM
unnest(ARRAY[1, 2])");
while (result.next())
{
  System.out.println(result.getInt(1));
}
```

This will unnest the passed array, and print each of its values on a new line.

Getting a ResultSet from a function returning a refcursor

If a function returns a `refcursor`, the invocation is similar to a standard function call. Because a cursor is going to be used, a transaction has to be opened first by disabling the connection's auto-commit flag as follows

```
connection.setAutoCommit(false);
```

Assuming that `refcursor_function` is an arbitrary function that returns a `refcursor`, it can then be called as follows:

```
String functionCall = "{ ? = call refcursor_function() }";
CallableStatement statement = connection.prepareCall(functionCall);
statement.registerOutParameter(1, Types.OTHER);
statement.execute();
```

 Note that the output parameter is registered as `Type.OTHER`, and not as a specific data type.

After executing the function call, `ResultSet` can be obtained from the statement. As there is no specific getter method for `ResultSet`, it is necessary to use `getObject` and type-cast the returned value to `ResultSet`:

```
ResultSet result = statement.getObject(1);
while(result.next())
{
  //process the results
}
```

Now, this `ResultSet` can be used like any other `ResultSet` returned from a query.

Design considerations

In many applications, the database structure is reflected by the application's architecture and vice versa. A table is mapped to a class, and an instance of such a class corresponds to one row of data. When designing such an application, the basics of database design and normalization can also be applied to the class design.

For such applications, an object-relational mapping library can be used to translate between the tabular representation in a database and objects that can be used from within an application.

An example of such a library is Hibernate, which will be introduced in the next chapter.

Summary

JDBC defines a vendor-independent API to access databases and execute SQL statements. It consists of four main components. The driver implements the communication with a specific type of database, while the `Connection` interface represents an open connection to a database server. Different kinds of `Statement` interfaces are provided to execute queries and updates on a database, and to call functions. Finally, `ResultSet` represents the results returned by a query. It also contains meta data about the queried table.

While JDBC is an easy way to interact with a database, there is still a mismatch of the tabular representation of data in a database and the object-graph of an object-oriented class design. The next chapter will introduce Hibernate as an example of an **object-relational mapping (ORM)** framework that adds a layer between the Java application and the database that translates between both the representations.

14
PostgreSQL and Hibernate

In the previous chapter, we discussed ways of using JDBC to access a database. In the context of object-oriented software design, it is often required to not only store simple values in a database but to also map the objects and their relations to the tables.

This chapter is an introduction to the concept of **Object-relational mapping (ORM)** and the Hibernate framework as an implementation of ORM. The first part describes the overall architecture of Hibernate, and gives guidelines for installing and configuring the framework.

Later in this chapter, the basic usage of Hibernate, such as performing CRUD operations, fetching strategies, and association mapping, will be covered.

Finally, the end of the chapter introduces advanced techniques such as caching, pooling, and using table partitioning in conjunction with Hibernate.

Introduction to ORM and Hibernate

While relational databases represent data in a tabular form, object-oriented programming languages organize the data in a graph of objects that reference each other. This results in different approaches for accessing and manipulating stored data.

An ORM framework translates between tabular and object representation, and creates a kind of *virtual object database* that can be used from within an application.

Hibernate overview and architecture

Hibernate is an open-source persistence framework for Java. Beside the ORM module, which will be discussed in the context of this chapter, it provides additional modules and tools for accessing the NoSQL data-stores, adding full-text search, or for validating data.

The Hibernate ORM module takes care of the mapping between the database tables and Java classes, and largely, reduces the amount of code needed to implement data persistence.

Hibernate inserts a layer between the Java application and JDBC, as shown in the following diagram. Along with JDBC, it uses the **Java Naming and Directory Interface (JNDI)** and the **Java Transaction API (JTA)** to allow integration with the J2EE application servers:

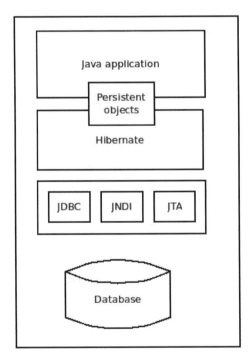

Hibernate ORM architecture

Installation and configuration

Before Hibernate can be used in an application, the library has to be installed and configured.

Installation of Hibernate

The Hibernate ORM can be downloaded from `http://hibernate.org/orm/` as a zip file containing a collection of JAR files that have to be added to the classpath manually.

As Hibernate depends on a couple of other open source libraries, it is recommended to let a build tool like Maven or Gradle resolve the dependencies automatically by adding a dependency to the hibernate-core module of the build file.

 The examples in this chapter refer to the Version 4.3.7.Final of Hibernate ORM.

Configuring Hibernate

Before Hibernate can be used, it has to be configured with the correct connection parameters and the database driver to use. This can be done either by using an XML file (`hibernate.cfg.xml`) or a properties file (`hibernate.properties`). In both cases, the file should be stored in the classpath, normally in `src/main/resources/`, if the Mavens standard directory structure is used.

A basic configuration in the XML format could look like this:

```xml
<?xml version='1.0' encoding='utf-8'?>
<!DOCTYPE hibernate-configuration PUBLIC
  "-//Hibernate/Hibernate Configuration DTD//EN"
  "http://www.hibernate.org/dtd/hibernate-configuration-3.0.dtd">
<hibernate-configuration>
  <session-factory>
    <property name="connection.driver_class">
      org.postgresql.Driver
    </property>
    <property name="connection.url">
      jdbc:postgresql://localhost/car_portal
    </property>
    <property name="connection.username">
      car_portal_app
    </property>
    <property name="connection.password"></property>
    <property name="dialect">
      org.hibernate.dialect.PostgreSQL9Dialect
```

```
      </property>
      <property name="show_sql">true</property>
    </session-factory>
  </hibernate-configuration>
```

When using a properties file, the configuration would be written in a `name=value` format (such as `connection.username=car_portal_app`).

In addition to specifying the parameters needed to connect to the database, two optional settings are configured in the example:

- **dialect**: This configures the specific SQL variant of the database. In most cases, Hibernate is able to resolve the used dialect by itself.

- **show_sql**: When this is set to `true`, Hibernate logs all the executed SQL statements to the console.

A complete list of the optional configuration properties is given in chapter 3.4 of the Hibernate reference documentation (`http://docs.jboss.org/hibernate/orm/4.3/manual/en-US/html/`).

Getting a session from the SessionFactory

Before a Java application can interact with the persistence store, it has to open a session. A session is a single-threaded object that holds a JDBC connection to the database. As with connections, a session should be closed as soon as it is no longer needed. A new session can be created by calling `openSession()` on the `SessionFactory`.

A `SessionFactory` is an immutable, thread-safe factory for session instances. It is recommended to instantiate it as a singleton object with the application-global scope.

Often, it is helpful to create a reusable helper class that provides the `SessionFactory`:

```
public class SessionFactoryHelper{
  private static final SessionFactory sessionFactory =
  createSessionFactory();

  private static SessionFactory createSessionFactory(){
    Configuration configuration = new Configuration().configure();
    StandardServiceRegistry registry =
      new StandardServiceRegistryBuilder()
      .applySettings(configuration.getProperties())
      .build();
```

```
      return configuration.buildSessionFactory(registry);
   }


   public static SessionFactory getSessionFactory(){
      return sessionFactory;
   }
}
```

Upon the first invocation of the `SessionFactoryHelper`, `createSessionFactory` is called to instantiate the `sessionFactory` object.

First, the configuration is loaded from the standard configuration file by calling configure on an instance of `Configuration`. The loaded properties are then used to create an instance of `StandardServiceRegistry`.

A `ServiceRegistry` instance manages services, which provide functionality in a pluggable manner. An example of a service is `ConnectionProvider`, which is an interface declaring methods for obtaining and releasing connections. Hibernate always references this interface, while the actual implementation is managed by the registry.

The `ServiceRegistry` is then used again to let the `Configuration` object build the `SessionFactory`.

Once this is done, the factory can be obtained by calling the `getSessionFactory` method.

Mapping classes to tables

In order to allow Hibernate to store objects in a table, a mapping between the Java class that represents the object and the table that it will be stored in has to be configured.

This can either be done by creating a mapping in the XML format or by adding annotations to an entity-class. In both cases, the mapping has to be added to the session-factory section in the configuration-file:

```
<mapping resource="Account.hbm.xml"/>
<mapping class="carportal.Account"/>
```

The first entry adds a mapping in the XML format, while the second entry specifies the fully-qualified name of an annotated entity class.

It is possible to add multiple mappings to the configuration, and use both methods at the same time.

Creating an entity class

A very basic entity-class for the `account` table could look like this:

```
package carportal;

public class Account{
  private int accountID;
  private String firstName;
  private String lastName;
  private String email;
  private String password;

  protected Account(){}
}
```

It contains a `private` field for each column in the table and a constructor without parameters. Hibernate needs this constructor to create an instance of the entity using Java reflection API.

For usage from within the application, the setter and getter methods for accessing the fields and a public constructor for initializing the entity should be added as needed.

Now, the next step is to configure the mapping.

Creating a mapping file

After creating the entity class, a mapping file (`Account.hbm.xml`) should be created in `src/main/resources/` with the following content:

```xml
<hibernate-mapping package="carportal" schema="carportal_app">
  <class name="Account" table="account">
    <id name="accountID" column="account_id">
      <generator class="identity"/>
    </id>
    <property name="firstName" column="first_name"/>
    <property name="lastName" column="last_name"/>
    <property name="email"/>
    <property name="password"/>
  </class>
</hibernate-mapping>
```

The top level element, `hibernate-mapping`, sets two optional parameters that define the default package name and the schema to be added to the unqualified class and table names.

Next, the class node maps a class name to the respective table. The table attribute is optional, and defaults to the class name if omitted.

There can be multiple class nodes in a mapping definition.

The mapping of columns to the fields is configured inside the class node using the `id` and `column` nodes. There has to be one `id` node for each primary key column of the table.

All other columns are defined as a `property` node. These are optional, and can be left out if a column will not be used inside the entity-class.

Both `id` and `property` nodes have a `name` attribute, which specifies the field name of the defined class. They can also have an optional `column` attribute if the names of the field and column do not match.

Additionally, the `id` node configures a `generator` class, which defines how the unique identifiers are created. The `generator` class can either be given as a shortcut name of one of Hibernate's built-in generators or the class name of an external implementation.

Some of the built-in generators are:

- **Assigned (default)**: This lets the application assign an identifier before storing an entity.
- **Identity**: It uses an identity or serial from the database.
- **Sequence**: This uses a sequence from the database. The name of the sequence is configured as a child of the generator node:
  `<paramname="sequence">account_id_seq</param>`.
- **UUID**: This uses a 128-bit UUID algorithm to create identifiers.

A complete documentation of the XML mapping can be found in *Chapter 5, SQL Language*, of the Hibernate reference manual.

Using annotation-based mapping

An alternative to XML mapping is to use annotations inside the entity class. Having the mapping inside the class makes it easier to maintain consistency when making changes, as there is only one file to edit.

The annotated version of the Account class looks like this:

```
package carportal;
import javax.persistence.*;


@Entity
@Table(name = "account")
public class Account{
  @Id
  @GeneratedValue(strategy = GenerationType.IDENTITY)
  @Column(name = "account_id")
  private int accountID;

  @Column(name = "first_name")
  private String firstName;

  @Column(name = "last_name")
  private String lastName;

  private String email;
  private String password;

  @Transient
  private int someInternalValue;

  private Account(){}
}
```

The following annotations were added to the `Account` class:

- **@Entity**: This tells Hibernate that a Java class is an entity that should be persisted. This is the only annotation that is mandatory in any case.

- **@Table**: This configures the name of the target table if it does not match the class name. The schema and catalog name can also be specified by setting the respective attributes of this annotation.

- **@Id**: The `@Id` marks a field as primary key. An entity class must define all the primary keys of a table.

- **@GeneratedValue**: This annotation configures the generator class for identifiers, as explained in the previous section. To specify a shortcut name, the strategy attribute is set, while an external generator class is configured using the generator attribute.

- **@Column**: This maps a column name to a field name in case they do not match. It is also used to define additional behavior like whether a column should be used in the insert or update statements or whether it can be null.

- **@Transient**: All the fields of a class that do not have a corresponding column in the database or that should not be persisted have to be marked transient

The fields `email` and `password` are not annotated in the example, as the account table has columns with matching names. Fields without annotations are automatically added to the mapping with a default configuration.

For the remainder of this chapter, annotation-based mapping will be used, as it is more convenient to use and XML mapping is now considered legacy.

Working with entities

In addition to adding a layer of abstraction above the database system, Hibernate introduces state management to entity objects. This shifts the focus of development from executing SQL statements to managing the state of entities.

States of an entity

In Hibernate, an entity can have one of the following four states:

- **Transient**: This is the initial state of an entity after instantiation. It does not have a representation in the database yet, and is not associated with a session.

- **Persistent**: An entity that is represented in the database and has an identifier assigned. A persistent entity is tied to a session.

- **Detached**: When closing the underlying session, a persistent entity will be detached. It will still exist as an object, but updates to it will not be reflected in the database. It can be reattached to a session later to persist it again.

- **Removed**: An object that is scheduled for deletion.

The transitions between the states are triggered by calling various methods on the session, as shown in the following diagram:

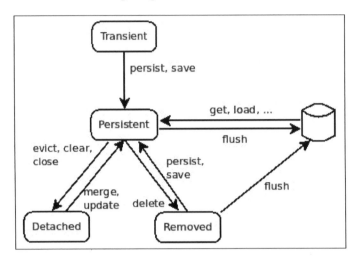

Transitions between Hibernate states

There are even more methods of loading an entity from the database using the query interface or a set of interfaces that retrieve an entity by its identifier. These are not shown in the diagram, but will be discussed together with the shown methods in the following sections.

Making a new entity persistent

New instances of an entity class start in the transient state. A transient entity can be persisted by associating it with a session and calling the save or persist method:

```
Account account = new Account("John", "Doe", "john@doe.com", "pass1234");
Session session = SessionFactoryHelper.getSessionFactory().openSession();
Transaction transaction = session.beginTransaction();
Serializable accountID = session.save(account);
transaction.commit();
session.close();
```

In this example, after creating a new account and obtaining an opened connection, a transaction is started. This is important for Hibernate to be able to roll back the changes that fail while cascading a `save` or `update` command over the object graph. It is possible to configure the connections to be in the autocommit mode by adding an appropriate property to the Hibernate configuration:

```
<property name="connection.autocommit">true</property>
```

This makes it unnecessary to wrap the save or update commands in a transaction. However, this should only be done in an application that does not need to cascade the changes over the object graph.

Once inside a transaction, the account can be persisted by passing it to the session's `save` method, which returns the generated identifier. Finally, the transaction is committed, which implicitly calls the `flush` method on the session. Then the session can be closed. Now the entity has a representation in the database.

Another way to persist an object is by using the `persist` method instead of `save`. Both methods differ slightly in their behavior outside of transactions and of assigning identifiers:

- `save`:
    - Immediately assigns an identifier
    - Calls flush if used outside a transaction

- `persist`:
    - Does not guarantee the assigning of an identifier immediately Depending on the configuration, this might not happen until you call the `flush` method
    - The `flush` method has to be called explicitly to write an object to the database

Loading an entity from the database

To load an entity from the database, either the `get` or `load` method can be used. Both expect the entity class and an identifier as parameters, and return an instance of an object, which must be cast to the target class type:

```
int accountID = 1;
Account account1 = (Account)session.get(Account.class, accountID);
Account account2 = (Account)session.load(Account.class, accountID);
```

It is also possible to load a database entry into an existing object:

```
Account account = (Account)session.load(Account.class, 1);
session.load(account, 2);
```

While the `get` method returns `null`, if no object with the given identifier exists in the database, load returns an instance of the target class in any case, and fails with an `ObjectNotFoundException` when accessing the entities fields. Thus, it should only be used when it is certain that the entry to be loaded exists in the database.

Finally, an entity can be reloaded from the database. This can be useful if a table uses triggers to calculate or modify values when inserting or updating an entry. This is done by calling the `refresh` method of the session:

```
session.refresh(account);
```

Loading a list of entries

It is often needed to get a list of entries from the database that match certain criteria. This can be done by letting a session create a `Query` object and calling its `list()` method:

```
Query query = session.createQuery("from Account");
List accounts = query.list();
```

The returned list will then contain all the entries from the table that is mapped to the `Account` class.

 The names in the query passed to the `createQuery` method refer to the entity class and its fields, not the mapped table and its columns!

To filter the result, a where constraint containing a single parameter or parameter-lists can be added to the query:

```
Query query = session.createQuery("from Account
    where lastName = :lastName and firstName in (:firstNames)");


query.setString("lastName", "Doe");
```

```
List firstNames = new ArrayList();

firstNames.add("John");

firstNames.add("Jane");

query.setParameterList(":firstNames", firstNames);


List accounts = query.list();
```

It is also possible to paginate the returned results by setting the first entry and/or the maximum number of rows returned by a query before calling the list method:

```
query.setFirstResult(20);

query.setMaxResults(10);

query.list();
```

Named queries

Besides specifying queries when calling the createQuery method, named queries can be defined by adding an appropriate annotation to the Entity class:

```
@Entity

@Table(name = "account")

@NamedQuery(name="Account.byLastName",

         query="from Account where lastName = :lastName")
         public class Account{

   //...

}
```

Such named queries are global within the scope of the SessionFactory, and an appropriate Query object can be created using the session's createNamedQuery method:

```
Query query = session.createNamedQuery("Account.byLastName");
```

This query can be used in the same way as the one created by explicitly specifying a query.

Creating dynamic queries

In many applications, it is useful to construct a where constraint at runtime. Rather than building the query string for such constraints, the `criteria` API in Hibernate can be used:

```
Criteria criteria = session.createCriteria(Account.class);
criteria.add(Restrictions.eq("lastName", "Doe"));
criteria.setMaxResults(10);
criteria.addOrder(Order.asc("lastName"));
List list = criteria.list();
```

After creating a criteria object for the `Account` class, an equals restriction is added to the `lastName` field. Then the result is limited to ten entries, and ascending ordering is applied. Finally, the query is executed by calling the `list()` method.

The `Restrictions` class provides methods for all the constraints that can be used in a WHERE statement. It also defines the Boolean operations that can be used to combine the constraints:

```
Restrictions.and(
  Restrictions.gt("number_of_owners", 1),
  Restrictions.le("number_of_owners", 3),
  Restrictions.not(
    Restrictions.in("car_id", new Integer[]{1, 5, 10})
  )
);
```

The preceding example creates a restriction for a query on the `car` table that translates to a WHERE constraint in the form of:

```
WHERE number_of_owners > 1 AND number_of_owners <= 3 AND car_id NOT in
(1, 5, 10);
```

To select cars with one to three owners, excluding certain `car_id`. Again, there is an equivalent for all Boolean operations that can be used in a WHERE constraint.

Modifying entities

Entities in a persisted state can be modified by updating the object's fields. Any changes will then be written to the database when the session is flushed by committing the transaction:

```
Account account = (Account)session.get(Account.class, 18);
Transaction transaction = session.beginTransaction();
account.changePassword("newPass123");
transaction.commit();
```

However, this requires loading and updating of an entity to happen within the same session. This might be inefficient if there is a longer period of time between loading and updating, for example, when displaying an entry in a user interface for entering the changes. In such cases, a more efficient approach is to update a detached entity:

```
public void updateAccount(int accountID){
    Session session =SessionFactoryHelper
        .getSessionFactory().openSession();
    Account account = (Account)session.get(Account.class,
    accountID);
    session.close();


    displayUI(account);


    session =
    SessionFactoryHelper.getSessionFactory().openSession();
    Transaction transaction = session.beginTransaction();
    session.update(account);
    transaction.commit();
    session.close();
}


private void displayUI(Account account){
    //display user-interface to modify the account
}
```

This loads the account in the first session, and then detaches it by closing the session. After that, the user interface can be displayed without blocking any database connections. Finally, the entity is reattached, and the updates are written to the database by calling the `update` method on a second session.

When reattaching an entity, it is important that a persistent entity with the same identifier loaded within the sessions scope does not exist already. Otherwise, an exception will be thrown.

To reattach an entity in any case, the `merge` method can be used; doing so will overwrite an already existing entity.

Deleting entities

To delete an entity, the session interface provides the `delete` method:

```
Transaction transaction = session.beginTransaction();

session.update(account);

transaction.commit();
```

After calling `delete`, the entity is in a detached state. It will only be deleted from the database when the session is flushed during the committing of the transaction. The application can still hold a reference to the object, which can be used like any other object in transient state.

Using association mapping

In relational databases, a table can reference the entries from another table. This is usually done by defining a foreign key constraint that references a unique identifier of the referenced table. There are four kinds of mappings, which will be introduced in the following sections.

One-to-many and many-to-one mappings

In a one-to-many mapping, one entity can be associated with multiple entities, while in a many-to-one mapping, several entries of one table are mapped to an entry in another one. In the `car_portal_app` schema, the tables `account` and `account_history` are associated this way. To implement such a relation with Hibernate, the `Entity` class for `account_history` has to be created and added to the Hibernate configuration first:

```
@Entity

@Table(name = "account_history")
```

```
public class AccountHistory{

  @Id
  @GeneratedValue(strategy = GenerationType.IDENTITY)
  @Column(name = "account_history_id")
  private int accountHistoryID;
  @Column(name = "search_key")
  private String searchKey;

  @Column(name = "search_date")
  private Date searchDate;

  @ManyToOne
  @JoinColumn(name="account_id")
  private Account account;

  AccountHistory(){}

  public AccountHistory(String searchKey, Date searchDate,
        Account account){
    this.searchKey = searchKey;
    this.searchDate = searchDate;
    this.account = account;
  }
}
```

The implementation is very similar to the Account class, the only difference being the account field which references the associated account. This field is annotated with @ManyToOne indicating the kind of association. Also, the column referenced by the foreign key constraint is defined using the optional @JoinColumn annotation. If this annotation is omitted, Hibernate will expect a column name in the format of `<referenced table>_<referenced column>`, which would be account_account_id in this case.

Referencing the Account entity in AccountHistory defines a unidirectional relation. An entity of AccountHistory knows about the account it is associated with, but an entity of Account does not know its history.

To achieve this, a bidirectional relation has to be created. This is done by complementing the `Account` class with a field referencing the associated `account_history` entries, and a method to access the mapping:

```
@OneToMany(cascade = CascadeType.ALL, mappedBy = "account")
private List<AccountHistory> accountHistory = new LinkedList<>();


public Set<AccountHistory> getHistory(){
   return accountHistory;
}
```

The `@OneToMany` annotation is configured with the `mappedBy` attribute, which refers to the account field in `AccountHistory`. This tells Hibernate that the foreign key constraint is contained in the `account_history` table, and thus, makes `AccountHistory` the owner of the relation.

Also, the `@OneToMany` annotation is configured with the optional `cascade` attribute, which causes Hibernate to cascade transitions between the states of an `Account` entity to the associated `AccountHistory` entities. Without defining a cascade type, this would have to be done explicitly. There are `CascadeTypes` for each transition between states (`MERGE`, `PERSIST`, `REFRESH`, `DETACH`, `REMOVE`) that can be used if only certain transitions should be cascaded. `CascadeType.ALL` combines all of them.

Hibernate will now load the associated history items when an account is read from the database. To add entries to the history from within the application, a new instance of `AccountHistory` has to be created and added to the account that it is associated to:

```
Session session = SessionFactoryHelper.getSessionFactory().openSession();
Transaction transaction = session.beginTransaction();
Account account = (Account)session.load(Account.class, 1);


AccountHistory history = new AccountHistory(
        "search term", new Date(), account);
account.getHistory().add(history);


session.update(account);
transaction.commit();


session.close();
```

In the preceding example, the `AccountHistory` item is still transient after creating it and adding it to the account. It is persisted once the account is updated.

One-to-one mapping and component mapping

In a one-to-one mapping, an entity is associated to exactly one entity of another table and vice versa. The implementation does not differ much from that of the one-to-many and many-to-one mapping shown in the previous section. The only difference is that the respective fields are objects, and have to be annotated with `@OneToOne` on both sides.

Since the entries in a one-to-one mapping are often very strongly related to each other, they can alternatively be stored in the same table. In the `car_portal` database, the address data in the `seller_account` table is such a case. On the Javaside, it is nonetheless possible to group the columns that belong together in a dedicated class. For the address data, such a class could be implemented like this:

```
@Embeddable
public class Address{
  @Column(name = "street_name")
  private String streetName;

  @Column(name = "street_number")
  private String streetNumber;

  @Column(name = "zip_code")
  private String zipCode;

  private String city;
}
```

The `@Embeddable` annotation tells Hibernate that the `Address` class will be used in a component mapping. It can then be referenced from an entity class using the `@Embedded` annotation:

```
@Embedded
private Address address;
```

The embeddable entity cannot use the `@Id` annotation to define an identifier, nor can it be associated with a specific table using the `@Table` annotation. Instead, both are inherited from the enclosing entity class.

Moreover, as with value types, shared references are not being used. Even if two `seller_accounts` have the same address data, their entities will contain independent instances of `Address`.

Many-to-many mapping

In a many-to-many mapping, both sides of the association can reference multiple entries of the other side. In the `car_portal_app` schema, the table `favorite_ads` defines such a relation by associating the `account` tables and advertisement using their primary keys. Implementing the `Advertisement` entity, this table is configured using the `@JoinTable` annotation:

```
@Entity
@Table(name = "advertisement")
public class Advertisement{
  @Id
  @GeneratedValue(strategy = GenerationType.IDENTITY)
  @Column(name = "advertisement_id")
  private int advertisementID;

  @Column(name = "advertisement_date")
  private Date advertisementDate;

  @Column(name = "car_id")
  int carID;

  @Column(name = "seller_acount_id")
  int sellerAccountID;

  @ManyToMany(cascade = CascadeType.ALL)
  @JoinTable(name="favorite_ads",
    joinColumns={@JoinColumn(name="advertisement_id")},
    inverseJoinColumns={@JoinColumn(name="account_id")})
  private Set<Account> accounts = new HashSet<>();

  Advertisement(){}
```

```
    public Advertisement(Date advertisementDate, int carID,
            int sellerAccountID){
        this.advertisementDate = advertisementDate;
        this.carID = carID;
        this.sellerAccountID = sellerAccountID;
    }
}
```

The `name` attribute of the `@JoinTable` annotation sets the table containing the mapping, while the attributes `joinColumns` and `inverseJoinColumns` configure the columns referring the primary keys of the entity owning the association and that of the associated entity, respectively.

In the `Account` class, the association is added in a similar way, but with the names of `joinColumns` swapped:

```
@ManyToMany(cascade = CascadeType.ALL)
@JoinTable(name = "favorite_ads",
    joinColumns={@JoinColumn(name = "account_id")},
    inverseJoinColumns={@JoinColumn(name = "advertisement_id")})
private Set<Advertisement> advertisement = new HashSet<>();
```

Now, modifying the set of associated entities in either of the classes and committing those changes will automatically update the mapping-table accordingly.

Fetching strategies

When loading an entity from the database, there are several strategies regarding when and how to load the associated entities. Choosing the right strategy is important, because choosing the wrong strategy might result in inefficient queries, or the loading of a huge portion of the database if there are associations between a lot of tables. While the default strategies in Hibernate offer a good performance in most cases, it is possible to override them for each mapping.

Hibernate distinguishes between two types of strategies: the `fetch` type, which configures when the associated entities are loaded, and the `fetch` mode, which defines how the database is queried.

Configuring the fetch type

The `fetch` type defines when the associated entities are to be loaded, and is configured as an attribute of the annotations that define the mapping type:

`@OneToMany(fetch = FetchType.EAGER)`

`FetchType` defines two strategies:

- `FetchType.EAGER`: This loads the associated entities immediately
- `FetchType.LAZY`: This loads the associated entities when they are accessed for the first time

By default, one-to-one and many-to-one relations are configured with `FetchType.EAGER`, while one-to-many and many-to-many relations are configured with `FetchType.LAZY`. For most cases, this is a good choice.

Configuring the one-to-many or many-to-many relations for eager fetching should be done with care, because loading all the associated entities might have a significant impact on performance.

Configuring the fetch mode

The fetch mode defines how Hibernate creates SQL queries to load the associated entities from the database. It can be configured by adding the `@Fetch` annotation to a mapping field:

`@OneToMany`

`@Fetch(FetchMode.JOIN)`

`FetchMode` defines the following modes:

FetchMode.SELECT

This is the default mode. It creates two separate queries similar to the following:

`SELECT * FROM account WHERE account_id = ?;`

`SELECT * FROM account_history WHERE account_id = ?;`

The first query loads the entity, and the second one loads the mapped entities (lazy or eager).

FetchMode.JOIN

Loads the entity and also the mapped entities using a `JOIN` query on both the tables:

```
SELECT * FROM account LEFT OUTER JOIN account_history
  ON account.account_id = account_history.account_id
  WHERE account.account_id = ?;
```

 Using `FetchMode.JOIN` disables lazy fetching!

FetchMode.SUBSELECT

Loads the associated entities for all the entities of a type using a subselect:

```
SELECT * FROM account;
SELECT * FROM account_history WHERE account_history.account_id IN
  (SELECT account_id FROM account);
```

Depending on the configuration, this can be done using lazy or eager, which can be added to a mapping.

In addition to the fetch modes, Hibernate provides the `@BatchSize` annotation:

```
@OneToMany
@BatchSize(size = 5)
```

This defines the number of mappings that should be preloaded when iterating over the entities, but not the number of entities in a single mapping. When iterating over accounts and accessing their history, this would result in the following queries:

```
SELECT * FROM account;
SELECT * FROM account_history WHERE account_id IN (?, ?, ?, ?, ?);
```

Then, after accessing the histories of five accounts, the second query will be executed again to preload the histories for the next accounts, as needed.

Tuning the performance of Hibernate

In applications that have a lot of users or that have to access large databases, it is often necessary to optimize the database usage in order to limit the used resources or to increase the application's response time.

This section shows how to configure Hibernate to use caches and connection pools, and how to deal with partitioned tables.

Using caching

A cache is a layer between the application and the database that stores queried data to minimize database access when accessing such data again. Hibernate uses a multi-level caching schema with a session acting as a first-level cache, which caches the changes to an object and delays the write operations as long as possible.

Optionally, Hibernate can be configured to use a second-level cache which is consulted after a lookup if the first-level cache yields no result and before the underlying database is queried. Any third-party cache that implements Hibernate's CacheProvider interface can be used. Hibernate is bundled with EhCache and Infinispan; other frequently used opensource implementations of CacheProvider are *OSCache* and *Terracotta*.

The CacheProvider to be used is configured by adding an appropriate property to the session-factory node of the Hibernate configuration:

```
<hibernate-configuration>
  <session-factory>
    <property name="hibernate.cache.provider_class">
    org.hibernate.cache.EhCacheProvider
    </property>
  </session-factory>
</hibernate-configuration>
```

Depending on the implementation used, it will also be necessary to create a configuration file for it. In case of EhCache, a file ehcache.xml has to be created in the application's classpath:

```
<diskStore path="java.io.tmpdir"/>
<defaultCache
  maxElementsInMemory="1000"
  eternal="false"
  timeToIdleSeconds="120"
  timeToLiveSeconds="240"
  overflowToDisk="true"
/>
```

The preceding configuration tells EhCache to store up to 1,000 entries for each entity-class in the memory. If this number is exceeded, cached data will be written to the disk. It also defines that entries should be removed from the cache if they have not been accessed for 120 seconds, or after 240 seconds regardless of whether they have been accessed or not.

After specifying the `CacheProvider`, the next step is to configure the concurrency strategy. The concurrency strategy defines the way data is stored in the cache, and how it is to be retrieved and configured by adding the `@Cache` annotation to a class or a collection:

```
@Entity
@Table(name="account")
@Cache(usage=CacheConcurrencyStrategy.READ_WRITE)
public class Account{
  //...
}
```

The possible strategies are as follows:

- **Read only**: Only allows read access. This is the optimal strategy when an application does not need to modify the instances of an entity class.

- **Read/write**: This allows the cached entries to be modified, and locks them until they have been completely written to the database. Access to a locked entry will be handled as a cache-miss and propagated to the database.

- **Non strict read / write**: An entry being changed will be marked as invalid in the cache and reread from the database upon the next access. However, there is no strict isolation between concurrent access and the changes that have not been written to the database yet, which might become visible to the other transactions. This strategy should not be used if strict transaction isolation is required.

- **Transactional**: Uses a two-phase commit, first to the cache and then to the database. This strategy is not supported by every cache implementation.

The decision if caching should be enabled and the strategy to use should be made separately for each entity class. As caching may sometimes even have a negative impact on performance, benchmarks should be taken and caching should only be used if the performance increases remarkably.

Using connection pools

Opening a connection to a database is an expensive operation in terms of runtime, and can have quite an impact on performance. Therefore, Hibernate allows the use of a connection pool that cares for creating connections as needed, and reuses the open connections instead of closing them after each operation.

Hibernate comes with a built-in connection pool that can be enabled by simply adding the `pool_size` property to the session-factory configuration:

```
<property name="connection.pool_size">
  100
</property>
```

However, Hibernate's pooling mechanism is not very efficient and is not meant to be used in a productive environment.

Instead, a third-party implementation like `c3p0`, which comes bundled with Hibernate, should be used. A third-party connection pool is configured by replacing the `pool_size` property with the implementation-specific configuration.

For `c3p0`, the following properties can be added to the session-factory configuration:

```
<property name="hibernate.c3p0.min_size">5</property>
<property name="hibernate.c3p0.max_size">20</property>
<property name="hibernate.c3p0.timeout">300</property>
<property name="hibernate.c3p0.max_statements">50</property>
<property name="hibernate.c3p0.idle_test_period">3000</property>
```

This configures the following parameters of `c3p0`:

- `min_size`: The minimum number of connections the pool should contain (default: 1).

- `max_size`: The maximum number of connections the pool should contain (default: 100).

- `timeout`: The number of seconds after which an unused connection expires and is removed from the pool. The default value of 0 never expires connections.

- `max_statements`: The number of prepared connections that are pooled (default: 0).

- `idle_test_period`: Sets the number of seconds after an idle connection is validated.

Applications running inside an application-server should use one of its configured data-sources instead of a third-party connection-pool. To use a data-source, its JNDI name has to be added to the session-factory configuration like this:

```
<property name="hibernate.connection.datasource">
   java:/car_portal_app/jdbc/test
</property>
```

It replaces the `connection.url` property.

Dealing with partitioned tables

To improve the performance from the database side, very large tables are often partitioned. In PostgreSQL, this is done by inheriting a child table from a parent table for each partition. The parent table typically uses triggers or rules to redirect access to the desired partition. The master table itself is usually empty.

As there are no rows inserted into the parent table, PostgreSQL returns a row count of 0. However, Hibernate interprets this as a failed update operation, and throws an exception.

To prevent this problem, the method of checking the returned row count can be changed by adding the `@SQLInsert` annotation to the entity class, which defines the query used for inserting a new row and the type of check that will be performed:

```
@SQLInsert(
   sql="INSERT into account (first_name, last_name, email,
   password)
      VALUES (?,?,?,?)",
   check=ResultCheckStyle.NONE)
public class Account{
   //...
}
```

The possible values for the check attribute are:

- `ResultCheckStyle.COUNT`: Checks the row count returned by an insert operation
- `ResultCheckStyle.NONE`: Does not perform any check
- `ResultCheckStyle.PARAM`: Checks the row count that is returned as an output parameter when using a function to insert new rows

For updates, the `@SQLUpdate` annotation can be used in the same way.

Summary

Hibernate is an open-source persistence framework for Java. Its ORM module provides interfaces for translating data between a tabular and an object-relational representation. This shifts the focus of development from executing the SQL statements as is the case when using pure JDBC for handling transitions of an entity between its different states of persistence.

Index

Thank you for buying
Learning PostgreSQL

About Packt Publishing

Packt, pronounced 'packed', published its first book, *Mastering phpMyAdmin for Effective MySQL Management*, in April 2004, and subsequently continued to specialize in publishing highly focused books on specific technologies and solutions.

Our books and publications share the experiences of your fellow IT professionals in adapting and customizing today's systems, applications, and frameworks. Our solution-based books give you the knowledge and power to customize the software and technologies you're using to get the job done. Packt books are more specific and less general than the IT books you have seen in the past. Our unique business model allows us to bring you more focused information, giving you more of what you need to know, and less of what you don't.

Packt is a modern yet unique publishing company that focuses on producing quality, cutting-edge books for communities of developers, administrators, and newbies alike. For more information, please visit our website at www.packtpub.com.

About Packt Open Source

In 2010, Packt launched two new brands, Packt Open Source and Packt Enterprise, in order to continue its focus on specialization. This book is part of the Packt Open Source brand, home to books published on software built around open source licenses, and offering information to anybody from advanced developers to budding web designers. The Open Source brand also runs Packt's Open Source Royalty Scheme, by which Packt gives a royalty to each open source project about whose software a book is sold.

Writing for Packt

We welcome all inquiries from people who are interested in authoring. Book proposals should be sent to author@packtpub.com. If your book idea is still at an early stage and you would like to discuss it first before writing a formal book proposal, then please contact us; one of our commissioning editors will get in touch with you.

We're not just looking for published authors; if you have strong technical skills but no writing experience, our experienced editors can help you develop a writing career, or simply get some additional reward for your expertise.

[PACKT] open source
PUBLISHING community experience distilled

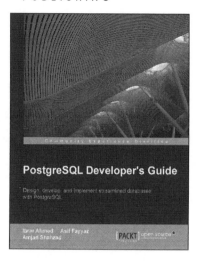

PostgreSQL Developer's Guide

ISBN: 978-1-78398-902-7   Paperback: 270 pages

Design, develop, and implement streamlined databases with PostgreSQL

1. Design efficient, real-world database solutions and extend your knowledge of database concepts.

2. Learn how to program using native PostgreSQL procedural languages to write custom functions.

3. Explore database partitioning and learn about query optimization techniques.

PostgreSQL for Data Architects

ISBN: 978-1-78328-860-1   Paperback: 272 pages

Discover how to design, develop, and maintain your database application effectively with PostgreSQL

1. Understand how to utilize the most frequently used PostgreSQL ecosystem-related tools and technologies.

2. A hands-on guide focused primarily on providing a practical approach to learning about architecture and design considerations for database architects.

3. The book covers PostgreSQL from a data architect's perspective – covering topics from installation from source to designing tables using SQL Power Architect, as well as deciding replication and failover strategies.

Please check **www.PacktPub.com** for information on our titles

Made in the USA
San Bernardino, CA
18 April 2016